CHILDREN'S RIGHTS IN SCOTLAND

AUSTRALIA
LBC Information Services—Sydney

CANADA and USA
Carswell—Toronto

NEW ZEALAND
Brooker's—Auckland

SINGAPORE and MALAYSIA
Sweet and Maxwell Asia
Singapore and Kuala Lumpur

CHILDREN'S RIGHTS IN SCOTLAND (2ⁿᵈ EDITION)

ALISON CLELAND,
LL.B. (Hons); Dip.L.P., LL.M.,
Lecturer in Law, Napier University,
and Convenor of the Scottish Child Law Centre

and

ELAINE E. SUTHERLAND,
LL.B. (Hons), LL.M.,
Reader in Law, School of Law, University of Glasgow, and
Professor, Lewis and Clark Law School, Portland, Oregon.

EDINBURGH
W. GREEN/Sweet & Maxwell
2001

Published in 2001 by W. Green & Son Ltd
21 Alva Street
Edinburgh EH2 4PS

Reprinted 2004

Typeset by YHT Ltd, London
Printed and bound in Great Britain by
Athenaeum Press Ltd., Gateshead, Tyne & Wear

No natural forests were destroyed to make this product;
only farmed timber was used and replanted

A CIP catalogue record for this book is available from the British
Library

ISBN 0 414 01349 2

© W. Green 2001

PREFACE TO THE SECOND EDITION

It is the unashamed position of the editors that children's rights matter and we were very gratified by the overwhelmingly positive response to the first edition of this book. The invitation from W. Green to produce a new edition of *Children's Rights in Scotland* was all that was needed to confirm what we already knew in our hearts—it was time. However, we were already thinking in terms of something far more radical than simply updating the first edition and we were delighted that our proposal to address children's rights from the perspective of both the European Convention on Human Rights and Fundamental Freedoms and the United Nations Convention on the Rights of the Child, along with other international instruments where relevant, met with such encouragement. Like any new edition, this volume reflects the fact that policy, law and practice are not static, but we hope it has moved into a new dimension in addressing the international context more comprehensively, with particular reference to domestic application. Since 1996, the law has undergone the inevitable process of reform and refinement. In that respect, perhaps the most important development is that we have been able to see what was 'new legislation', the Children (Scotland) Act 1995, in operation. However, the reform process was not confined to this statute, as the following chapters demonstrate. In short, there has been much (sometimes complete) rewriting and, in some cases, restructuring and redirection of individual chapters. In addition, it gave us the opportunity to add new chapters.

We were delighted that so many of the original contributors were able to make time to remain part of the team, not least because they are all busy professionals with demanding commitments. Where contributors could not continue, we were fortunate, indeed, to find new contributors of such high calibre and we welcome Colin Moodie ("The Right to a Safe Environment", with David Stone), Kenneth McK. Norrie ("The Child's Right to Care and Protection"), Shona Smith ("Child Abduction") and Kay Tisdall ("Equal Opportunities, Race, Gender, Disability—and Children"), as contributors to this edition. Elaine took over the chapter entitled "The Child in Conflict with the Law" and John P. Grant extended his contribution by co-authoring the chapter entitled "Scots Law and International Conventions" with her. This time, we decided we should share our thoughts with the reader from the outset in the chapter entitled "How Real are Children's Rights in Scotland?".

Of course, it has not been possible to deal at length with every aspect of children's rights in Scotland and we sought to concentrate on the principal ones. Given the fundamental point of the Kilbrandon philosophy (that children who do wrong should be treated along with children who are wronged), the editorial decision to devote separate chapters to each aspect may cause raised eyebrows in some quarters. However, we believe the separation was justified, not least because some international provisions apply to one or other area only, but also in order to devote sufficient space to the important issues involved in these fast-developing areas of law and practice.

We would like to express our sincere thanks to contributors for giving of their time, keeping to schedule and keeping to word limits. It is the constant challenge with a book of this kind that full exploration of the issues must be balanced with ensuring that the work is as widely accessible as possible. Given each author's desire to share his or her thoughts and expertise, it would have been all too easy to exceed the allocated space. On the other hand, accessibility requires that some attention be paid to economic reality; if the book was not to be prohibitively expensive, then limits had to be placed on length. We would also like to thank the staff at W. Green for their encouragement, assistance and support throughout the project. A final, and very special, word of thanks goes to John P. Grant whose extensive assistance, in the form of personal support, innovative suggestions, critical analysis and contribution to the editing process, was invaluable.

Alison Cleland & Elaine E. Sutherland
May 2001

PREFACE TO THE FIRST EDITION

The idea for this book came from earlier work of the editors. As Scottish Co-ordinator of the Children's Rights Development Unit, Alison has already written the *Scottish Agenda for Children,* which examined various aspects of Scots law in the light of the *United Nations Convention on the Rights of the Child.* Meanwhile, Elaine had given papers and written articles on the *Convention* and Scots Law. We both believed that there was a pressing need for a comprehensive examination of the extent to which Scots law has implemented the rights of children and young people which are set out in the *Convention.*

Given that the *Convention* operates on the levels of law, policy and practice, we felt it was important to address Scots law from all of these perspectives. Having identified the areas of law to be examined, we sought out individual contributors for each area and were delighted to find a wealth of enthusiasm for the project. That so many busy, eminent people were prepared to give of their time is a tribute to the commitment to children's rights in Scotland. The contributors include practising solicitors and advocates, academic lawyers and other relevant professionals. Given the experience and calibre of the contributors, it is no surprise that each chapter has something of a flavour of its own, and the views expressed by any one contributor do not necessarily reflect those of the others.

What has resulted is an assessment of all the major areas of Scots law as it is at present, and as it will be when the Children (Scotland) Act 1995 comes into force, from the perspective of the *Convention.* When Scots law satisfies the principles and standards of the *Convention,* that is noted. More important, however, is the highlighting of the many deficiencies in our law. What more we need to do is the crucial dimension which, we hope, will guide legislators in the future.

We would like to thank all of the contributors for their diligence, co-operation and generosity. Everyone has agreed to donate one half of their fee to the Scottish Child Law Centre. In addition, we would like to express our thanks to Louise Balmain and Moira Smith for their assistance with typing, to Emily Wiewiorka for her assistance with research, to Jane Mair for producing the index, and to the staff at Greens for their unflagging support. A special word of thanks goes to John P. Grant who gave generously of his time and experience to assist in editing.

A.C. & E.E.S.
January 1996.

CONTENTS

ABOUT THE CONTRIBUTORS

Alastair Bissett-Johnson is Professor of Private Law at the University of Dundee. Previously he taught at law schools in England, Australia and Canada, where he was a co-drafter of the Yukon Children's Act 1984 and the Children and Family Services Act of Nova Scotia 1990. He has written extensively on the subject of family law.

John Blackie is a Professor of Law at the University of Strathclyde. Within his work in connection with medical responsibility and the law, he has a special interest in the law relating to mental health. His other academic interests centre on the law of obligations generally. He is the author (with Hilary Patrick) of *Mental Health: A Guide to the Law in Scotland* (1990), the second edition of which is currently in preparation.

Alison Cleland is a lecturer at Napier University School of Law, teaching child and family law and a consultant with Mowat Dean, solicitors, where she advises on representation of clients under age 16, having spent four years with the firm working for clients under 16. She was the Scottish Child Law Centre's first advice worker and now chairs the Centre's Board of Trustees.

John Grant is a consultant in international law and Professor Emeritus of International Law at the University of Glasgow, where he was the Dean of Law for a total of eight years and founded the Lockerbie Trial Briefing Unit. He is also a professor at Lewis & Clark School of Law, Portland, Oregon, where he teaches and researches for six months each year, spending the remainder of the year in Scotland. He is a former member of the children's panel and has written extensively on the hearings system and on international human rights.

Peter Hunter is an employment and discrimination law specialist employed as the legal officer of Unison Scotland. He is the former director of the Scottish Low Pay Unit and currently sits as a lay member of the Employment Appeal Tribunal. He has written extensively on the legal position of many vulnerable groups in the labour market, including children and young people.

Kathleen Marshall is a solicitor, child law consultant and Visiting Professor to the Centre for the Child & Society, University of Glasgow. She was Director of the Scottish Child Law Centre from 1989 to 1994. She chaired the Edinburgh Inquiry into Abuse and Protection of Children in Care, which reported in February, 1999. Her consultancy work has addressed a wide range of children's rights issues, for example, in relation to support for children and families, child protection, health, education and the court system.

Much of her current work is connected with aspects of the UN Convention on the Rights of the Child.

Colin Moodie is a senior solicitor with Falkirk Council where he deals primarily with social work and education matters. Prior to working in Falkirk, he was the senior legal officer at the Scottish Child Law Centre. He is a member of the Board of Trustees of the Centre.

Kenneth Norrie is Professor of Law at the University of Strathclyde, having previously taught in Aberdeen and Dundee. He was also taught abroad in Germany, Austria and Australia. He is best known as the author of works such as *Parent and Child*, and *Children's Hearings in Scotland*, and has published extensively in these fields both at home and abroad. He was formerly a Board Member of the Scottish Child Law Centre and sat for many years on the children's panel for the City of Glasgow.

Hilary Patrick is Honorary Fellow, Faculty of Law, University of Edinburgh. She is co-author (with John Blackie) of *Mental Health: A Guide to the Law in Scotland*, and with Colin McKay, of *The Care Maze: A Guide to Community Care and the Law in Scotland*. She is also a contributor to Mays *Scottish Social Work Legislation*, and to Butterworths' *Elderly Client Service in Scotland*. She was a member of the Millan Committee, which recommended reform of Scottish mental health law.

Janys Scott is an advocate with a particular interest in the law relating to children. She has worked with the British Agencies for Adoption and Fostering as their Scottish legal adviser. She served as Convenor of the Scottish Child Law Centre and is currently Chair of Stepfamily Scotland. She has written about adoption in Butterworths' *Family Law Service*, Macphail's *Sheriff Court Practice* and Green's *Scottish Human Rights Service*.

Shona Smith is a solicitor in private practice at Balfour and Manson, Edinburgh. She has worked exclusively in the area of family law for a number of years and is accredited by the Law Society of Scotland as a family law specialist. The present chair of the Family Law Association and a former Board member of the Child Law Centre, she has a particular interest in cases involving children. She is a contributor to Butterworths' *Scottish Family Law Service*.

David Stone is Professor of Paediatric Epidemiology and Director of the Paediatric Epidemiology and Community Health (PEACH) Unit in the Department of Child Health at the University of Glasgow. His main research interests include the epidemiology of birth defects, injury surveillance and prevention, and health screening. He is a Trustee of the Child Accident Prevention Trust and was elected Chair of the International Society for Child and Adolescent Injury Prevention in 2000.

Elaine E. Sutherland is a Reader in Law at Glasgow University and a Professor at Lewis & Clark Law School, Portland, Oregon, spending six months of the year researching, writing and teaching at each. Presenting papers at conferences around the world is one of her great joys and privileges. Her publications include: *Child and Family Law* (1999); the Scottish chapter in Hamilton and Standley (eds), *Family Law in Europe* (1995); (with McCall Smith (eds)), *Family Law and Medical Advance (1994)*; "Parent and Child" in the *Stair Memorial Encyclopaedia of the Laws of Scotland* (1991). She is a former "safeguarder", participates in the law reform process through regular responses to consultation papers from government and other bodies, and serves on the Family Law Committee of the Law Society of Scotland.

Kay Tisdall is Lecturer in Social Policy, University of Edinburgh and Director of Policy & Research, Children in Scotland (the national agency for organisations and professionals working with children and their families). She is convenor of the MSc in Childhood Studies at the University and is active in policy development through her post at Children in Scotland. She is involved in a range of research projects, from the views of children in family law proceedings, to children affected by disabilities, to integrated services for children and their families.

TABLE OF CASES

TABLE OF STATUTES

TABLE OF STATUTORY INSTRUMENTS

TABLE OF CONVENTIONS AND TREATIES

CHAPTER 1

HOW REAL ARE CHILDREN'S RIGHTS IN SCOTLAND?

ELAINE E. SUTHERLAND AND ALISON CLELAND

Can it be asserted, with confidence, that children's rights have come **1.1** of age in Scotland? Certainly, the concept has passed beyond its infancy, the time when it was somewhat undeveloped and it was greeted either as a novelty or heralded as a "'hurrah' idea".[1] If children's rights have moved beyond their infancy, where are they now? This chapter will set the scene for the chapters which follow, highlighting the extent to which children's rights are, or are not, finding expression in Scotland, in terms of policy, law and practice.

The United Nations Convention on the Rights of the Child (UN **1.2** Convention) has been with us for over a decade and has now been ratified by all but two countries in the world.[2] The European Convention on Human Rights and Fundamental Freedoms (European Convention) has been with us much longer but, undoubtedly, its status was enhanced with the coming into force of the Human Rights Act 1998. A fundamental question for everyone committed to promoting children's rights is whether the European Convention will be a help or a hindrance. There is a danger that the due process requirements[3] and the right to respect for private and family life[4] could be interpreted in an adult-centric way, making the European Convention a dormant virus waiting to attack children's rights. Certainly, these concepts have been used to that effect in the United States.[5] While we must remain vigilant to ensure that children's rights are not diminished in this way, the picture is not entirely gloomy. The European Convention and the Constitution of the United States of America are very different documents, with different jurisprudential histories. Given the European Court's willingness to use other instruments, like the UN Convention and the

---

[1] M.D.A. Freeman, *The Rights and Wrongs of Children* (Frances Pinter, 1983), p. 6. See further, Chap. 2, *infra*.
[2] Somalia and the USA, see para. 3.28.
[3] Art. 6.
[4] Art. 8.
[5] See, *e.g.*, *Kingsley v. Kingsley*, 623 So 2d 780 (Fla., 1993).

Beijing Rules, as aids to interpreting its own provisions and ascertaining world standards, the European Convention may actually become a vehicle for the furtherance of children's rights. Perhaps the fundamental point to remember is that "children are people too"[6], so the rights found in the European Convention extend to them. Indeed, a number of the European Court's recent decisions, in the context of children's rights, have been encouraging.[7]

Policy

1.3 How far, then, does public policy demonstrate a regard for children's rights? One must grasp the fundamental limitations of the Conventions in this respect, since statements of policy are often couched in somewhat aspirational terms. International experience tells us that it is considerably easier to ensure respect for "hard" as opposed to "soft" rights; that is to say, civil rights often gain recognition more effectively than social rights.[8] Take, for example, the child's right to enjoy the 'highest attainable standard of health care' as required by the UN Convention.[9] Who defines what amounts to this "highest standard"? Is it some kind of absolute? Where does it rank alongside the other rights that children have, including the right to an adequate standard of living,[10] the right to freedom from abuse and exploitation,[11] and the right to education?[12] Given that government, of whatever hue, has limited resources, it must prioritise areas of expenditure.

1.4   Nor are children the only people who need resources allocated to them. Others, including adults with disabilities, older members of the community, and homeless adults, have legitimate rights as well. Again, governments must identify priorities. This makes it all the more important that the voices of children and those who work for and with them are heard when policies are being considered. Several voluntary organisations in Scotland concerned with child protec-

---

[6]   It may be no coincidence that this is the title of Peter Newell's excellent book making the case against physical punishment of children, a matter on which the European Court has made considerable, albeit slow, progress in getting closer to recognising the child's right to be protected from violence; P. Newell, *Children Are People Too: The Case Against Physical Punishment* (Bedford Square Press, 1989). See further, paras 6.30–6.33.

[7]   See, *e.g.*, *Z and others v. United Kingdom*, May 10, 2001 (rejecting the approach of the House of Lords in *X v. Bedfordshire County Council* [1995] 3 All E.R. 353), and *T.P. and K.M. v. United Kingdom*, May 10, 2001, both available on the European Court's website at < www.hudoc.echr.coe.int. >

[8]   See Chap. 16 for a very full discussion.

[9]   UN Convention on the Rights of the Child, Art. 24.1.

[10] *ibid.*, Art. 27.

[11] *ibid.*, Art. 34.

[12] *ibid.*, Art. 28.

tion and child welfare lobby effectively in relation to these matters.[13] An alliance of children's organisations[14] raises awareness in
relation to issues directly affecting children's rights and interests.
Who Cares? Scotland, the organisation for children looked after by
local authorities in Scotland, has been consulted on legislative
change, and it continues to be well supported by Scottish Executive
funding. Thus, there is pressure in relation to children's rights issues
from outside the Scottish Parliament.

Inside the Parliament itself, the need to promote children's rights   **1.5**
has been recognised in two distinct ways. First, there is a cross-
party group on children, which looks closely at policy issues affecting children and young people in Scotland. Second, there is a
Minister for Children, albeit that the portfolio is only part of the
remit of the Minister to whom the responsibility is allocated. While
these developments are encouraging, a further, highly significant,
step is being explored. The cross-party group has been considering
whether there should be a Children's Commissioner. The Scottish
Parliament's Education, Culture and Sports Committee is undertaking an enquiry into a Children's Commissioner for Scotland.
The Committee will consider whether such an office can be set up
without duplication or overlap with existing services and the
Scottish Parliament will naturally be concerned that, if there is to be
such an office, it will be providing added value.

The case for a Commissioner is often argued most strongly on the   **1.6**
basis that it provides an independent, non-governmental office
which can consider policy, law and practice as they affect, or may
affect, children and young people.[15] The case has been made that
the office, if given adequate funding and autonomy, could fulfill
both proactive and reactive roles. It might suggest where there is a
lack of research on matters affecting children[16] and where legislation is needed,[17] as well as advising against policies which would be

---

[13] *e.g.,* Save the Children, Barnardos, Children First (formerly Royal Society for the
Prevention of Cruelty to Children), Scottish Child Law Centre, National
Children's Homes.

[14] Children's Rights Alliance.

[15] M.G. Flekkoy, *A Voice for Children: Speaking Out as their Ombudsman* (Jessica
Kingsley, 1991); R. Gallagher, *Children's and Young People's Voices on the Law,
Legal Services, Systems and Processes in Scotland* (HMSO, 1999); K. Marshall,
Children's Rights in the Balance: the Participation—Protection Debate (HMSO,
1997); M. Rosenbaum and P. Newell, *Taking Children Seriously: A Proposal for a
Children's Rights Commissioner* (Caslouste Gulbenkian Foundation, 1991).

[16] *e.g.,* research is required into children's experience of being involved in court cases
and of instructing solicitors and in relation to services available for children and
young people with mental health problems.

[17] *e.g.,* the matter of physical punishment of children, on which the Scottish Law
Commission recommended the abolition of the parental right of reasonable
chastisement, but on which no action has so far been taken.

detrimental to children's rights and welfare.[18] Clearly, the jury in Scotland is still out on this issue.

1.7   How might children influence local authority decision-making? Many authorities have children's rights officers who deal with complaints brought by children looked after by these local authorities. It is encouraging that some authorities have given this priority to children, and it may be that children's committees within the local authority structure would allow elected members to become more aware of the concerns of the young people in their communities.

Law

1.8 One of the pillars of the UN Convention is the child's right to be heard.[19] Of course, this has to be read in the light of the importance of the child's welfare, the child's own evolving capacity, and the role of other family members in the child's life. It has long been recognised that the Convention itself contains an inherent tension between rights and welfare—something that poses a challenge to legislators. The European Convention is, perhaps, narrower, but nonetheless, it recognises the right to a fair and public hearing by an independent and impartial tribunal in the determination of one's civil rights and obligations and in respect of criminal charges.[20] To what extent is the child's right to have a voice respected in the various stages of the legal process in Scotland?

1.9   The first stage is consultation on possible reform of the law and, of course, there is a clear overlap with the development of policy in this respect. To what extent have children been consulted when new legislation has been considered? There was an encouraging start in relation to the Scottish Office consultation on child care policy and law. In the proposals published in 1993,[21] there was a commitment to the view that "children have the right to express views about any issues or decisions affecting or worrying them"[22] and young people were consulted on the proposals.[23] One revelation to emerge from the consultation was that, in relation to children's hearings, many young people found it very difficult, and sometimes impossible, to

---

[18] *e.g.*, the Hamilton "Child Safety Initiative", which saw curfew imposed on children in one area in Scotland, could have been scrutinised for its effects on children's civil liberties and for the possibility of alienating children from their communities; see J. McGallagey, K. Power, P. Littlewood and J. Meikle, *Evaluation of the Hamilton Child Safety Initiative* (2001), Scottish Executive, Central Research Unit.

[19] Art. 12.

[20] Art. 6(1).

[21] *Scotland's Children: Proposals for Child Care Policy and Law* (HMSO, 1993).

[22] *ibid.*, para. 2.8

[23] *Scotland's Children: Speaking Out, Young People's Views on Child Care in Scotland* (HMSO, 1995).

make hearings dealing with their cases aware of their feelings when their parents were present in the room. As a result, hearings were given the power to exclude parents and other "relevant persons" from hearings in order to allow children to speak more freely.[24]

Anticipating the creation of the Scottish Parliament, the Scottish **1.10** Office published *Improving Scottish Family Law,*[25] a consultation document exploring options for reform of various aspects of child and family law. Much of the material contained in the consultation paper revisited proposals of the Scottish Law Commission which had not found their way into legislation,[26] although some of the issues explored were new.[27] No real attempt was made on that occasion to involve children and young people in the consultation process, despite the fact that many of the reforms being considered would affect their lives.

There are some positive signs that the Scottish Executive is **1.11** learning from the experience in relation to child care reform proposals and moving towards greater involvement of children and young people in the legislative process. For example, prior to introducing the Standards in Scottish School, etc. Bill, there was extensive consultation with adults.[28] Concern was expressed at the lack of consultation of children, albeit the Executive was at pains to point out that it had commissioned Save the Children to undertake a series of focus groups with children and young people.[29] Rather more attention was given to feedback from children and young people when the Review of Youth Crime[30] was launched in December 1999. This project is seeking to identify the most effective strategies for preventing youth offending and for dealing with children and young people who offend. Views were sought from the usual range of organisations, but there was a specific focus on input from persons under 18 years old.[31]

What of the legislation which results? A leader in the field when it **1.12** comes to recognising the importance of the European and UN Conventions is the Scottish Law Commission. As early as 1992, its

---

[24] Children (Scotland) Act 1995, s. 46.
[25] Scottish Office, 1999.
[26] *e.g.,* parental responsibilities and rights of non-marital fathers, judicial separation, and the grounds for divorce, were revisited.
[27] *e.g.,* the possibility of giving full parental responsibilities and rights to step-parents by simple agreement between the step-parent and the birth parents, was discussed.
[28] The whole process is detailed in *Standards in Scotland's Schools, etc. Bill,* Research Paper 00/02, February 15, 2000, available on < http://www.scotland.-gov.uk/library/ > .
[29] *ibid.,* at p. 34.
[30] The website for the project is < http://www.scotland.gov.uk/youth/crimereview > and this will be updated as the consultation process progresses.
[31] Initial consultation produced 290 responses with 170 of these coming from young people. A significant number of the responses from young people came from residents in young offenders institutions.

recommendations on law reform in respect of the child in the family setting showed a keen awareness of both the Conventions' core provisions and how they could find expression in legislation.[32] It is no surprise, then, that the Children (Scotland) Act 1995, Part I of which was based substantially on the Commission's recommendations, should attempt to give children a voice when decisions were being taken about their future.[33] In Part II of the Act, dealing with child protection, the place of the child's voice is again recognised.[34] Similarly, the Act seeks to recognise the importance of the child's welfare and the centrality of family in a child's life.

1.13   Of course, not all legislation lives up the standards of the UN Convention. In the field of child abduction, for example, the goal of the law is to effect the speedy return of the child to the appropriate jurisdiction. This leaves little room for the child's views on return to be considered by the court.[35] In the field of education, and despite some recent legislative improvements, the child's voice is something of a whisper, since there is no principle of allowing children to be heard in education decisions affecting them.[36] The very limited concession to the requirements of Article 12 of the UN Convention is the right of appeal recently given to pupils to appeal against their exclusion from school. [37] However, this concession is effectively negated by the lack of any due process at the first instance since the pupil's appeal will be heard by an appeal committee of the education authority who made the decision to exclude.[38]

1.14   What of the courts? Of course, they are currently somewhat preoccupied with, some might say besieged by, the European Convention. The courts at all levels in Scotland, like their counterparts in many other jurisdictions,[39] are embracing the UN Convention.[40] Whether they always interpret it in a way that the present authors might advocate cannot be guaranteed, but that can be true of any authority cited to a court. That the UN Convention

---

[32] *Report on Family Law* (Scot. Law Com. No. 135, 1992), para. 3.24.
[33] s. 6. See paras 6.17–6.21–and 10.26–10.39.
[34] s. 16. See para 8.4 and 8.21.
[35] See paras 7.22–7.33.
[36] See para. 12.75.
[37] Standards In Scotland's Schools (Scotland) Act 2000, s. 41.
[38] See paras 12.63–12.68.
[39] A flavour of the use made of the UN Convention can be gleaned from searching Lexis for cases where reference is made to it. Such a search, conducted in mid-March 2001, produced the following results: Scotland (8 cases), England and Wales (93), Australia (224), Canada (166) and New Zealand (73). While there may be an element of duplication, in respect of cases being reported at each level, the point is clear.
[40] See, *e.g., Sanderson v. McManus* (1997) S.C. (H.L.) 55 *per* Lord Clyde at p. 65 (parental right to contact with children and the legitimate limits thereon); *Dosoo v. Dosoo*, 1999 S.L.T. (Sh. Ct) 86, *per* Sheriff Robertson at p. 87 (child's right to express views on contact with a parent and the right to confidentiality); *White v. White*, 1999 S.L.T. 106, *per* Sheriff Principal Nicholson at p. 110 (different position of marital and non-marital father); *Re B.*, 1996 S.L.T. 1370.

is now an accepted part of the legal landscape was reinforced by Lord McCluskey, borrowing from and paraphrasing Lord Hope,[41] when he said:

> "[T]he presumption to be applied when interpreting legislation found to be ambiguous is that Parliament is to be presumed to have legislated in conformity with the [European] Convention, not in conflict with it. The same general approach has to be taken when construing and applying legislation dealing with the subject matter of the UN Convention".[42]

In a sense, there is nothing radical in this observation, since it **1.15** simply confirms the established position of Scots law. However, it was helpful that a senior member of the judiciary should issue the reminder, since only a year earlier the Scottish Executive seemed rather confused on the point. Dismissing the UN Convention as "not having the force of law in Scotland", it saw no need to ensure that its proposals for reform of the law on physical punishment of children met that Convention's standards.[43] Lest we become complacent over judicial enthusiasm for the UN Convention, we must remember that the judiciary works largely with what is argued to it and, in this respect, the recent decision in *S. v. Miller*[44] is disappointing, since no mention is made in the judgments of the UN Convention or, indeed, other relevant international instruments. That brings us to a fundamental point in ensuring respect for children's rights. Sound policy foundations are important, as are laws which have explicit regard to children's rights. However, what actually happens in practice, at all levels and in every aspect of a child's life, is what matters to the individual child.

Practice

Perhaps the greatest practical obstacle to the realisation of chil- **1.16** dren's rights is ignorance—on the part of children, parents and professionals. It is not known how many children and parents are aware of the obligation to take the child's views into account when a major decision is being taken in the context of parental responsibilities and rights,[45] but the suspicion exists that there is widespread ignorance of this requirement. In the context of education

---

[41] In *Sanderson v McManus*, 1997 S.C. (H.L.) 55, commenting on the position of the UN Convention prior to passage of the Human Rights Act 1998.
[42] *White v. White*, 2001 S.L.T. 485 at p.494.
[43] *Physical Punishment of Children in Scotland* (Scottish Executive, February 2000), at para. 3.24.
[44] 2001 S.L.T. 531.
[45] Children (Scotland) Act 1995, s. 6.

and health care, there are, again, strong suspicions, supported by anecdotal evidence, that children's rights are not always respected. Of course, suspicion alone is not enough and anecdotal evidence is no evidence at all.[46] Nonetheless, there is a need for far greater public education of both children and adults, whether the latter are parents or professionals involved with children.

1.17   Rights are of little value unless the holder not only knows their content and implications but also has an effective means of enforcing them. This requires that children should have real access to legal advice and representation. In this respect, the UN Convention and the European Convention may be pointing in the same direction. While neither requires legal representation in all circumstances, each anticipates it being necessary in some situations. This would be clearest, perhaps, in the case of a child facing an accusation of his or her own criminality. For children attending a children's hearing, there is, as yet, no guarantee of such representation, although the decision in *S v. Miller* gives some cause for optimism.

1.18   In theory, there is no legal barrier to representation for children in civil proceedings, other than, perhaps, the availability of legal aid.[47] However, if the child's right to be heard is to become a reality, children and young people must know they can consult a solicitor, they must know how to gain access to a solicitor, and they must be guided towards solicitors who are capable of communicating effectively with them. Does the legal system currently offer this to children? It does not.

1.19   In an already over-stretched school curriculum, there is no mandatory course on children's rights and many children do not know of their right to seek legal advice or to be heard in the myriad of possible settings where the law requires that they should. While the Scottish Office published a booklet advising children of their rights in family court cases,[48] a child is likely to see it only when a court case affecting him or her is pending.

1.20   For the limited number of children who do seek legal advice, the issue must be one of the quality of the representation available to them. As the wealth of textbooks and articles in the field of child law demonstrate, the law relating to children is complex, demanding and one which has undergone tremendous development over the last few decades. It is not a field in which a practitioner can dabble, not least because the outcome of a case can have an enormous impact on a child's life. In addition, children have the right to expect that the solicitors whom they consult will have had some training on dealing with child clients. No such requirement exists at

---

[46] This makes research into public and professional awareness of children's rights all the more urgent.

[47] See paras 10.35–10.50.

[48] "You Matter" (1996, The Scottish Office), produced by the Scottish Child Law Centre and jointly commissioned and funded by the Scottish Office Home and Health Department and Scottish Courts Administration.

present in Scotland. While the Law Society of Scotland took the welcome step of introducing a recognised specialism in child law, it does not require that a designated specialist has undergone any additional training. It does not even demand that the accredited specialist should ever have met a child client.

What of the child who makes it through the obstacle course and **1.21** gets as far as a court? If the child's views are to have any influence, judicial attitudes are crucial. While there are encouraging signs of a greater willingness on the part of judges to listen to children,[49] the trend is far from universal.

Quite apart from access to the legal system, a whole range of **1.22** matters of practice remain of concern. While the law seeks to protect children from dangerous employment and the policy-makers appear genuinely concerned,[50] children continue to be employed in illegal occupations, outwith the legally permitted hours, and few prosecutions ever take place. Children with, and affected by, disabilities and those with special needs could be forgiven for thinking that they have no legal rights because the practical effects of any legal safeguards are so limited.[51] Provision for these children remains woefully inadequate and the mechanisms to ensure their views are heard in matters affecting them are, at best, ineffective.

The verdict

Clearly, children's rights in Scotland have moved beyond infancy **1.23** but, to return to the question posed at the beginning of this chapter, where are they now? Of course, it is for the reader to reach his or her own conclusion on the stage of development of children's rights in Scotland and it is to be hoped that the following chapters will assist in that process. While the editors would not wish to reveal the whole plot of the book, it may be too early to describe children's rights as having come of age. Rather, it can be argued, the concept is experiencing adolescence: a time of exciting development, coupled with a degree of uncertainty and anguish.

---

[49] Contrast the opinion in *Henderson v. Henderson*, 1997 Fam. L.R. 120 with that in *Fourman v. Fourman*, 1998 Fam. L.R. 98.
[50] See paras 13.14–13.20.
[51] See paras 4.19 *et seq.* and 12.69 *et seq.*

CHAPTER 2

THE HISTORY AND PHILOSOPHY OF CHILDREN'S RIGHTS IN SCOTLAND

KATHLEEN MARSHALL

The History of Children's Rights in Scotland

Early History

It is difficult to be sure about the content of Scots law before the **2.1**
union of parliaments of 1707. No official records were kept before
1424, and from that date up to 1707 they are described as "patchy
and unreliable", with some improvement after 1578.[1]

Nevertheless, there is support for the view that, between the de- **2.2**
parture of the Romans in 410 A.D. and the introduction of the
feudal system in the 12th century, Scottish law had the character
largely of "customary law". This was traditionally backed by no
official sanctions, but based on the general consensus of the community.[2] Adjudication might be by a hereditary caste or by identified "just men" who provided a succession of "sages". It is perhaps
not surprising that there is little substantive evidence about the
content of these laws. There is speculation that the Scottish laws
may have been similar to the Irish Brehon laws, which consisted
largely of a tariff of compensatory fines for wrongs done.

What little we do know has some relevance to the law relating to **2.3**
children. Thus, a Gaelic "contract of fosterage" by Sir Roderick
MacLeod in 1614 would seem to provide evidence for the lingering
in Scotland of a Celtic legal custom whereby children of one family
were brought up and educated by another.[3] This arrangement is
referred to in a history of the islands of Colonsay and Oronsay:

> "It was a common custom in those days for ruling families to
> exchange children, who were fostered out until they were old

---

[1] Thankerton, *The Statutory Law,* in The Stair Society, *The Sources and Literature of Scots Law* (1936), pp. 5–10.

[2] *Bruce v. Smith*, 1890, 17 R. 1000, quoted by St Vigeans, *Custom,* in The Stair Society, *op. cit.,* p. 163.

[3] J. Cameron, *Celtic Law,* in The Stair Society, *op. cit.,* p .351.

enough to reclaim their birthright. One purpose behind this custom may have been to minimise clan feuding by building up personal contacts between neighbours".[4]

Thus children could play an important role based on the needs of the community rather than their own individual development.

2.4   There appear also to have been some laws (cáins) which were specifically promulgated, as opposed to growing slowly out of custom. In the seventh century a law for the protection of non-combatants was promulgated by Adomnán, Abbot of Iona. Whilst associated largely with the protection of women, it extended also to children, up to the point where they themselves took up arms for the first time.

> The enactment of the *Cáin Adomnáin* stands as an everlasting *cáin* for clergy and women, and for innocent children until they are capable of killing a man, till they have a place in the tribe and till their first armed conflict is known.[5]

Thus, even at this early stage of development, the law recognised the innocence and vulnerability of children, and the need to extend some protection to them, and identified an indicator of when that protection should end.

The Feudal System

2.5   The establishment of the feudal system provided a more comprehensive legal structure, and it is claimed that in 1400, "all churchmen, widows, orphans and pupils might resort to the King for redress".[6] The important distinction in status in feudal times was based, not on the age of a person, but on their relationship to their superiors. A Poor Law Commissioner, writing in 1856, observed that:

> "The feudal serf, villein or slave was there, as elsewhere, an article of property. He had no rights, individual or social. Himself, his children and his children's children for ever, were the property of another, who might sell and dispose of them when, where, and as he thought fit".[7]

---

[4]   N.S. Newton, *Colonsay and Oronsay* (David and Charles, 1990), p. 108.
[5]   Para. 34 of the *Cáin Adomnáin*. It survives in its Irish version, which represents some discernible modifications of the original Iona material. See G. Márkus, *Adomnán's Law of the Innocents* (1997), pp. 3 and 6.
[6]   Thomson, *Acts of the Parliaments of Scotland 1124–1707*, I, 576, quoted by R. K. Hannay, *Early Records of Council and Session, 1466–1659*, The Stair Society, *op. cit.*, p. 18.
[7]   Sir G. Nicholls, *A History of the Scotch Poor Law, in Connection with the Condition of the People* (John Murray, 1856), p. 4.

Fraser[8] also refers to the period in which " the superior had the custody of his minor vassals".

It could therefore be argued that children were the property of their superiors.

The Reception of Roman Law

The development in Scotland of Roman law principles was not a **2.6** legacy of the earlier presence of the Roman legions, but the result of a much later "reception" of the Roman system by legal academics and the judiciary. In the intervening centuries, there had been some Roman influence through the application of Canon Law, the law of the Roman Catholic Church.

The attractiveness of the Roman system lay in the fact that it **2.7** provided a readily available body of principles which could be drawn upon to help shape a comprehensive, national system of law. In pursuing this aim, the Court of Session drew heavily on the work of Stair who regarded Roman law as very close to the law of nature. [9]

Despite this respect for the law of Rome, it was not received **2.8** indiscriminately. General principles were adopted, but "elaborate refinements" were dropped. The Roman law that was received has been described as a "simplified product".[10]

The reception of Roman law was significant for Scotland's chil- **2.9** dren. Roman law was based on a family structure resting upon the authority of the male head of the extended family, the *paterfamilias*. In earlier days, the status of the descendants, of whatever age, could be described as a "condition of utter subjection",[11] equivalent to that of slaves. It amounted to ownership of the child as a piece of property and extended even to the power to put the child to death. The law softened with the passage of time.

The Scottish reception did not include the harsher notions as- **2.10** sociated with the authority of the father of the family—the *patria potestas*—but did include some of the characteristics of ownership, together with a high notion of the rights of the father.

Alongside the overarching power of the head of the family, there **2.11** developed a two-fold distinction between children, based on the assumed age of puberty. This was relevant largely when the *paterfamilias* was dead and a system was required for regulating guardianship of the child. Children under the age of puberty were called "pupils" and were subject to their guardians (tutors) as regards to both their property and their persons. On attaining puberty, they became "minors". Their guardians, known as "curators",

---

[8] P. Fraser, *A Treatise on the Law of Parent and Child*, (3rd ed., 1906, by James Clark, Advocate, W. Green & Son), p. 283.

[9] Thomson, *op. cit.*, p. 180.

[10] D.B. Smith, *Roman Law, The Stair Society, op. cit.*, p. 179.

[11] J. Muirhead, *Roman Law* (2nd ed., 1899, Adam and Charles Black), p. 28.

acted with the children in the administration of their affairs, but had no control over their persons. Puberty was held to have occurred at age 12 for girls and 14 for boys.

2.12   Roman law was not in fact as clear on the capacity of children as this neat division might suggest. Fraser[12] states that:

> "A pupil who was near the age of puberty did not, by the Roman law, labour under the same disabilities as a pupil *proximus infantiae*. After he had passed the age of ten and a half, he was said to be *proximus pubertati*, and his powers were in a great measure commensurate with those of a minor who had attained to puberty".

2.13   Fraser proceeds to cite authorities for his claim that "This distinction was formerly recognised in Scotland to its full extent". Moreover, he argues that:

> "By the ancient constitutions of Scotland, the age of capacity to discharge the business of life was regulated in some measure by the status of the party, and the property which he possessed, and not entirely by the number of years he might have lived. But there is no distinction of this nature in existence at the present day".

2.14   It would seem that Scotland adopted the Roman law notion of the child as property of the father, as well as the two-stage approach to the maturity and capacity of children. In the course of the reception of that law, however, Scotland adopted a softer and more discretionary approach to the powers of the father, and a more rigid and legalistic approach to the capacity of children.

Modification of Roman Law

2.15   Scotland's adherence to the Roman law continued to change with the times. The leading case in Victorian times was *Harvey v. Harvey*.[13] A boy of 15 and a girl of 14 had been in the custody of their mother for 12 years. The parents had been divorced following the father's adultery with his wife's sister. The father petitioned for custody and access. The children expressed a strong desire to have nothing to do with him. The father argued that he had an absolute legal right to custody up to the age of majority and that the court could not interfere unless it was shown that this would place the children in serious moral or physical danger. The respondents argued that a minor child was entitled to choose his own place of

---

[12]   Fraser, *op. cit.*, p. 199.
[13]   (1860) 22 D. 1198.

residence unless seeking maintenance from the father. In any event, they considered that the father's character and conduct were such as ought to dissuade the court from placing the children in his care.

In surveying the contemporary legal situation, the court ac- **2.16**
knowledged that the law had developed from its earlier application:

> "The very capacity of complete emancipation shows how fee-
> ble is the hold of the *patria potestas* over a child in puberty, as
> compared not only with the same authority during the child's
> pupillage, but with its exercise at all ages of children in the
> earlier Roman law, and at one time even in the law of Scot-
> land".

In refusing the father's petition, the court referred to the children's **2.17**
clear wishes on the matter, supported by the report of a curator *ad
litem,* appointed to protect their interests. It set out four "practical
propositions" in support of its decision:

1. That the control to which a *minor pubes* is subjected, does
   not proceed on any notion of his incapacity to exercise a
   rational judgment or choice, but rather arises, on the one
   hand, from a consideration of the reverence and obedi-
   ence to parents which both the law of nature and the
   divine law enjoin, and, on the other hand, from a regard
   to the inexperience and immaturity of judgment on the
   part of the child, which require friendly and affectionate
   counsel and aid.
2. That the power of a father, at this age, is conferred not as
   a right of dominion, or even as a privilege for the father's
   own benefit or pleasure, but merely, or at least mainly,
   for the benefit, guidance and comfort of the child.
3. That, therefore, the father's authority and right of control may at this age of the child be easily lost, either by an
   apparent intention to abandon it and leave the child to
   his own guidance, or by circumstances or conduct
   showing the father's inability or unwillingness to discharge rightly the parental duty towards his child.
4. That in all questions as to the loss of the parental control
   during puberty from any of these causes, the wishes and
   feelings of the child himself are entitled to a degree of
   weight corresponding to the amount of intelligence and
   right feeling which he may exhibit.

This judgment contains the seeds of the modern view of parental **2.18**
rights as existing for the benefit of the child. The welfare of the child
is the main consideration, and the wishes of mature children are to
be taken into account.

How relevant was the law to the actual lives of children?

Introduction

2.19 Much of the case law regarding the tutory and curatory of children had to do with the administration of property. Many examples are cited in Fraser. There was less legal activity concerned with the welfare of children. Some matters did come before the court, and might be concerned with the custody or protection of a child. Insofar as the upper classes were concerned, these were centred mainly on the extent to which the court was willing to interfere with the father's *patria potestas*. This might arise in the context of a dispute between parents, or a concern about the child's moral or physical welfare. In the lower ranks of society, legal interest was centred on the operation of the Poor Laws.

The Upper Classes

2.20 Inter-familial disputes often centred on the rights of the mother to custody, access and guardianship. Whilst the courts were hesitant to concede any qualification of the natural right of the father, the case of Harvey, set out above, shows how the passage of time did see an increasing willingness to look to the welfare of the child and the wishes of the mother and the children as relevant considerations.

2.21   Disputes other than those between parents might also centre on perceptions of the welfare of the child, although in some of the following cases there might also be an element of the child as a tool of social change.

2.22   Until the current century, the law did not interfere in family life to any great extent. This was partly a consequence of the notion of the privacy of the family under the authority of the *paterfamilias*. Whilst the courts would interfere in the case of a vicious father, there was a lack of systems for surveillance of children and identification of concerns. Only relatives of the child could apply to the court to take measures aimed at the child's protection. Neither strangers, nor the Crown, had any right to intervene.[14]

2.23   The power of the Court of Session in these cases was inherited from the jurisdiction of the Scotch Privy Council who, Fraser tells us,[15] "claimed the right of superintending the morals and education of the community". Thus, in 1665, "Scott of Raeburn and his wife being infected with the error of Quakerism, had their children taken from them",[16] and the young Marquis of Huntly was removed from

---

[14] Fraser. *op. cit.,* p. 93.
[15] *ibid.,* p. 90.
[16] Quoted *ibid.,* p. 90.

the custody of his mother and guardians, "they being popishly in-clined".

By 1775, the right of the Court to control parental authority was **2.24** well established. From that date also are seen cases based on the cruelty of the father towards his children. The case of *Bailie v. Agnew,*[17] was based upon the drunkenness of the father, Sir Stair Agnew of Lochnaw, and his "high acts of ferocity and maltreat-ment to his children".[18] Still it was doubted whether the court would intervene if the father had merely been neglectful of matters such as the education of the child, or of provision beyond what was strictly necessary for subsistence.

The Poor Laws

The law was also relevant to the lives of poorer children. Much of **2.25** what we know from the 15th and 16th centuries was concerned with putting an end to vagrancy. An Act of 1579 sought to remove the children of beggars from the assumed immoral influence of their parents and place them in an industrious and honest state. It pro-vided that:

> "If any beggar's bairns (male or female), being above the age of five years and under fourteen, shall be liked of by any subject of the realm of honest estate—such person may have the bairn by direction of the provost and bailies within burgh, or the judge in landward parishes, if he be a manchild to the age of 24 years, and if a womanchild to the age of 28 years. And if they depart or be taken or enticed from their master's or mistress's service, the master or mistress shall have the like action and remedy as for their 'feit' servant or apprentice, as well against the bairn as against the taker or enticer thereof".[19]

This seemed to aim at containing and reforming the children of **2.26** beggars, at great cost to their liberty. A further Act of 1617 ex-tended their period of bondage up to the age of 30 for both sexes. This Act did refer to the need to "care for" children, but its pro-visions were described as "modified slavery" leading to "evils of no inconsiderable magnitude".[20]

The author of these derogatory comments also noted however that:

> "It checked the growth of vagrancy by arresting one main source of supply, and at the same time promoted the increase

---

[17] 5 Sup. 526 (1775). Quoted Fraser, *op. cit.,* p. 92.
[18] *ibid.,* p. 92.
[19] Quoted Nicholls, *op. cit.,* p. 22.
[20] *ibid.,* p. 43.

of industrial power; and these were operations assuredly
tending to the general weal".

It might be argued that, here also, the child was being used as a tool
of social change.

2.27 Concern about vagrancy was high on the agenda of lawmakers of
that time. Indeed, the first moves towards provision of relief for the
poor arose out of a desire to put an end to vagrancy and begging.
Contributions to the Poor Law Fund were initially voluntary, and
relief was available for those who were infirm or disabled. There
was, in Scotland, to a greater extent than in England, a resistance to
provision of relief for the able-bodied.[21]

In 1843, a Commission of Inquiry appointed to survey the operation of the Poor Law in Scotland expressed concern for the
moral welfare of the children of beggars:

> "The low lodging houses which beggars frequent, and the bad
> habits of the class of persons with whom they necessarily as-
> sociate, soon familiarise their minds with vice and debauchery;
> and if such (it is asked) be the effects upon those of mature
> years, what must be the result with children, whom it is the
> common practice of the parents to send to beg?"[22]

2.28 The Commission's report led to the passing of the Poor Law
Amendment Act of 1845.[23] This levied a compulsory rate of contribution to the Poor Law Fund and made specific provision for the
education of pauper children.[24]

Mackay, writing in 1907, noted that:

> "...although the main function of the early Poor Law Acts was
> repressive, they held the germ of that kindlier spirit which
> animates the great Act of 1845".[25]

2.29 In practice, some of the more restrictive conditions of the Poor
Laws were not observed.[26]

2.30 Whilst Poorhouses were set up to accommodate various categories of needy people, orphaned and deserted children were generally boarded-out with relatives, friends, or other persons willing
to take charge of them.[27] Institutions were regarded as having a bad

---

[21] Nicholls, *op. cit.*, p. 112.
[22] Quoted *ibid.*, p. 164.
[23] An Act for the Amendment and better Administration of the Laws relating to the Relief of the Poor in Scotland (*8th and 9th Vict. cap. 83.*).
[24] Nicholls, *op. cit.*, p. 169.
[25] Mackay, *Practice of the Scottish Poor Law*, p.1–2.
[26] *ibid.*, p. 70.
[27] Nicholls, *op. cit.*, p. 141.

effect on children.[28] Nevertheless, this had to be balanced in some cases by the advantages to the child of remaining in a family, where that family was not "vicious". Speaking of the reception into the poorhouse of a "vicious" parent with children, Mackay says that, wherever possible, these children should be boarded out. He reflects that:

> "It would be an immense advantage if Parish Councils in Scotland had, as in England, statutory power to separate children from depraved and vicious adults".[29]

The system of boarding-out was said to have grown naturally, and **2.31** was "not regulated, or even suggested, by Statute".[30] Reference was made to the desirability of avoiding the use of local Poor Law inspectors to visit children boarded-out, on the grounds that this would make their status known and attract stigma. Nor was contact with their indigent families encouraged. Guardians of boarded-out children were reminded that:

> "...the object of the Council in boarding out children is to remove the children from all pauperising influences......No communications from, nor visits by, relatives or friends to children should be allowed without the sanction of the Inspector..."

Those children who did enter the poorhouse were given special diets **2.32** appropriate to their stage of development. They were also accorded specific rights with regard to religion. If a child was registered as adhering to one religion and was deserted or orphaned, the parochial board was not to alter the register without the child's consent.[31]

There is a further specific reference to the rights of children with **2.33** regard to the provision of relief. It had traditionally been held that relief to a child amounted to relief to a parent. There was therefore a reluctance to provide relief for a child whose parent was poor but able-bodied. Nevertheless, writing in 1856, Nicholls refers to a "recent" decision of the Sheriff of Lanarkshire, upheld by the Court of Session, to the effect that such children had a "legal right" to be relieved independently of their parents.[32]

A great amount of legal activity around the Poor Laws concerned **2.34** the issue of "settlement". As relief was provided by parishes, some system was required for determining the parish to which relief

---

[28] Mackay, *op. cit.*, p. 120.
[29] *ibid.*, p. 64.
[30] *ibid.*, p. 65.
[31] Nicholls, *op. cit.*, p. 265/6.
[32] *ibid.*, p. 220.

should be chargeable. Rules were developed based on the length of residence or "settlement" in a parish. Insofar as children were concerned, their legal status as pupils or minors and the application of the doctrine of *forisfamiliation* (emancipation from parental control) were relevant to determining their place of settlement for the purpose of relief.

So the law was relevant to the situations of rich and poor children, but in different ways.

Illegitimacy

2.35 Straddling the lives of rich and poor was the stigma of illegitimacy. Children born out of wedlock have traditionally been legally disadvantaged. In setting out the legal disabilities of these children, Fraser asserts:

> "It is the policy of law to discourage every other connection than that of marriage, by not acknowledging, as to any legal effect, the relations which spring from connections unsanctioned by marriage".[33]

2.36 The law acknowledged the relationship of father and child only to the extent of imposing an obligation of aliment on the father. Neither could a father marry an illegitimate daughter. Beyond that, the child remained unrecognised and was not entitled, for example, to succeed to the father's estate. The disadvantages extended beyond the private sphere, for, in earlier times at least, bastards were barred from holding public office.

2.37 In this way, some children were clearly disadvantaged on the basis of the greater good of the community. Children were used as a tool of social control.

Legislative Reform

Parental Rights

2.38 While the courts were increasingly placing emphasis on the welfare of children at the expense of the *patria potestas,* parliament was enacting laws to the same effect.

2.39 The Conjugal Rights (Scotland) Amendment Act 1861 allowed the Court of Session to make arrangements for the custody of pupil children within the process of divorce or separation rather than through a separate application to the *nobile officium.* [34]

---

[33] Fraser, *op. cit.,* p. 144.
[34] Fraser, *op. cit.,* p. 175.

The Guardianship of Infants Act 1886, provided that mothers **2.40**
would take over the tutory of pupil children on the death of the
father. It also allowed the mother of a pupil child to make application to the court for custody or access, the court being empowered by section 5 to "make such order as it may think fit...having
regard to the welfare of the infant, and to the conduct of the parents, and to the wishes as well of the mother as of the father...".
The Act applied to England as well as Scotland. In a subsequent
case, it was referred to by Lindley, L. J., as "essentially a mother's
Act."[35] In respect that it opened up more options for children and
referred to the welfare of the child as at least one of the considerations to be taken into account, it could be regarded as being in
some respects also a children's Act.

The Guardianship of Infants Act 1925 went further in making the **2.41**
welfare of the child the "first and paramount consideration", irrespective of the claims of the mother or father.

However, these Acts applied only to pupil children and it was felt **2.42**
that provision should also be made for custody awards to be made
in relation to older children to relieve them of the burden of choice
between parents. As a result, the Custody of Children (Scotland)
Act 1939 gave courts the power to make orders relating to the
custody, maintenance and education of, and access to, minor children under the age of 16.

Illegitimacy

In 1986, The Law Reform (Parent and Child) (Scotland) Act sought **2.43**
to remove as far as possible the consequences related to the stigma
of illegitimacy. To that extent it could be seen as a statement that
children were no longer to be used as a tool of social control, but to
be regarded as individuals in their own right, regardless of the
circumstances of their birth.

Child Protection and Welfare

On the child protection front, the Custody of Children Act 1891, **2.44**
which applied throughout the United Kingdom, was a protective
Act in respect that it allowed the Court to resist applications by a
parent for "production" of a child on the basis that the parent had
abandoned or deserted the child "or has otherwise so conducted
himself that that the court should refuse to enforce his right to the
custody of the child". In these circumstances the Court was not to
make an order for delivery of the child to the parent "unless the
parent has satisfied the Court, that, having regard to the welfare of
the child, he is a fit person to have the custody of the child". The

---

[35] *In Re A. And B., Infants*, 1897, 1Ch. 786. Quoted Fraser, *op. cit.*, p. 181.

1891 Act was however essentially reactive in nature.

2.45   More proactive was a series of Acts between 1889 and 1908 which developed and consolidated the law on the prevention of cruelty to children.[36] These made provision for a police constable to remove to a place of safety a child in need of immediate protection and for children to take refuge there. Where a parent or other person with custody, charge or care of a child was convicted of cruelty to the child, the court could order the child to be removed from that person's custody and placed with a relative or other "fit person". The child could also be removed when the parent was committed for trial for cruelty, but if the parent was acquitted, the order fell.

2.46   Further milestones are to be found in the Children and Young Persons (Scotland) Act 1932, consolidated in the 1937 Act of the same name, and the Children Act 1948, which contains provisions recognisable to the modern practitioner. In 1963, a further Children and Young Persons Act imposed on local authorities a broader duty to promote social welfare.

2.47   The law relating to child protection and welfare was substantially reformed by the Social Work (Scotland) Act 1968 which, in its relation to children, arose largely out of the recommendations of the Kilbrandon Commission.[37] The Commission's remit had been:

"to consider the provisions of the law of Scotland relating to the treatment of delinquents and juveniles in need of care or protection or beyond parental control and, in particular, the constitution, powers, and procedure of the courts dealing with such juveniles".

2.48 The Commission's 1964 report led to the establishment of Scotland's unique system of children's hearings. Members of hearings are drawn from a panel of trained community volunteers. Their task is to determine whether children referred to them on proven or admitted grounds require compulsory measures of care. Their operating principle is based on the Commission's philosophy that children who offend require care rather than punishment. Once referred, there is no difference in approach between those referred for offending behaviour and others who may have been offended against.[38]

---

[36] The Prevention of Cruelty to, and Protection of, Children Act 1889; The Prevention of Cruelty to Children (Amendment) Act 1894; The Prevention of Cruelty to Children Act 1894; the Prevention of Cruelty to Children Act 1904; and the Children Act 1908.

[37] *Children and Young Persons: Scotland* (1964) Cmnd. 2306.

[38] See Chaps 8 and 15.

The Current Position

Introduction

At the time of writing, the most important pieces of legislation **2.49** relative to the rights of children are:

1. Age of Legal Capacity (Scotland) Act 1991.
2. Children (Scotland) Act 1995.

The Law Reform (Parent and Child) (Scotland) Act 1986 retains significance as regards the presumed paternity of a child.

The Age of Legal Capacity (Scotland) Act 1991

This Act largely replaced the common law rules relating to the **2.50** tutory and curatory of children which had been based on the law of Rome. The age of legal capacity was fixed at 16. There were some specific exceptions relating, for example, to the right to make a will and to give or withhold consent to one's own adoption (both of which were fixed at 12). There were also less specific exceptions relating to consent to medical examination and treatment and to minor contracts commonly entered into by children under 16. In relation to these, a gradualist approach was introduced, requiring individual assessment of the child's actual capacity in order to determine legal capacity. In a sense this represents a return to the more flexible approach of the Romans referred to above.

The Children (Scotland) Act 1995

This legislation amends both the private law relating to children **2.51** within the family, and the public law relating to state intervention and support. It aims to take account of international standards set out in the European Convention on Human Rights and the United Nations Convention on the Rights of the Child. It shifts the focus from parents' rights to responsibilities, with a correspondingly greater emphasis on the rights of the child.

The Philosophy of Children's Rights

The Child as Property

It would seem that across the centuries, children have, at various **2.52** times, been seen as the property of the tribe, or clan, of the feudal

superior, of the father, and, more recently, of the mother too. They
have been used in some respects as the property of the state, as tools
of social control and reform, as bastards whose rights must be
negated in order to uphold the favoured social and moral structure,
or as potential inheritors of the moral degeneration of their parents,
who must be separated from them for the sake of the advancement
of society.

Approaches to Welfare

2.53 This is not to say that there has been no concern for the welfare of
the child as an individual.[39] The difference between the past and the
present lies in the way in which the welfare issues are addressed.
There seems in the past to have been a clearer common acceptance
of the factors to be assessed in making a determination about the
child's interests. What is striking about the rationale set out for
decisions about children is the willingness of decision-makers to be
judgmental about parents, and to base their decisions on their own
explicit values and Christian beliefs, which are assumed to be
shared by the community. This makes it difficult to disentangle
individual and social reasons for a particular decision.

2.54   From the 18th to the mid-19th century, Scottish academics
proposed a philosophy of "common sense." This was described as
being "based on the proposition that the common reason of man-
kind consists of certain fundamental judgements which the structure of language itself implies and which are intuitively recognised
by the mind as true".[40] Does such a "common sense" exist in
twenty-first century Scotland? Even the structure of language is
subject to criticism, precisely because it reflects fundamental judgments which are no longer acceptable to affected sections of society.
In a secular and heterogeneous society, one must question the basis
for decisions about the welfare of children. On what criteria are
they based? Does the perception of decision-makers match that of
those on the receiving end? Are our judges the equivalent of the
"sages" of yesteryear? How can one challenge discretionary decisions based on the undisclosed, and perhaps unacknowledged,
values of the decision-maker?

The Right to Welfare

2.55 There have been attempts to set out a value base on which decisions
about children could be based. In the course of this century there

---

[39] Indeed the *Cáin Adomnáin*, referred to above, is evidence for some early concern
for the vulnerability of children.

[40] S.J. Kermack, *Jurisprudence and Philosophy of Law*, in The Stair Society, *op. cit.*,
p. 441.

have been a number of charters and statements of the rights of children which aim to set out basic acceptable standards. 1924 saw the first international recognition of children's rights when the Assembly of the League of Nations passed the Declaration of the Rights of the Child. This proclaimed the rights of children to the means needed for material and spiritual development, to food and to help in times of sickness, to shelter and succour when orphaned or homeless, and to be "reclaimed" when they erred. In general, the rights proclaimed were protective in character. This approach was largely replicated by the UN's 1948 Declaration on the Rights of the Child, and expanded upon in a further Declaration in 1959.

The Right to Participate

The major contribution of the 1989 United Nations Convention on **2.56** the Rights of the Child is Article 12 which sets out a new right of children to participate in matters affecting them. The trigger condition is that the child must be capable of forming views. If this is the case, the child must be given the opportunity to express those views, and they must be taken into account in the decision making process, the weight given to them being dependent on the age and maturity of the child. This new right has a two-fold significance. Article 12(1) is a basic statement of principle about the right of the child as an individual to express views and have them taken into account. To that extent it is an innovation and a recognition of the individuality of a child. Article 12(2) sets out the child's right to be heard in judicial and administrative proceedings affecting him. The Traveaux Preparatoires[41] indicate that this was based on the insight that ascertainment of the child's views was an essential part in coming to a decision which was in the child's interests. It therefore retains the character of a welfare provision, and leaves room for the exercise of individual discretion subject to the concerns set out above.

Since the introduction of the Children (Scotland) Act 1995, the **2.57** Scottish legal system has been taking laudable steps to make the right of participation a reality. The principles within the Act have been fleshed out by rules of court which offer a number of options to those seeking to ascertain the views of children. It is essential that the research programme, already initiated, continues to monitor the impact of these provisions on the experience of children and young people.

---

[41] S. Detrick (ed.) *The United Nations Convention on the Rights of the Child—A Guide to the Travaux Préparatoires* (Martinus Nijhoff, 1991).

Participation and Protection

2.58 The Children Act 1995 was based on the need to take account not only of the UN Convention, but also of the European Convention on Human Rights. This document, drawn up initially in 1950, proceeds on the assumption that children are people too and should also benefit from the safeguards set out in it. As a basic principle, that approach is to be welcomed. There has been some concern that, in addressing children in the same way as adults, the European Convention risks a failure to take account of the status of children as dependent and vulnerable human beings which requires that they be granted extra rights to secure their protection. There is little reference in the European Convention to the specific and complicating needs of children.

2.59   There are two basic dilemmas—of substance and process. With regard to substance, the dilemma is that basic human rights presuppose and uphold the status of humans as autonomous individuals. Children have an additional right, the right to protection and to promotion of their welfare. Autonomy and welfare are incompatible concepts. Either the welfare must be qualified for the sake of the autonomy, or the autonomy must be qualified for the sake of the welfare. It is notable that the UN Convention does not give children the right to autonomy but the right to participation; decisions will ultimately be based on the best interests of children.

2.60   With regard to process, tension between the UN Convention and the European Convention became clear in Scotland in the debates surrounding procedures for the emergency protection of children. The 1995 Act introduced new procedures and appeals designed to safeguard the rights of parents and children under the European Convention on Human Rights. The concern expressed at that time, that the resultant complex procedure and extent of legal process might ultimately be to the disadvantage of children, does not so far appear to have been borne out by experience, although, at the time of writing, there has been little research into this matter.

2.61   The significance of the European Convention has been increased by the passing of the Human Rights Act 1998, which effectively incorporates that Convention into domestic law. Scottish courts are now required to take account of European case law when considering relevant matters. It is comforting to note the extent to which the European Court of Human Rights has progressively taken account of the specific needs and rights of children, to the extent of making frequent reference to the UN Convention on the Rights of the Child. At the time of writing, the problem appears to lie more in domestic ignorance of the developing European jurisprudence, than in that jurisprudence itself. There is a perception that the European Convention is largely about parents' rights, which may, if unchecked, lead to too great a caution on the part of those charged with protecting the rights of children.

Conclusion

The centre of power in relation to children appears to have shifted **2.62** from the clan, to the feudal superior, to the father (latterly shared with the mother). Today, it could be argued that that power is shifting to the state. In our world of increasing individualism, children can no longer be defined mainly in terms of their relationship to stable family groups. Insofar as parents are driven to pursue their individual needs at the expense of the group, so must children be conceded the status of individuals. More and more the state is being called upon to adjudicate on the rights and welfare of children. The state may therefore be said to be the new guarantor of, and therefore threat to, those rights.

Any power is vulnerable to misuse and abuse. It is essential **2.63** therefore that the burgeoning power of the state be monitored and checked. This could be achieved, first, by empowering children through educating them about their rights and making processes accessible to and comprehensible by them; and, secondly, by establishing an office of Children's Commissioner to promote the rights and interests of children.

CHAPTER 3

SCOTS LAW AND INTERNATIONAL CONVENTIONS

JOHN P. GRANT & ELAINE E. SUTHERLAND

The principal international standards against which children's **3.1**
rights under Scots law and practice are to be judged are the European Convention on Human Rights (European Convention) and
the United Nations Convention on the Rights of the Child (UN
Convention). In some ways these two instruments could not be
more different in their approach. At first glance, the European
Convention is very much an adult document, whereas the UN
Convention is, quite deliberately and expressly, child-centred.
However, once one notes the obvious fact that children are human
beings, it becomes clear that the European Convention is far from
irrelevant to children's rights. While the European Convention has
always had a powerful enforcement mechanism, first, through the
European Court of Human Rights and, now, through domestic
courts under the Human Rights Act of 1998, the UN Convention
has the softer enforcement mechanism of self-reporting. This
chapter sets the scene for those which follow by examining the
genesis, structure and content of these two conventions and the
impact they have had, and will have, on children's rights.

Drafting of the European Convention on Human Rights

The Council of Europe was established in 1949 among the states of **3.2**
Western Europe as a political and ideological bulwark against
communism. One of its aims is the "maintenance and further realisation of human rights and fundamental freedoms".[1] To reinforce
the importance of human rights to the entire Council of Europe
endeavour, acceptance of human rights is a pre-requisite of membership.[2] This effectively means that any applicant state must
subscribe to the European Convention on Human Rights.
  One of the first tasks undertaken by the Council of Europe was **3.3**

---

[1] Statute of the Council of Europe, *ETS* No. 1, Art.1(b).
[2] *ibid.*, Art. 3.

the elaboration of an agreement on human rights.[3] Two months after the Council's Statute was signed in London in May 1949, a group of distinguished statesmen, including Sir David Maxwell-Fyfe of the United Kingdom,[4] submitted a draft European convention on human rights to the Committee of Ministers.[5] While this early initiative was defeated in the Committee of Ministers,[6] the human rights movement in Europe could not be long delayed. The Consultative Assembly remitted the matter to its Committee on Legal and Administrative Questions which, on September 5, 1949, supported the formulation of a European convention based on the Universal Declaration of Human Rights.[7] Its draft convention enumerated twelve substantive rights and made provision for the creation of a European commission and court to oversee the implementation of these rights.[8] The enforcement machinery was to include the right of individuals who were the victims of human rights violations to petition the commission.[9] After endorsement by the Consultative Assembly, this report was remitted to the Committee of Ministers which, in turn, appointed a Committee of Experts to draw up its own convention. This Committee, apparently in some confusion as to its mandate and the political support among the member states, produced an ambivalent report and alternative texts.[10]

3.4   The Committee of Ministers then appointed yet another body, this time a Conference of Senior Officials of the members states, with the mandate "to prepare the ground for the political dimensions to be taken by the Committee of Ministers".[11] The Conference reported in a spirit of compromise. While four states, including the United Kingdom, wished the rights in the convention to be defined in detail, four others favoured a mere list of rights. The Conference, in its proposed text, adopted a middle position between definition and enumeration,[12] a position maintained in the European Convention itself. Nine states supported the right of individual petition, while three, including the United Kingdom, reserved their position on the basis that individual petition might lead to abuse.[13] The establishment of a court was supported by only four

---

[3]   A.H. Robertson, *The Council of Europe* (1956), 1.
[4]   G. Marston, "The U.K.'s Part in the Preparation of the European Convention on Human Rights", (1993) 42 I.C.L.Q. 796.
[5]   Council of Europe, *Collected Edition of the Travaux Preparatoires* (1975), Vol. 1, xxiv.
[6]   Essentially on the ground that the matter was already dealt with at the UN level: *ibid.*, 10–11.
[7]   *ibid.*, 218.
[8]   *ibid.*, 228–34.
[9]   *ibid.*, 224.
[10] *Collected Edition etc.*, Vol. 2, 274–86.
[11] *ibid.*, 290.
[12] *ibid.*, 248.
[13] *ibid.*, 252.

states, with seven states, including the United Kingdom, opposed. The Committee of Ministers addressed the thorny issues of individual petition and the court by the simple expedient of making both optional and therefore subject to separate acceptance by states.[14]

The European Convention for the Protection of Human Rights **3.5** and Fundamental Freedoms[15] was signed on November 4, 1950 and, having been ratified by the requisite ten states, entered into force on September 3, 1953. There are now 41 parties to the Convention.[16]

Structure of the European Convention

The European Convention is divided into three sections: I—Rights **3.6** and freedoms; II—European Court of Human Rights, and III—Miscellaneous provisions. This structure differs slightly from the 1950 text. Originally, there were four sections, one concerning rights, two concerning enforcement and a final section dealing with miscellaneous matters. As from November 1, 1998, Protocol 11[17] has been in effect, making sweeping changes in the enforcement mechanism by eliminating the Commission and making the Court the sole enforcement organ; and thereby also eliminating a section of the Convention.

The substantive rights in the Convention are augmented by rights **3.7** from four of the eleven protocols adopted to date,[18] but are to be read as distinct from the core Convention, given that they bind only those states which have accepted them. The United Kingdom, for example, has ratified, and is therefore bound by, Protocols 1 and 6; but it has not ratified, and is therefore not bound by, Protocols 4, 7 and 12. So, the United Kingdom has recognised the right to property, to education and free elections under Protocol 1[19]; and has abolished the death penalty in conformity with Protocol 6.[20]

---

[14] *Collected Edition etc.*, Vol. 1, xxvi–xxviii.
[15] *ETS* No. 5.
[16] Albania, Andorra, Austria, Belgium, Bulgaria, Cyprus, Croatia, Czech Republic, Denmark, Estonia, Finland, France, Georgia, Germany, Greece, Hungary, Iceland, Ireland, Italy, Latvia, Liechtenstein, Lithuania, Luxembourg, Malta, Maldova, Netherlands, Norway, Poland, Portugal, Romania, Russia, San Marino, Slovakia, Slovenia, Spain, Sweden, Switzerland, Former Yugoslav Republic of Macedonia, Turkey, Ukraine and the United Kingdom.
[17] *ETS* No. 155.
[18] Protocols 2 (*ETS* No. 44), 3 (*ETS* No. 45), 5 (*ETS* No. 55), 8 (*ETS* No. 118), 9 (*ETS* No. 140), 10 (*ETS* No. 146) and 11 (*ETS* No. 155) all deal with procedural matters and, insofar as they remain relevant, are incorporated into the current text of the Convention.
[19] *ETS* No. 9.
[20] *ETS* No. 114.

The United Kingdom is not subject to Protocol 4,[21] ensuring protection against the deprivations of liberty for contractual debt, freedom of movement and residence, and prohibitions on the expulsion of nationals and the collective expulsion of aliens. Nor is the United Kingdom subject to the range of rights provided for in Protocol 7,[22] including the right of aliens to procedural guarantees, compensation for miscarriages of justice and equality of rights and responsibilities between spouses. Nor is the United Kingdom subject to Protocol 12[23] establishing discrimination standing alone, and not in relation to another right in the Convention, as a breach of the Convention.

3.8   The Council of Europe's principal foray into the area of children's rights resulted in the European Convention on the Exercise of Children's Rights of 1996.[24] This Convention confines itself to procedural rights before any "judicial authority, providing for explicit rights" for a child to be informed, to express views and to have these views given "due weight" (Arts 3 and 6) and for the appointment of a representative where the child's interests conflict with those of the parents (Arts 9 and 10). Intended to supplement the rights in the UN Convention, this Convention has attracted little support, with four parties. The United Kingdom has not even signed this Convention. In other areas of endeavour, the Council of Europe, through recommendations by its Parliamentary Assembly, has contributed more to the emerging corpus of children's rights.[25]

3.9   The rights protected by the European Convention are a fairly standard exposition of civil and political rights,[26] based on the Universal Declaration of Human Rights.[27] Thus, protection extends to the right to life (Article 1), to freedom from torture (Article 2) and slavery (Article 3), to the right to liberty and security (Article 5) and to a fair trial (Article 6), to respect for private and family life (Article 8) and the right to marry (Article 12), and to the freedoms of thought, conscience and religion (Article 9), of expression (Article 10) and of assembly and association (Article 11).

---

[21] *ETS* No. 46.

[22] *ETS* No. 117.

[23] *ETS* No. 177.

[24] *ETS* No. 160. The Convention entered into force in July 2000 having been ratified by the requisite 3 states.

[25] See Parliamentary Assembly Recommendation 1121 (1990) on the rights of children; Recommendation 1286 (1996) on a European strategy for children establishing the "first call for children" principle; Recommendation 1371 (1998) on abuse and neglect of children; and Recommendation 1460 (2000) on an ombudsman for children.

[26] The European Social Charter of October 18, 1961 (*ETS* No. 35) is the European instrument encompassing social and economic rights. The United Kingdom is a party. The Charter has been amended and augmented on two occasions (*ETS* Nos 142 and 155); and will be replaced in due course by the European Social Charter (Revised) of April 2, 1966 (*ETS* No. 163).

[27] This was acknowledged during the negotiation of the Convention; and is made explicit in the Preamble and Section I.

Fundamental European Principles

The European Convention is based upon a number of inter-related **3.10** fundamental principles which, while invariably described as principles, are often no more than canons or techniques of interpretation.

Central to the European Convention on Human Rights is the **3.11** obligation contained in Article 1, *viz.* that the parties "shall ensure to everyone within their jurisdiction the rights and freedoms defined in Section I..." Article 1 applies equally to negative and positive obligations on states in respect of the rights contained in Section I. Thus, for many rights, state action in fulfilment of this obligation will be negative in the sense that states merely have to abstain from certain action—as abstaining from torture (Article 3) and from placing illegitimate restrictions on trade union membership (Article 11(1)). However, some Convention rights require positive action on the part of states—as in ensuring that conditions in public institutions like prisons and schools are not inhuman and degrading (Article 3) and that accused persons have legal representation (Article 6(3)(c)). In the landmark *Marcks* case, the European Court ruled that Belgium, in order to secure the applicant's right to family life under Article 8, was required to remove all legal impediments to an illegitimate child being a member of the mother's family[28]. In *Johnston v Ireland*, the European Court stated that "there may ... be positive obligations inherent in an effective respect for family life" under Article 8.[29]

Another fundamental principle in the European Convention is **3.12** contained in Article 14, prohibiting any discrimination in the enjoyment of the rights set out in Section I. The prohibited discrimination is on "any ground such as sex, race, colour, language, religion, political or other opinion, national or social origin, association with national minority, property, birth or other status" (Article 14(1)). This provision is not free-standing and can be used only in relation to one of the Convention's substantive rights.[30] Until the entry into force of Protocol 12, adopted in November 2000, discrimination *per se* is not prohibited.[31] That does not mean, however, that there must be a violation of the other substantive right for Article 14 to be violated. There may be a violation of Article 14 where, considered along with the Convention right, there is discriminatory or differential treatment, even although no

---

[28] *Marcks v. Belgium* (1979) 2 E.H.R.R. 330.
[29] *Johnston v. Ireland* (1986) 9 E.H.R.R. 203 at para. 20.
[30] *Abdulaziz, Cabales & Balkandali v. United Kingdom* (1985) 7 E.H.R.R. 471.
[31] Protocol 12 (*ETS* No. 177) provides that any discrimination by a public authority on grounds set out in Art. 14 is a violation of the Convention.

violation of the Convention right is found.[32] The violation of Article 14 must fall within the "ambit" of a substantive Convention right.[33] For example, in the *Belgian Linguistics Case,*[34] the Court ruled that, while Belgium was not obliged under Article 2 of Protocol 1 to maintain any particular system of education, it was required by Article 14 to operate the system it adopted in a non-discriminatory manner. However, discrimination will not be unlawful under Article 14 if it is capable of reasonable and objective justification.[35] Thus, in *Rasmussen*[36], in paternity proceedings in Denmark, the fact that the time limit for making application was shorter for fathers than for mothers, while *prima facie* discriminatory, was justified by the state's determination that there be legal certainty and that the child's best interests be served. This justification, in turn, points to two other fundamental principles underlying the European Convention: the margin of appreciation and proportionality.

3.13   Margin of appreciation is the term used to describe the discretion, subject to European supervision, left to states in taking legislative, administrative and judicial action in an area covered by a Convention right. As commentators have said, margins of appreciation "are the outer limits of the schemes of protection which are acceptable under the Convention."[37] This doctrine was first articulated by the European Court of Human Rights in *Handyside* [37a] where it was acknowledged that, in relation to some Convention rights, national authorities are in a better position to judge their content and any limitations on them than international judges. So, in *Handyside*, the Court allowed a margin of appreciation to the United Kingdom courts in determining whether possession of an allegedly obscene publication was exempt from the right of free expression through the limitation concerning "protection of morals" in Article 10(2). However, there is no unlimited power of appreciation left to states, and any margin of appreciation will be subject to the supervision of the European Court.[38] Margin of appreciation is particularly relevant to those Convention rights, like those in Articles 8—11, which have inbuilt limitations. The scope of the margin of appreciation will be greater when there is no common ground in the law and policies of

[32] See F.G. Jacobs and R.C.A. White, *The European Convention on Human Rights,* (2nd ed., 1996), pp. 285–6.
[33] *Abdulaziz, Cabales & Balkandali v. United Kingdom, supra.*
[34] (1968) 1 E.H.R.R. 252.
[35] See, *e.g.,* the *Belgian Linguistics Case, supra.*; *Lithgow and Others v. United Kingdom* (1986) 8 E.H.R.R. 252.
[36] (1984) 7 E.H.R.R .372.
[37] P. Jacobs & R.M. White, *The European Convention on Human Rights* (2nd ed., 1996), 37. For further discussion of the margin of appreciation, see the special issue in (1998) 19 *Hum. Rts. L.J.* 1.
[37a] (1976) 1 E.H.R.R. 737.
[38] *ibid.,* para. 49.

the parties to the Convention and lesser when such common ground exists.[39]

Proportionality has become an important principle in the Eur- **3.14** opean Court of Human Rights. This principle is based upon the recognition that European human rights standards are not—and cannot be—absolutes and that a balance must be struck between the interests of an individual invoking a Convention right and the broader public interest.[40] Again, it applies particularly to those Convention rights, like those in Articles 8—11, which themselves contain limitations. Proportionality requires that any state action limiting a Convention right must be proportionate to the legitimate aim being pursued. Thus, in *Berrehab*,[41] the European Court weighed the Dutch decision to deport a divorced father against the right of his daughter to family life under Article 8 and, finding that the effect on the child would be serious, condemned the Dutch action as disproportionate.

Enforcement

As core obligations in the European Convention the states parties **3.15** are required to secure the rights set out in section 1 to all persons within their jurisdiction (Article 1) and to provide effective remedies (Article 13). These obligations imply, but do not mandate, that the states parties to the Convention incorporate the Convention into their domestic law. Most of the states parties have done so, and their citizens, including their children, can invoke Convention rights before domestic agencies and courts.

Until the entry into force of the Human Rights Act 1998, the **3.16** European Convention was, as a matter of strict law, in no different position than any other treaty which has not been made part of United Kingdom law by statute. Treaties which are not made part of the law by statute have no force and effect in the United Kingdom.[42] This rule has been somewhat relaxed where domestic legislation has been enacted to give effect to an international instrument, where there is a presumption that Parliament intended to fulfil its international obligations; and, hence, an ambiguous or unclear statutory provision can be read in the light of the international instrument.[43] In relation to the European Convention, the courts have been prepared over the last thirty years to use it as an

[39] *Rasmussen v. Denmark, supra.*
[40] *Soering v. United Kingdom* (1989) 11 E.H.R.R. 439.
[41] *Berrehab v. United Kingdom* (1988) 11 E.H.R.R. 322.
[42] *The Parlement Belge* [1880] 5 P.D. 197; *Walker v. Baird* [1892] A.C. 491; *Attorney-General for Canada v. Attorney-General for Ontario* [1937] A.C. 326 at 347 *per* Lord Atkin.
[43] *Saloman v. Commissioners of Customs and Excise* [1967] 2 Q.B. 116; *Post Office v. Estuary Radio* [1967] 1 W.L.R. 1396.

aid to construction of a statute where the wording of the statute allows.[44] In this regard, the position in Scotland appears to be identical to that in England.[45] These rules about the effect of treaties within United Kingdom law are of no enduring significance as the Human Rights Act 1998 has enacted all the substantive Convention rights set out in section 1, along with the Protocols which have been ratified by the United Kingdom,[46] into the law of the land.[47]

3.17   Essentially, the Human Rights Act will operate at three levels. At the first level, proposed legislation will be subject to pre-scrutiny to determine its compatibility with the Convention. Where legislation is being introduced at Westminster, any incompatibility must be declared.[48] The Scottish Parliament is precluded from legislating in a manner inconsistent with the Convention.[49] Secondly, the courts will be able to issue a "declaration of incompatibility" in respect of Westminster legislation,[50] while Acts of the Scottish Parliament will be declared unlawful if they are inconsistent with the provisions of the Convention.[51] Thirdly, acts of public authorities—very broadly defined—may be challenged and declared unlawful where they violate the Convention.[52] Significantly, the Human Rights Act expressly mandates that all legislation is, wherever possible, to be read so as to be compatible with the European Convention;[53] and that Convention rights are to be interpreted with full regard to the interpretation of the European organs, particularly the European Court of Human Rights.[54] Of course, the real importance of the Human Rights Act lies in the fact that remedies for infractions of the European Convention will be available in the United Kingdom. Indeed, it is no exaggeration to say that the Convention "will move into the very core of our legal system".[55]

3.18   Until October 2000, people within the United Kingdom could only get redress for violations of the European Convention on Human Rights through the mechanism established by the

---

[44] *R. v. Home Secretary ex parte Brind* [1991]1 A.C. 696; *Attorney-General v. Associated Newspapers* [1994] 2 A.C. 238.

[45] *T. Petitioner*, 1997 S.L.T. 724 at 728 *per* Lord President Hope. *c.f. Kaur v. Lord Advocate*, 1981 S.L.T. 322 at 329 *per* Lord Ross.

[46] *viz.* Protocols 1 and 6.

[47] Human Rights Act, s. 1(1). The Convention rights appear as Schedule 1 to the Act.

[48] *ibid.*, s. 19.

[49] Scotland Act 1998, s. 35.

[50] Human Rights Act 1998, s. 4(2). This declaration does not affect the validity or continued operation of the legislation: *ibid.*, s. 4(6).

[51] Scotland Act 1998, s. 29.

[52] Human Rights Act, s. 6.

[53] *ibid.*, s. 3(1).

[54] *ibid.*, s. 2(1).

[55] H. Swindells, A. Neaves, M. Kushner and R. Skilbeck, *Family Law and the Human Rights Act 1998*, (1999), 3.

Convention for its enforcement.[56] In brief, the Convention initially established a Commission and a Court to "ensure the observance of the engagements undertaken" by the parties.[57] The mechanism allowed for a state to make a complaint in respect of another state's violation of the Convention;[58] and, subject to separate agreement, for an individual to make a complaint (called a petition) in respect of a state's violation of the Convention,[59] provided certain admissibility criteria were met.[60] The Commission's task was to attempt to find a "friendly settlement"[61] while the Court, to which cases might ultimately be referred, gave a final and definitive ruling on the interpretation and application of the Convention.[62]

With the entry into effect of Protocol 11[63] to the Convention in **3.19** November 1998, sweeping changes have been made in the enforcement machinery of the Convention. The Commission has been abolished and the Court, now a full-time rather than a part-time body, is the sole organ of enforcement.[64] All states parties to the Convention have to recognize the right of individual petition[65] and the jurisdiction of the Court.[66] The criteria for the admissibility of individual petitions remain unchanged.[67] This enforcement mechanism, while not beyond criticism, is generally regarded as the most sophisticated and successful for any human rights treaty.[68]

The European Convention and Children

The European Convention is applicable to *all* people within the **3.20** territories of the contracting states: Article 1 requires that the parties "secure to everyone within their jurisdiction the right and freedoms defined in Section I..." While the Convention benefits

---

[56] Discussed in Chap. 16, *infra*.
[57] Original ECHR, Art. 19.
[58] *ibid.*, Art. 24.
[59] *ibid.*, Art. 25.
[60] *ibid.*, Arts 26 and 27(1) and (2). All domestic remedies must be exhausted and the petition must not be anonymous, substantially the same as a previous petition, already submitted to another form of settlement, manifestly unfounded or an abuse of the rights of petition.
[61] *ibid.*, Art. 28.
[62] *ibid.*, Art. 45.
[63] *ETS* No. 155. Protocol 11 is now an integral part of the European Convention on Human Rights, and the Convention must be read with the inclusion of the relevant provisions of the Protocol as part of its text.
[64] Amended ECHR, Art. 19.
[65] *ibid.*, Art. 34. Inter-state complaints are now regulated by Art. 33.
[66] *ibid.*, Art. 32.
[67] *ibid.*, Art. 35.
[68] See, *e.g.*, M. Janis, R. Kay and A. Bradley, *European Human Rights* (1995) 3; F.G. Jacobs and R.C.A. White, *The European Convention on Human Rights* (2nd ed., 1991) 403; R. Beddard, *Human Rights in Europe* (3rd ed., 1993) 1.

clearly extend to children, there are very few express references to children. In relation to the right to liberty and security, Article 5(2) permits the detention of a minor for educational supervision and for attendance at a court or tribunal. In relation to the right to a fair trial, Article 6(1) recognises that the requirement that judgment be pronounced publicly may be dispensed with "where the interests of juveniles... so require". Article 7 to Protocol 7, in requiring equality of spouses between themselves and in relation to their "children" in marriage and in the event of dissolution, allows states to take measures necessary in the interests of "children". Amazingly, in Article 2 of Protocol 1, entitled "Right to education", the terms "child", "minor", or "juvenile" do not appear at all. This provision merely states that "[n]o person shall be denied the right to education". Thereafter, the very next sentence requires that contracting parties respect parents' religious and philosophical convictions in their educational provision. Happily, the European Court of Human Rights has made it clear that the right to education set out in the first sentence of Article 2 vests in the child[69] and that the second sentence must be read in the light of the primary obligation contained in the first sentence.[70]

3.21   Yet the basic point remains: the European Convention on Human Rights was not intended to be, and is not, child-specific. It is an international instrument guaranteeing a range of civil and political right to everyone in the territories of the contracting states. One authority has cautiously suggested that "[i]n theory, Convention rights are guaranteed to all, and there is little to prevent their application to children".[71] In fact, through the jurisprudence of the Commission (until its abolition in 1998) and the Court, the Convention has been shaped and adapted to have regard for children where its terms allow.

3.22   The Court has stated on numerous occasions that the Convention is a dynamic instrument. Thus, in the *Tyrer* case concerning corporal punishment of school children, the European Court of Human Rights confirmed that "the Convention is a living instrument which must be interpreted in the light of present-day conditions".[72] Similar statements can be found in *Marcks,*[73] dealing with the status of a child born out of wedlock, and in *Dudgeon,*[74] dealing with homosexual acts. While this kind of expansive canon of interpretation cannot be utilised against clear and precise wording, it does lend itself to those provisions of the Convention which are loosely worded, such as Article 8 (the right to respect for private

---

[69] *Campbell & Cosans v. United Kingdom* (1982) 4 E.H.H.R. 293.
[70] *Kjeldsen, Busk, Madsen & Pedersen v. Denmark* (1976) 1 E.H.H.R. 711.
[71] E. Kilkelly, *The Child and the European Convention on Human Rights* (1999), 3–4.
[72] *Tyrer v. United Kingdom* (1978) 2 E.H.H.R. 1.
[73] *Marcks v. Belgium* (1979) 2 E.H.H.R. 330.
[74] *Dudgeon v. United Kingdom* (1981) 4 E.H.H.R. 149.

and family life), a provision likely to be used by children.[75] The normal method by which effect is given to the dynamic and "living" nature of the European Convention is through reference to the laws and policies in the member states of the Council of Europe. In the *Marcks case*, for example, the Court recognised that, while it may have been acceptable to treat children differently according to their parents' marital status when the Convention was drafted, the attitude within countries had changed by 1979.

Reference has also been made to other international instruments. **3.23** So, for example, the *Marcks* Court looked to the European Convention on the Legal Status of Children Born out of Wedlock of 1975.[76] Most significantly, both the Commission and the Court have, on appropriate occasions, used the Convention on the Rights of the Child. In *Costello-Roberts v. United Kingdom*,[77] the Court rather curiously utilised Article 16 of the UN Convention, concerning a child's right to privacy and family life, to assist it in interpreting Article 3 (prohibition of torture) and Article 8 (right to respect for private and family life) of the European Convention in a case involving corporal punishment of a seven-year-old boy. In *Keegan v. Ireland*,[78] the Court looked to Article 7 of the UN Convention, in particular the requirement that a child has "the right to know and be cared for by his or her parents", in examining the rights under Article 8 of the European Convention that an unmarried father has in relation to a proposed adoption. After a thorough review of the European case law, Kilkelly concludes that, in the absence of child-specific standards in the European Convention, it is permissible to turn to the UN Convention for "guidance" to fill gaps and to clarify ambiguities, but not so as to frustrate the object and purpose of the Convention.[79]

Drafting the United Nations Convention on the Rights of the Child[80]

The acceptance that children have rights—and real attempts to **3.24** define the content of these rights—is a process which can best be

---

[75] Kilkelly, *supra.*, 14.

[76] *ETS* No. 85.

[77] (1993) 19 E.H.H.R. 112.

[78] (1994) 18 E.H.R.R. 342.

[79] Kilkelly, *supra*, 15–16. This approach is very much in line with the Council of Europe's endeavours to align state law and practice and European human rights law with international standards, particularly those of the Convention on the Rights of the Child. See the Parliamnetary Assembly's recommendations mentioned in fn. 25, *supra.*

[80] For a detailed discussion of the drafting process, see, C.P. Cohen and H.A. Davidson (eds), *Children's Rights in America: UN Convention on the Rights of the Child compared with United States Law* (1990, American Bar Association); LeBlanc, *supra*; Van Bueren, *The International Law on the Rights of the Child* (1995, Martinus Nijhoff); Veerman, *supra*.

described as somewhat uneven and haphazard in a world context.[81]
Progress was made in 1959 when the Declaration on the Rights of
the Child was adopted by the General Assembly of the United
Nations.[82] While not a legally binding instrument, it is clear from
the terms of the Declaration that it was intended to have normative
effect. Twenty years later, as part of the International Year of the
Child, the Polish government proposed the drafting of a convention
to elevate the principles embodied in the Declaration to the status
of enforceable rights. It submitted two draft models to the Commission on Human Rights, the UN body which drafts human rights
instruments. The second model formed the basis of the deliberations for the drafting of what became the Convention on the Rights
of the Child.

3.25   The drafting of the Convention did not get off to a good start. As
Van Bueren points out, the majority of member states had opposed
the call for a binding treaty on the rights of the child in 1959 and,
while their opposition was withdrawn in 1979, "a withdrawal of
opposition ... ... is not the same as enthusiastic support".[83] She
continues, however, with the encouraging observation that "dele-
gates began to realise the importance of their work". While much of
the Convention has its origins in the second Polish draft presented
to the Commission on Human Rights in 1979, some articles were
the result of drafts tabled by government delegations or sponsored
by non-governmental organisations.[84] During the first reading de-
liberative process, most articles were amended to some extent, while
amendment during the second reading stage appears to have varied
from intense to haphazard.[85] Drafting of the Convention proceeded
on the basis of consensus, consensus being described by Cohen as
"a process which does not so much denote support, as it does a lack
of objection".[86]

3.26   A good illustration of what the drafting process involved can be
found in relation to Article 1. Since all lawyers know that the very
definition of terms used is an essential prerequisite for discussing

---

[81] For a detailed discussion of the history of children's rights, see P. Veerman, *The Rights of the Child and the Changing Image of Childhood* (1992).
[82] General Assembly Res. 44/25.
[83] Van Bueren, *supra*, at p. 13.
[84] For a discussion of the activities of non-governmental organisations, see Cohen, "The Role of Non-Governmental Organisations in the Drafting of the Convention on the Rights of the Child", 12 *Human Rights Quarterly* 137 (1990). Indeed, Van Bueren suggests that the initial reluctance of some governments to accord high priority to the drafting of the Convention had the beneficial result that the Working Group was able to adopt its own methods of working including close co-operation with non-governmental organisations, *supra*, at p. 13, n. 97.
[85] Cohen, "A Guide to Linguistic Interpretation of the UN Convention on the Rights of the Child" in Cohen and Davidson, *op. cit.* at p. 40.
[86] *supra*, at p. 42.

substantive issues, it is hardly surprising that finding an acceptable definition of the child provoked much debate throughout the drafting process,[87] and indeed continues to reflect division of opinion amongst states which have signed or ratified the Convention.[88] Debate focussed on three issues: the beginning of childhood; the end of childhood; and the age of majority, although it was the first of these which proved to be most controversial. The second Polish model referred to a child as "every human being from the moment of his[89] birth to the age of 18 years".[90] This prompted a sharp division during the deliberations of the Working Group between states who wanted to protect the child from the moment of conception and those whose domestic law permitted abortion. Agreement was reached by the adoption of the proposal by the Moroccan government to delete the words "from the moment of birth". During the second reading, Malta and Senegal, supported by the observer from the Holy See, proposed the insertion of the words "moment of conception", but the proposal was dropped in the face of strong opposition. To some extent, the willingness of Malta and Senegal to concede the matter resulted from the agreement to include in the preamble to the Convention mention of the child's need for "appropriate legal protection before as well as after birth". While the preamble must be read in the light of the substantive articles in the Convention, this mention of the pre-birth period injected a point of principle enabling consensus. In effect, each state is left to decide the matter for itself.

From the point of view of Scots law, it is significant that the **3.27** United Kingdom delegation to the negotiations included no Scots lawyer. This explains why the difficulties which arose later in respect of Article 37(d), which requires that every child deprived of his or her liberty should have prompt access to legal and other appropriate assistance, were not noticed at an earlier stage. The way in which the children's hearings system operated at the time raised real problems over compliance and the United Kingdom was forced to enter a reservation in respect of the system. Had there been a Scots lawyer present the difficulty would have been noticed and attempts would have been made to avoid the ensuing embarrassment. Subsequent changes to the hearings system, introduced by the Children (Scotland) Act 1995 and the rules made thereunder, enabled the United Kingdom to withdraw its reservation in respect of the children's hearings system.

---

[87] *supra,* at pp.41–43. See also, Van Bueren, *supra,* at pp. 32–38.
[88] The U.K. Reservation and Declarations (CRC/C/2/Rev.4, p. 32) which provides, "The United Kingdom interprets the Convention as applicable only following a live birth".
[89] Gender neutrality found its way into the Convention in the course of the drafting process.
[90] UN Doc. E/CN.4/1.1542 (1980), paras 30–31.

3.28   The United Nations Convention on the Rights of the Child[91] was adopted unanimously by the General Assembly of the United Nations on November 20, 1989. After ratification by more than the required twenty states, it came into force on September 2, 1990. It has now been ratified by every country in the world except the United States and Somalia.[92] Somalia currently has no effective government to proceed with ratification, and it is tempting to sum up the overall position on non-ratification by saying simply that Somalia has too little government and the United States has too much.[93]

Structure of the UN Convention

3.29 The Convention is unique in a number of respects. Not only does it deal with an unprecedented range of rights, it also applies both during peace and in time of war. It came into force more quickly than any other UN human rights convention. Various attempts have been made to categorise the many different rights embodied in the Convention and one of the clearest is provided by Muntarbhorn[94] who classified the rights as follows:

1. *General rights* (the right to life, prohibition against torture, freedom of expression, thought and religion, the right to information and to privacy).
2. *Rights requiring protective measures* (including measures to protect children from economic and sexual exploitation, to prevent drug abuse, and other forms of abuse and neglect).
3. *Rights concerning the civil status of children* (including the

---

[91]   1577 UNTS 3; (1989) 28 I.L.M. 1448.
[92]   A current list of the parties to the Convention can be found at < http:// www.unhchr.ch/html/menu3/b/treaty15_asp.htm >
[93]   This is, of course, an oversimplification of the opposition to the Convention in the United States. While some opposition stems from issues of domestic U.S. government, politics and law, much proceeds from the misconception that the UN Convention gives children autonomy and fails to respect the role of parents in raising children; see, *e.g.*, B.C. Hafen and J.O. Hafen, Abandoning Children to their Autonomy: The United Nations Convention on the Rights of the Child, 37 *Harv. Intl. L.J.* 449 (1996). It should be noted that there is considerable support in the "U.S. for ratification of the Convention; see, *e.g.*, S. Kilborne, U.S. Failure to Ratify the UN Convention on the Rights of the Child: Playing Politics with Children's Rights", 6 *Transnatl. & Contemp. Probs.* 437 (1996).
[94]   Muntarbhorn, "The Convention on the Rights of the Child: Reaching the Unreached?" (1992) 91 *Bulletin of Human Rights* 66, quoted in Freeman, "Laws, Conventions and Rights", (1993) 7 *Children and Society* 37, at pp. 43–44. See also, L.J. LeBlanc, *The Convention on the Rights of the Child: United Nations Lawmaking on Human Rights* (University of Nebraska Press, 1995), where the author discusses the Convention in terms of survival rights, membership rights, protection rights and empowerment rights.

right to acquire nationality, the right to preserve one's identity, the right to remain with parents, unless the best interests of the child dictate otherwise, and the right to be reunited with the family).

4. *Rights concerning government and welfare* (including the child's right to a reasonable standard of living, the right to health and basic services, the right to social security, the right to education and the right to leisure).

5. *Rights concerning children in special circumstances* or in "especially difficult circumstances". These extend to such children as handicapped children, refugee children and orphaned children. Included are special regulations on adoption, the cultural concerns of minority and indigenous children, and rehabilitative care for children suffering from deprivation, as well as a prohibition on the recruitment of soldiers under 15 years of age.

6. *Procedural considerations*, particularly the establishment of an international committee of ten experts to monitor implementation of the Convention".

In all of this, the importance of a particular provision will depend **3.30** on the circumstances confronting the individual child. The right to have one's views taken into account may be of little significance to a child whose immediate concern is the elimination of the suffering he or she is experiencing due to malnutrition or disease. The rights of a child during armed conflict may be of little immediate concern to the Scottish child who wants to participate in the decision about where he or she goes to school. Nonetheless, it is the fact that the Convention provides for the rights of all children around the world in the diverse circumstances in which they find themselves that makes it so special. The precise impact of the rights conferred by the Convention and their impact on Scots law will be discussed in the following chapters. However, it is worth taking a little time to examine three principles, fundamental to the Convention—the rights to freedom from discrimination, to protection and to participation.

Fundamental Principles of the UN Convention

Central to the Convention is the principle that the child is entitled **3.31** to be protected from all forms of discrimination. While Article 2(1) confines its prohibition on discrimination to that in respect of the rights set out in the Convention, Article 2(2) is broader in scope and requires states to "take all appropriate measures to ensure that the child is protected against all forms of discrimination or punishment on the basis of the status, activities, expressed opinions, or beliefs of the child's parents, legal guardians, or family members". Thus, the ambit of Article 2(2) goes beyond the specific rights covered by the Convention and includes any other matters.

44   *Children's Rights in Scotland*

3.32   It is when one considers the remaining two fundamental principles of the Convention, the right to protection and the right to
participation, that what is sometimes seen as the internal conflict in
the Convention becomes apparent. Article 3 provides as follows:

   1.   In all actions concerning children, whether undertaken by
        public or private social welfare institutions, courts of law,
        administrative authorities or legislative bodies, the best
        interests of the child shall be a primary consideration.
   2.   States Parties undertake to ensure the child such pro-
        tection and care as is necessary for his or her wellbeing,
        taking into account the rights and duties of his or her
        parents, legal guardians, or other individuals legally re-
        sponsible for him or her, and, to this end, shall take all
        appropriate legislative and administrative measures.
   3.   States Parties shall ensure that the institutions, services
        and facilities responsible for the care or protection of
        children shall conform with the standards established by
        competent authorities, particularly in the areas of safety,
        health, in the number and suitability of their staff, as well
        as competent supervision.

3.33 It is worth noting that the Convention, unlike the Declaration and
Scots law, requires that the child's welfare should be a "primary"
rather than "the primary"or "the paramount" consideration. How
the position of the child's best interests came to be watered down in
this way has never been satisfactorily explained and there is the
danger that it would permit a state to find another primary consideration, such as economic interests, which takes precedence.
However, Van Bueren[95] has suggested that, since Article 3 embodies a broad principle of interpretation, there may be occasions
(such as the granting to parents of a decree of divorce) when the
child's interests are only one of a number of legitimate concerns.[96]
Furthermore, at various points throughout the Convention, the
principle of "the best interests of the child" is restated in other ways.
In Article 18, which recognises the parental responsibility for the
upbringing and development of the child, it is noted that, "The best
interests of the child will be their basic concern". Interestingly,
when the matter of adoption is being addressed in Article 21, the
best interests of the child is stated to be "the paramount consideration". A very real concern about the concept of the "best
interests of the child" is that there is so little consensus about what
this involves when applied in particular cases and that it can become nothing more than a short-hand phrase for the views of a
particular dominant group of adults.[97]

---

[95] *supra*, at p. 46.
[96] See paras 6.22 *et seq* for further discussion of this point.
[97] See paras 6.27–6.28 for further discussion of concerns surrounding the "best
interests" standard.

Having attempted to guarantee protection for the child, Article **3.34**
12 of the Convention turns to the right of participation. It provides
that:
1. States Parties shall assure to the child who is capable of
    forming his or her own views the right to express those
    views freely in all matters affecting the child, the views of
    the child being given due weight in accordance with the
    age and maturity of the child.
2. For this purpose, the child shall in particular be provided
    the opportunity to be heard in any judicial and admin-
    istrative proceedings affecting the child, either directly, or
    through a representative or an appropriate body, in a
    manner consistent with the procedural rules of national
    law.

This principle reflects acceptance of the fact that the holding of **3.35**
rights can become something of an empty concept in the absence of
the opportunity to participate in the exercise of these rights.[98]
However, it should be noted that the child is given nothing more
than the right to have his or her voice heard and any views expressed taken into account. Article 12 does not give the child autonomy. To leave unfettered decision-making power with children
would fly in the face of the responsibility of the adult members of
any community, not only to protect children from other adults, but
to protect them from their own inexperience.

While participation is a child's right, protection and, to some **3.36**
extent, decision-making are adult responsibilities. This right to
participation becomes all the more meaningful when the nature of a
child's evolving capacity is emphasised, as it is in both Article 12
and Article 5. Recognising the role of family members in providing
direction and guidance to the child, Article 5 again notes the
evolving nature of the child's capacity. Indeed, it can be argued that
it is through enabling a child to exercise this evolving capacity that
he or she will become fully able to participate in the community as
an adult.

Ratification and Reservations

The United Kingdom signed the Convention on April 19, 1990 and **3.37**
ratified it on November 16, 1991. Ratification was subject to a
number of Reservations and Declarations.[99] The reservations re-

---

[98] See, M.G. Flekkoy and N.H. Kaufman, *Rights and Responsibilities in Family and
    Society* (Jessica Kingsley, 1987), which examines the child's right to self-
    expression and the development of the decision-making function, and K.
    Marshall, *Children's Rights in the Balance* (HMSO, 1997) which looks at
    children's rights and focuses on participation in the decision-making process.
[99] CRC/C/2/Rev.4, p.32. The current texts of all the reservations to the Convention
    can be found at < http://www.unhchr.ch/html/menu3/b/treaty15_asp.htm >

lated to: confining the Convention's application to the period after the child's birth; restrictions on the meaning of the word "parent"; citizenship and the right of entry into the United Kingdom; employment legislation; the mixing of adult and young offenders; and the children's hearings system.[1]

3.38   An enduring concern of the Committee on the Rights of the Child ("CRC") has been the number and extent of reservations; nearly every set of concluding observations condemn the reservations made by the reporting state, coupled with a request that they be withdrawn. In terms of international treaty law, reservations are only permissible if they are compatible with the object and purpose of the treaty;[2] the United Kingdom reservations seem to satisfy that test.[3] It is equally clear that a distressingly large number of reservations are so extensive and far-reaching that they cannot be compatible with the object and purpose of the Convention. In excess of a dozen states have reservations which effectively negate any commitment to the obligations in the UN Convention.[4] None of these reservations qualifies as a permissible—and therefore valid—reservation. What is significant is that the states which have objected to these reservations have not taken advantage of the rule[5] which permits them to regard the state with the impermissible reservations as not a party to the Convention. Clearly, these objecting states recognise the importance of the universality of the UN Convention, however abhorrent and illegal they may regard the reservations.

3.39   While the ratification of the Convention does not make its provisions directly applicable in Scotland or, indeed, any other part of the United Kingdom, it is accepted that every attempt will be made to honour our international obligations. As we have seen, where a statute is ambiguous, it will be interpreted in a way that will lead to compliance with, rather than the flouting of, such obligations.[6] However, where a provision of Scots law is clear, the fact that it is

---

[1]   In the somewhat over-optimistic belief that the Children (Scotland) Act 1995 made the children's hearings system Convention compliant, the reservation with respect to children's hearings was withdrawn on April 18, 1997.

[2]   Vienna Convention on the Law of Treaties 1969 (1151 *UNTS* 331), Art. 19(c). See also, UN Convention, Art. 51(2).

[3]   The present United Kingdom reservations are set out in Appendix 3.

[4]   Saudi Arabia, *e.g.*, has entered "reservations with respect to all such articles as are in conflict with the provisions of Islamic law". Brunei Darussalam goes even further with reservations "on the provisions of the said Convention which may be contrary to the Constitution of Brunei Darussalam and to the beliefs and principles of Islam, the State, religion..."

[5]   Vienna Convention on the Law of Treaties 1969, Art. 20(4)(b).

[6]   See, *e.g.*, *Mortensen v. Peters* (1906) 8F. (J.) 93; *Waddington v. Miah* [1974] 1 W.L.R. 683; *ex p. Brind* [1991] 2 W.L.R. 588. The recent specific reference to the UN Convention is encouraging: *White v White* (I.H.), 2001 S.L.T. 458, *per* Lord McCluskey at p. 494.

unambiguously inconsistent with the CRC will not diminish the validity of Scots law within Scotland.[7]

While it represents a landmark in the development of children's **3.40** rights, the Convention should not be seen as an end-point, but rather as the foundations for future developments. In one sense, the Convention has this built into its own provisions, since States Parties are required to report their progress to the UN Committee on the Rights of the Child at regular intervals.[8] In addition, the United Nations continues its work on children's rights. Work was underway throughout the 1990s on the substantive provisions of the Convention through two optional protocols, one on children in armed conflict[9] and the other on the sale of children, child prostitution and child pornography.[10] The General Assembly adopted both the Optional Protocol on the Sale of Children, Child Prostitution and Child Pornography[11] and the Optional Protocol on the Involvement of Children in Armed Conflict[12] on May 25, 2000. Neither optional protocol has yet been ratified by a sufficient number of states to come into force, although both the United Kingdom and the United States have signed the former, but not the latter. Work is planned on yet another optional protocol, this time dealing with the issue of enforcement and monitoring of the CRC through the right of individual petition.[13]

---

[7] See, *e.g.*, *Kaur v. Lord Advocate*, 1980 S.C. 319; *Salomon v. Commissioners of Customs and Excise* [1967] 2 Q.B. 116; *I.R.C. v. Collco Dealings Ltd* [1962] A.C. 1.

[8] See *infra*, Chap. 16.

[9] The Human Rights Commission established an inter-sessional open-ended working group on the optional protocol; E/CN.4/1994/91. This was followed by a report of the Expert of the Secretary-General, Ms. Graca Machel; *Impact of Armed Conflict on Children*, August 1996, UN Doc A/51/306 and an interim report by the Special Rapporteur of the Secretary-General, Mr. Olara A. Otunna; *Children in Armed Conflict*, March 1998, UN Doc E/CN.4/1998/119. The open-ended working group submitted the text of the draft protocol to the Commission on Human Rights; E/CN.4/2000/74.

[10] The Human Rights Commission established an inter-sessional open-ended working group on the optional protocol; E/CN.4/1994/90. This was followed by *Report of the Special Rapporteur [Mrs. Ofelia Calcetas-Santos] on the Sale of Children, Child Prostitution and Child Pornography*, January 1996 UN Doc. E/CN.4/1996/100. The open-ended working group submitted the text of the draft protocol to the Commission on Human Rights; E/CN.4/2000/75.

[11] Adopted by GA Res. 54/263; (2000) 39 I.L.M. 1285. As of mid-March 2001, there is one party (Bangladesh) and 74 signatories.

[12] Adopted by GA Res. 54/263; (2000) 39 I.L.M. 1285. As of mid-March 2001, there are three parties (Bangladesh, Canada and Sri Lanka) and 36 signatories.

[13] See, Report of the Committee on the Rights of the Child to the General Assembly 2000, A/55/41, para. 1558(j). Discussed further in para 16.12.

Enforcement

3.41 The UN Convention requires states parties to make the Convention's provisions "widely known, by appropriate and active
means, to adults and children alike".[14] However, if the UN Convention lacks anything, it is a powerful enforcement mechanism.[15]
In contrast with the European Convention, there is no court to
receive individual complaints of violations. Instead, enforcement is
through the softer method of self-reporting by states.

What difference can the European and UN Conventions make?

3.42 In a sense, it is premature to address this question here, since that is
what the remainder of this book is about.

3.43   A tantalising prospect for the increased importance of the UN
Convention for domestic law is coming from a rather circuitous
route. It will be recalled that the European Convention on Human
Rights has been incorporated into the law of the various parts of
the United Kingdom. Thus, compliance with the European Convention will effectively become mandatory. The European Court
has become increasingly willing to use the UN Convention as an aid
to construction.[16] Most recently, in *T. v. United Kingdom* and *V. v.
United Kingdom*,[17] the case brought by the two boys convicted of
killing James Bulger in 1993, the Court made reference to the
provisions of the UN Convention when considering the rights of
children being tried for a criminal offence. Granted, the articles of
the UN Convention addressing this issue were given additional
weight by the fact that the Committee of Ministers of the Council of
Europe had specifically endorsed them by Recommendation.[18]
However, it is clear that the Court was willing to use the UN
Convention as an indication of internationally accepted standards
and, as such, something which could flesh out the European Convention when it did not address a particular issue explicitly. When
one remembers that the European Convention was drafted with the
atrocities of the holocaust and the needs of post-war Europe in
mind, it is not surprising that it did not focus on the rights of
children. It can be anticipated that it will need refinement when

---

[14] Art. 42.
[15] For a very full discussion of enforcing international conventions, see Chap. 16.
[16] See, *e.g.*, *Costello-Roberts v United Kingdom* (1994) 19 E.H.R.R. 112; *Keegan v
Ireland* (1994) 18 E.H.R.R. 342.
[17] The cases are reported on the European Court web site: http://www.echr.coe.int/.
[18] Recommendation No. R (87) 20.

children's rights are being examined. In this respect, the UN Convention has much to offer and, if it is used by the Court increasingly in the future, the indirect impact of the UN Convention will increase.

CHAPTER 4

EQUAL OPPORTUNITIES? RACE, GENDER, DISABILITY—AND CHILDREN

E. KAY M. TISDALL

"If I were First Minister, I would make sure that all children were treated equally." (Donna Maciver, Corrodale Back School, Isle of Lewis)[1]

The standard "trio" of identities in equal opportunities has become **4.1** "race", gender and disability. Fuelled by civil rights movements, people from black and minority ethnic groups, women and disabled people are recognised as being at particular risk of endemic and institutionalised discrimination in the United Kingdom. Legal provisions making it unlawful to discriminate on the grounds of "race", gender and disability are contained in the Race Relations Act 1976 ("RRA"), the Sex Discrimination Act 1975 ("DSA") and the Disability Discrimination Act 1995 ("DDA"). Rights are to be protected and promoted through the relevant commissions (Commission of Racial Equality, the Equal Opportunities Commission and the Disability Rights Commission), as well as through recourse to the courts. These legal structures are set within a broader European and international human rights agenda, which has numerous conventions and declarations seeking to address discrimination by "race", gender and disability.

The children's rights movement is a more recent arrival on the **4.2** civil rights scene. This new movement is beginning to question how well anti-discrimination and equal opportunities legislation has promoted children's rights and how well legislation affecting children has recognised anti-discrimination and equal opportunities issues.

The discussion of the extent of discrimination on the grounds of **4.3** "race", gender and disability has resulted in heated debates about these concepts and categories. The policy debates have been highly politicised.[2] "Race", for example, has been accused of reifying the

---

[1] Reported in *Children in Scotland, "If I Were First Minister"* (2000) *Children in Scotland* (Edinburgh), p. 20.
[2] The term "politicised" is used here in reference to the sensitivity within these debates and the difficulties at times of expressing alternative views.

idea of separate and fixed human "races",[3] relying on scientifically disproved notions of genetic inheritability and difference[4]. "Race" has traditionally focused on differences in skin colour, when in fact discrimination due to combinations of cultural, class and religious background can have more impact[5]. More flexible, changing and contextualised identities and differences must therefore be considered[6]. Since the 1970s, a conceptual distinction was drawn made between "sex" (biological difference) and "gender" (the social construction of sex). This allowed a consideration of socialisation and gender-role stereotyping. More recently, that distinction has been challenged[7], with both the fixedness of sex and the feasibility of separating sex from gender being questioned and reappraised.

4.4   In relation to discussion about disability, in the 1970s and 1980s the disability advocacy movement first argued for a conceptual move away from a medicalised, individual-impairment model towards a recognition of social barriers and the social "creation" of disability to suit a capitalist society.[8] That approach has itself been challenged, as failing to recognise the "body"—the role of pain and impairments and the need to consider transition and change.[9]

4.5   The use of the terms "race", gender and disability are therefore subject to caveats throughout this chapter. The debates noted above raise conceptual questions that will be returned to below. The chapter will sketch the International, European and United Kingdom framework for non-discrimination and equal opportunities. The extent to which UK and Scottish law and policies meet the needs and rights of disabled children, of male and female children, and of children from black and minority ethnic groups will be considered by examining three specific issues: child care services under the Children (Scotland) Act; aspects of the state school system; and the transition into "adulthood". It will conclude by questioning the present framing of anti-discrimination and equal opportunities, posing particular problems faced by children and young people as demonstrated by research.

[3]   D. Gillborn (1995) *Racism and Antiracism in Real Schools*, (Buckingham, Open University Press).
[4]   B. Bagilhole (1997) *Equal Opportunities and Social Policy: Issues of Gender, Race and Disability*, (London, Routledge).
[5]   T. Modood, S. Beisohn, and S. Virdee (1992) *Changing Ethnic Identities*, (London, Policy Studies Institute).
[6]   M. Mac an Ghaill, (1999) *Contemporary Racisms and Ethnicities: Social and Cultural Transformations* (Buckingham, Open University Press).
[7]   *e.g.* see M. Barrett, and A. Phillips, (eds) (1992) *Destablizing Theory*, (Policy Press: Oxford).
[8]   *e.g.* see P. Abberley, (1987) "The concept of oppression and the development of a social theory of disability", *Disability, Handicap and Society*, 2(1): 5–19; M. Oliver, (1990) *The Politics of Disablement: a Sociological Approach*, (Basingstoke, Macmillan).
[9]   *e.g.* see J. Morris, (ed) (1996) *Encounters with Strangers: Feminism and Disability*, (London, Women's Press).

Overarching legal principles: race, gender and disability

The importance of "race", gender and disability as equal oppor- **4.6**
tunity "identities" is exemplified by their extensive consideration
within International Conventions. The UN Convention on the
Rights of the Child ("UN Convention") requires all rights under the
Convention to be respected and ensured without "discrimination of
any kind", with particular mention of race, colour, sex, language,
religion, national, ethnic or social origin and disability (Article
2(1)). Numerous articles within the Convention deal with aspects of
culture, religion, ethnicity and/ or language, ranging from the right
to have a name from birth (Article 7), to adoption (Articles 20 and
21), to education (Article 29) and juvenile justice (Article 40), to
special measures for immigrant and refugee children (Articles 10
and 22). Article 23 recognises "handicapped" children's right to
special care, education and training designed to help them to
achieve the greatest possible self-reliance and to facilitate their
"active participation in the community".

Despite the attention to gender and race within Article 2(1), the **4.7**
UN Convention has been accused of being ethno- and gender-
centric: "To the extent that the Convention deals with children as
unspecified, unsituated people, it tends in fact to deal with white,
male, relatively privileged children".[10] For example, Ennew states
that the child in the Convention is a Northern child, which has
damaging consequences for Southern children who can be excluded[11]. Partly as a result of such criticisms, the UN Committee on
the Rights of the Child has focused considerable attention on issues
of race, gender and disability, in General Discussions (*e.g.* January
1995 on the girl child[12] and October 1997 on disabled children[13])
and when considering States' Reports. The Guidelines for State
Periodic Reports specifically ask for disaggregated statistics by
gender, disability, race and for information on measures to prevent
and eliminate potentially racist attitudes and prejudice.[14]

The European Convention on Human Rights ("European Con- **4.8**
vention") contains very similar non-discrimination articles to those
in the UN Convention. The enjoyment of European Convention

[10] F. Olsen, (1992) "Social Legislation. Sex Bias in International Law: The UN
Convention on the Rights of the Child", Indian Journal of Social Work, 53 (3):
509.

[11] J. Ennew, (1995) "Outside Childhood: Street Children's Rights", in B. Franklin,
(ed.) *The Handbook of Children's Rights,* (London, Routledge).

[12] See Committee on the Rights of the Child (1995) *Report on the Eighth Session*
1.95, CRC/C/38.

[13] See Committee on the Rights of the Child (1997) *Report on the Sixteenth Session*
26.11.97 CRC/C/69 http://www.unhchr.ch/tbs/doc.nsf/(symbol)/CRC.C.69.

[14] R. Hodgkin, and P. Newell, (1998) *Implementation Handbook for the Convention
on the Rights of the Child* (Geneva,) (UNICEF).

rights is not to be subject to discrimination on any ground such as "sex, race, colour, language, religion, political or other opinion, association with a national minority, property, birth or other status".[15] "Other status" has been determined as including the criterion of age. Express recognition of other grounds such as sexuality and disability has not been made. Kilkelly, however, argues that the European Court of Human Rights has given tacit approval for inclusion of such grounds, as they have been considered the basis for discriminatory treatment.[16] Article 14 does have limitations. First, it applies only in respect of the other articles of the European Convention.[17] Second, alleged discrimination does not contravene Article 14 if there are "reasonable and objective" grounds for treating children differently.[18] Third, the principles of the European Convention as incorporated into domestic law apply to "public authorities".[19]

4.9   Further articles are contained in the European Conventions that directly relate to language and religion. People detained or charged with a criminal offence have a right to information in their own language. Rights are protected to freedom of thought, conscience and religion[20] and freedom of expression.[21] Such rights, if they were to be exercised by children, might potentially conflict with parents' rights.[22] Article 8 (respect for person's private and family life) and Article 2 Protocol 1 (respect for parents' rights to ensure education and teaching in conformity with their religious and philosophical convictions) could be used to assert parents' rights, possibly at the expense of children's rights. Kilkelly notes that the Convention authorities have not yet addressed a conflict between a parent and child in regards to the child's religion.[23] In the European Convention and the UN Convention, there may be an unresolved tension between parental and children's rights

4.10   The principles of non-discrimination and the positive promotion of culture are also contained within other international instruments such as the International Covenants on Civil and Political Rights[24] and on Economic, Social and Cultural Rights;[25] the Declaration of Rights of Persons belonging to National or Ethnic, Religious and

---

[15] Art. 15.
[16] U. Kilkelly, (1999) *The Child and the European Convention on Human Rights* (Dartmouth, Ashgate).
[17] *Abdulaziz, Cabaut and Balkandale v. United Kingdom* (1985) 7 E.H.R.R. 471. Also see para. 3.12 *supra*.
[18] See, *e.g., Marcks v. Belgium* (1979) 2 E.H.R.R. Also see para. 3.12 *supra*.
[19] s. 6, Human Rights Act.
[20] Art. 9.
[21] Art. 10.
[22] for discussion of this issue, see paras 3.20–3.23
[23] *op.cit., supra.*
[24] 999 UNTS 171; (1967) 6 I.L.M. 368.
[25] 999 UNTS 3; (1967) 6 I.L.M. 360.

Linguistic Minorities;[26] and the International Convention on the Protection of the Rights of all Migrant Workers and Members of their Families.[27] The Amsterdam Treaty, Article 13, allows (but does not require) the European Community to take a proactive approach towards the elimination of discrimination based on sex, racial or ethnic origin, religion and belief, disability, age or sexual orientation. The rights of girls are additionally addressed in the Convention on the Elimination of All Forms of Discrimination against Women.[28] The rights of ethnic minorities are considered in the International Convention on the Elimination of All Forms of Racial Discrimination.[29] Disability is not mentioned in the International Covenants on Civil and Political Rights or in those on Economic, Social and Cultural Rights but is within their commentaries and within the Universal Declaration of Human Rights.[30] Following various Declarations, the UN General Assembly adopted the Standard Rules on the Equalization of Opportunities for Persons with Disabilities[31](1993) and the Salamanca Statement and Framework for Action on Special Needs Education[32] (1994). Various rules in the Salamanca Statement refer directly to children, including a promotion of inclusion and education of all children.[33]

In the United Kingdom, RRA makes it unlawful to discriminate **4.11** directly or indirectly on racial grounds.[34] "Racial grounds" means colour, race, nationality, or ethnic or national origin.[35] The Act also makes it unlawful to apply requirements or conditions that are disadvantageous to people of a particular racial group that cannot be justified on non-racial grounds. All public authorities are subject to the Act in regards to their employment practices and their activities in the areas of education, housing and the provision of goods, facilities and services. There is a general duty on local authorities to carry out their functions "with due regard to the need (a) to eliminate unlawful racial discrimination; and (b) to promote equality of opportunity, and good race relations, between persons of different racial groups".[36]

The Race Relations (Amendment) Act 2000 has extended the **4.12** scope of the RRA, so that it will be illegal for any public authority

---

[26] I GA. Res. 47/135; (1993) 32 I.L.M. 911.
[27] G.A.Res. 45/158; (1991) 30 I.L.M. 157.
[28] 1249 UNTS 13; (1980) 19 I.L.M. 33.
[29] 660 UNTS 195; (1966) 6 I.L.M. 350.
[30] G.A. Res. 217A (III).
[31] G.A. Res. 48/96.
[32] G.A. Res. 49/153.
[33] For further comparison between the expression of these articles in various international conventions and associated documents, see Hodgkin and Newell, *op. cit.*
[34] Race Relations Act 1976, s. 1.
[35] *ibid.*, s. 3(1).
[36] Race Relations Act 1976, s. 71.

to discriminate on racial grounds in respect of any of its functions. The Act will make it unlawful for any police officer to discriminate on racial grounds in carrying out any policing functions[37] and will give greater enforcement powers to the Commission for Racial Equality. The CRE will be able to serve a compliance notice on public authorities that do not comply with the above duty. Compliance with the new duty will also be subject to inspections or audits by existing inspectorates/ offices.

4.13   Under the SDA, it is unlawful to discriminate on the grounds of sex,[38] marriage[39] and gender reassignment[40] in employment, training, education, housing, and in the provision of goods, facilities and services to members of the public. As with the RRA, discrimination can be either direct or indirect. Co-educational schools, colleges and universities must not discriminate in the way they provide facilities or in the way they admit students.[41] The Careers Service must not discriminate between boys and girls in the way the service provides advice and assistance.[42] Single-sex schools may restrict admissions to boys or girls, but they must not restrict the types of subjects they teach as a result.[43] The Equal Opportunities Commission can help individuals prepare and present complaints and take legal proceedings. It can also hold inquiries and investigations, issue non-discrimination notices and take preliminary action in action in employment matters and cases involving advertising or "instructions or pressure to discriminate". Currently, the Commission can order unlawful acts of sex discrimination to stop but cannot impose changes in practice.[44]

4.14   Under DDA, a "disabled person"[45] has the right not to be discriminated against in employment,[46] the provision of goods, facilities and services,[47] public transport[48] and in the sale or lease of land and property.[49] Various exemptions and qualifications are, however, applied. Where any arrangement or physical feature of the premises place the disabled person at a substantial disadvantage, employers have a duty to take such steps as is reasonable to prevent

---

[37] CRE (2000) CRE 2000 "The Race Relations (Amendment) Bill Questions and Answers", Edinburgh/ London: CRE.
[38] Sex Discrimination Act 1975, s. 1.
[39] *ibid.*, s. 3.
[40] *ibid.*, s. 2A.
[41] *ibid.*, s. 22.
[42] *ibid.*, s. 23.
[43] *ibid.*, s. 26.
[44] EOC (1998) *Equality in the 21st Century*, Manchester: EOC.
[45] "Subject to the provisions of Schedule 1, a person has a disability ... if he [sic] has a physical or mental impairment which has a substantial and long-term adverse effect on his ability to carry out normal day-to-day activities" (Section 1(1)).
[46] Disability Discrimination Act 1995, s. 4.
[47] *ibid.*, s. 19.
[48] *ibid.*, ss. 33 and s. 40.
[49] *ibid.*, s. 22; this applies only where an estate agent or public advertisement is used.

them having that effect.[50] However, the term "reasonable" is used and the duty presently only applies to employers of 20 employees or more.[51] Unlike in England and Wales, the DDA does not apply in state schooling. Further education is required to meet the educational needs of disabled students and produce disability statements.[52] Scottish Higher Education Funding Council grants and other payments are subject to conditions, including the provision of disability statements. The Disability Rights Commission has a range of enforcement powers: *i.e.*, to conduct formal investigations, to serve non-discrimination notices, to enter into an agreement, to apply to a sheriff court for an order in certain circumstances, to provide assistance to individuals and to provide conciliation.[53]

The RRA, SDA and DDA are all United Kingdom wide legis- **4.15** lation and discrimination is a reserved matter. The Scottish Parliament can, however, take some action in relation to equal opportunities. The Scotland Act 1998 allows the Parliament "the encouragement (other than by prohibition or regulation) of equal opportunities, and in particular of the observance of the equal opportunity requirements".[54] This was used to argue successfully for amendments to the Standards in Scotland's Schools etc. Act 2000.[55]

All legislation affecting children can be analysed for its promo- **4.16** tion of equal opportunities and avoidance of discrimination. However, for reasons of space, and because of their potentially profound impact on children's lives, this chapter will focus on child care services under the Children (Scotland) Act 1995 ("the 1995 Act") and on education services under the Education (Scotland) Act 1980 ("the 1980 Act") and the Standards in Scotland's Schools etc. Act 2000.

Child care services

The 1995 Act saw the first comprehensive revision of Scottish child **4.17** care law since the Social Work (Scotland) Act 1968. It consolidated different areas of law affecting children—family, child care and adoption law—and attempted to rationalise and co-ordinate them. The Act was implemented in two stages, with virtually all sections implemented by April 1, 1997.

---

[50] *ibid.*, s. 6(1).
[51] *ibid.*, s. 7.
[52] *ibid.*, s. 31.
[53] For full description of enforcement powers, see http://www.drc-gb.org/drc/AboutTheCommission/Page212.asp.
[54] Scotland Act 1998, Sched. 5, s. L2.
[55] For example, the requirement for local authorities' annual statements of improvement objectives to include an account of how the authority will encourage equal opportunities and observe equal opportunity requirements. (s. 5.)

4.18   How well has the 1995 Act, heralded as bringing the key principles of the UN Conventions into Scottish law,[56] recognised anti-
discrimination and equal opportunities?

Children with Disabilities

4.19 The 1995 Act is revolutionary in that, for the first time in Scottish
legislation, children with and affected by disabilities are included
within "mainstream" child care legislation. Local authorities have
been placed under new duties towards "children in need".[57] That
important category includes children with disabilities and those
adversely affected by the disability of any other person in the child's
family.[58] Local authorities must safeguard and promote the welfare
of "children in need" in their areas, preferably by promoting children's upbringing within their families, by providing a "range and
level of services appropriate to the children's needs".[59] The only
specific service required by the 1995 Act for "children in need" is
daycare,[60] which includes after-school and holiday care.[61]

4.20   The general duties owed to "children in need" by local authorities
must be read alongside their specific duties towards disabled children.[62] "Children in need" services must be designed: to minimise
the effect of his/her disability on a disabled child; to minimise the
effect of the disability of another family member, on any child
adversely affected; and to give those children "the opportunity to
lead lives which are as normal as possible".[63]

4.21   These requirements promote an "integrative" or "inclusionary"
approach to services (albeit perceiving "disability" as inherently
negative) and would seem to mitigate against the provision of
segregated or stigmatising services for children with or affected by
disabilities. Further, local authorities are defined corporately under
the Act[64] and thus include services such as housing, education and
leisure and recreation. The words "to minimise" and "as normal as
possible" in themselves are qualified and imprecise in the 1995
Act—but the potential is worth exploring.

4.22   A person is disabled if that person is "chronically sick or disabled

---

[56] U.K. Government (1999), *The UN Convention on the Rights of the Child. The
U.K's Second Report to the UN Committee on the Rights of the Child* (London,
HMSO), http://www.doh.gov.uk/unchild.htm.
[57] Children (Scotland Act 1995, s.22.
[58] *ibid.*, s. 93(4).
[59] *ibid.*, s. 22.
[60] *ibid.*, s. 27.
[61] *ibid.*, s. 27(3).
[62] *ibid.*, s. 23.
[63] *ibid.*, s. 23(1).
[64] *ibid.*, s. 93(1)—"local authority" means a council constituted under s. 2 of the
Local Government etc. Scotland Act 1994.

or suffers from a mental disorder (within the meaning of the Mental Health (Scotland) Act 1984)".[65] This definition of disability has the advantage of being familiar to local authorities. Conceivably, it could be quite wide, with non-life threatening chronic diseases included. Its appropriateness to children, however, is questionable, as "chronicity" can be difficult to establish in young children and few children are classed as mentally ill. Perhaps most problematically, the definition focuses the disability on the individual child and thus remains firmly within the "medical model" of disability. Even though the Acts were being legislated for coterminously, the 1995 Act fails to incorporate the more up-to-date definition of disability as provided for in the Disability Discrimination Act 1995.[66] Disability legislation itself could be accused of failing adequately to consider its applicability to children, but it does recognise the contribution made to an individual's disability by their social context.

Duties towards children with and affected by disabilities are **4.23** further specified in the 1995 Act. A local authority must assess the needs of such children in relation to the provision of support services, when requested to do so by a child's parent or guardian.[67] Other family members can also be assessed. Further, a local authority must assess a carer's ability to care when requested to do so by a carer.[68]

Broadly, inclusion of services for children with and affected by **4.24** disabilities within mainstream legislation has been welcomed. The need for assessments was not disputed. However, the particular formulation does have some inherent problems. First, the parent or guardian, and not the child, is the only one who can initiate an assessment. What if a child wishes to have an assessment but his/her parent or guardian refuses? Second, no specific reference is made in legislation about taking into account of children's views, a breach of UN Convention Article 12. Third, despite the government's good intentions, the assurances given in Parliament that carer assessments for young carers were covered by the Carers (Recognition and Services) Act 1995 proved incorrect. For children under 16 in Scotland, their right to such a carer's assessment is presently insecure (although promoted in guidance).[69] Fourth, the carer's assessment is dubiously worded in the context of children. The assessment is to consider the "carer's ability to continue to

---

[65] *ibid.*, s. 23(2).
[66] Disability Discrimination Act 1995, s. 1(1) states that "a person has a disability for the purposes of this Act if he has a physical or mental impairment which has a substantial and long-term adverse effect on his ability to carry out normal day-to-day activities.
[67] Children (Scotland) Act 1995, s. 23(3).
[68] *ibid.*, s. 24.
[69] Scottish Office, Social Work Services Group (1997) The Children (Scotland) Act (Edinburgh, HMSO).

provide, or as the case may be, to provide, care for a child". This may be appropriate for adults but, if a carer is not able to care, a local authority may feel obliged to instigate child protection proceedings[70] or refer a child to a children's hearing. A more appropriate wording would have been to assess carers for their need of services, in order to support their caring.[71]

4.25   Other legislation (e.g. the Education (Scotland) Act 1980 as amended) is more prescriptive in terms of assessment requirements, in linking services to assessments, appeals, and parental receipt of reports—so precedents did exist for greater specificity, on such issues, within the 1995 Act. Given the difficulties found in both community care and education in relation to these issues, firm requirements would have been better expressed in the legislation. Fortunately, certain of these matters (*e.g.* information to carers about their right to assessment) are set out in guidance on the Act.[72]

4.26   How are these provisions working in practice? Comprehensive Scottish research is not yet available. The Children (Scotland) Act requires local authorities to publish children's services plans; a review of them does indicate attention to children affected by disabilities.[73] Many plans note their need to review inter-agency assessments, to increase services and to involve children and parents. Surveys of the voluntary sector indicate a high commitment to services for disabled children and continued concern that their needs be met.[74] A fundamental issue remains, however, that the dramatically smaller local authorities, cut in size after local government reform in 1996, lack economies of scale to provide specialist resources. English experience of parallel provision in the Children Act 1989 shows continued gaps (and some examples of good practice): barriers to gaining services, including service- rather than needs-led assessments; a limited range of services; and lack of measurable objectives for services.[75] In short,

---

[70]   An application for a Child Assessment Order (s. 55) or a Child Protection Order (s. 57) under the Children (Scotland) Act 1995 may be granted where a local authority has reasonable cause to suspect (for CAO) or to believe (for CPO) that a child is suffering or is likely to suffer significant harm.

[71]   Such a viewpoint is given further strength by the recent volume of criticism by disabled parents, against the discourse around "young carers" as "victims'. The discourse leads to a limited level, of usually recreational, services for the young people, posits the fault as poor parenting and an inappropriate reversal of roles, and fails to address the central problem—*i.e.* lack of support for the disabled parent. See for example R. Olsen, (1996) "Young Carers: Challenging the Facts and Politics of Research into Children and Caring", Disability and Society, 11(1), pp. 41–54.

[72]   Scottish Office, Social Work Services Group (1997) The Children (Scotland) Act, (Edinburgh, HMSO.)

[73]   Scottish Office, Social Work Services Group (1999) "Children (Scotland) Act 1995: Review of Children's Services Plans". (Letter 11.1.99.)

[74]   Children in Scotland (1998) *Making the Act Work*, (Edinburgh, CIS.)

[75]   Social Services Inspectorate (1998) *Removing Barriers for Disabled Children*, (Wetherby, Department of Health).

while some information is available, systematic research needs to be undertaken to know how these provisions are working in practice.

Race, religion and culture

There is little Scottish research available that charts the im- **4.27** plementation of "due regard" to a child's "religious persuasion, racial origin and cultural and linguistic background". This principle is applied in three places within the Act: for children "looked after" by local authorities,[76] for "children in need" services[77] and in adoption decisions.[78] The Scottish Office review of the first children's services plans notes that, while numbers of children from ethnic minorities were often stated, their specific needs were rarely included.[79] In a backward step, the requirement for a children's hearing to have regard to a child's religious persuasion has not been repeated in the 1995 Act, although it was within earlier legislation. If such a consideration, however, were recognised as part of a child's welfare, the children's hearing can still have regard to it.. Religion, though, is not often argued as a determining factor in modern family law cases.[80]

To assist service providers, the Social Work Services Inspectorate **4.28** for Scotland commissioned guidance on the delivery of services to groups of children, "*Valuing Diversity: Having Regard to the Racial, Religious, Cultural and Linguistic Needs of Scotland's Children*".[81] The guidance covers a range of contentious issues that have become areas of controversy, particularly in England and Wales. It refers to the issues of identity for black and mixed race parentage children, especially in relation to "looked after" children and adoption. It recommends that relevant statistics be gathered for strategic planning.[82] Consultation with black and minority ethnic groups is advocated.[83] Intercountry adoption has since been addressed by Adoptions (Intercountry Aspects) Act 1999, which allows the United Kingdom Government to ratify the Hague Convention on Protection of Children and Co-operation in Respect of Intercountry Adoption.[84]

---

[76] Children (Scotland) Act s. 17(4).
[77] *ibid.*, s. 22(2).
[78] *ibid.*, s. 95.
[79] Scottish Office, Social Work Services Group (1999). Letter: Children (Scotland) Act 1995: Review of Children's Services, (Edinburgh, The Scottish Office).
[80] L. Edwards and A. Griffiths, (1997) *Family Law* (Edinburgh, W. Green).
[81] (1998, Edinburgh, HMSO.)
[82] Social Services Inspectorate (1997a) *Responding to Families in Need* (Wetherby, Department of Health); Social Services Inspectorate (1999) *Getting Family Support Right* (Wetherby, Department of Health).
[83] Social Services Inspectorate (1997b) *Children in Need* (Wetherby, Department of Health).
[84] See paras 9.44–9.46.

Gender

4.29 The Children (Scotland) Act 1995 does not make reference to gender (with one exception): its reference to a child as "him" is defined officially as gender-neutral. The exception lies with children's hearings, which cannot have a panel of only one sex (s. 39 (5) Children (Scotland) Act 1995). The index for the 1995 Act guidance indicates six references to gender. The three references to children are in relation to assessments: assessments for disabled children, assessments carried out under Child Assessment Orders, and "steps for consideration" by a local authority before applying for a Child Protection Order. In relation to staff, gender is also mentioned: to have a balance of male and female staff in residential care and secure accommodation; and to take account a child's wish for a female or male doctor when a child is medically examined in secure accommodation.

4.30 While these mentions of gender are undoubtedly welcome, they do not address comprehensively particular aspects of gender. Statistics are collected that indicate considerable differences in the proportions of girls and boys that experience aspects of child care services. For example, more boys than girls are "looked after"[85] and are in residential care and, within that category, secure accommodation.[86] Questions arise due to these gender differentials, that are unaddressed by the legislation and guidance: questions about underlying differences in experiences, potential differences in how systems identify or respond to these experiences, and the problems caused by small populations of one gender within services.

4.31 The Children (Scotland) Act 1995 thus takes three different approaches, in addressing disability, "race" and gender. The Act can be seen as revolutionary for disabled children, sensitive to issues on ethnicity and culture, and virtually silent on gender. The Act considers services for disabled children, concentrating on new assessments and how services should be designed. For children from black and minority ethnic groups, their backgrounds, religious persuasion and racial origin are factors in decision-making, in relation to being "looked after" and/ or adopted, and in the design of "children in need" services. Only in guidance is some reference made to gender, in terms of assessments, examinations and staffing.

---

[85] Scottish Executive (1999a), *Information on Children Looked After as at 31st March 1999*, http://www.scotland.gov.uk/library2/kd01/info-01.htm.

[86] Scottish Executive (1999b), *Information on Children in Residential Accommodation in the Year to 31st March 1998*, http://www.scotland.gov.uk/library2/kd01/info-note-98.htm.

Education services

If research is presently limited on the implementation of the Chil- **4.32**
dren (Scotland) Act 1995, a sharp contrast is the research volume
on equal opportunities and education. Three issues will be considered here within education, that have caught considerable media,
public and policy attention in the past decade: differentials in
school achievement; bullying; and school exclusions/ inclusions.
Much of the discussion will be in respect of research and policy,
rather than case law.[87] Cases under the non-discrimination acts are
rare in relation to children and education.[88] The Special Educational Needs and Disability Act 2001 now extends DDA to cover
Scottish education and legal cases on special educational needs are
common.

Differentials in school achievement

As stated above, the Sex Discrimination Act made it illegal to deny **4.33**
educational access on the basis of sex.[89] Measor and Sikes, however, note that cases that have been taken to court have been hard
to prove.[90] The focus on differential achievements, however, has
been considerable. While in past decades concerns were expressed
on girls' leaving qualifications, recent headlines have raised the
alarm of boys' underachievement in schools.[91]

Girls are gaining higher examination results than boys, as a **4.34**
group. Young women in the Scottish School Leavers Survey (2000)
achieved significantly higher exam results than young men: 60 per
cent compared with 47 per cent had the highest grades (five or more
Standard Grades at grades 1–3). Boys are twice as likely as girls to
leave school at age 16 or 17 with no qualifications at all.[92] Younger
and colleagues outline the various explanations offered for such
differences,[93] including: boys' disregard for authority, academic
work and formal achievement; "masculinity", which comes into

---

[87] The cases on education law are considered in Chap. 12.

[88] Equal Opportunities Commission (1998) *Equality in the 21st Century: A New Sex
Equality Law for Britain* (Manchester, EOC).

[89] Note the exception in s. 44 of the Sex Discrimination Act, allowing for the
division of girls and boys into sports "traditional" to their sex. The Equal
Opportunities Commission advocates this exception be removed.

[90] (1992) Gender and Schools (London, Cassell).

[91] *e.g.* see "Bid to put boys in the hot seat" T.E.S., May 14, 1999, "Girls make the
grade more often than boys", *The Scotsman*, July 28, 2000.

[92] Scottish School Leavers Survey (2000) 17 in 1997, http://www.scotland.gov.uk/
library3/education/ssls-02.asp#t1.

[93] M. Younger, M. Warrington, and J. Williams, (1998) "The Gender Gap and
Classroom Interactions: Reality and Rhetoric?', British Journal of Sociology of
Education, 20 (3) at pp. 325–417.

conflict with school ethos; the wider social context of changing labour markets, de-industrialisation and male unemployment; girls' increased maturity and more effective learning strategies; and the apparent success of equal opportunities programmes in schools.

4.35   Younger and colleagues also identify two concerns arising from the present alarm. First, the focus on the gender gap fails to recognise the overall rising performance levels of both girls and boys. Second, the debate risks seeing the "superior attainment on the part of girls as somehow also constituting a problem, rather than seeing it as a cause for celebration and congratulation".[94] A further concern should be noted. Socio-economic background remains far more determinative of academic success than gender; combined with gender, boys from the lowest socio-economic backgrounds are missing out on the rise of performance levels—they are the one group whose attainments are actually decreasing.[95] Gorard, however, suggests that a closer look at the statistical data does demonstrate differentials but that the gaps, despite what politicians and even researchers have stated, are actually diminishing.[96]

4.36   The gendered patterns of classroom interaction and assessment have been a research focus for at least two decades. Measor and Sikes encapsulate the concerns of the 1980s: "Classroom research makes it clear that boys dominate girls in the classroom and secure greater attention than them, leaving the girls at a disadvantage".[97] Recent research continues to find the predominance of teachers' interactions with boys. But they also note that this predominance is over classroom management; when academic interactions are considered, girls' requests result in more teacher interaction with them than boys. As Younger and colleagues write:

> "...certain characteristics which girls have always exhibited but which have sometimes been subtly denigrated, such as diligence and application, are being re-evaluated as they come to be associated with a range of perceivably newer and more positive characteristics—for example, that girls are more confident, are self-learners, are more articulate and are more inclined to take the initiative in promoting their own learning."[98]

4.37 Statistical analysis reveals a continued subject polarisation at higher

---

[94] *ibid.*, p. 326.

[95] *e.g.* see: J. Bynner, and S. Parsons, (1997) "Getting on with Qualifications", in J. Bynner, E. Ferri, and P. Shepherd, (eds) Twenty-something in the 1990s, (Aldershot, Ashgate); D. Gillborn, and C. Gipps, (1996) *Recent Research on the Achievement of Ethnic Minority Pupils,* (London, HMSO).

[96] S. Gorard, (1999) "Keeping a Sense of Proportion: The 'Politician's Error' in Analysing School Outcomes", British Journal of Educational Studies, 47(3) at pp. 235–246.

[97] *ibid.*, p. 87.

[98] *ibid.*, p. 327.

educational levels, with girls concentrating on humanities and languages while boys dominate in the sciences and technical subjects.[99]

As the SDA does in relation to sex, the RRA makes it unlawful **4.38** to discriminate against a person, directly or indirectly, in the field of education on grounds of race.[1] The research on differentials by ethnic background has become more sophisticated in its disaggregation of statistics; most publications now identify that people from Indian parentage as a group have higher academic achievements while those with a Bangladeshi or an African-Caribbean background can be particularly disadvantaged.[2] Local education authorities in England were found to have very different attainment results by ethnic groups. Worryingly, Gillborn and Mirza found that African-Carribean pupils' positions tended to be worse, relative to their white peers, between the start and end of their compulsory schooling. Further, these statistics are detailed by gender, demonstrating that girls tend to achieve more qualifications than boys within each group. These findings, however, are based on English data. Little analysis is available in Scotland on the achievements of children from black and minority ethnic groups.

Unlike gender and race, potential discrimination in qualification **4.39** achievements has been neither substantially debated nor researched for disabled children within Scotland. Riddell and colleagues did examine the 5–14 Development Programme for children with special educational needs. They noted the benefits—that these children were included in the "mainstream" curriculum—but also the costs—certain inflexibility in meeting these children's educational needs and recognising their achievements.[3] Research is now being undertaken on more individualised educational planning for each child with special educational needs, which may in the longer term be used alongside other performance targets comparing schools. At present, however, the debate about disabled children's education is mainly ideological, with some advocating children's inclusion in mainstream schooling and others pressing for the continuation of specialist schools.

---

[99] EOC (1998), *ibid.*
[1] Race Relations Act 1976 (c.24).
[2] D. Gillborn, and C. Gipps, (1996), *ibid.*, D. Gillborn, and H.S. Mirza, (2000) *Educational Inquality: Mapping Race, Class and Gender*, (London, OFSTED).
[3] S. Riddell, (1996) "Theorising special educational needs in a changing political climate" in L. Barton, (ed.) *Disability and Society, Emerging Issues and Insights,* (London, Longman.)

Bullying

4.40 Bullying is rarely brought into the legal arena[4] but the media has reported some recent retrospective cases that have raised issues of disability and recent concentration on bullying of girls.[5] Further, the Law Society of Scotland has issued leaflets through schools, advertising the availability of legal services in relation

4.41   Bullying has received considerable policy-maker and public attention in the past decade, with fears expressed both for the bullies and the bullied.[6] Bullies and victims differ in a variety of ways which are relevant to this chapter. For example, girls are less likely to be identified as bullies and when they are, they rarely bully boys.[7] Children with "special needs" are reported as twice as likely to be bullied as other children.[8] Disabled children report being bullied both within mainstream and special schools.[9] English research shows that Asian pupils are more likely to be "racially" teased than white pupils and Asian boys are more likely to be considered bullies than white boys.[10] Concerns have been raised about racism in Scottish schools.[11] Advice has been provided to schools on promoting and evaluating an ethos of equal opportunities and schools will now need to record all incidents in schools with a racist motivation.[12]

4.42   Most of the research on bullying has two related deficits: it is not founded on children's own definitions of bullying and (therefore) it may under-represent differences by gender. While girls are less likely to be bullies, the research does demonstrate that girls are more likely to receive verbal forms of bullying than boys and that boys are more likely to be bullied physically than girls.[13] Research by Björkqvist and colleagues[14] takes such findings a step further, by using a typology that includes physical, direct verbal and indirect

---

[4]   For discussion of the few relevant cases, see Chap. 12, paras 12.50–12.51.
[5]   For example, see "Bullied Girl's mother to stand guard for exams", *The Scotsman*, March 26, 1998.
[6]   Commission on Children and Violence (1995), *Children and Violence* (London, Calouste Gulbenkian Foundation).
[7]   P.K. Smith, and S. Sharp, (eds) (1994) *School Bullying: Insights and Perspectives*, (London, Routledge).
[8]   See "Scope exposes bullying", Community Care 11–17 June, 1998.
[9]   N. Watson, T. Shakespeare, S. Cunningham-Burley and C. Barnes, (1999) "Life as a Disabled Child", ESRC Report, Nick.Watson@ed.ac.uk.
[10] M. Boulton, (1995) "Patterns of bully/victim problems in mixed race groups of children", Social Development 4 (3) at pp. 277–293.
[11] *The Herald*, "Racism in school is at its worst in primaries five and six", December 4, 1999.
[12] Scottish Executive (1999) *The Stephen Lawrence Inquiry: An Action Plan for Scotland*, http://www.scotland.gov.uk/.
[13] Smith and Sharp (1994), *ibid.*
[14] For example, see K. Björkqvist, (1994), "Sex Differences in Physical, Verbal, and Indirect Aggression: A Review of Recent Research", Sex Roles 30 (3/4) at pp. 177–188.

aggression. Using this typology, girls' aggression against their peers is far closer to boys—and that the impact of such aggression may be under-estimated. Sexual harassment of girls has been noted by researchers for some time, seen as "so common that it comes to be accepted as part of ordinary life in school".[15] Gillborn notes the combination of sexual and racial harassment for girls: "The harassment of Asian girls and young women, for example, frequently embodies a range of complex, sometimes contradictory, racist and sexist stereotypes as at once demure yet licentious, alluring yet ugly".[16] Bullying policies may benefit from a closer look at "race", gender and disability.

School Exclusions

Exclusion from school[17] is yet another issue that has comerapidly **4.43** into the attention of policy-makers and the public. The official number of permanent exclusions remains small in Scotland, although the numbers of temporary exclusions rose in the early 1990s. Official statistics, however, are likely to underestimate exclusions substantially.

Research demonstrates that exclusions are neither equally dis- **4.44** tributed amongst the school population nor among schools.[18] In England, considerable alarm has been raised about potential discrimination against African-Caribbean pupils who are disproportionately excluded. Research has sought through qualitative methodology to unveil the dynamics behind such potential discrimination, that may be equally important for Scottish schools to consider. Teachers may expect "trouble" from African-Caribbean students, particularly boys, and may react quickly;[19] a reinforcing cycle can emerge, with boys adopting a "macho form of masculinity" that is "not conducive to academic success".[20] With a very small population in Scotland, however, the concern is not paralleled by statistical findings. For the first time, 1998–99 statistics reported on school exclusion by ethnic background. Of those children for whom background was known, 97.8 per cent were white.[21]

---

[15] Measor and Sikes, *ibid.*, p. 86.

[16] D. Gillborn, (1998), "Race and Ethnicity in Compulsory Schooling", in T. Modood, and T. Acland, (eds.) *Race and Higher Education*, (London, Policy Studies Institute), p. 21.

[17] For discussion of the legal mechanisms relating to exclusion, see Chap. 12, para. 12.56–12.68.

[18] See P. Munn, M.A. Cullen, M. Johnstone, G. Lloyd, (1997) *Exclusions and In-School Alternatives*, (Edinburgh, HMSO).

[19] D. Gillborn, and C. Gipps, (1996), *ibid.*

[20] A. Pilkington, (1999) "Racism in Schools and Ethnic Differentials in Educational Achievement: a brief comment on a recent debate", British Journal of Sociology of Education, 20 (3), p. 415.

[21] Scottish Executive (2000), Exclusions from Schools 1998/99, http://www.scotland.gov.uk/stats/bulletins/00007-00.asp.

4.45 Given the qualitative research and the findings on classroom management described above, the greater number of school exclusions for boys compared to girls is unsurprising. More boys than girls are excluded (9:1 in primary schools and 4:1 in secondary schools).[22] Vandalism was more often cited as a reason for boys than girls (11:1) while truancy had a lower ratio (24 boys to 15 girls). The gender ratios, however, are not constant from school to school (from nine boys to every one girl, in certain schools, to one boy to one girl in others). Do such differences raise potential concerns about discrimination?

4.46 Feminist criminological literature has developed the idea of "double discrimination" against women who not only conduct a deviant act but who are also seen as going against traditional stereotypes of feminine roles. Lloyd described evidence of this for girls identified as "troublesome". Problems further arise in terms of service availability. With a smaller population of "troublesome girls", services may be organised primarily to meet boys' needs rather than girls and girls may be "escalated" up the disciplinary options as being seen as particularly difficult or manipulative.[23] There are few residential schools, for example, for girls; this may require girls to be far away from home.

4.47 Increasingly, the lines are seen as artificial between children who are identified as having "social, emotional and behavioural difficulties" through the special needs system, who are excluded from school as discipline problems and may go through the children's hearing system for this and other reasons, and those who may be labelled as having a mental health problem.[24] But the lines can have substantial difference in terms of rights to services, appeals and other protective mechanisms. For example, parents have some (albeit limited) rights to school choice if their child had a record of special educational needs[25] that they do not have under child care law within children's hearings. The assessment rights of children with special educational needs leaving school are far stronger than those for children leaving local authority care. Children have rights to be heard in child care proceedings,[26] and now education—at least in respect of exclusion from school—that they do not have in mental health law.

4.48 The Scottish school system is under pressure to become more

---

[22] Munn *et al.* (1997), *ibid.*

[23] G. Lloyd, (1999) "Gender and exclusion from school" in J. Salisbury, and S. Riddell, (eds) *Gender, Policy and Educational Change*, (London, Routledge). See also C. Baines, and M. Adler, (1996) "Are girls more difficult to work with? Youth worker's perspectives in juvenile justice and related areas", Crime & Delinquency 42 (3) at pp. 467–485.

[24] For example, see: T. Booth, (1996) "Stories of exclusion: Natural and unnatural selection", in E. Blyth, and M. Milner, (eds) *Exclusion from School*, (London, Routledge) G. Lloyd, (1999), *ibid.*

[25] See para. 12.77

[26] Children (Scotland) Act 1995, ss. 16 and 17.

inclusive. Article 23 (1) of the UN Convention states that a disabled child should "enjoy a full and decent life, in conditions which ensure dignity, promote self-reliance, and facilitate the child's active participation in the community". An even stronger commitment to inclusive education is found in the Salamanca Statement, arguing that regular schools with an inclusive orientation are:

"the most effective means of combating discriminatory attitudes, creating welcoming communities, building an inclusive society and achieving education for all; moreover, they provide an effective education to the majority of children and improve the efficiency and ultimately the cost-effectiveness of the entire education system".[27]

In the United Kingdom, the Special Educational Needs and Disability Act 2001 should provide another impetus towards inclusion. The consultation paper outlined the proposal to:[28] **4.49**
make it unlawful for education providers to discriminate against a disabled child by:
  (i) treating a child less favourably on the grounds of the disability than a non-disabled child, without justification, in the arrangements made for the provision of education;
  (ii) failing to take reasonable steps to change any policies, practices or procedures which place a disabled children at a substantial disadvantage compared to a non-disabled child; and
  (iii) failing to take reasonable steps to provide education using a reasonable alternative method where a physical feature places a disabled child at a substantial disadvantage compared to a non-disabled child.
The problematic qualifiers of "reasonable" remain and Scottish **4.50** children's organisations have reacted unfavourably to the failure to require physical adjustments (as is proposed for post–16 education). In principle, the extension is strongly supported.

With the Standards in Scotland's Schools etc. Act 2000, Scottish **4.51** educational law has now caught up with other United Kingdom education legislation in having some promotion of integration/ inclusion. The Scottish Executive introduced an amendment into the Bill as it went through Parliament, to create a presumption for mainstream schooling. This amendment was subject to considerable controversy, with many confused by the legal wording (so the media ran stories that the parents' right to choose a mainstream school

---

[27] UNESCO, (1994), The Salamanca Statement and Framework for Action on Special Education, ED-94/WS/18.
[28] Department for Education and Employment (DfEE), Scottish Executive, Scotland Office, The National Assembly for Wales (2000) SEN and Disability Rights in Education Bill, London: DfEE.

was actually *worsened* by the amendment) and others critical of the "get out" clauses in subsection (15(3)) and the deficit-based wording. Nonetheless, the Scottish Executive indicated a wish to underline their support for an inclusive education policy.

4.52   Past European case law would not suggest that the European Convention can be used to go further than the new section 15. Article 2 of the First Protocol is not violated if the proposed placement (in a special school) is consistent with the properly assessed needs of the child and, as far as possible, with the parents' views about their child's needs. Further, the United Kingdom had entered a reservation to this Article, with similar wording to Section 15(3) of the Scottish legislation: i.e., making it subject to the provision of effective instruction and training and the avoidance of unreasonable public expenditure. The policy balance is likely to remain, at least in the short-term, between a broad promotion of school inclusion but a continued support of special schooling for some children.

Moving on?

4.53 The inclusion debate is fuelled by disabled adults who have had very negative experiences of segregated schooling,[29] that were both damaging in themselves and failed to equip them for the world after school. There is little doubt that young people leaving special schools have poor levels of qualifications.[30] If local career statistics are considered, they tend to reveal very different post-school destinations for special schools.

4.54   Young people with records of special educational needs[31] have particular rights to assessments under Scottish law,[32] that were intended to address the transitional difficulties.[33] Despite all the assessments legally required by law, research has repeatedly and definitively mapped the transitional difficulties for young people with disabilities. In an extensive United Kingdom survey, Hirst and Baldwin reported the considerable disadvantage faced by the majority of disabled young people.[34] Most young disabled people

---

[29] For example, see C. Barnes, and M. Oliver, (1998), *Disabled people and social policy: from exclusion to inclusion*, (London, Longman).

[30] M. Hirst, and S. Baldwin, (1994), *Unequal Opportunities: Growing Up Disabled*, Social Policy Research Unit, (London, HMSO.)

[31] For a description of recording and definition of special educational needs, see A. Closs, (1997), "Special Educational Provision" in M.M. Clark, and P. Munn, (eds) *Education in Scotland*, (London, Routledge).

[32] See paras 12.69–12.81.

[33] For a discussion of difficulties in co-ordinating such assessments, see E.K.M. Tisdall, (1997) *The Children (Scotland) Act 1995: developing policy and law for Scotland's children*, (Edinburgh, HMSO.)

[34] M. Hirst, and S. Baldwin, (1994) *ibid.*

quickly fell behind their non-disabled peers in terms of income. Their employment prospects were bleaker and their friendship and recreational opportunities more limited. Service co-ordination continued to be a problem for many young people, who lost contact with specialist therapy and health resources in the transition from child to adult services. The Beattie Committee's Report in 1999[35] continues to emphasise the need for considerable changes in professional training, co-ordination of services and extended opportunities.

Just as the transitional problem has been extensively researched **4.55** for young disabled people, information is available on transitions by gender and by race. More young women than young men are involved in further and higher education (although more men participate in science programmes and higher degrees)[36]. United Kingdom statistics find that more young people from black and minority ethnic populations participate in further and higher education than white young people.[37] But leaving the educational system, women and people from black and minority ethnic groups continue to have lower incomes (as a group).[38]

While the transitional problems have been extensively mapped **4.56** for disability, gender and race, the problems for young women and young people from black and minority ethnic backgrounds have not been addressed by proactive legislation.[39] But would legislation effectively address the problems? The bureaucratic processes translated into legal rights in Scottish law have not resulted in a reversal of disabled young people's disadvantage and a radical extension of their opportunities. As disability advocates/ studies are increasingly arguing, changes in attitudes are fundamental to inclusion.[40]

Questionable concepts, contested identities **4.57**

Anti-discrimination and equal opportunities as it applies to children **4.58** thus has a limited legal history. Cases have rarely been taken on behalf of or by children, in relation to the Race Relations Act or the

---

[35] Beattie Committee Report (1999), *Implementing Inclusiveness, Realising Potential*, (Edinburgh, Scottish Executive).
[36] EOC (1999), *Facts about Women and Men in Scotland 1999*, (Glasgow, EOC.)
[37] T. Modood, R. Berthoud, J. Lakey, J. Nazaroo, P. Smith, S. Virdee, and S. Beisohn, (1997), *Ethnic Minorities in Britain*, (London, Policy Studies Institute.)
[38] *e.g.* see EOC (1999), *Facts about Women and Men in Scotland 1999*, (Glasgow, EOC) Commission for Racial Equality website http://www.cre.gov.uk/publs/crepubs.html.
[39] Note that the RDA and SDA do apply to further and higher education.
[40] N. Watson, and J. Davis, (2000), "The Voice of the Disabled Child", at Disability Studies Seminar, Edinburgh, July 5–7, 2000.

Sex Discrimination Act, to test Scottish law, policy or practice. Court decision-making has given some explicit recognition to race, gender and disability when making decisions on children's lives but the Scottish list of reported cases is short. Only in cases on special educational needs is case law more extensive.

4.59   Certain areas of children's services have attracted particular policy attention, in relation to "race", gender and disability: inter-agency services for disabled children; local authority care and adoption for children from black and minority ethnic groups; and education for all three groups. Research raises concerns about differential opportunities that remain despite efforts to improve services. A policy comparison notes differences in approaches. For disabled children, parents or guardians have rights to assessments and (to a lesser extent) services. The incremental approach over time has created a potentially confusing plethora of assessments, that risk individualising the problem and failing to address societal barriers and lack of opportunities. The "due regard" principle encourages a positive promotion of identity for children from black and minority ethnic groups in child care legislation while English research and now the MacPherson Report[41] has created a policy awareness of institutional racism. Gender is not accorded positive rights in the Children (Scotland) Act 1995. Except for the Sex Discrimination Act on education, legislation affecting children tends to be officially "gender-neutral". Research, though, demonstrates that legislation, policy and practice can indeed have different impacts on boys and girls; these accusations can be levelled as much against the UN Convention as they can be to Scottish legislation. "Gender-neutral" can, at times, result in gender-bias.

4.60   Both small and large group differences pose particular service problems and questions about under-lying discrimination. Why are so many boys excluded from school and/or identified as having social-emotional behavioural difficulties? How well do child care services meet the needs of a child, who comes from the only family with a particular cultural background in a community? Are "troublesome" girls who are identified as "doubly deviant" more likely to receive harsher penalties yet have fewer services that meet their needs?

4.61   The legal structures camouflage the heated debates about what constitutes "race", gender and disability, with legislation freezing in time particular and often contested conceptualisations. A challenge to all three concepts is poststructural and postmodern theorisations that have argued against fixed notions of identity, recognising the multiplicity and overlapping nature of identities, their fluidity and

---

[41] MacPherson (1999), The Stephen Lawrence Inquiry, Cm. 4262-I, http://www.official-documents.co.uk/document/cm42/4262/4262.htm.

their interaction with societal structures.[42] For example, children from certain ethnic minorities are disproportionately likely to have certain disabilities.[43] Boys are more likely to be identified as disabled than girls.[44] The "politics of identity" have raised other potential identities—that equally may be discriminated against—such as sexual orientation. Geography and mobility can be the basis for discrimination: such dimensions as rural versus urban, displaced people and refugees. The Government's emphasis on "social exclusion" has recognised the potential overlaps in disadvantage. Whether as a cause or as a result, underlying these exclusions tends to be socio-economic disadvantage, that continues to have an stronger overall influence on differential life expectations than any other factor.

What remains largely unquestioned in Scottish society is discrimination by age. One can find stores that display signs prohibiting children to come in unattended, discrimination that would be legally prohibited if they referred to sex or race. Legal "chastisement" of children by their parents could be constituted as assault except for that relationship. While the need for a disability, racial equality and equal opportunities commission is recognised, an equivalent commission for children has not yet been created in Scotland. Perhaps this ignorance of age discrimination, however, will be changed due to European influences in the European Convention and the Amsterdam Treaty.   **4.62**

Law and policy arguably need to catch up with the present theorisations of identities, recognising their multiplicities and corresponding multiple disadvantages and dimensions of equal opportunities. They need to recognise that diversity benefits from being officially recognised, as ideas of "equal treatment" or "gender neutrality" in fact can result in discrimination. They can perhaps learn from new theorisations on school inclusion, which perceives that schools need to value all aspects of diversity: "an inclusive approach under which all pupils should be treated equally, should be valued and should be offered an educational experience which they value".[45] If so many people, so many children, risk being discriminated against and excluded by our "mainstream" services, should not the premises of these services be questioned?   **4.63**

---

[42] For discussion, see P. Moss, and P. Petrie (1999), *From Children's Services to Children's Spaces: Two Perspectives On Public Policy, Children and Childhood*, (London, Thomas Coram Research Unit. Discussion Paper).

[43] W.I.U. Ahmad, and K. Atkin (1996), "Ethnicity and Caring for a Disabled Child: The Case of Children with Sickle Cell or Thalassaemia", British Journal of Social Work 26 at pp. 755–775.

[44] Riddell Report (1999), *Report into the education of children with severe low incidence disability*, (Edinburgh, Scottish Executive).

[45] The Scottish Office Education and Industry Department (1998), *Special Educational Needs in Scotland*, Discussion paper, (Edinburgh, SOEID), p. 10.

CHAPTER 5

THE CHILD'S IDENTITY

ALASTAIR BISSETT-JOHNSON*

(* With thanks to Morven Callum, Ben Wickens and Margaret Barron Linton who provided research assistance on various parts of this chapter.)

This chapter examines what the United Nations Convention on the Rights of the Child (the UN Convention) and the European Convention on Human Rights and Fundamental Freedoms (the European Convention) require in terms of respect for the child's right to identity and the extent to which Scots law complies with the requirements. The principal statute discussed is the Children (Scotland) Act 1995 ("the 1995 Act").

The Child's Sense of Identity

A necessary prelude to any discussion of law is evidence from the **5.1** behavioural sciences about a child's sense of identity. Identity, which is not defined in either Convention, is a complex mix of factors including nature and nurture[1] contributing to a sense of self-knowledge, self-awareness and self-esteem. It may include identity within the family but, as the child develops, can encompass outside influences such as racial, linguistic and religious identity[2] as a child proceeds through a series of as many as eight stages, of which the turbulence of adolescence is a key, from which the child emerges as an integrated adult personality.[3] Although the process starts with

---

[1] On attachment theories, see: Bowlby, *Attachment and Loss: Volume 1, Attachment* (Pelican, 1991) (favouring early years influences); Clarke & Clarke, *Early Experience and the Life Path* (Jessica Kingsley, 2000) (cautioning against undue emphasis on the early years).

[2] Hodgson, "The International Legal Protection of the Child's Right to a Legal Identity and the Problem of Statelessness" (1993) 7 International Journal of Law and Family 255 at p. 264

[3] Erikson's work is perhaps the most influential: see Erikson, *Identity, Youth & Crisis* (Nahol & Co., 1968); *Childhood & Society* (W. Norton & Co., 1993). For a Different theoretical perspective, see Gilligan, *In a Different Voice—Psychological Theory and Women's Development* (Harvard University Press, 1982). For a legal perspective see, Masson and Harrisson, "Identity: Mapping the Frontiers", in Lowe and Douglas (eds), *Families Across Frontiers*, (Martinus Nijhoff, 1996).

the birth of the child and links to the child's birth parents, it gradually expands to encompass a widening series of influences such as the extended family, friends and, ultimately, to the child relating to factors of race, language and religion. The 1995 Act, in sections 7(4), 22(2) and 95, talks in terms of the need to protect a child's religion, race and nationality, but this is not always easy in the context of a differential willingness amongst racial and religious groups to offer themselves as foster or adoptive parents. The skill in operating the new Act will be to ensure that, in trying to respect these ties, a child is not left in limbo without a family. The child's sense of time[4] is important to children of all races, religions and cultures. Almost certainly, the provisions in sections 17(4), 22(2) and 95 will involve the need for redoubled efforts at an early stage to involve the extended family of the child. These provisions should also be seen in the context of the need to take into account the child's wishes wherever practicable. The words "wherever practicable" have, in the past, been used to undermine a child's right to information which was crucial to his or her identity. In *C., Petrs*,[5] an application was made to adopt a six-year-old child by his mother and the man the child believed to be his father although the child had in fact been conceived during a brief affair which the mother had with another man. When the social work department was asked to provide a report to the court, the applicants refused to co-operate with the social work authorities for fear of the child discovering the truth. The adoption order was made after a finding by the sheriff that it was impracticable to ascertain the wishes of the child. Sutherland[6] rightly describes this as judicial participation in the applicants' deception of the child.

Birth

5.2 Having established that identity is made up of a host of factors relating to "who you are," it becomes apparent that, in legal terms, this is closely related to the concept of parental rights and responsibilities. These are defined in sections 1 and 2 of the 1995 Act, as a set of obligations which parents have towards their children and the corresponding powers they have to enable them to discharge these obligations. However, while this legal relationship is accorded to both parents where the couple is married, the same is not true where the parents are unmarried. In these circumstances

---

[4] See Goldstein, Solnit and Freud, *Beyond the Best Interests of the Child* (Free Press, 1973), Chap. 3, and the same authors, *Before the Best Interests of the Child* (Free Press, 1979), at pp. 40–41 and 50–51.

[5] 1993 S.L.T. (Sh. Ct) 8.

[6] "Adoption: The child's view", 1994 S.L.T. (News) 37.

the child has automatic "legal identity" only *vis-à-vis* the mother.[7] This represents a change from the position advocated by the Scottish Law Commission which recommended[8] that all parents, including the non-marital father, should have parental rights and responsibilities. However, in recognition of the significance of many non-marital fathers' participation in their child's life,[9] the Act made it easier for a non-marital father to acquire parental rights and responsibilities. He can apply to the court for a general order imposing parental rights or responsibilities[10] or for specific responsibilities or rights. In addition, section 4 offers the acquisition of parental rights and responsibilities by a non-marital father if both parents enter into and register an irrevocable parental responsibilities and rights agreement (PRRA) in the prescribed form. This approach had merit, offering a quick alternative to court action for non-marital fathers to show commitment to their children, while simultaneously allowing mothers with real concern over their children's safety to withhold agreement. However, the evidence shows this has not happened. Only 426 agreements were made between November 1996 and December 1998 where, during the same period, around 30,000 births were jointly registered.[11] While ignorance of the provision may be a partial explanation for the small number of agreements registered, even if the agreements were widely known about they would still never work. The main problem must surely be that during the happy days of the relationship the cumbersome formalities of a section 4 agreement seem unnecessary, and, should the relationship deteriorate, there seems little incentive for the mother to concede her consent to the agreement. The existence of thousands of fathers with no "legal link" to their children means that it can be argued that we fail to conform to our international obligations.

Many agree with Lowe's contention that "there is a strong case **5.3**

---

[7] 1995 Act, ss. 3(1)(a) and (b). It is important to note that the non-marital father, although not holding automatic rights and responsibilities, does have a financial obligation to the child in terms of the child support legislation and the Family Law (Scotland) Act 1985.

[8] *Report on Family Law* (Scot. Law Com. No. 135, 1992), Rec. 5.

[9] During 1987 and 1997 the number of births to unmarried parents nearly doubled. Three quarters of those births were jointly registered, indicating those fathers wished to acknowledge commitment to their child. In the majority of those cases, the mother and father were registered at the same address, indicating a cohabiting relationship. See *Improving Scottish Family Law* (Scottish Office, 1999), pp. 24 and 51.

[10] 1995 Act, s. (2)(b). The correct procedure according to the dicta of Sheriff Principal Nicolson is for the unmarried father to first seek an order for parental rights and responsibilities under s. 11(2)(d) before seeking to enforce it under s.11(7)(2)(d). However, Edwards ("*White v. White*: Fathers, Families and Parental Rights", 46 Fam. L.B. 3) notes that this approach might prolong proceedings and that Sheriff Principal Bowen has rejected this approach in *Horsfall v. Horsfall*, 2000 G.W.D. 14-518.

[11] *Improving Scottish Family Law*, supra, p. 51.

for arguing the UN Convention does oblige the UK...to treat all fathers equally".[12] Articles 2(1), 8(1), 9(3) and 18(1) all lend weight to this assertion. According to Article 2(1), States should "respect and ensure the rights set forth in the ...Convention to each child...without discrimination of any kind, irrespective of the child's or his or her parent's...sex...birth or other status". As Sutherland indicates, we do not just breach this once but achieve "a hat trick".[13] Identity is the focus of Article 8(1), requiring states to ensure children "know who they are". Masson and Lowe[14] argue that, as the birth certificate is the legally recognised statement of identity, then requiring the unmarried father to obtain the consent of the mother before being able to register his name as father adversely affects the child's protected right to identity. Article 9(3) requires "respect [for] the right of the child who is separated from one or both parents to maintain personal relations and direct contact with both parents on a regular basis, except if it is contrary to the child's best interests." While a married father has this obligation imposed upon him by section 1(1)(c) of the 1995 Act, the same is not true of the unmarried father. It could be argued that requiring unmarried fathers to go to court, or have the consent of the mother, before being subject to this obligation is a necessary safeguard, in-built to ensure that the contact is in the best interests of the child, as required by the Article. However, in light of today's social statistics, it could hardly be argued that in all cases of unmarried fathers it is against the child's best interests to maintain personal relation and direct contact with the father. "Recognition of the principle that both parents have common responsibilities for the upbringing and development of the child" is advocated in Article 18(1). Arguably, Scots law breaches this article. Lowe however notes that it has been queried whether "common responsibilities" means common and equal or common but different.[15] As the idea behind this is to provide children with two parents to look to for protection and guidance, Norrie rightly states that "there is no justification in treating the children of unmarried parents differently from the children of married parents...the child of an unmarried father can only look to her or his mother".[16] It could be argued that imposing a financial obligation on unmarried fathers fills this purpose. However, it is doubtful that a financial obligation can constitute "upbringing and development".

---

[12] Lowe, "The Meaning and Allocation of Parental Responsibility: A Common Lawyer's Perspective", (1997) 11 International Journal of Law, Policy and the Family 192, at 202.

[13] Sutherland, "The Unequal Struggle—Fathers and Children in Scots Law: *Brixey v. Lynas* and *Sanderson v. McManus*", (1997) 9 C.F.L.Q. 191.

[14] Masson and Harrison, "Identity—Mapping the Frontiers", in Lowe and Douglas (eds), *Families Across Frontiers,* (Martinus Nijhoff Publishers, 1996), p. 283.

[15] Lowe, *supra*, p. 201.

[16] K. Norrie, *Children (Scotland) Act 1995* (W. Green, Edinburgh, 1998) s. 15 at p. 14.

Whether Scotland breaches the European Convention on Human **5.3**
Rights is more contentious.[17] It narrowly complies with Article 6(1)
by allowing an unmarried father living with the mother of his child
the right to attend a children's hearing system.[18] However, placing
an onus on the unmarried father to obtain the same "rights" as his
married counterpart could be contrary to Articles 8 and 14. Article
14 provides that "the enjoyment of the rights and freedoms set forth
in this Convention shall be secured without discrimination on any
ground such as sex...birth or other status". One of these "rights and
freedoms" is enshrined in Article 8(1), providing "respect for family
life". However, States are allowed a margin of appreciation in this
context. Whilst no case has actually required that unmarried fathers
be accorded the same rights as married fathers, for a number of
reasons, movement is edging in that direction. First, whilst "family
life" was originally perceived by the Convention as the nuclear family,[19] only recently the Court reaffirmed that "the notion of family
life in Article 8 is not confined solely to families based on marriage
and may encompass other de facto relationships". [20] As can be seen
from the cases, the unmarried family is gradually being accorded
more recognition. In *Marckx v. Belgium*,[21] it was decided that
"family life" could also include a mother and child born out of
wedlock where they lived together. In *Johnston v. Ireland*,[22] the recognition has expanded to cover an unmarried father and his child
through his cohabitation with the mother. *Kroon v. The Netherlands*[23] concerned an unmarried father who had never cohabited
with the mother or child. However, this was a stable relationship.
Keegan v. Ireland[24] found that not only established relationships
should come within the scope of Article 8, but also potential relationships which may develop, so long as the father has shown
some prior commitment to the child. This idea was furthered in the
recent case of *Söderback v. Sweden*.[25] There the Commission indicated that an unmarried father's right to "family life" now starts
from the moment the child is born, even if there is limited contact.

A second reason for feeling that we may soon see a case requiring **5.5**
unmarried fathers be afforded the same rights as married fathers is

---

[17] See Norrie, "Parental Responsibilities and Parental Rights Agreements", 1996
SCOLAG 94 at 95 and Meulders-Klein, "Cohabitation and Children in Europe",
29 American Journal of Comparative Law 359. For a rejoinder see, Deech, "The
Unmarried Father and Human Rights" (1992) 4 J.C.L. 3.
[18] Children's Hearings (Scotland) Rules 1996 (S.I. 1996 No. 3261).
[19] O'Donnell, "Parent–Child Relationships within the European Convention", in
Lowe and Douglas (eds), *Families Across Frontiers* (Martinus Nijhoff, The
Hague, 1996), p. 138.
[20] *X., Y. & Z. v. United Kingdom* [1997] 2 F.L.R. 892, 900 A.
[21] 1979 E.C.H.R. Series A No. 31.
[22] (1985) 9 E.H.R.R. 203.
[23] (1994) 19 E.H.R.R. 263.
[24] (1995) 20 E.H.R.R. 342.
[25] (1998) 23 E.H.R.R. 342.

the fact that the Convention is a "live instrument".[26] As such it has
to be interpreted in light of present day conditions. This has led one
commentator to suggest that, "the Court and Commission are not
justified in adopting a restrictive interpretation of the concept of
family life". [27] If the Court is recognising that unmarried families
have a "right to respect for family life" they should recognise that
discrimination against unmarried fathers, whilst it may have a legitimate aim, constitutes interference which is not proportionate to
that aim. The case of *McMichael v. United Kingdom*[28] accepted that
the different treatment afforded to married and unmarried fathers
was to pursue the legitimate aim of identifying meritorious fathers.
However whether this was correctly decided or not has been
questioned. As stated in *Inze v. Austria*,[29] there is a breach of the
Convention if the aim of the legislation could be achieved in another way.[30] It is wrong to say that unmarried fathers are necessarily unmeritorious. The fact that the majority of births outside
wedlock are jointly registered shows that most unmarried fathers
are demonstrating some commitment to their child. Surely the aim
of the legislation could be better achieved by all unmarried fathers
gaining automatic rights and responsibilities and these being revoked by a court if necessary. Branchflower[31] follows this argument, pointing out that it is surely the exclusion not identification of
unmeritorious fathers which advances the interests of the child.
Norrie maintains[32] that the decision may have been different had
the case been argued on the basis that there is different treatment
afforded to unmarried women than unmarried men. Following
Schmidt v. Germany,[33] "very weighty reasons" would have to be
advanced before the Court would accept that a difference of
treatment based on sex was compatible with the European Convention *Inze v. Austria* stated that "very weighty reasons had to be
advanced before differences of treatment on account of birth out of
wedlock could be justified under the Convention".[34] In *Keegan*, the
Commission stated that "[the] mutual enjoyment by parent and
child of each others company constitutes a fundamental element of
family life". It could be argued that, as United Kingdom law affords the unmarried father a method of obtaining rights and responsibilities, then this is all that is necessary to comply with the
Convention. However, as Bainham[35] explains, this may be so if

[26] See *Inze v. Austria* (1987) 10 E.H.R.R. 393.
[27] O'Donnell, *supra*, at p. 150.
[28] February 24, 1995 (European Court of Human Rights).
[29] (1987) 10 E.H.R.R. 394.
[30] (1987) 10 E.H.R.R. 394 at 407.
[31] "Parental Responsibility and Human Rights" [1999] Fam. Law 34 at 36.
[32] K. Norrie, *Children* (Scotland) Act 1995, *sup. cit.*, s. 13 at p. 14.
[33] (1994) 18 E.H.R.R. 513.
[34] (1987) 10 E.H.R.R. 393 at 406.
[35] Bainham, "When is a Parent Not A Parent?" 3 (1989) International Journal of Law and the Family 208 at 208.

Article 8 imposed a negative obligation. However, from the cases it appears that something of positive obligation is required by the state to allow the integration of the unmarried family into normal life. It would appear that O'Donnell agrees stating, "[the approach of the Court and Commission to offer restrictive interpretations is] difficult to justify, given that the Convention imposes positive obligations upon states to respect family life". [36]

It is therefore not surprising that the Lord Chancellor and more recently the Scottish Office issued consultation papers which accepted that the law required revision.[37] The Lord Chancellor's Department concluded that rights and responsibilities should be conferred where the birth certificate is jointly signed and this is the position taken by the Scottish Executive in its recommendations.[38] **5.6**

In the case of step-parents, the Scottish Executive propose the possibility of both parents making an agreement with the step-parent, similar to the section 4 agreement, giving the step-parent parental responsibilities and rights. This would have the effect of providing a child with an additional parent figure without cutting an existing parent figure of the child's life, as presently happens in step-parent adoption, and would be less expensive than applying for a section 11 order. The White Paper considered the possibility of allowing similar agreements to unmarried "step-parents" but rejected it. Given that the break-up rate of second marriages is high, the White Paper recognised that a child needed to know where he or she stood on a breakdown of a second marriage, and possibly the child at 12 should have an equal right to that of the parent and step-parent about whether there should be any termination of a step-parent PRR agreement.[39] This would be consistent with the Scottish law of adoption under which a Scottish child has had the right to consent to their own adoption if he or she is over the age of 12 save where they are incapable of giving a consent to their adoption in which case the court may dispense with the need for the child's agreement.[40] A possible alternative to this was to restrict termination of the agreement to the courts. The idea of termination by one of the parties giving an appropriate period of notice was rejected. The White Paper seems to conclude that court hearings provide the best forum for resolving contested cases, and could easily cope with uncontested cases, but views were sought on this issue. **5.7**

---

[36] O'Donnell, *op. cit.*, p. 135.

[37] "Procedures for the Determination of Paternity and the Law on Paternal Responsibilty for Unmarried Fathers", Lord Chancellors Department, March 6, 1998, Chap. 5 and *"Parents and Children: A White Paper, Improving Scottish Family Law"*, (Scottish Executive, 2000), para. 2.13.

[38] See further, para. 6.8.

[39] See para. 6.16 *et seq* on the difficulties inherent in children participating in the original decision.

[40] Adoption (Scotland) Act 1978, s. 10(8).

Artificial Reproductive Technology

5.8 It has been assumed to this point that the child has been born to parents without recourse to artificial reproductive technology. Where a child is born to a "gestational mother" as the result of the donation of an ovum by another woman, the law provides that it is the gestational mother who is the legal mother notwithstanding that the genetic mother is another woman.[41] Where a man consents to the insemination of his wife or partner with semen provided by another man, then the genetic father is not the legal father of the child. The social father who consented to the insemination of the mother becomes the legal father.[42]

5.9   Thus far, we have been focusing on children's *legal* identity, *i.e.* their identity in terms of the status in law of themselves and those around them. In the context of both adopted children and children born as a result of assisted reproduction, it is important to consider also what information children have the right to know about their biological origin even where they have had no contact with a genetic parent. The need to know who one's biological parents are, is not mere curiosity, but rather a part of our identity and who we are as persons. In the field of adoption, the former practice of bringing a child up in ignorance of his or her being adopted has been replaced by the practice of telling children that they were specially selected by their new parents when their birth parents were unable to care for them. Increasingly, non-identifying information is given to adopted children and, where older children who have recollections of their birth parents are concerned, the practice of open adoption sometimes coupled with contact orders made under section 12(6) of the Adoption (Scotland) Act 1978 is growing.[43] The significance of a child knowing who its birth parents were was underlined by the work of McWhinnie[44] and Triseliotis[45] who revealed that, in Scotland, where adopted people had had access to the information on their birth records for many years,[46] in contrast to England where a right of access only dates back to the Children Act 1975, most adopted persons used great care and sensitivity in trying to

---

[41] Human Fertilisation and Embryology Act 1990, s. 27(1).
[42] *ibid.* s. 28
[43] *Editorial*, 43 Fam.L.B. 1.
[44] *Adopted Children: How They Grow Up* (Routledge, 1967).
[45] *In Search of Origins* (Routledge, 1973).
[46] The Adoption (Scotland) Act 1978, s. 45, allows access by the adopted person at age 16. In the case of children conceived by assisted reproduction, the Human Fertilisation and Embryology Act 1990, s. 32, requires the authority to keep information about donors and persons to whom treatment services were provided. It also regulates the circumstances under which the information may be disclosed. A person over 18 may be provided with information provided that it is authorised by regulations under s. 45(4), although no such regulations seem to have been made.

trace their birth parents. Often the search by a female adoptee was undertaken when she was pregnant and was thinking of the characteristics her child might have. Certainly, considerable problems can result when the first revelation to a child of being adopted was done in an "unhelpful way", for example, where the telling was a taunt by another child in the school playground.[47]

The problem of revelation of who is one's genetic parent is **5.10** particularly acute in cases of artificial reproductive technology, where the name of the sperm donor or ovum donor has traditionally been kept confidential in the United Kingdom, unlike the position in Scandinavia[48] and increasingly in the United States. Golombok[49] has claimed that, on the evidence currently available, keeping this information secret from the children conceived by assisted reproduction presents no particular problem. However, since the first such children have only just begun to reach adolescence in significant numbers, it may be too early to be clear about this.[50] Although Mason and McCall Smith[51] argue that "telling" is different for children conceived by assisted reproduction, as opposed to adopted children, since they may never need to question their parentage, an opposite view can be advanced. Increasingly, genetic screening for inherited diseases may open up the question of parentage[52] and the possibility of an "unhelpful" revelation of parentage is just as possible in cases of assisted reproduction as adoption. One could imagine the destructive possibilities to a child who only learns of the existence of a genetic parent in adulthood, and that the person they have treated as a parent is only a social parent. Their whole life would have been a lie.[53] More recently,

---

[47] Triseliotis, *supra*, p. 26 *et seq.* Perhaps even worse would be the angry words spoken to a naughty child by its from an adopted parent "you would never have done that if you had been my child".

[48] In 1985, Sweden enacted a law giving children born by donor insemination the right to receive identifying information about the donor when the child was sufficiently mature.

[49] Golombok, Cook, Bish and Murray, "Families created by the new reproductive technologies" (1995) 64 Child Development 285–288; Golombok, Brewaeys, Cook, Giavazzi, Mantovani, van Hall, Crosignani and Dexues, "The European Study of Assisted Reproduction Families" (1996) 11 Human Reproduction 101–108; Golombok, Murray, Brinsdren and Abdalla, "Social versus Biological Parenting" (1999) J. Child Psychol. Psychiat. 519–527.

[50] A number of children conceived by donor insemination are now approaching 30 years old and may well have sensed that there was something behind their families' refusal to talk openly about the inherited aspects of their families. See A. McWhinnie, "Families from Assisted Conception" (2000) 3 Human Fertility 13–19.

[51] Law and Medical Ethics (5th ed., 1999), p. 66.

[52] McWhinnie, "Should offspring from donated gametes continue to be denied knowledge of their origins and antecedents?", Human Reproduction, May 2001 (in press); Roberts, "A Right to Know for Children by Donation", 2000 C.F.L.Q. 371.

[53] McWhinnie is about to release a series of videotapes entitled "Families from Assisted Conception: how have they fared? Six families tell their stories".

work by Turner and Coyle[54] suggests that donor offspring had experienced mistrust with their family, negative distinctiveness, lack of genetic continuity and feelings of frustration in their quest for their biological fathers as well as a need to talk to another person who could understand their feelings. In Sweden, an adult conceived by donor insemination has the right to receive information about the sperm donor. However, the right to receive the information presupposes that the person concerned knows that he or she was conceived by donor insemination. Recent research[55] shows that 89 per cent of parents had not informed their child, though 59 per cent of them had told someone else. Since the right to receive the identity of the genetic father presupposes that children conceived in this way needs to know of the means of their conception, this seems to suggest a significant gap in the Swedish law.

5.11   It is questionable whether this current approach by the law to such matters conforms to the child's right to an identity under the UN Convention. Although the right to identify is less well established under the European Convention, it was recently announced in *The Scotsman*[56] that Liberty, the civil rights group, were backing a test case brought by two siblings born as a result of donor insemination to use Article 8 of the European Convention on Human Rights to discover details of their biological fathers.

5.12   It is true, of course, that the genetic father of many children may, to his and the child's ignorance, be different from the husband of the child mother, even where he has assumed (in ignorance) the role of father. New techniques for genetic testing of illness have only recently become available. The statistics on this have been estimated at around 10 per cent[57] but, where there are reasons for suspicion about paternity,[58] the figure may rise to as much as 30 per cent.[59] Since DNA tests require the co-operation of the parent with whom the child resides (or that of the child if mature enough) the question has arisen whether the courts powers[60] to order blood tests and draw adverse inferences in cases of non-co-operation with the court order should be exercised. In *Smith v. Greenhill*[61] the court was concerned that it might be contrary to a child's best interest and to her mother's marriage to learn that conception had occurred at a

---

[54] "What does it mean to be a donor offspring?" (2000) 15 Human Reproduction 2041–51.

[55] C, Gottlieb O. Lalos and F. Lindblad, "Disclosure of donor insemination to the child, etc" (2000) 15 Human Reproduction 52–56.

[56] September 12, 2000.

[57] McIntyre and Sooman, "Non-paternity and prenatal genetic screening" (1991) *The Lancet* 869.

[58] For example, where a man has a belief that he is not the father of the child and is prepared to pay a fee in the order of £450 for DNA fingerprinting in the hope of defeating a child support claim.

[59] *The Sunday Times*, June 11, 2000.

[60] Law Reform (Miscellaneous Provisions) (Scotland) Act 1970, s. 70(1)(a).

[61] 1993 S.C.L.R. 944.

time when the mother was estranged from her husband and having sexual intercourse with both him and another man who might be the genetic father. When the affair ended, she was reconciled with her husband who acted as if the child was his. When the other man sought blood tests to show that the child was his, the request for blood tests to establish the child's paternity was refused.

Adoption

It is a fundamental feature of Scots adoption law that, for the most **5.13** part, adoption operates as a guillotine to sever the legal links between a child and the child's birth parents and extended family and to replace these with new legal links to the adoptive parents.[62] For this reason, the birth parents of a child born within marriage must normally agree to the adoption of their child or the need for their agreement must be dispensed with by a court order. However, as we have seen, ties do not exist between a father and his non-marital child unless he has taken the additional step of executing an agreement with the child's mother or obtaining an order from the court.

In the context of post-adoption contact, it should be noted that **5.14** the 1995 Act does not permit applications from certain categories of persons, including any parent who has had his or her parental responsibilities or rights terminated or transferred in the adoption setting.[63] This attitude may be inconsistent with moves towards open adoption, though it is crucial to stress the maintenance of these ties should be restricted to cases where there is evidence of long-term benefit to the child.[64] In these circumstances, the birth parents or siblings of a child may well wish to have contact with him or her subsequent to the time of adoption. The matching of adoptive parents with older children is complex and such arrangements run a higher risk of breakdown if the children have suffered emotional trauma prior to the adoption or if their age reduces their

---

[62] By way of exception to this general rule, the Children (Scotland) Act 1995, s. 97, amends the Adoption (Scotland) Act 1978 and introduces a new procedure for step-parent adoptions in which the natural parent of a child being adopted by his or her new spouse (the child's step-parent) will not be required to join in the adoption but will retain his or her rights over the child arising from being the birth parent.

[63] 1995 Act, s. 11(3) and (4), reinforcing the decision of the House of Lords in *D v. Grampian Regional Council*, 1995 S.C.L.R. 516. See also para. 6.13.

[64] See, "Adoption—the Future," Cm. 2288 (1993), paras 4.14 *et seq*. The risk is that in insisting that adoptive parents have to agree to "open adoption" will pressurise them into accepting an arrangement about which they have covert misgivings. The search for adoptive parents might even delay finding suitable couples, thus replicating the problem of Rowe and Lambert's, "Children Who Wait", ABAFA (1975).

ability to integrate into the new family. It is unclear how courts will view applications for post-adoption contact by members of the extended birth family who have been significant positive figures in the child's life.[65] It is understandable that social workers should be concerned about disruptions in planning the future of children if birth parents or their extended family, who have had their ties to the child broken by "freeing for adoption" or the acquisition of parental rights by others, can seek to resurrect those ties. Nevertheless it might well have been preferable to have allowed parents to make an application for contact with their child, subject to having to show cause in the sheriff court that this would be in the child's best interest, rather than to leave such applications (with a slim chance of success) to the *nobile officium*. This would recognise that the risk of breakdown of adoptions of older children,[66] or those who are both older and from a minority background, or those who may have been subjected to physical or emotional trauma or neglect, is higher than with adoptions involving younger children who have not been subjected to the tribulations often suffered by older children. Placement of older children who have recollections of their birth family with adoptive families who are best able to meet their needs requires particular skills as well as the provision of post-adoption support. This is not widely available at present. Although adoption societies are to be encouraged to develop post-adoption services under the Act, the availability of resources for such services is unclear. For those children placed for adoption from minority backgrounds, section 97 requires not only that a court is satisfied that adoption will promote the child's welfare throughout his or her life, but also that regard has been taken of the child's religious persuasion, racial origin and cultural and linguistic background. In practice, the consideration of these matters is more likely to have significance at the time of placement for adoption and fostering of the child and to be governed by section 17 of the Act. There is no doubt that finding racially or culturally appropriate adopters or fosterers is now a matter of significance, provided the child is not

---

[65] The extended birth family might include grandparents, siblings, aunts and uncles. There have been allegations that, in the context of "open adoption", contact orders under s. 12(b) of the Adoption (Scotland) Act 1978, s. 12(b), are becoming more common in Edinburgh; *Editorial* 43 Fam. L.B. 1.

[66] *The Times*, August 10, 2000, based on the Prime Minister's Review of Adoption, Cabinet Office Performance & Innovation Unit, 2000 (for more detail see C. Barton, "The Prime Minister's Review" (2000) 30 Fam. Law 731), reported growing numbers of children being sent back by adopters to foster parents or children's homes because they cannot cope. The rate of failure for children aged 11 and 12 was alleged to be as high as 50 per cent although an overall failure rate of 15–20 per cent has been suggested, reflecting the fact that adoption was being contemplated for children was 20 years ago would have been considered unacceptable. See further, Barton, "The Prime Minister's Review" (2000) 30 Fam. Law 731.

left in limbo for excessive amounts of time whilst these matters are attended to.[67]

The problems of finding homes and parents for children suffering **5.15** from severe physical or mental disabilities is epitomised by *Re AMT*[68] in which the only adopter who could be found for a profoundly disabled child was a male nurse living in a stable homosexual union. Unfortunately, his partner could not become a joint adopter of the child since section 14 of the Adoption (Scotland) Act 1978 restricts joint adoption to married couples. It is doubtful whether the child was capable of comprehending that his adopter's partner could, at best, rely on parental rights granted under section 11 of the 1995 Act. The partner might feel conscious of his lesser position especially if the child's father by adoption was to die. This perception might have subtle effects on the child and the parents concerned.

The requirement under section 6 of the 1978 Act[69] for courts at **5.16** the time of adoption to consider the need to "safeguard and protect the welfare of the child...throughout his life as the paramount consideration" is equally consistent with the need for courts to take a long-term view and not prematurely to sever racial, ethnic, linguistic or religious ties which are a significant part of the child's sense of identity. The need for courts and adoption agencies to consider these factors before making any decisions relating to adoption is specifically mentioned in section 95. Careful balancing will be necessary to prevent children without families waiting so long in the hope of preserving their racial and other links that they become unadoptable in the process.

Name

In western developed countries the name by which a child is known **5.17** has an important symbolism in establishing the link between father and child. However, the norm of giving the child the father's last name is purely a matter of custom and tradition,[70] though this may not be understood by the general public. Where a couple are married, this tends not to be a problem, with the father's surname being chosen and presumably all siblings using the same name. Even where children are born to unmarried parents, the majority of these are to cohabitants where both parents have registered the name of the child in the father's name. Problems tend to arise where the mother with custody or residence rights in respect of a child after divorce wishes to change the name of her child to that of her

---

[67] See Prime Minister's Review on Adoption.
[68] 1997 S.L.T. 94.
[69] The 1995 Act introduced a new s. 6(1)(a) of the Adoption (Scotland) Act 1978.
[70] See Thomson, *Family Law in Scotland* (3rd ed., 1996), p. 193.

new partner.[71] As Sutherland points out, this decision is one of, "more...than mere preference".[72] Thomson agrees stating that, as the name symbolises this important link with the child's identity, it should not be prematurely abandoned unless the use of the father's name gives rise to distress for the children.[73] This view received judicial acknowledgement in the dissenting opinion of Lord Jauncey in the House of Lords recently[74]: "the surname is ...a biological label which tells the world at large that the blood of the name flows in its veins. To suggest that a surname is unimportant because it may be changed at any time by deed poll when the child has obtained more mature years ignores the importance of initially applying an appropriate label for that child".[75] While agreeing with this, Sutherland[76] acknowledges that it may help a child to integrate into a new family if they all have the same surname. Presumably, this would be of more relevance in the case of younger children.

5.18   At one time, the case law tended to favour the right of the custodial parent to change the name of any child resident with her (as it usually was). Thereafter, the courts were reluctant to force the mother to change the child's surname back to its original one since this might be contrary to the best interests of the child.[77] More recently, the English Courts have taken a more interventionist role to preserve the link with the father epitomised by a child carrying the father's name. *Re T*[78] is, of course, an English decision, which

---

[71] See Bissett-Johnson, "Children in Subsequent Marriages—Questions of Access, Name and Adoption" in Eekelaar and Katz (eds), *Marriage and Cohabitation in Contemporary Societies* (Butterworths, 1980).

[72] Sutherland, *Child and Family Law* (T&T Clark, 1999), p. 53.

[73] Thomson, *supra*, p. 193.

[74] *Dawson v. Wearmouth* [1999] 2 All E.R. 353 (H.L.). The case concerned the child of cohabitants in which the father did not have parental rights.

[75] *supra*, at 361C.

[76] *supra*, at p. 53.

[77] See for example the coverage of this issue in the first edition of Thomson, *Family Law in Scotland*, Butterworths (1987).

[78] [1998] Fam. Law 531. A mother had five children; two were known by the surname of her former husband, the third was known by that name, though the former husband was not the father, and the fourth and fifth children, twins, were known by the name of their father, T, a man with whom the woman had cohabited before the relationship ended as a result of violence but with the father being granted parental responsibility in the form of contact. The mother then changed the name of the twins by deed poll to that of her former husband so that all the children bore the same surname. T then sought to contest this by means of a specific issue order. The trial judge held that since the mother had residence of the children she was entitled to change their name but was reversed by the Court of Appeal. The Court of Appeal held that as both parents had parental responsibility the mother could not change the child's family name without either the consent of the father or of the court. The mother was told to change the children's name back notwithstanding that they had, in the interim, become known by their new name. This contrasts with the earlier decision in *Re PC* [1997] 2 F.L.R.730 in which the decision to leave the child with his new name seemed to reflect the wishes of the child. See further, Ogle, "What's in a Name" [1998] Fam. Law 80.

might not be followed in Scotland. It does, however, emphasise the difference in those cases where the father has, or has not, been granted parental responsibilities and rights and the importance of the views of a child who is old enough to express them. Nor have the English Courts been overly impressed by arguments that it would be embarrassing for a mother to have a different name from her child. This could be either as a result of her marriage after divorce or, as in *Re C. (Change of Surname),*[79] where a mother sought to confer her own name on her child after the breakdown of cohabitation, at which time the father acquired parental responsibility for the child by agreement.

According to the 1995 Act, the most important consideration is **5.19** what is in the best interests of the child. These may not necessarily be the same as the wishes of the custodial parent. The 1995 Act has implemented the desire of the UN Convention that the wishes of the child be taken into account. However, on a practical note, it is probably still important to distinguish the child's real wishes from mere mirroring of the wishes of the parent with a right to have the child live with him or her.[80]

Conclusion

In summary, despite there being many good things in the Children **5.20** (Scotland) Act 1995, there will be a need to monitor its application in practice to see whether the detail in the, as yet unpublished, regulations meets the high aspirations of the international conventions. Sometimes, meeting conventional obligations requires the expenditure of funds. Whether the funds will be made available in times of economic restraint must be open to question.

---

[79] [1998] 2 F.L.R. 656.
[80] *W. v. A (Child: Surname)* [1981] Fam. 14, and *Cosh v. Cosh*, 1979 S.L.T. (Notes) 72.

CHAPTER 6

CARE OF THE CHILD WITHIN THE FAMILY

ELAINE E. SUTHERLAND

In Scotland and, indeed, many other jurisdictions there is no single **6.1**
"family setting" in which children find themselves. While 41 per
cent of children born in 1999 were to unmarried parents,[1] 83 per
cent of the births were registered jointly by the child's parents, with
73 per cent of these parents living at the same address.[2] This suggests that the traditional notion of unmarried parenthood meaning
lone parenthood is far from accurate. Of course, the fact that a
child is born to married parents is no guarantee that he or she will
grow up living with both parents since many children experience
parental divorce.[3] Given that over a quarter of divorcees remarry,[4]
while others go on to cohabit with a new partner, it can be assumed
that some of their children will find their way into either *de jure* or
de facto step-families. This is borne out by the fact that over half of
all adoptions are step-parent adoptions.[5] In addition, many children live in extended families or apart from family members. The
permutations seem endless. Nonetheless, it is for all of these permutations that Scots law must cater, not least because all of these
children have rights under both the United Nations Convention on
the Rights of the Child (the UN Convention) and the European
Conventions on Human Rights and Fundamental Freedoms (the
European Convention).

The UN Convention starts from the position that the family **6.2**
setting is generally the best place for the child[6] and, while it does not
attempt to define a "family", notes the place of "parents or, where

---

[1] Registrar General for Scotland, *Annual Report 1999* (General Register Office for
Scotland, 2000), Table 3.1.
[2] *Annual Report 1999, supra*, Table 3.3.
[3] The Registrar General for Scotland, *Annual Report 1996*, was the last to record
the number of children under 16 involved in divorce and the *Civil Judicial
Statistics* do not provide this information. It would be helpful if one of these
publications did so. In 1996 alone, 6,658 children under 16 were affected by
divorce, being present in 34 per cent of divorces.
[4] *Annual Report 1999*, Table 7.4.
[5] *Annual Report 1999*, Table 9.2.
[6] Art. 9.

applicable, the members of the extended family or community as provided for by local custom".[7] It acknowledges that families are not always intact, nuclear families when it stresses the need for the child's right to "maintain relations and direct contact" with a parent when the child is separated from that parent, unless such contact is contrary to the child's best interests.[8] Reinforcing the notion of parental equality and the need for continued parental involvement even after parental separation, it places the onus on the state to use "best efforts to ensure recognition of the principle that both parents have common responsibilities for the upbringing and development of the child".[9] All of this must of course be read in the light of Article 3 (giving paramountcy to the child's best interests), Article 5 (acknowledging the child's own evolving capacity), and Article 12, giving the child a right to participate in the decision-making process.

In providing that "everyone has a right to respect for his private and family life",[10] the European Convention, again, gives no definition of the family. However, the European Commission and the European Court have had the opportunity to develop a very considerable jurisprudence on what these elements mean. Certainly, what amounts to "private life" has been interpreted broadly.[11] In terms of "family life" the Court's thinking has evolved and just how far the thinking has developed is a theme to which we will return throughout this chapter. Suffice it to say, at this stage, that the Court looks to the reality of relationships rather than any necessary formal basis for them. Respect for the right to family life places positive and negative obligations on the state; that is to say, the state must not only actively recognise the right, it must also desist from taking action to obstruct the right. States are permitted a degree of latitude, known as the "margin of appreciation", in implementing their obligations. In addition, state interference with these rights may be permitted in certain limited circumstances,[12] but only to such an extent "as is in accordance with the law and as is

---

[7] Art. 5.
[8] Art. 9(3).
[9] Art. 18(1). This carries with it the reminder that "The best interests of the child will be [the parents'] basic concern."
[10] Art. 8(1). The article also gives the individual a right to respect for "his home and his correspondence". Given the Convention is of some antiquity, the drafters might (just about) be forgiven for its lack of gender neutrality.
[11] Thus, it can include such matters as an individual's sense of personal identity (*Gaskin v. United Kingdom* (1989) 12 E.H.R.R. 6), moral or physical integrity (*X and Y. v. The Netherlands* (1985) 8 E.H.R.R. 235), and sexual activities (*Dudgeon v. United Kingdom* (1981)) 4 E.H.R.R. 149.
[12] The circumstances are: the interests of national security; public safety or the economic well-being of the country; the prevention of disorder or crime; the protection of health or morals; or the protection of the rights and freedoms of others; Art. 8(2).

necessary in a democratic society".[13] Thus, the onus falls on the state to demonstrate that the circumstances warranted interference with the individual's right and that the degree of interference was proportionate to the end being achieved. Two further provisions of the European Convention are of particular importance in the context of the family: Articles 6(1) and 12. Essentially, Article 6(1) requires that the individual be afforded a fair and public hearing within a reasonable time before an independent and impartial tribunal, in the determination of civil rights and obligations.[14] Article 12 provides that "Men and women of marriageable age have the right to marry and to found a family, according to the national laws governing the exercise of this right".[15]

Part I of the Children (Scotland) Act 1995 (the 1995 Act), largely **6.3** a product of the recommendations of the Scottish Law Commission,[16] regulates the care of the child in the family setting, although some issues are still dealt with in other statutes.[17] In this chapter, we will examine the extent to which Scots law complies with the various international obligations.

What are parental responsibilities and parental rights?

For the first time in Scotland, the 1995 Act defines what is meant by **6.4** parental responsibilities and parental rights.[18] Central to the Act is the emphasis on parental responsibilities, with parental rights existing only in order to enable parents and others to fulfill these responsibilities.[19] "Parental responsibilities" are defined as the responsibility: to safeguard and promote the child's health, development and welfare; to provide direction and guidance to the child in a manner appropriate to the child's stage of development; where the child is not living with the parent, to maintain personal relations

---

[13] Art. 8(2).
[14] Article 6 is discussed more fully in paras 15.15–15.37.
[15] See para. 6.XXX, *infra*, for further discussion of this provision.
[16] *Report on Family Law* (Scot. Law Com. No. 135, 1992).
[17] For example, financial support for children is governed by the Family Law (Scotland) Act 1985, the Child Support Acts 1991 and 1995, and the Child Support, Pensions and Social Security Act 2000, while the provision of some forms of substitute care is governed by the Children Act 1989.
[18] While the Act talks of *parental* responsibilities and *parental* rights, these are simply convenient short-hand terms and, as we shall see, each may be owed or held by persons other than parents; *F. v. F.*, 1991 S.L.T. 357, *per* Lord Hope at p. 361, dealing with the earlier relevant legislation.
[19] 1995 Act, s. 2(1).

and direct contact with the child on a regular basis; and to act as the child's legal representative.[20] The child-centred approach here reflects Article 3 of the UN Convention, while the responsibility to maintain personal relations and direct contact mirrors Article 9(3).

6.5   These parental responsibilities exist subject to two important qualification. They apply only so far as is practicable and in the interests of the child, again reflecting the welfare principle. Parental responsibilities terminate when the child reaches the age of 16, except the responsibility to provide guidance, which lasts until the child reaches 18.[21] On one hand, the 1995 Act can be seen as failing to live up the letter of Article 1 of the UN Convention which defines a child as a person "below the age of eighteen years". On the other hand, when the Scottish Law Commission grappled with the issue,[22] it justified its stance on the argument that it recognises reality and the child's evolving capacity under Article 5. The child, or anyone acting on the child's behalf, has title to sue or defend in proceedings in respect of parental responsibilities[23] thus giving teeth to the provision. Enforcing parental responsibilities against an unwilling parent must, of course, be considered in the light of the qualification on parental rights in terms of both practicability and the child's interests. Thus, for example, it may often be the case that forcing an unwilling parent to have contact with the child would not serve the child's interests at all.

6.6   "Parental rights" mirror parental responsibilities and are defined as the right: to have the child living with him or her or otherwise to regulate the child's residence; to control, direct or guide the child's upbringing in a manner consistent with the child's stage of development; if the child is not living with the parent, to maintain personal relations and direct contact with the child on a regular basis; and to act as the child's legal representative.[24] All parental rights give the child or a person acting on his or her behalf title to sue[25] and terminate when the child reaches the age of 16.[26] Again, the argument can be made that, in bringing parental rights to an end at 16, the Act fails to meet the requirement of Article 1 of the UN Convention. However, the recognition of the child's evolving capacity becomes all the more significant in the context of rights a person may have in respect of the child.

---

[20] 1995 Act, s. 1(1).
[21] 1995 Act, s. 1(2).
[22] *Report on Family Law, supra,* paras 2.7–2.13.
[23] 1995 Act, s. 1(3).
[24] 1995 Act, s. 2(1).
[25] 1995 Act, s. 2(4).
[26] 1995 Act, s. 2(7).

Who holds them automatically?

Only mothers[27] and "married fathers"[28] acquire responsibilities and **6.7**
rights automatically.[29] Automatic acquisition of parental responsibilities from the moment of the child's birth is not subject to any
test of merit. Of course, it would be possible for the law to require
everyone wishing to become a parent or, at least, wishing to acquire
parental responsibilities and parental rights, to pass some kind of
test. While this might be consistent with Article 3 of the UN
Convention, it is not envisaged by Article 5, which notes the centrality of the family in the child's life, and it would be inconsistent
with the right to found a family, guaranteed by Article 12 of the
European Convention. In any event, the opportunity to exercise
these automatically-endowed parental responsibilities and rights
can be seriously restricted from the outset, where there is cause for
concern over the child's welfare.[30] Even at a later stage in a child's
life, parental responsibilities and rights may be restricted or removed by a court in the context of private law (usually intra-family)
proceedings[31] or at the instance of the authorities charged with
child protection.[32]

At the outset, the invidious position of children of unmarried **6.8**
parents and non-marital fathers should be noted. Unlike mothers
and married fathers, non-marital fathers do not acquire parental
responsibilities and rights automatically.[33] The Scottish Law
Commission recommended an end to this discrimination,[34] but
Westminster chose to reject this rational approach and, instead,

---

[27] "Mother" means the woman who gives birth to the child, regardless of the genetic
origins of the child: Human Fertilisation and Embryology Act 1990, s. 27(1).
Thus a surrogate who carries a foetus produced entirely from donated gametes is
the mother of the child, nonetheless. This does not preclude an individual whose
genetic material was used from seeking parental responsibilities and rights under
section 11 of the 1995 Act. The decision would be taken ultimately on the basis of
the paramountcy of the child's best interests, any views the child wished to express
and the presumption on non-intervention; see paras 6.17–6.28, *infra*. To date, the
European Court has not had the opportunity to consider surrogacy.
[28] Such fathers are defined as being "married to the mother at the time of conception
or subsequently"; 1995 Act, s. 3(1)(b).
[29] 1995 Act, s. 3 (1).
[30] See, *e.g.*, *A. v. Kennedy*, 1993 S.L.T. 1188, where the Second Division upheld the
reporter's right to refer a baby to a children's hearing because she was about to
become part of the same household where an older sibling had died as a result of
being assaulted some eight and a half years previously. A similar view was taken
in *Re D. (A minor) v. Berkshire County Council* [1987] 1 All E.R. 20, where the
mother had continued to use heroin during the ante-natal period.
[31] 1995 Act, s. 11, discussed at paras 6.24–6.28, *infra*.
[32] Child protection and the mechanisms employed to that end are discussed in Chap.
8.
[33] 1995 Act, s. 3(1)(b).
[34] *Report on Family Law, supra*, paras 2.36–2.50.

threw a sop to non-marital fathers in the form of the, little used, parental responsibilities and rights agreements.[35] The position of the non-marital father is discussed fully in Chapter 5, along with the relevant provisions of the European and UN Conventions and the European Court caselaw, and reference should be made to that and other discussions of the issue.[36] Suffice it to say that the current state of Scots law is undoubtedly in breach of Articles 2 and 18 of the UN Convention. Despite the views of the Lord Chancellor's Department to the contrary,[37] it is also arguably in breach of Articles 8 and 14 of the European Convention.[38] The trend of European Convention caselaw is firmly in the direction of greater recognition for the non-marital father and, in the light of the increasing use made of the UN Convention by the European Court, that trend can only continue. Certainly, judicial notice has been taken of our failure to comply with the UN Convention.[39] The position of non-marital fathers was considered again in 1999[40] and it might have been hoped that the Scottish Executive would take the opportunity to reform the law, along the lines recommended in 1992 by the Scottish Law Commission. However, in yet another "compromise solution", the Scottish Executive proposes to extent automatic parental responsibilities to certain non-marital fathers, but only if the father registers the birth jointly with the child's mother.[41] It has consulted further on whether any new legislation should have retrospective effect.[42] As it stands, the Executive's proposal would continue to discriminate against a group of non-marital children and leave the decision to the child's mother, since whether joint registration takes place is wholly at her discretion. In addition, it makes a mockery of the Executive's claim that its proposals would "remove the last vestiges in the law concerning the

---

[35] 1995 Act, s. 4.
[36] See paras 5.2–5.6. The present author has also written at length on the matter; see E. E. Sutherland, *Child and Family Law* (T & T Clark, 1999), paras 5.44–5.5.67; E. E. Sutherland, "The Unequal Struggle: Fathers and Children in Scots Law", 1997 C.F.L.Q. 191; E. E. Sutherland, "Parental Responsibility and Rights Agreements: Better Half a loaf than none at all?",1998 S.L.P.Q. 265.
[37] In the Consultation Paper, *The Law on Parental Responsibility for Unmarried Fathers* (Lord Chancellor's Department, 1998), at para. 62, the view is expressed that "the current law which does not give responsibility automatically to unmarried fathers on the birth of the child complies with articles 8 and 14 of the Convention".
[38] *Marcx v. Belgium* (1979) 2 E.H.R.R. 330; *Johnston v. Ireland* (1986) 9 E.H.R.R. 203; *Kroon v. The Netherlands* (1994) 19 E.H.R.R. 263; *Sonderback v. Sweden* [1999] 1 F.L.R. 250.
[39] In *White v. White,* 1999 S.L.T. (Sh. Ct) 106, at p. 110H (overturned on a different point), Sheriff Principal Nicholson expressed the view that it "appears to be at odds with the United Nations Convention on the Rights of the Child".
[40] *Improving Scottish Family Law* (Scottish Office, 1999), paras 5.1–5.8.
[41] *Parents and Children: A White Paper on Scottish Family Law* (Scottish Executive, 2000), paras 2.12–2.14 and Proposal 1. The Adoption and Children Bill 2001, Cl. 91, contains a similar provision for England and Wales.
[42] *Parents and Children, supra,* para. 2.18 and Question 1.

status of illegitimacy".[43] Thus, Scots law would remain in breach of the UN Convention and, arguably, the European Convention.

One further category of father, the donor father, merits mention. **6.9** Most often, donated sperm is used to inseminate a woman who hopes to become pregnant as a result. However, donated sperm can be used to fertilise an ovum, whether from the woman intending to use it or a donor, the fertilised embryo then being implanted in a woman.[44] Donor fathers are, by definition, non-marital fathers, but they warrant separate consideration since Scots law will often afford them even less recognition than other non-marital fathers. Where a married woman has a child as a result of donor insemination, her husband will be treated in law as the father of the child, unless the husband can show that he did not consent to the treatment.[45] Parallel provisions exist where an unmarried woman is treated along with her male partner in the course of treatment services provided by a person who is licensed to provide such services.[46] Where either of these provisions applies, the donor is simply excluded from the legal picture.[47] Where neither provision applies, then the donor will simply qualify as a non-marital father. Disputes have arisen elsewhere when a donor later wanted to acquire parental responsibilities and rights in respect of the child and found that the child's mother opposed his wishes. Certainly, some donor fathers in the United Staes have been afforded a degree of recognition, where they had formed a personal relationship with the child.[48]

The whole field of assisted reproduction presents new challenges **6.10** to international instruments, just as it has presented challenges to domestic law. Essentially, there are two separate issues to consider; first, to whom should, or must, fertility services be made available and, secondly, what recognition, if any, of "family" is extended where the means of reproduction involve the assistance of technology? The UN Convention is silent on reproductive technology as, not surprisingly, is the European Convention.

---

[43] *Parents and Children, supra*, para. 1.2.

[44] For a discussion of the various techniques that can be used to assist in reproduction, see, J.K. Mason, *Medico-Legal Aspects of Reproduction and Parenthood* (Dartmouth, 1998), Chaps 8 and 9, and Sutherland, *Child and Family Law, supra*, at paras 4.28–4.73.

[45] Human Fertilisation and Embryology Act 1990, s. 28(2).

[46] 1990 Act, s. 28(3).

[47] 1990 Act, s. 29(1) provides that a person treated as a parent is so treated "for all purposes".

[48] See, for example, *Jhordan C. v. Mary K.*, 224 Cal. Rptr. 530 (Ct. App. 1986), where the father provided the mother with sperm for self-insemination and they had an oral agreement that he surrendered all parental rights. Despite this, he had been allowed to form a relationship with the child by regular visits and the court refused to divest him of his parental rights. A similar decision was reached in *Thomas S. v. Robin Y.*, N.Y.S. 2d 357 (App. Div. 1994).

6.11   Since it applies to "every human being below the age of eighteen years",[49] the UN Convention may not apply to the provision of fertility services. However, it does apply once a child is born, regardless of the mode of conception, and decisions about the child's life are no different to decisions about the life of a child born by ordinary means of conception. Thus, Article 3 requires that the best interests test is applied in decisions about the child, including the role of any donor. Once the child is old enough to express a view, Article 12 will apply to his or her right to participate in the decision-making process. In terms of the availability of assisted reproduction, the only legislative provision in the United Kingdom is somewhat couple- and hetero-centric in nature, stating "a woman shall not be provided with treatment services unless account has been taken of the welfare of any child who may be born as a result of the treatment (including the need of that child for a father)"[50]. Article 12 of the European Convention and its protection for the right "to found a family", when read with Article 14, suggests that any discrimination against particular groups in the provision of fertility services might not pass muster. Thus, denying the service to women over a particular age or to same-sex couples or single women would probably be open to challenge[51]. For completeness, the issue of cloning of humans should be addressed. It can be speculated that human cloning might fall foul of Article 2 of the European Convention, if the right to a separate genetic identity is read into the right to life; article 14, if clones are treated less favourably than other persons; or Article 3, if clones are created with a view to their being organ donors.[52]

6.12   The European Convention provides the tools to deal with the issue of recognition of family relationships through the application of Articles 8, 12 and, 14, albeit use of these tools is in its early stages. In *G. v. The Netherlands,*[53] the European Commission took the view that the biological link between the donor and the child was not sufficient to amount to family life and, thus, the protection afforded to it under Article 8, despite the fact that the donor had acted as babysitter for the child. In the light of the US caselaw on that issue, it is likely that further European Convention challenges will be made on this point. It must be remembered that the

---

[49] Art. 1.

[50] 1990 Act, s. 15(3).

[51] While in *X. v. Belgium and Netherlands* (1975) 7 DR 75, the European Commission did not find a breach of Article 12 in respect of denying unmarried people the opportunity to adopt, this should be read in the light of there being no obligation on the state to provide a system of adoption nor to recognise any particular form of adoption; *X. and Y. v. United Kingdom* (1977) 12 DR 32.

[52] H. Swindells, A. Neaves, M. Kushner and R. Skilbeck, *Family Law and the Human Rights Act 1998* (Family Law, 1999), para. 5.49.

[53] (1993) 16 E.H.R.R. CD 38.

European Court recognises *de facto*, and not simply *de jure*, family relationships. Consistent with this approach, in *X., Y. and Z. v. United Kingdom*,[54] the Court was prepared to accept that such a relationship existed between a woman, the child she had as a result of donor insemination and her female-to-male transsexual partner.[55] Thus, they were protected from arbitrary interference with family life and had to be afforded the opportunity for the child to be integrated into the family. However, since the position of the male partner could be recognised through the legal mechanism of parental responsibilities and rights, the Court was not prepared to find a breach of Articles 8 and 14 in the United Kingdom's refusal to allow him to be registered as the child's father. Central to the Court's decision was the lack of consensus amongst Member States of the Council of Europe on this point and the margin of appreciation this gave to individual states. It follows that, were a particular consensus to emerge, then the Court might reach a different conclusion in the future.

Who can make applications to a court in respect of parental responsibilities and parental rights?

Any person who "claims an interest" may apply to the court for an **6.13** order relating to parental responsibilities and rights, unless the person falls within the excluded categories, as can any person who already has parental responsibilities or rights.[56] A person falls within the excluded categories if his or her parental responsibilities or rights have been extinguished by an adoption order[57] or transferred to an adoption agency or a local authority.[58] Certainly, the exclusion in the context of adoption accords with the European Convention on the Adoption of Children,[59] which favours permanency and the "closed" model of adoption. This can be contrasted with "open" adoption, where there may be some contact between the child and the birth parents or, more often, other birth

---

[54] (1997) 24 E.H.R.R. 143.
[55] This is an advance on the decision in *Kerkhoven, Hinke and Hinke v. The Netherlands*, May 15, 1992, unreported, No. 15666/89, where the Commission did not find a family relationship to exist between two women and the child born to one of them as a result of donor insemination.
[56] 1995 Act, s. 11(3)(a).
[57] This includes the expedited adoption proceedings applicable to surrogacy cases under the Human Fertilisation and Embryology Act 1990, s. 30(9).
[58] 1995 Act, s. 11(3) and (4). This gives statutory expression to, and widens the scope of, the decision of the House of Lords in *D. v. Grampian Regional Council*, 1995 S.L.T. 519.
[59] 1967, Cmnd. 3673; ETS No. 58, Art. 10.

relatives.[60] It should be remembered, however, that it is only the parent who is prevented from applying to the court for an order in relation to parental responsibilities or rights. It remains competent for the child or other interested persons to apply. The child's right to apply to the court for an order under section 11 is, of course, entirely consistent with Article 12 of the UN Convention. However, it should not be forgotten that children face very real practical difficulties in using the legal system[61]. For completeness, it should be noted that a local authority cannot make applications under this provision, since it has a wide range of measures open to it under Part II of the 1995 Act.[62]

6.14   While section 11 provides the opportunity for the pursuer to seek regulation of another person's parental responsibilities and rights, it is frequently used by pursuers who are asking to be given responsibilities and rights. The very wide ambit of the section does no more than allow a person to get a case into court, but it does ensure the widest opportunity for issues of concern to be raised. Section 11 provides non-marital fathers with the opportunity to acquire some or all of the parental responsibilities and rights. It has also been used by grandparents,[63] step-parents[64] and others who have had some involvement with a child. Thus, a woman was able to apply for contact with her former partner's child after the couple's same-sex relationship had come to an end.[65]

---

[60] The term "open adoption" should be used with care since it can mean anything from a simple exchange of information between the birth parent(s) and the adopters to what is really "adoption with contact", with there being some contact between the child and the birth parent(s). For a full discussion of open adoption, see, J. Triseliotis, J. Shireman and M. Hundleby, *Adoption: Theory, Policy and Practice* (Cassell, 1997), Chap. 4. It can certainly be argued that "open" adoption may serve the child's best interests. For example, an older child may benefit from continued contact with birth relatives generally and, in some cases, birth parents. See further, paras 5.14 and 9.6

[61] See paras 10.35–10.50 for a full discussion of the position of children as parties in litigation.

[62] 1995 Act, s. 11(7), giving effect to the recommendation of the Scottish Law Commission and overturning the decision in *M. v. Dumfries and Galloway Regional Council*, 1991 S.C.L.R. 481. See futher, paras 8.13–8.17 and 8.31–8.33.

[63] See, for example, *Senna-Cheribbo v. Wood*, 1999 S.C. 328, discussed *infra*. The grandparent's right to apply to the court is separate to the situation where the parent, often a young non-marital father, applies for a residence order and the fact that his mother will be assisting him in caring for the child is central to his case; *Brixey v. Lynas*, 1996 S.L.T. 908.

[64] See, for example, *Robertson v. Robertson*, Outer House, December 7, 1999, unreported, where, in addition to seeking residence of one child and contact with two others, a man sought parental responsibilities and rights in respect of his step-daughter.

[65] The case, *R. v. F.*, which was heard in Dunfermline Sheriff Court is unreported, but an account of it can be found in J. Fotheringham, "Parental Responsibilities and Rights as for Homosexual Couples", 1999 S.L.T. (News) 337.

In the light of this, the recent decision of the United States Su- **6.15**
preme Court in *Troxel v. Granville*,[66] striking down a Washington
state law which allowed grandparents to apply to a court for visitation rights (contact), was thus greeted with some surprise in
Scotland. There, a dispute arose between the mother of two girls
and their paternal grandparents, with whom the children had an
established relationship, over the amount of visitation the grandparents could have with the girls. After six and a half years of
litigation, the Supreme Court found that the Washington statute, as
applied in the particular case, violated the substantive due process
rights of a fit parent to decide whom her children should see and
when. The Court indicated that there is a presumption that a fit
parent will act in the best interests of her children and that, in such
circumstances, the state is not justified in intruding on private
(parental) decision-making within the family. All but one of the
justices, quite astonishingly, failed to discuss the case from a children's rights perspective.[67] The plurality opinion was critical of a
decision being taken solely on the basis of a, judicially determined,
best interests test.[68] For our present purpose, the real interest lies in
the fact that the case turns on the substantive due process—essentially *privacy*—right of the parent. Could a similar challenge to
section 11 of the Children (Scotland) Act 1995 be mounted successfully under Article 8 of the European Convention? It is submitted that it could not. The European Court has expressly
recognised the importance of the relationship between grandchildren and grandparents[69] and, indeed, the child and other relatives.[70] Secondly, the Court has shown a willingness, in

---

[66] *Troxel v. Granville,* 120 S. Ct. 2054 (2000). The Supreme Court's decision is less
helpful than it might have been, not least because it is a 4-1-1-3 plurality decision.
Thus, it is open to a variety of interpretations and, indeed, the literature
surrounding the case grows by the day. In addition, it strikes down the statute "as
applied" and does not address the general question of whether such a statute
would always fail to pass constitutional muster.

[67] Justice Stevens (dissenting), at p. 2072, observed, "The constitutional protection
against arbitrary state interference with parental rights should not be extended to
prevent the States from protecting children against the arbitrary exercise of
parental authority that is not in fact motivated by an interest in the welfare of the
child".

[68] Justice O'Connor observed, "The Washington nonparental visitation statute is
breathtakingly broad ..... [I]n the state of Washington a court can disregard and
overturn any decision by a fit custodial parent concerning visitation whenever a
third party affected by the decision files a visitation petition, based solely on the
judge's determination of the child's best interests". (p. 2061.)

[69] *Marckx v. Belgium* (1979) 2 E.H.R.R. 330, at para. 45, where it said, "'family life'
within the meaning of Article 8 includes at least the ties between near relatives, for
instance, those between grandparents and grandchildren, since such relatives may
play a considerable part in family life". See also, *Price v. United Kingdom* (1988)
55 D.R. 224.

[70] *Boyle v. United Kingdom* (1994) 19 E.H.R.R. 179 (uncle and nephew);
Moustaquim v. Belgium (1990) 13 E.H.R.R. 802 (siblings); *Olsson v. Sweden*
(1988) 11 E.H.R.R. 359 (siblings).

attempting to ascertain internationally-accepted standards, to look at the UN Convention. While the UN Convention acknowledges the importance of parents in a child's life, it makes frequent mention of the role of other family members,[71] subject always to the paramountcy of the child's best interests.

6.16   While a step-parent may play an important practical role in a child's life, he or she has only very limited legal standing in respect of the child.[72] As we have seen, step-parents can use section 11 to acquire parental responsibilities and rights or they can apply to adopt the step-child through the special provision introduced by the 1995 Act specifically for them[73]. The Scottish Executive is now proposing that a new kind of Parental Responsibilities and Rights Agreement, along the lines of that available to unmarried parents,[74] should be introduced to enable step-parents to acquire parental responsibilities and rights without the need to go to court.[75] Since a whole range of questions were left unresolved in the original proposal, it is consulting further on the matter.[76] The Executive seems to think that the child's right to participate in the making of this important decision, as required by Article 12 of the UN Convention, could be dealt with adequately through section 6 of the 1995 Act. As we shall see presently, section 6 is fraught with problems and, most certainly, does not provide the child with adequate protection when a decision of this magnitude is being taken.

The child's views

6.17   Having established who the adult players are, in terms of parental responsibilities and rights, it falls to consider the input of the most important person in the picture: the child concerned. Article 12 of the UN Convention, requiring that the child should be given the opportunity to express his or her views freely on all matters affecting the child and that due weight should be given to these views in accordance with the child's age and maturity, puts the child's role in decision making beyond doubt. It further requires that the child is heard, either directly or through a representative or other appropriate body, in all judicial or administrative proceedings affecting the child. The 1995 Act attempts to comply with this requirement in two distinct ways, one of general application and the other in the context of litigation.

---

[71] See, for example, Art. 5.
[72] For example, a step-parent may qualify as a "relevant person" under Part II of the 1995 Act.
[73] 1995 Act, s. 97 amending the Adoption (Scotland) Act 1978.
[74] 1995 Act, s. 4, discussed at paras 5.2 and 6.8, *supra.*
[75] *Parents and Children: A White Paper on Scottish Family Law* (Scottish Executive, 2000), paras 2.25–2.45 and Proposal 2.
[76] Such questions as whether a parent with sole responsibilities and rights should be able to make this agreement and whether only a court should be able to terminate these agreements were posed, but not answered, in the White Paper.

The general provision, found in section 6 of the 1995 Act, requires **6.18**
any person who is making a major decision in the course of fulfilling
parental responsibilities or exercising parental rights to give the child
the opportunity to express his or her views and to take account of
them in the light of the child's age and maturity. What constitutes a
"major decision" is not defined and there is a dearth of judicial decisions to act as a guide. One might speculate that, for example, the
instruction to a child to tidy his or her room is probably not a major
decision, whereas which school a child should attend is, particularly
where the child is older.[77] The first problem with section 6 is that
most parents and almost all children are probably unaware of its
existence or the obligation it creates. Even if parents are aware of it,
we have no way of knowing how many are complying, although there
is a strong suspicion, at least amongst children's rights activists, that
many parents who did not consult their children in the past have not
mended their ways. Nor is there any real enforcement mechanism,
short of the child taking the decision in question to a court for
resolution. The cosmetic nature of section 6 is confirmed further by
the fact that a third party who deals in good faith with a child's
representative is protected from the transaction being challenged on
the ground that the child's views were not sought.[78]

Section 6 will undoubtedly apply when future arrangements are **6.19**
being made for the care of a child after the parents separate, since it
seems inconceivable that such arrangements could be anything
other than a major decision.[79] Of course, again, there is the problem
of parental ignorance of the provision. However, here there should
be a check. Where a court is called upon to give effect to a parental
agreement on the future arrangements for a child, by means of a
court order, the court ought to ensure that any views the child
wishes to express are before it. It is far from clear from the reported
cases that this is always done.[80]

---

[77] The Act does not make clear whose perception of "major" is to be applied, that of
a hypothetical reasonable child of that age, or that of a hypothetical reasonable
adult.

[78] 1995 Act, s. 6(2).

[79] In *Smith v. Woodhead*, Outer House, January 23, 1996, unreported, a pre-1995
Act case, Lord Osborne observed, in respect of Article 12, "Custody disputes
provide a typical example of decisions that affect a child in a fundamental way".
While he was commenting on the court's obligation to take the child's views into
account, his observation holds true for decisions made by parents themselves.

[80] In *McAdam v. McAdam*, Outer House, November 30, 1999, unreported, the Lord
Ordinary simply granted the pursuer's application and noted that the defender
had not opposed it. No indication is given of what evidence was before the court
regarding the four-year-old's wishes. Similarly, in *Robertson v. Robertson*, Outer
House, December 7, 1999, unreported, the parents had eventually agreed that two
of the children should reside with the mother while a third should reside with the
father. There, the Lord Ordinary, while referring to the evidence of the parents
and another relative, made no reference to the views of the children, the eldest of
whom was 11 years old.

6.20   The second way in which the Act seeks to comply with Article 12 of the UN Convention is through section 11 which requires that, when a court is considering making an order in relation to parental responsibilities or rights, it shall give the child the opportunity to indicate whether he or she wishes to express any views on the matter and, if so, give the child the opportunity to do so. Again, the court is to have regard to the child's views, taking account of the child's age and maturity. How this is done, and with what effect, is discussed fully in chapter 10.[81] Suffice it to say that there are very real problems with the mechanism used by the courts which relies on sending a form out to the child and leaving the onus on the child to respond.

6.21   Another mechanism for ascertaining a child's views, through a reporter acting as intermediary, highlights a further problem for children who want to have an input into the decision-making process. While a child may have views about future arrangements, he or she may prefer that these should not be disclosed to the parents, often to avoid hurting their feelings or, sometimes, due to fear of the parents' reactions. Can a court offer a child confidentiality in these circumstances? Would giving a child the benefit of confidentiality infringe the right of the parent, under Article 6(1) of the European Convention, in terms of equality of arms? There are a number of conflicting or inconclusive decisions on this point in Scotland[82]. The final possibility is for the child, with sufficient information and organisation, to become a party in the proceedings. While this has been done successfully, it requires that the child be provided with a solicitor, and the right kind of solicitor at that, obtain legal aid and, in some cases, overcome judicial resistance[83].

The child's welfare and the issue of divorce

6.22   Almost a quarter of a century ago, Judith Wallerstein began to question a popular and, for many parents, convenient, myth about the impact of divorce on children.[84] As California led the world in introducing no-fault divorce, it was believed that, if the divorce made the parents happier, then the children would be happier too.

---

[81]   See paras 10.26–10.29.
[82]   *Dosoo v. Dosoo*, 1999 S.L.T. 86 (two boys aged 12 and 14 described by the reporter as having "a palpable fear of their father", confidentiality allowed); *McGrath v. McGrath* 1999 S.L.T. 90 (seven-year-old girl requesting her views not be disclosed to her father, confidentiality refused); *Oyeneyin v. Oyeneyin*, 1999 G.W.D. 38-1836 (reporters should explain to children that confidentiality cannot be guaranteed); *Grant v. Grant*, 2000 G.W.D. 5-177 (no breach of natural justice, opinion reserved on issue of confidentiality).
[83]   See paras 10.53–10.59 for a full discussion of these issues.
[84]   J.S. Wallerstein and J.B. Kelly, *Surviving The Breakup: How Children and Parents Cope With Divorce* (Basic Books, 1980).

Working with children experiencing parental divorce in California, she found that the vast majority of children had not wanted their parents to separate and were unhappy that they had. In her latest book,[85] she charts the progress, as adults, of a number of children who participated in her earlier studies and, using a control group of children whose parents stayed together, despite relationship problems, debunks what she describes as the "second myth" about the impact of divorce on children; that any adverse effect of parental divorce on children is short-lived. She demonstrates that many children of divorce experience lasting adverse effects, particularly in forming successful relationships of their own. Of course, California is not Scotland but research here mirrored Wallerstein's earlier findings,[86] so her latest work cannot be dismissed lightly. In addition, divorce often has an adverse economic impact on children[87] and, as we know, poverty diminishes an individual's life chances.

If parental separation and divorce have an adverse impact on the child, not only throughout his or her childhood, but lifelong, what is the solution for the legal system? Remember Article 3 of the UN Convention requires that the child's best interests be a paramount consideration in all matters affecting the child. Could it be argued that respect for the child's rights requires that divorce is simply prohibited where the couple has children below the age of 16 (or, perhaps, 18)? Leaving aside domestic violence cases where there might well be a separate argument centred on the child's welfare, should we legislate to the effect that, where a court decides that the parents' relationship "is not all that bad", they should simply put up with it until the children grow up? There are a number of reasons why this simplistic solution is untenable and it must be stressed that Wallerstein does not suggest this *is* the solution. First is the practical matter that, short of creating some kind of "relationship police", insisting that couples remain married would not prevent them from separating[88] and, in any event, there would be no practical method of scrutinising the parting of unmarried parents.[89] Sec-

6.23

---

[85] J.S. Wallerstein, J.M. Lewis and S. Blakeslee, *The Unexpected Legacy of Divorce: A 25 Year Landmark Study* (Hyperion, 2000).

[86] A. Mitchell, *A Child in the Middle: Living Through Divorce* (Tavistock Publications, 1985).

[87] While the leading U.S. treatise on this point, L.J. Weitzman, *The Divorce Revolution: The Unexpected Social and Economic Consequences for Women and Children in America* (Free Press, 1985), has come under attack, the fundamental point remains valid. See further on this point, Sutherland, *Child and Family Law, supra*, paras 14.26 and 14.27.

[88] It should be remembered that actions for adherence were simply a device whereby the pursuer could obtain aliment from the defender. Such actions were abolished by the Law Reform (Husband and Wife) (Scotland) Act 1984, s. 2(1).

[89] It must be acknowledged that, unless someone brings the issue to a court, there is at present, no scrutiny of the arrangements unmarried parents make for the care of their children after they separate. In the majority of cases, it is questionable that there is any scrutiny in the vast majority of cases where married parents divorce and agree the future arrangements for the care of their children.

ondly, the UN Convention, in putting the child's welfare no higher than "a" paramount consideration clearly countenances other valid considerations and, indeed, in Article 9, provides specifically for the possibility of parental separation. Thirdly, we must consider the provisions of the European Convention, Article 12, guaranteeing the right to marry and to found a family 'according to the national laws governing the exercise of this right'. This should not be read literally to mean that a state is free to pass *any* law it pleases and thus be free from challenge, since that would effectively rob the right of all content. What, then, is and is not permissible? In *Johnston v. Ireland*,[90] the Court found no breach of Article 12 in Ireland's absolute prohibition on divorce. However, it is clear from its decision just one year later, in *F. v. Switzerland* that, once a state opens the door to divorce, it may not then place 'unreasonable restrictions' on remarriage.[91] At issue there was a Swiss law that prevented a party who had been found solely responsible for the breakdown of the marriage from remarrying for a period of three years, something the Court found, by a nine to eight majority, to be in breach of Article 12. Where would that leave a law which prohibited divorce until the children grow up? It is submitted that any such law would place an unreasonable restriction on the right to marry.[92] However, we must not lose sight of Wallerstein's fundamental point. Divorce and, sadly, its frequent occurrence, may be here to stay and the challenge for the legal system is to find an approach which puts the interests of the children to the fore.[93]

Decisions on parental responsibilities and parental rights

6.24 Where parents agree on future arrangements for the care of their children, there is little court scrutiny of these arrangements. Where

---

[90] (1986) 9 E.H.R.R. 203. There, the husband had left his wife, formed a new relationship and had a child with his new partner. The Court find no violation of Art. 8 in respect of his inability to create an equivalent relationship with his new partner although it did find a violation of Art. 8 in respect of his daughter's status as an "illegitimate" child under Irish law. Divorce is now permitted in Ireland.

[91] (1987) 10 E.H.R.R. 411. See also *Hamer v. United Kingdom* (1979) 24 D.R. 5 and *Draper v. UK* (1980) 24 D.R. 72, where the Commission found that, while English law at the time did not prohibit prisoners from marrying, the fact that they could not actually do so in prison meant that they had to wait until they were released. The delay amounted to an infringement of the substance of their rights. Prisoners may now marry in prison in England.

[92] One is reminded of Mary Ann Glendon's observation that "the fundamental right to marry .... has now to be understood as the right to marry, and marry and marry"; M.A. Glendon, *The New Family and the New Property* (Butterworths, 1981), at p. 72.

[93] There is a wealth of literature in Scotland and elsewhere addressing this issue. See the materials cited in Sutherland, *Child and Family Law, supra*, paras 1.49–1.50 and 6.98–5.100 and, more recently, M.A. Mason, *The Custody Wars: Why Children Are Losing The Legal Battle and What We Can Do About It* (Basic Books, 2000).

parents do not agree, the matter has traditionally been dealt with in adversarial court proceedings. It has long been recognised that the traditional court system is seriously flawed as a means of helping families to arrive at a workable solution for them. With the birth of the alternative dispute resolution (ADR) movement, it became apparent that mediation, in particular, had something to offer in helping families find a solution with which everyone could live and, since it was "their" solution, one to which the individuals involved might be more committed.[94] Mediation undoubtedly has much to offer to many families, but concern has been expressed that the child's views may get lost in the mediation process.[95] While the primary obligation to take the child's views into account lies with the parents, it is incumbent on mediators to ensure and facilitate the inclusion of the child's views. Where the parents are unable to resolve their dispute, whether through mediation or otherwise, the matter will proceed to court.

As we have seen, a very wide range of people, including the child **6.25** concerned and the parents, may seek an order from a court in relation to parental responsibilities and parental rights. Essentially, the court can bestow any of the parental responsibilities and rights on an individual; remove them from a person who has them; or regulate their exercise.[96] This is usually done through the granting of a residence order, a contact order, a specific issue order, or a combination thereof.[97] In addition, the court may grant interdict, appoint a judicial factor to manage the child's property or remove a person as the child's guardian.[98] In reaching its decision, the court must be guided by three principles: the paramountcy of the child's welfare; the obligation to take account of any views the child wishes to express, in the light of the child's age and maturity; and the presumption of non-intervention.[99] As we have seen, Scots law does a somewhat imperfect job of meeting its obligation under Article 12 of the UN Convention in respect of the child's views. What, then, of the other two principles?

The requirement that a court should not make an order unless to **6.26** do so would be better for the child than making no order at all,

---

[94] The roots of ADR being applied to family disputes can be traced to a seminal article; R.H. Mnookin and L. Kornhauser, "Bargaining in the Shadow of the Law", 88 Yale L.J. 950 (1979). See further, Sutherland, *Child and Family Law*, *supra*, paras 1.42–1.50 and J. Lewis, *The Role of Mediation in Family Disputes in Scotland* (CRU, 1999).

[95] See, *Alternative Dispute Resolution in Scotland* (CRU, 1996); *Giving Children a Voice in Family Mediation* (National Family Mediation and the Gulbenkian Foundation, 1994); C. Bruch, "And how are the children? The effect of ideology and mediation on child custody and children's well-being in the United States" (1995) I.J.L.F. 106.

[96] 1995 Act, s. 11(2)(a)–(c).

[97] 1995 Act, s. 11(2)(c)–(e).

[98] 1995 Act, s. 11(2)(f)–(h).

[99] 1995 Act, s. 11(7).

reflects a move away from the notion, prevalent in the past, that one parent would have residence while the other would be permitted contact with the child, at best. The current approach accords with Article 19 of the UN Convention and recognises the continued involvement of both parents in a child's life even after divorce. Until recently, it was believed that the result of this principle is that the onus is now placed firmly on the pursuer to demonstrate to the court why the order sought will serve the child's best interests,[1] albeit, once the court has the evidence before it, "the matter then becomes one of overall impression".[2] The extraordinary decision of the Inner House, in *White v. White*,[3] calls that belief into question. The Lord President found the proposition that a child generally benefits from contact with a parent to be part of "certain common values and assumptions as to the upbringing and welfare of children",[4] supported by Article 9(3) of the UN Convention. Furthermore, he read Lord Hope's opinion in *Sanderson v. McManus* in the House of Lords, wrongly it is submitted, as giving no indication of where the onus of proof lay under the 1995 Act. All of this supported his conclusion that, since the court can make an order for parental responsibilities and parental rights *ex proprio motu*, where onus of proof is inapplicable, then similarly, there is no onus of proof where a person actually asks the court to make a particular order. It would appear that either, there is no onus of proof in such cases, or, given the Lord President's starting point, that the onus will fall on the person seeking to prevent contact. It is to be hoped that the House of Lords is given the opportunity to clarify its thinking on the matter.

6.27   While the application of the welfare principle accords entirely with the requirement of Article 3 of the UN Convention, the principle or, at least, its operation, has come under attack. Essentially, it is criticised as a vague and arbitrary standard that, at best, allows a judiciary with no special knowledge or training in child welfare to impose its, sometimes contradictory, views on a population with which it is all too often out of touch.[5] At worst, it is seen as the imposition, by a male dominated judiciary, of its own prejudices.[6] In addition, it has been criticised as attempting to predict

---

[1] *Porchetta v. Porchetta*, 1986 S.L.T. 105; *Sanderson v. McManus*, 1997 S.C. (H.L.) 55. It should be remembered that, while it is competent for a court to regulate parental responsibilities and rights when a supervision requirement from a children's hearing is in place, the practical effect of the court's decision is subject to the supervision requirement; *P. v. P.*, 2000 SCLR 477 (I.H.).
[2] *Sanderson v. McManus, supra, per* Lord Hope at p. 62G.
[3] 2001, S.L.T. 485.
[4] *ibid.* at p.490
[5] The literature here is vast but R.H. Mnookin, "Child Custody Adjudication: Judicial Functions in the Face of Indeterminacy", 39 Law and Contemp Prob. 227 (1975), is often regarded as the seminal article. Despite its shortcomings, the welfare principle at least claims to be child-centred; B.B. Woodhouse, "Child Custody in the Age of Children's Rights: The Search for a Just and Workable

future events and for promoting litigation due to the uncertainty of its content[7]. In Scotland[8], unlike many other jurisdictions, there is no statutory checklist of factors to guide the court on what will contribute to, or detract from, the child's welfare. This might suggest that the welfare principle, as operating here, is more arbitrary than most. However, when one notes that virtually every checklist has the final criterion of "all the circumstances of the case", it becomes apparent that the presence or absence of a checklist probably makes little difference. Certainly, how the welfare principle has been applied by the Scottish courts in the past has been analysed extensively in the literature and there is no shortage of "unofficial checklists".[9]

If the operation of the welfare principle is, indeed, arbitrary, this **6.28** puts it in real jeopardy when examined in the light of Article 8(2) of the European Convention which, it will be remembered, permits interference with the right to family life only in certain circumstances. The European Court has made clear that the removal of parental rights can be interference with the right to respect for family life.[10] It then falls to the state to demonstrate that it has acted lawfully and proportionately in the pursuit of one of the ends set out in Article 8(2). Resolution of a contact or residence dispute could be so justified as protecting "the rights and freedoms of others". However, the question remains the lawfulness of the intervention. While the Court has been prepared to strike down a custody decision where the criteria for the decision amounted to

---

Standard", 33 *F.L.Q.* 815 (1999).

[6] F. Olsen, "The Politics of Family Law", 2 Law and Inequ. 1 (1984); M.A. Fineman, *The Illusion of Equality: The Rhetoric and Reality of Divorce Reform* (1991); J.C. Murphy, "Legal Images of Motherhood: Conflicting Definitions from Welfare "Reform", Family, and Criminal Law", 83 Cornell L. Rev. 688 (1998).

[7] M. S. Melli, "Towards a Restructuring of Custody Decision-making at Divorce: an Alternative Approach to the Best Interests of the Child", in J. Eekelaar and P. Sarcevic, *Parenthood in Modern Society* (Martinus Nijhoff, 1993), where the author prefers the "primary caregiver" standard. That standard has, in turn, been criticised as a thinly disguised version of the maternal preference; R. Neely, "The Primary Caretaker Parent Rule: Child Custody and the Dynamics of Greed", 3 Yale Law and Policy Rev. 167 (1984).

[8] After consideration, the Scottish Law Commission rejected a statutory checklist of factors which the court would be required to consider in assessing welfare on the basis that such a checklist would be necessarily incomplete, might divert attention from other factors which ought to be considered, and might result in judges taking a mechanical approach to decision making; *Report on Family Law*, paras 5.20–5.23. That the opposite view was taken by the Law Commission in England and Wales is demonstrated by the list found in the Children Act 1989, s.1(3) and (4); see *Report on Guardianship and Custody* (Law Com. No. 172, 1988), paras 3.17–3.21.

[9] See, for example, Sutherland, *Child and Family Law, supra,* paras 5.106–5.129 and A.B. Wilkinson and K.McK. Norrie, *The Law of Parent and Child in Scotland* (2nd ed., 1999, W. Green), paras 10.11–10.37.

[10] *Hoffman v. Austria* (1993) 17 E.H.R.R. 293.

discrimination,[11] it has had no difficulty in accepting the welfare test and the precise content of that test will usually fall within the margin of appreciation permitted to the individual state. Accordingly, despite the criticisms levelled against it, the welfare test would appear to be safe from challenge. This would seem to be all the more the case given that it is precisely the standard set out in the UN Convention.

Exercise of parental responsibilities and parental rights

6.29 There are a host of contexts in which decisions have to be made in respect of children and disputes may arise between the child and the parents, the parents themselves, other family members, and the various organs of the state which are charged with addressing the issue. What role does the child play when the ultimate decision on parental responsibilities and rights, the child's possible adoption, is being taken?[12] Can a mother who has remarried change the child's last name so that the child has the same as her own and that of the step-father?[13] Can a fourteen- year-old young woman seek contraceptive advice and feel secure that she will receive this without her parents knowing?[14] Where a child may require special provision in the context of education, who makes the final decision?[15] Individual chapters of this book are devoted to these areas and reference should be made to them for discussion of the relevant law, policy and practice at work. For now, the example of physical punishment of children will be examined as an illustration of Scots law and the relevant international conventions in operation.

Physical punishment of children

6.30 While Scots law makes strenuous efforts to protect children from abuse and neglect, a glaring anomaly remains the right of parents to inflict a certain amount of violence on children under the euphemistic and vague umbrella of "reasonable chastisement". The right to chastise a child stems from the notion of parental power[16] and, as such, can be delegated to others entrusted by parents with the care of the child.[17] It should be noted that children are the only

---

[11] *ibid.*

[12] See paras 9.28–9.33.

[13] See paras 5.17–5.19.

[14] See paras 11.35–11.45.

[15] See paras 12.13–12.75.

[16] Erskine, Institutes, I, v, 53.

[17] *Stewart v. Thain,* 1981 J.C. 13. The issue of physical punishment within the context of education was severely limited and, finally, eliminated, by statute; Education (No. 2) Act 1986, s. 48; Education Act 1993, s. 295; Standards in Scotland's Schools etc (Scotland) Act 2000, s. 13. Early restrictions were largely as a result of the European Court decision in *Campbell and Cosans v. United Kingdom* (1982) 4 E.H.R.R. 293.

category of persons against whom such violence is permitted.[18] What amounts to "reasonable chastisement" is somewhat unclear, and depends on the circumstances of the individual case and, in particular, on the age of the child and the extent of the violence.[19]

The issue of physical punishment of children provides a **6.31** particularly clear example of the way the European Court's thinking on a given issue can develop. Article 3 of the Convention prohibits "inhuman or degrading treatment or punishment" and, having concluded, initially, that corporal punishment of children did not necessarily qualify as a breach, the Court gradually edged its way towards countenancing the possibility that it might be so classified in particular circumstances.[20] Finally, in 1998, in *A v. United Kingdom,*[21] the Court had the opportunity to consider physical punishment in the family. There, a nine-year-old boy had been caned by his step-father with considerable force on a number of occasions. In 1994, while not denying the factual allegations, the step-father argued that his actions amounted to "reasonable chastisement" and was acquitted of the charge of occasioning actual bodily harm (broadly equivalent to assault, in Scotland). In a unanimous judgement, the European Court found that there had been a breach of the child's rights under Article 3 and awarded him £10,000 in damages. While it stopped short of condemning all

---

[18] While robust physical contact is an inherent part of many sports, the criminal law remains applicable. See *Ferguson v. Higson,* unreported, October 11, 1995, where a football player who was convicted of assaulting another player on the pitch was sentenced to three months imprisonment.

[19] The right is subject to a "reasonableness test", a rather vague standard which is not understood by all parents. Thus, for example, in *B. v. Harris,* 1990 S.L.T. 208, it was held to be reasonable for a mother to hit her nine-year-old daughter with a belt, but, in *Peebles v. McPhail,* 1990 S.L.T. 245, it was held unreasonable for a mother to slap a two-year-old on the face with such force as to knock him over. In 1999, a father, himself a school teacher, was convicted of assaulting his eight-year-old daughter, having slapped her buttocks when she became hysterical in a dentist's waiting room. That case cause considerable public outcry not, as one might have hoped, because a child had been assaulted by a parent, but because the father was subsequently struck off the teaching register by the General Teaching Council for Scotland.

[20] *Campbell and Cosans v. United Kingdom* (1982) 4 E.H.R.R. 293 (physical punishment in school not a breach of Article 3 but was a breach of Article 2 of the First Protocol, which requires respect for the parents' religious and philosophical convictions in the course of a child's education); *Tyrer v. United Kingdom* (1978) 2 E.H.R.R. 1 ("judicial birching" was a breach of Article 3); *Warwick v. United Kingdom* (1986) D.R. 60. (Commission decided that caning at school was degrading punishment); *Costello-Roberts v. United Kingdom* (1994) 19 E.H.R.R. 112 (corporal punishment could involve a breach of Article 3, but minimum level of severity had not been reached in that case). See also *Z. and others v. United Kingdom,* May 10, 2001.

[21] (1999) 27 E.H.R.R. 611.

physical punishment of children,[22] the message is clear. Physical punishment of children is growing less acceptable and will be subject to more rigorous scrutiny.

6.32   That the European Court's thinking should develop in this way is hardly surprising in the light of the provisions of the UN Convention. Article 19(1) is quite explicit in requiring States Parties to "protect the child from all forms of physical or mental violence". Unlike some other rights accorded to the child under the Convention,[23] no qualification is placed on the child's right to protection from violence. Thus, the usual justifications for parental physical punishment of children, like the suggestion that it is somehow in the child's interests or serves some educational purpose, are no response to the Convention's very clear prohibition. In addition, Article 37(a) requires States Parties to ensure that "no child shall be subjected to torture, or other cruel, inhuman or degrading treatment or punishment". As we have seen, that phrase is found in the European Convention and, while the Court has not yet found that it prohibits all physical violence against children, it does afford some protection. In the context of the UN Convention, in a sense, this is less important given the very clear prohibition on violence found in Article 19. Certainly, the Committee on the Rights of the Child was critical of the continued acceptance of corporal punishment of children in the United Kingdom and pointed out the incompatibility with Articles 3, 19 and 37.[24] The Committee would rightly have expected this issue to be addressed squarely when the United Kingdom next reported. If that was the case, it must have been disappointed by the *Second Report*. On the issue of physical punishment of children, the Report, having noted the Committee's concern, simply indicates that consultation on the matter is underway; records that physical punishment is no longer permitted in respect of a child in state care; and notes the opposition of some NGOs to all physical punishment of children.[25]

6.33   Prompted by the European Court's decision in *A v United Kingdom*, the Scottish Executive published a consultation paper, *Physical Punishment of Children in Scotland*.[26] Eight years earlier, the Scottish Law Commission's had proposed that the right of

---

[22] The Commission, at para. 55, had indicated that its finding "did not mean that Article 3 is to be interpreted as imposing an obligation on States to protect, through their criminal law, against any form of physical rebuke, however mild, by a parent of a child."

[23] For example, the child's right to freedom of thought, conscience and religion is subject to the rights and duties of parents to provide the child with direction in the exercise of these right; Article 14.

[24] Committee on the Rights of the Child, *Concluding Observation on the United Kingdom*, C.R.C./C./15/Add.34 (February 15, 1995), para. 16.

[25] *Second Report*, paras 7.12.1–7.13.3.

[26] February 2000.

physical chastisement should be defined and restricted,[27] but the Executive felt that the passage of time warranted fresh consultation. What is astonishing is the Executive's cavalier dismissal of the UN Convention as "not having the force of law in Scotland"[28]. While the UN Convention has not been incorporated into domestic law in the same way as the European Convention, it is far from irrelevant and domestic courts are paying increasing attention to it. In any event, the Executive was consulting over possible law reform, not the application of existing law and, as such, ought to have been thinking in terms of compliance with international obligations. What will result from the consultation is unknown but, certainly, the Executive has the opportunity to join the many developed countries in the world which have, or are in the course of, prohibiting all physical violence against children.[29]

Conclusions

For the most part, Scots law governing the care of the child in the **6.34** family setting provides an encouraging example of compliance with international obligation. Given that Part I of the 1995 Act was drafted with the provisions of the European and UN Conventions in mind, this is hardly surprising. Where Scots law falls down is over the treatment of children of unmarried parents and non-marital fathers, on the issue of physical punishment of children and on that most challenging of all tasks, enabling children to participate in the decision-making process in a meaningful and non-intimidating way. While there are concerns that the flexible and largely child-centred approach of Scots law might be threatened by particular applications of the concepts of privacy and due process inherent in the European Convention, it is likely that any such challenges could be resisted and that is perhaps a tribute to the European Convention itself and to the European Court.

---

[27] It had proposed that, in both civil and criminal proceedings, it should not be a defence that a person struck a child in the exercise of a purported parental right if he or she struck the child, (i) with a stick, belt or other object, (ii) in such a way as to cause, or risk causing, injury, or (iii) in such a way as to cause, or risk causing, pain or discomfort lasting more than a very short time; see *Report on Family Law* (Scot. Law Com. No. 135, 1992), paras 2.67–2.105, Rec. 11 and draft Children (Scotland) Bill, cl. 4.

[28] At para. 3.24.

[29] Sweden led the way, banning all physical punishment of children in 1979 and seven other European countries (Austria, Croatia, Cyprus, Demark, Finland, Latvia and Norway) have followed suit. Belgium, Bulgaria, Germany, Ireland, New Zealand and Switzerland are considering such a ban.

CHAPTER 7

CHILD ABDUCTION

SHONA SMITH

Introduction

Article 9 of the UN Convention on the Rights of the Child directs **7.1**
State Parties to ensure that children shall not be separated from
their parents against their will except when competent authorities
subject to judicial review determine that it is in the best interests of
the children. Article 11 instructs state parties to take measures to
combat the illicit transfer and non-return of children abroad. The
UN Convention specifically provides that State parties should take
all appropriate measures to prevent the abduction of children.[1]

The abduction of children by one parent from another, across **7.2**
international boundaries has become increasingly common over
recent years and cases involving applications to return children
often draw much attention from the media. However, when the
philosophy and objective of much of the law governing this area is
not to determine what is in children's best interests but to secure
their return to the country of their habitual residence, what rights
does a child have and what measures have been put in place to
protect them?

In looking at the rights of children in relation to child abduction, **7.3**
it is necessary to understand the background to child abduction law
in Scotland. The law derives from two international treaties known
as the Hague Convention[2] and the European Convention[3], accepted into United Kingdom law by the Child Abduction and
Custody Act 1985. Both Conventions apply to abductions from
outwith the United Kingdom. Abductions within the United
Kingdom are dealt with by the Family Law Act 1986 and the Child
Abduction Act 1984 in relation to criminal matters. All of them

---

[1] UN Convention on the Rights of the Child, Art. 35.
[2] Convention on the Civil Aspects of International Child Abduction signed at the
Hague on October 25, 1980.
[3] European Convention on Recognition and Enforcement of Decisions Concerning
Custody of Children and on the Restoration of Custody of Children signed in
Luxembourg on May 20, 1980.

assume that an abducted child's best interest is normally to be returned forthwith to the country of the child's habitual residence and
for the welfare principle to be applied in that country.

7.4　　If neither the Hague nor European Convention applies, recourse
may be had to some non reciprocal provision, not embodied in a
bilateral or multi-lateral treaty, such as the United States Uniform
Child Custody & Jurisdiction Act. Prevention of child abduction is
however better than cure. Unfortunately space here forbids more
than passing reference to the practical steps which a fearful parent
might take.[4]

The Hague Convention

7.5　The aim of this Convention is to secure the immediate return of
children who have been taken across international borders in
breach of the custody rights given by the law of the child's habitual
residence.[5] Its basic premise is that the country to which a child has
been abducted should not decide the custody issue, but rather
should decide where custody jurisdiction should be exercised. The
Convention enforces all custody rights, whether they flow from a
court order or an agreement between the parties or by operation of
the law. The grounds on which a State can refuse to return a child
are detailed in Articles 12(2)[6] and 13 of the Convention. It can
refuse to return if the applicant was not in fact exercising custody
rights at the time of the removal or consented to or acquiesced in
the removal. Another justification for non-return is that there is a
grave risk that the return would expose the child to the risk of
physical or psychological harm or otherwise place the child in an
intolerable situation.[7] In addition the court may refuse to return if
the child objects to the return and has reached an age and level of
maturity at which it is appropriate to take account of his or her
views.[8]

7.6　　If the child is abducted into Scotland then an application should
be made by the bereft parent for return of the child to the appro-

---

[4]　Useful leaflets appear from time to time–try the Citizens' Advice Bureaux. For
detailed papers contact Reunite (International Child Abduction Centre), P.O.
Box 24875, London, E1 6FR, Tel. 020 7375 3440, or the Scottish Child Law
Centre, 23 Buccleuch Place, Edinburgh, Tel. 0131 667 6333.
[5]　For details of the countries which have ratified the Convention, contact either the
Justice Department, Hayweight House, 23 Lauriston Street, Edinburgh, Tel. 0131
221 6814 or Reunite. Reasonably up to date lists are also printed in the
Parliament House book at pp. K252 (Hague) and K258 (Europe).
[6]　Art. 12(2) Child has settled in new environment.
[7]　Hague Convention, Art. 13.
[8]　See *Urness v. Minto*, 1994 S.C.L.R. 392; *Re S.* (child abduction) (child's views)
[1993] 2 All E.R. 683.

priate jurisdiction.[9] The procedure is aimed at ensuring that cases are dealt with as quickly as possible. The longer the delay, the greater the risk of the child becoming attached to the abductor and detached from the bereft parent. On receipt of the application, the Justice Department of the Scottish Executive will automatically issue a certificate which entitles the bereft parent to free legal aid in Scotland.[10] The certificate covers all legal costs and can cover the costs of return of the child to the jurisdiction of origin. It should be noted, however, that the abducting parent has to apply for legal aid in the usual way and is subject to the usual tests in relation to financial eligibility.

If a child is abducted from Scotland to another country which **7.7** has signed the Convention, then an application can be made for the return of that child through the Scottish Executive.[11] They will then liaise with the Central Authority in the country to which the child has been abducted. The Central Authority in that country will appoint a solicitor to act on behalf of the bereft parent. The entitlement to legal aid for the bereft parent will unfortunately be determined by the domestic arrangements in force in that country.

The European Convention

The European Convention differs from the Hague Convention in **7.8** two respects. It only enforces custody orders actually made in the country of origin[12] in contrast to the Hague Convention which enforces custody rights irrespective of whether an order has been made. Secondly it recognises orders obtained even after the abduction has taken place,[13] once again contrasting with the Hague Convention which only enforces rights exercisable at the time of the abduction. In this context "decisions relating to custody" means decisions relating to the care of the child and includes the right of access to the child.[14] A foreign decision must under no circumstances be reviewed by the state addressed[15] and the enforcement of

---

[9] The application is made to the Justice Department, Hayweight House, Edinburgh.

[10] All that is needed is a letter, signed by the applicant or solicitor, and accompanied by a brief memorandum and the Certificate issued by the Secretary of State following upon receipt of the application in terms of Reg. 46(2) of the Civil Legal Aid (Scotland) Regulations 1996.

[11] Statistics in respect of incoming and outgoing applications under the Hague Convention are available from the Justice Department, Hayweight House, Edinburgh.

[12] "Decisions relating to custody" means a decision of an authority relating to the case of a child, including the right to decide the place of the child's residence or the right of access to the child—Art. 5(1).

[13] Art. 12.

[14] Art. 5(1).

[15] Art. 9(3).

the order may only be refused under very limited circumstances. Enforcement can be refused if the service of the initial proceedings was invalid,[16] if jurisdiction was unsound[17] or if the decision is incompatible with a decision relating to custody which became enforceable in the state addressed before the removal of the child unless the child was habitually resident in the requesting state for one year prior to removal.[18] Enforcement may also be refused on a number of welfare grounds.[19]

7.9   Of the two Conventions the Hague Convention, with its wider remit, is the more popular. Bereft parents may of course choose not to invoke either Convention and apply for custody of an abducted child using the domestic system. There are, however, practical disadvantages in proceeding in that manner. In the first instance the assistance of the Central Authority will not be available to them. In addition a private action will not attract any automatic grant of legal aid. Using the domestic proceedings will also open up the welfare question in the court where the child is located rather in the court of habitual residence.

Family Law Scotland Act 1986

7.10 The abduction of children is as much a problem between the different legal systems of the United Kingdom as it is with foreign legal systems. Scotland, England and Wales and Northern Ireland are independent countries in international law and accordingly the Family Law Act 1986 was set up to discourage abduction between different parts of the United Kingdom. It permits any person who has a Part 1 order[20] in any country in the United Kingdom to have it recognised and enforced in the other countries. In this respect it is more like the European Convention than the Hague Convention. The recognition of the original order is automatic. In the event that an order has not existed prior to the abduction it is open to the bereft parent to seek an urgent order from the local court and the apply to that court for the papers to be transferred to the jurisdiction that the child has been abducted to enable enforcement to take place. Like the European Convention it cannot be enforced without a petition to the court in Scotland.[21] That petition can only be presented once the papers have been received from the originating court and an order for enforcement will not be granted prior to service of the petition being made on the abducting parent. In the

---

[16] Art. 9(1)(a).
[17] Art. 9(1)(b).
[18] Art. 9(1)(c).
[19] Art. 10.
[20] Family Law Act 1986, s. 1
[21] cn. 7.8, *supra*.

event that a child has been abducted from Scotland to another part of the United Kingdom the procedure is the same.

Common Law

It is of course necessary for bereft parents to be located in states **7.11** which are signatories to the Hague and European Conventions for the conventions to apply. If children are abducted into Scotland from overseas countries which are not signatories to the Hague or European Conventions, Scottish courts have since the early part of the last century recognised and enforced custody orders from the country where the child was habitually resident provided that the orders accord with the best interests of the child.[22] Foreign orders will not be automatically or blindly enforced but will be given consideration with the court treating the child's welfare as the paramount consideration. Unfortunately if Scottish children are abducted overseas to countries which are not party to either Convention and which do not have non reciprocal legislation of their own, and if the criminal law does not apply there is nothing which Scottish law can do. Return is dependent upon the internal law of the other country. Its courts are likely to uphold the social and cultural values of the country concerned, such as the automatic supremacy of the father's claim and the importance of the extended family. Bereft parents should find out what parental rights exist under local law and what, if anything, might influence the local courts decision.[23] The consular department of the Foreign and Commonwealth Office can help by providing a list of local lawyers who correspond in English, but neither the consular department nor British Consulate officers abroad can give legal advice or act as legal representatives.

The Objectives of the Legislation

As is apparent from the foregoing, the overriding emphasis behind **7.12** the law in this area is to ensure the return of the child to the country of their habitual residence to enable the legal system of that country to determine questions of welfare. The justification behind that

---

[22] Starting with *Westergaard v. Westergaard,* 1914 S.C. 977; through *Radoyevitch v. Radoyevitch,* 1930 S.C. 619; 1930 S.L.T. 404; *MacLean v. MacLean,* 1947 S.C. 79, *Kelly v. Marks,* 1974 S.L.T. 118; *Campbell v. Campbell,* 1977 S.C. 103; 1977 S.L.T. 125; *Sinclair v. Sinclair,* 1988 S.L.T. 87; 1988 S.C.L.R. 44.
[23] See, *e.g.* Report, "Child abduction and the principles of Islamic Law" available from Department of Law, University of London, Queen Mary and Westfield College, Mile End Road, London, E1 4NS.

emphasis is to protect children against abduction or wrongful re-
tention and accordingly protect their rights in terms of Articles 11
and 35 of the UN Convention. In relation to those rights the law in
Scotland can be seen to be working well, but what of other rights?
What of the right under article 12 for a child who is capable of
forming his or her own views to express those views freely and for
due weight to be given to them and of the right of the child in those
circumstances to be provided with the opportunity to be heard in
any judicial proceedings affecting the child? What of the right to a
fair trial as provided for by the European Convention on Human
Rights or the obligation on States to hold that the best interests of
the child be the primary consideration in terms of Article 3 of the
Convention on the Rights of the Child?

The Welfare Principle—Article 3

7.13 The domestic law of Scotland in relation to children is regulated by
the Children (Scotland) Act 1995. Section 11(7)(a) directs that
courts in making orders in relation to children shall regard the
welfare of the child concerned as its paramount consideration. Thus
our domestic law is fully in harmony with Article 3 of the UN
Convention which provides that " the best interests of the child
shall be a primary consideration". The welfare principle has also
been approved in the case law which has proceeded under the
European Convention on Human Rights.

7.14   However, the conventions and the Family Law Act 1986 are
based on the assumption that it is not for the State to which a child
has been abducted to investigate the merits of a dispute and come to
a decision based on the best interests of a child by reference to the
welfare principle, but rather that the best interest of an abducted
child is normally to be returned immediately to the country of
origin. Indeed, international agreements would be nullified if
countries to which abductors fled explored the merits of a custody
dispute.

7.15   Nevertheless, two of the grounds on which the Hague Convention permits non-return touch on welfare. The first of these is the
grave risk of physical or psychological harm or other element which
would place the child in an intolerable situation.[24] However, it is
important to stress that the cases in which this ground has been
founded upon have made it extremely clear that this is not by any
means a mechanism for simply allowing the welfare principle to be
applied in abduction cases. The majority of cases defended under
this ground are unsuccessful. Accordingly, to use its discretion to
return on this basis, the court must be satisfied that the risk is in
reality a grave one and it is only in the clearest of cases that an order

---

[24] Art. 13(b).

to return will not be granted.[25] In the words of Temporary Judge Horsburgh:

> "In most cases that come before this court involving a dispute **7.16** between parents as to custody of a child, the overriding and paramount consideration is the welfare of the child. In this type of case under the 1985 Act the court is not enjoined to conduct an enquiry into that matter. The matter before this court is restricted to determining whether or not the party opposing the return of the child establishes a grave risk of the kind specified... A court of competent jurisdiction in Ontario is already considering the case and has made an interim order granting custody to the petitioner. If the question of the welfare of the child has to be litigated it would appear that that would be the appropriate court to deal with the matter".[26]

It is accepted that an order to return will frequently bring with it **7.17** some element of emotional damage but that in itself will not justify a refusal to return.[27] It has in fact been suggested that it is the abduction itself which causes the distress on return.[28] In *Cameron v. Cameron*,[29] it was acknowledged that to make an order for return would increase the risk of psychological harm but that that did not satisfy the "grave risk" test. Accordingly the test is an exceptionally high one.

However, welfare considerations were taken into account in **7.18** *Singh v. Singh*.[30] In that case the parties had three children aged 14, nine and three. At the time the application was made, the youngest child was with the petitioner in Canada and the mother and two older children were in Scotland. It was found that the mother had wrongfully retained the two older children in Scotland. The return of the children was however ultimately refused. Both children expressed a wish not to return. It was held that the both children had reached an age and degree of maturity at which it was appropriate to take account of their views, but it was only the eldest child for whom the order for return was refused. On appeal it was held that once the door was opened to the exercise of discretion by the objection of a sufficiently mature child the court required to have regard to the welfare of the child in the wider sense.

The second ground which touches on welfare is the discretion to **7.19** refuse to return where a period of more than one year has elapsed and it can be shown that the child has now settled into a new

---

[25] *Taylor v. Ford*, 1993 S.L.T. 654.
[26] *ibid.* at p. 658B.
[27] *Starr v. Starr*, 1998 S.L.T. 335.
[28] *Freidrich v. Freidrich*, 78F (3d.) 1060 (1996).
[29] 1997 S.L.T. 206.
[30] 1998 S.L.T. 1084.

environment to such an extent that it overrides the duty to return.[31] The justification for this ground is that the Convention seeks to minimise disruption in a child's life. However, in practice, given that the majority of cases are raised within twelve months of abduction, such defences are rare.

7.20 It can safely be concluded that the applicability of the welfare principle to Hague Convention cases is minimal.

7.21 The European Convention and the Family Law Act 1986 approach the welfare question in a different way primarily because the receiving court is asked to enforce a decision of another court which has, it is hoped, already considered the best interests of the child. The European Convention directs the receiving state not to refuse an incoming custody order unless it is "manifestly no longer in accordance with the welfare of the child."[32] The Family Law Act 1986 gives the court the power to make interim directives about matters concerning the welfare of the child and in general provides a far greater latitude for welfare aspects to be taken into account.[33] The common law has also shown a greater emphasis on welfare in the manner in which it has recognised custody decrees from other countries over the years provided that those decisions conformed to the welfare principle.

The Views of the Child

7.22 Article 12(1) of the UN Convention provides:

> "States Parties shall assure to the child who is capable of forming his or her own views the right to express those views freely in all matters affecting the child, the views of the child being given due weight in accordance with the age and maturity of the child."

7.23 Once again, that Article has been incorporated into our domestic law in terms of section 11(7) of the Children (Scotland) Act 1995. However, the Family Law Act 1986 makes no provision for ascertaining the views of the child, leaving that to the court of habitual residence. The European Convention mentions it only once. It provides that if a change in circumstances makes it "manifestly no longer in accordance with the welfare of the child" to order return, then the state addressed should ascertain the child's views if possible.[34]

7.24 There is of course nothing to stop any court from making such enquiries as it sees fit during the course of an action but it is only the Hague Convention which specifically permits a receiving state to

---

[31] Art. 12(2); *Souci v. Souci*, 1995 S.L.T. 414.
[32] Art. 10(1)(b).
[33] cn. 8.40, *supra*.
[34] Art. 15.

refuse to return if a child having reached a sufficient age and maturity at which it is appropriate to take account of his or her views objects to being returned. The views by themselves are however not conclusive and the cases demonstrate that the child's reasoning and whether the views are substantiated must also be considered.[35] In the English case of *In Re S* it was stated that:

> "It will usually be necessary for the judge to find out why the child objects to being returned. If the only reason is because it wants to remain with the abducting parent, who is also asserting that he or she is unwilling to return, then this will be a highly relevant factor when the judge comes to consider the exercise of his discretion."[36]

In addition a court will give little weight if the child's views have **7.25** been influenced by the abducting parent:

> "...it would be naïve to ignore the ability of intelligent children to manipulate circumstances so as to please parents."[37]

There have been a number of reported decisions in this regard. In **7.26** *Urness v. Minto*,[38] the court, having heard the evidence of boys aged twelve and nine and also of psychologists concluded that the older child was of an age and maturity for his views to be taken into account. The younger child was also against the return but the court concluded that he did not have the necessary maturity. However, in that case it was held that to return one child without the other would have placed the younger child in an intolerable situation and for that reason the return was refused in respect of both children.

In *Matznick v. Matznick*,[39] which concerned three children aged **7.27** eleven, nine and four the views of the two older children were sought and it was submitted that account should be taken of their views and of their objection to returning to the United States. In ordering the return Lord Cameron of Lochbroom indicated that:

> "Each case must of course depend on its own facts. But it is also necessary for the court to be satisfied that the child has put forward valid reasons for its objections to return. In the present case it is plain that the basis upon which the objections were taken to a return have disappeared with the acceptance of the mother that if an order for their return is made, she is prepared to return to the United States with the children."[40]

---

[35] *Singh v. Singh*, 1998 S.L.T. 1084.
[36] Balcombe L.J., 1993 F.M. 242 at 251.
[37] *Joffre v. Joffre*, 1989 G.W.D. 13-536 and 1992 G.W.D. 27-1522.
[38] 1994 S.L.T. 988.
[39] 1994 G.W.D. 39-2277.
[40] Judgment of Lord Cameron, p. 38.

7.28 In the case of *Marshall v. Marshall*[41] the court once again ordered a return against a 13-year-old girl's objection where although the objection was heartfelt and genuine it did not necessarily point to her having the requisite degree of maturity.

7.29 In *O'Connor v. O'Connor*[42] an order was once again made to return a 13-year-old child against her wishes where it Lord Morton of Shuna held that:

> "I do not consider that the child's objection is of sufficient materiality to cause me to exercise the discretion in Article 13 to refuse to order the return of the child."

7.30 In *Cameron v. Cameron*[43] it was stated that although the seven-year-old child who expressed her views was both articulate and confidant there was no basis for attributing a level of maturity to her greater than her years and accordingly it was concluded that she had not reached the necessary age or level of maturity in terms of the article.

7.31 In *Singh*[44] following upon the eldest child's objection, she was allowed to stay in Scotland. In that case the court had the benefit of the child giving evidence to the court orally and also the benefit of a report from a child psychologist in relation to the assessment of her level of maturity. She was described as being "bright, articulate and thoughtful" and unlike in some of the cases referred to above provided the court with a clear, reasoned, detailed and substantial basis for not wishing to return to Canada. Lord Macfadyen summarised that:

> "She was, for all the reasons she gave unhappy there, but is happy here. I have no doubt as to the genuineness, and depth of her feelings on these matters. It did not appear to me that her preference was merely a preference to be with her mother."[45]

7.32 The most recent case on this matter is the as yet unreported decision of *P. v. S. and A.*[46] which concerned the abduction of a nine-year-old boy from the United States. In that case it was held both that the child objected to the return and further that he had reached an age and degree of maturity at which it was appropriate to take account of his views in terms of Article 13. However, the court then went on to consider the basis of the objection, in which it found certain weaknesses. Following upon consideration of the numerous

---

[41] 1996 S.L.T. 429.
[42] Court of Session, December 1, 1994 Lord Morton of Shuna, at p. 7.
[43] 1997 S.L.T. 206.
[44] cn. 8.18, *supra*.
[45] 1998 S.L.T. 1084 at 1092.
[46] As yet unreported decision of Lord Bonomy 2000.

other factors in what was a particularly difficult case, the court finally ordered the return of the child against his wishes.

It can be seen from the reported cases that it is only in a minority **7.33** of those cases that a child's objection to return has been upheld. The important aspect however is that their views have been taken into consideration and have been considered in accordance with their age and maturity. Thereafter, ultimately, as in our domestic law, they have been considered as one factor amongst other factors and when the age and level of maturity are appropriate and the reasoning sound, as in *Singh*, those views have been complied with.

The Opportunity for a Child to be Heard in Judicial Proceedings

Article 12(2) provides that in relation to a child's right to express **7.34** views that:

"...the child shall in particular be provided the opportunity to be heard in any judicial and administrative proceedings affecting the child, either directly, or through a representative or an appropriate body, in a manner consistent with the procedural rules of national law."

It is clear from the foregoing section that Scotland does endeavour **7.35** in considering cases under the Hague Convention to take the views of the child into account but how are those views ascertained?

In our domestic law children are advised of the existence of the **7.36** proceedings when the action is raised and at that time they can decide whether they wish to advise the court of their views in writing, whether they wish to instruct a solicitor and on occasion whether they wish to enter the proceedings as a party to the action. Unlike domestic proceedings, actions in relation to child abduction are not intimated to children. Their views are accordingly normally only brought to the attention of the court if they are advised of the position by the abducting parent and for that reason alone it is probably not surprising that there has been so much discussion in the case law about the influence of the abducting parent and whether the child's view is in reality only to stay with the abducting parent.

Views have been given in different ways in the cases. They are **7.37** often obtained by a report being instructed by a child psychologist. In *P. v. S. and A.* Lord Bonomy observed:

"A report by a court appointed psychologist agreed by the parties should in most cases provide sufficient opportunity for the child's views to be relayed to the court."[47]

---

[47] Judgment of Lord Bonomy, p. 11.

He went on to say in some cases a local authority reporter may be instructed, that in others the court could take the views of the child directly or in the form of a letter written by the child and indeed those methods have also been used in cases of this type. Unlike in our domestic law[48] what has happened less frequently is that children have actually been separately represented. In *Singh,* although the eldest child was separately represented her application to enter the action as a party was refused. In the European Convention case of *Dehn v. Dehn*[49] the child who had entered process was allowed to withdraw at the start of the action. In *Cameron* a more unusual approach was taken in that, in the later stages of the action, counsel represented the child, who had instructed her own solicitor, although she did not formally enter process as a party. In *P. v. S. and A.* Lord Bonomy expressed doubts about the direct representation of children in child abduction hearings given that views could be expressed in other ways, indicating that he made those observations:

> "...lest it be too readily assumed that children should be separately represented in proceedings under this Convention and insufficient thought is given to the question whether separate representation is appropriate in the circumstances of the case."[50]

7.38 One exceptional case was that of Re M. (Child Abduction: Child's Objection to Return)[51] where a 13-year-old child successfully appealed in his own name against an order to return.

Human Rights

7.39 Following upon the coming into force of the Human Rights Act 1998 in October 2000,[52] the opportunity may arise for the practise of the courts in this area of law to be brought under scrutiny. The practice of the Court of Session is to facilitate speed in this type of action by ensuring that matters are dealt with by way of affidavit evidence and written reports. Against that background, a number of questions may well arise in terms of the European Convention on Human Rights in respect of the right under Article 6 to a fair trial. Difficulties will be encountered by children in relation to being

---

[48] For discussion of children's right to legal representation in other types of cases affecting them, see Chap. 10

[49] Lord McFadyen November 26, 1997.

[50] Judgment of Lord Bonomy, p. 12.

[51] (1995) 1 F.C.R. 170.

[52] For discussion of children's legal aid applications, see Chap. 10, paras 10.40–10.50.

properly advised of the proceedings and thereafter in being separately represented before the court. The evidence will largely be in the form of affidavits and difficulties may arise in relation to children being allowed to give oral evidence to explain their position or in relation to their ability to challenge and have cross-examined on their behalf evidence presented by other parties. Children wishing to be separately represented in this regard also face the further obstacle of having to apply for Legal Aid. Unlike the petitioner there is no automatic grant of Legal Aid made available to them and they are required to apply in the normal and accordingly disadvantaging them in the proceedings.

In the case of *Glaser v. United Kingdom*[53] an application was **7.40** made to the European Court of Human Rights by a father who had obtained a contact order in respect of his child in England. Following upon the removal of the mother with the children to Scotland, the father had sought to enforce the order in Scotland under the provisions of the Family Law Act 1986. In that case the human rights arguments arose in the context of a situation in which the court had in fact examined the question of welfare rather than blindly enforcing an order for contact. The proceedings in England had taken some considerable time prior to the mother's unexpected removal to Scotland. Once she had been located and the father was aware of her whereabouts he made the application to the Court of Session for enforcement in August 1994. The application was defended and the Court ordered a report on the children's welfare which became available in late January 1995. A contact order was made in June 1995 but once that was available there were further difficulties both in practice and procedure.

The result was that although the father sought to enforce a **7.41** contact order of June 1993, the first contact visit to actually be arranged was in February 2000. The father's complaints to the court included a complaint under Article 8 in relation to his inability to secure contact with the children from 1993 onwards and in relation to Article 6 the lack of availability to him of Legal Aid and the unreasonable delay in enforcement of contact with his children. The complaints were not upheld. The court commented that:

"While the applicant submitted that it was their (the Scottish and English Courts) absolute responsibility to enforce his rights, the Court reiterates that where other individuals are concerned, particularly children, the courts must ensure that the steps taken do not infringe their rights. Their decision-making process must inevitably involve a balancing of the respective interests, as coercive measures may in themselves present a risk of damage to the children."[54]

---

[53] Unreported—Judgement Strasbourg, September 19, 2000, available on http://www.echr.coe.int.
[54] p. 18.

7.42   The Court did not find that there had been unreasonable delay in the circumstances. In relation to the complaint about the lack of availability of Legal Aid it found that the Convention did not provide a right to receive Legal Aid in civil proceedings but that in some circumstances the lack of Legal Aid may deprive an applicant of affective access to court. In this case the father had been represented throughout and had accordingly had not been prevented from appropriately presenting his claims.

Conclusion

7.43   There is an inbuilt tension in attempting to apply the UN Convention on the Rights of the Child to child abduction in balancing Articles 11 and 35, which support international treaties, with Articles 3 and 12 which lay down the welfare principle and the rights of the child to be heard. There is a similar tension in relation to applying the provisions of the European Convention of Human Rights. The present legislation assumes that the best interests of children are generally served by a policy of the prompt return to enable the court of habitual residence to decide the issue of welfare. There are cogent reasons for that philosophy. If welfare is explored in the country to which a child has been abducted then there is an incentive to abductors to go window shopping to whichever country suits them best which is the very problem that States have sought to address by entering into such international treaties. Furthermore time is on the side of the abductor, as the longer a child is in the country addressed the more it will be contrary to that child's welfare to be returned.

7.44   Potential abductors will be deterred, or so the philosophy goes, only if all countries agree that a child's best interests are served by a prompt return. That alone, it is thought, gives the clear message to the world that there is no advantage in abducting a child, only disadvantage. How, it may be asked does that position accord with the decision in *Glaser* where the court found that the father's rights had not been infringed by the courts delay in investigating issues in relation to welfare? Although an argument can be advanced that in certain respects abduction legislation does not protect the rights of the child, equally it could be argued that it does little to protect the rights of the adults involved. What it does do is concentrate on the welfare of children generally in taking the view that their welfare is served by the return to their state of habitual residence. To concentrate on the welfare of children generally must by definition limit the scope for considering the welfare of the individual child.

7.45   One concern is certainly the ability of children to be represented and express their views in proceedings and the weight given to those views. If however children's objections, provided that they had reached the necessary age and maturity, were accepted without analysis, would that not in itself simply open the way to abducting parents to proceed as they wish and defeat the purpose of the legislation? Ultimately the rights of a far greater number of children may be affected and then what of the rights of those children to maintain contact with both parents and to remain free of abduction against their wishes?

CHAPTER 8

THE CHILD'S RIGHT TO CARE AND PROTECTION

KENNETH MCK. NORRIE

It is necessary in every society, particularly democratic societies, **8.1** that there be legal mechanisms in place whereby the state can step in to protect weak and vulnerable individuals from those who, deliberately, carelessly, negligently or unintentionally, may cause them harm. Children, axiomatically, are vulnerable to harm and are less able to protect themselves than adults: that, together with the unpalatable truth that children are most at risk of harm from members of their own family, makes it all the more important that the state has the power, and indeed the duty, to step in to protect children, even when that involves interference with that "hallmark of a democratic society",[1] family autonomy. The legal mechanisms in Scotland under which such protection is provided are mostly to be found in Part II of the Children (Scotland) Act 1995. Though, famously, this statute in its terms confers few substantive rights on children,[2] its drafting was, to some extent at least, driven by the requirements of the international conventions to which the United Kingdom is a party and which do, directly or implicitly, recognise the concept of children's rights.

Where Do Children's Rights to Protection Come From?

Notwithstanding the lack of substantive provision in the 1995 Act, **8.2** a child in Scotland can trace rights to be protected from neglect or abuse to at least three different sources.

Rights as Concomitants of Duties

First, the 1995 Act imposes numerous duties on local authorities **8.3** and state institutions to protect children, and it is a necessary

---

[1] Thomson, *Family Law in Scotland* (3rd ed. 1996) at p. 255.
[2] The only substantive child's "right", as such, contained in the Act is the right under s. 45(1)(a) to attend his or her own children's hearing.

concomitant of such duties that children have a right to be protected.[3] So, for example, local authorities have a statutory duty to provide accommodation to children who require such accommodation because no-one has parental responsibility for the child or because those who have been caring for the child are prevented for whatever reason from providing accommodation or because the child has been lost or abandoned:[4] such a child necessarily has a right to be so accommodated. As well, local authorities have a duty to safeguard and promote the welfare of children in need, that is to say those who are unlikely to achieve or maintain a reasonable standard of health or development without the provision of local authority services;[5] children so "in need" have a right to be provided with such services. Similarly, local authorities have a duty to institute proceedings which might lead to compulsory measures of supervision by giving information to the children's reporter whenever it appears that such measures may be necessary;[6] and if the reporter comes to the view, after investigation, that compulsory measures of supervision are necessary in the child's best interests, then he or she is under a duty to arrange a children's hearing to consider and determine the child's case.[7] These procedures too confer upon the child the right to be protected.[8]

The UN Convention

8.4 Secondly, the United Kingdom has ratified the United Nations Convention on the Rights of the Child,[9] thereby undertaking an international obligation to protect children in a number of ways,

---

[3]   s. 45 of the Court of Session Act 1988 allows the court to impose such penalty as it thinks fit on any body that fails to fulfil its statutory duty. An action for judicial review of a decision by a local authority not to provide a child with such services as statute requires is also open. An action for damages against a local authority for their failure to fulfil their statutory duties, though it may sometimes be excluded as not being fair, just and reasonable (*X. v. Bedfordshire County Council* [1995] 3 All E.R. 353) remains competent in circumstances in which it is fair, just and reasonable: See *e.g. W. v. Essex County Council* [1998] 3 All E.R. 111 and *Barrett v. London Borough of Enfield* [1999] 3 W.L.R. 79.

[4]   1995 Act, s. 25(1).

[5]   1995 Act, ss. 22(1) and 93(4)(a).

[6]   1995 Act, s. 53(1).

[7]   1995 Act, s. 56(6).

[8]   It is true that compulsory measures of supervision are compulsory in the sense that they can be imposed upon a child unwilling to accept them voluntarily, and in that sense the language of children's "rights", which will normally, by definition, include an element of choice, is less appropriate. But just as a child's right to education can only be properly secured by denying the child the right to decline education, so too a child's right to protection can only be properly secured by permitting measures taken even against the child's wishes.

[9]   (1989) 28 *International Legal Materials* 1448, adopted on November 28, 1989 and ratified by the United Kingdom on December 16, 1991 (two months and two days after the coming into force of the (English) Children Act 1989, many of the provisions of which were designed to allow for United Kingdom ratification).

such as for example, to take measures to combat the illicit transfer and non-return of children abroad;[10] to provide children with the protection of the law against arbitrary or unlawful interference with their privacy, family, home or correspondence;[11] to take measures to protect children from economic exploitation or forms of work likely to be hazardous or interfere with the child's education, health or development;[12] to take measures to protect children from the illicit use of drugs and to prevent the use of children in the illicit production and trafficking of drugs;[13] to protect children from all forms of sexual exploitation and sexual abuse;[14] and to protect children from the sale of or traffic in children.[15] More generally, the United Kingdom is obliged "to take all appropriate legislative, administrative, social and educational measures to protect the child from all forms of physical or mental violence, injury or abuse, neglect or negligent treatment, maltreatment or exploitation, including sexual abuse, while in the care of parent(s), legal guardian(s), or any other person who has the care of the child".[16] The legislative measures in Scotland, that is to say Part II of the Children (Scotland) Act 1995, were taken partly in response to, and reflect various provisions in, the UN Convention.[17] This is seen most particularly with the three "overarching principles" in section 16. Section 16(1) provides that the welfare of the child shall be the court's or the children's hearing's paramount consideration: this may be compared with Article. 3(1) of the UN Convention, under which in all actions concerning children, whether undertaken by public or private social welfare institutions, administrative authorities, legislative bodies or courts of law, "the best interests of the child shall be a primary consideration".[18] Section 16(2) provides (i) that the child

---

[10] Art. 11(1). The most important measure in Scots law with this aim is the Child Abduction and Custody Act 1985, which brings into domestic law the provisions of the Hague Convention on International Child Abduction. See further, Chap. 7.

[11] Art. 16, which is in similar but not identical terms to Art. 8 of the European Convention, considered below.

[12] Art. 32. Section 28 of the Children and Young Persons (Scotland) Act 1937 prohibits the employment of children below the age of 14 and contains other protective prohibitions for children above that age.

[13] Art. 33. This article led to the insertion of a new ground of referral to the children's hearing in s. 52(2)(j) of the 1995 Act.

[14] Art. 34. See the Criminal Law Consolidation (Scotland) Act 1995, ss.1–6; Sexual Offences (Amendment) Act 2000, ss.3 & 4.

[15] Art. 35. See the Adoption (Intercountry Aspects) Act 1999, especially Art. 32 of the Convention on Protection of Children and Co-operation in Respect of Intercountry Adoption, reproduced in Sched. 1 to the Act.

[16] Art. 19(1).

[17] See Sutherland, *Child and Family Law* (1999) at paras 3.12–3.40 for an analysis of how the 1995 Act has attempted to respond to the UN Convention.

[18] Whether "a primary consideration" places less emphasis on welfare than "the paramount consideration" is a matter of some dispute, but both formulations require courts and other decision-making bodies to treat the child's welfare as always relevant and always important. This matter is considered further later in this chapter: see post at paras 8.20, *infra*.

be given an opportunity to indicate whether he or she wishes to express views, (ii) that the child be given an opportunity to express views if he or she does so wish and (iii) that the court or hearing shall have regard to such views as the child may express:[19] this can be traced to Article 12 of the UN Convention[20] under which states parties must assure to the child who is capable of forming his or her own views the right to express those views freely in all matters affecting the child, the views of the child being given due weight in accordance with the age and maturity of the child.[21] And section 16(3) sets out the so-called "no order presumption", that is to say that the court or hearing shall make no order unless they consider that it would be better for the child that the order be made than that none should be made at all. This principle does not find its origins in the UN Convention, but it does reflect the important principle of proportionality within the European Convention on Human Rights, discussed below. A combination of the no-order presumption and the principle of proportionality creates a new concept–the minimum intervention principle, that is to say the court or hearing should presume that it is to make no order[22] (or that it is to terminate any existing order), but that if any order is to be made (or continued) it must be designed in such a way as constitutes the minimum intervention necessary to achieve its purpose.

8.5   As well as these direct legislative consequences to the United Kingdom's ratification of the UN Convention, there is in addition a requirement that courts resolve matters of ambiguity in favour of conformity with the United Kingdom's international obligations

---

[19] Of course the whole point of children's hearings has always been to give the child just such an opportunity, though the legislation under which the hearings system was established (the Social Work (Scotland) Act 1968) nowhere explicitly required the hearing to listen to children. And before the 1995 Act there was no requirement, and very little practice, for courts to take account of the views of children. Now, in addition to the requirement under s. 16(2), courts and children's hearings are prohibited from making an order or decision before having regard to the views of a child who has indicated a desire to express views: see Ordinary Cause Rules 1993, r. 33.19; Rules of the Court of Session 1994, r. 49.20, Act of Sederunt (Child Care and Maintenance) Rules 1997, r. 3.5(1)(b) and Children's Hearings (Scotland) Rules 1996, r. 15(3)(b).

[20] In addition, "all interested parties" (which must, surely, include the child) must be "given an opportunity to participate in the proceedings and make their views known" in all child protection proceedings which might result in the child being removed from the parent against their will: UN Convention, Art. 9(2).

[21] Whether the fact that there is no provision made for paid legal representation for the child at children's hearings deprives the child of an *effective* opportunity to express views remains open to doubt. See further paras 15.30 –15.33.

[22] The First Division, in *White v. White*, 2001 S.L.T. 485, did not interpret the provision in Part I of the 1995 Act equivalent to s. 16(2) as creating any presumption. However, different considerations are relevant in public law cases and the conclusion in *White* is not, it is suggested, applicable here. See further, Norrie, writing at 5 S.L.P.Q. 2001.

rather than otherwise. This principle, first accepted by the Scottish courts in *T., Petitioner*[23] in relation to the European Convention, was applied to the UN Convention in *White v. White*.[24]

The Human Rights Act 1998

Thirdly, substantive rights to protection have been conferred on **8.6** children by the Human Rights Act 1998, which incorporates the European Convention on Human Rights into Scots domestic law. The European Convention, while by no means child-centred—and hardly even child-friendly[25]—does confer rights on "everyone" (which clearly includes children) and these rights, though enforceable only against the state,[26] require that the legal system has sufficient means of protecting children and others against infringements of their rights. So infringements of rights by private individuals can be challenged by the victim seeking better protection than the law actually gives.[27]

While the UN Convention does not have the direct effect that the European Convention now has, it does have effect on the interpretation of the latter. The UN Convention has been used by the European Court to flesh out some of the skeleton principles in the European Convention—it is particularly appropriate to do so since the latter says little on children and the UN Convention says, of course, a lot. Examples include *Costello-Roberts v. United Kingdom*[28] when the UN Convention was used to explain the European

---

[23] 1997 S.L.T. 724.
[24] 2001 S.L.T. 485 especially *per* Lord McCluskey at p. 494F.
[25] "The nadir of the jurisprudence of the European Court of Human Rights" (in the words of Van Beuren, "Protecting Children's Rights in Europe" (1996) E.H.R.L.R. 171 at n. 33) is the case of *Nielsen v. Denmark* (1989) 11 E.H.R.R. 175 in which it was held that there was no breach of Art. 5 (right to liberty) when a mother had her 12-year-old child placed in a closed psychiatric ward on the basis of *her* assessment that he was neurotic since he persistently ran away from her to live with his father. Van Beuren points out that the judgment was delivered before the final draft of the UN Convention was adopted and suggests that that Convention would make it difficult for the Court to come to the same decision on the same facts today.
[26] The role of Art. 8 is "essentially that of protecting the individual against arbitrary interference by the public authorities in his private or family life": *Belgian Linguistics Case* (1979) 1 E.H.R.R. 252 at p. 282.
[27] See, for example, *A. v. United Kingdom* (1998) 27 E.H.R.R. 611, in which a step-father had been acquitted by a criminal court for beating a step-child after pleading the defence of "reasonable chastisement". The European Court held that the state was in breach of Art. 3, which requires states to take measures designed to ensure that individuals within their jurisdiction are not subject to the sort of treatment prohibited by Art. 3 even when such treatment is administered by private individuals (para. 22). And in *Z. v. United Kingdom*, May 10, 2001, the European Court held that there had been a breach of Art. 3 when the state failed to enforce its protection mechanisms with sufficient vigour to protect children from suffering a catalogue of serious abuse at the hands of their parents.
[28] (1993) 19 E.H.R.R. 112 at para. 35.

Convention right to private life; *A. v. United Kingdom*[29] when Articles 19 and 37 of the UN Convention were cited as elaboration of the right to physical integrity (itself part of the right to private life); and *T. v. United Kingdom*[30] where the Court referred to both the Beijing Rules[31] and Article 40 of the UN Convention in assessing whether an 11-year-old child had suffered degrading treatment (contrary to Article 3) during his trial on a charge of murder.[32]

8.7   In relation to care and protection, the right at issue is the right to physical and moral integrity of the person, which is an aspect of both the right to private life found in Article 8 of the European Convention,[33] and the right to be free from torture and inhuman or degrading treatment or punishment, found in Article 3 thereof[34] (and in Article 37(a) of the UN Convention). Because it is likely that most challenges in the future will come through this route, it is appropriate to spend some little time further exploring the substantive provisions of the European Convention.

The Operation of the European Convention on Human Rights

8.8 Apart from cases involving challenges to the legality of physical chastisement of children,[35] the jurisprudence of the European Court

---

[29] (1998) 27 E.H.R.R. 611 at para. 22.

[30] December 16, 1999, especially para. 74.

[31] That is to say the United Nations Standard Minimum Rules for the Administration of Juvenile Justice, adopted by the UN General Assembly on November 29, 1985.

[32] See also *Nortier v. Netherlands* (1993) 17 E.H.R.R. 273, *per* Judge Morenilla (concurring) at para. 2 and *Olsson v. Sweden (No. 2)* (1994) 17 E.H.R.R. 134, *per* Judges Pettiti, Matscher and Russo (dissenting) at p. 192.

[33] *X. & Y. v. The Netherlands* (1985) 8 E.H.R.R. 235 at para. 22; *Costello-Roberts v. United Kingdom* (1993) 19 E.H.R.R. 112 at para. 36; *Stubbings v. United Kingdom* (1994) 23 E.H.R.R. 213 at para. 59. Kilkelly points out (*Children's Rights and the ECHR* at p. 172) that Art. 8 imposes a positive obligation on the state to have in place mechanisms for the protection of children from abuse, neglect and maltreatment. See also Connelly, "Problems of Interpretation of Article 8 of the E.C.H.R." (1986) 35 I.C.L.Q. 567 at pp. 572–575. At the very least, the domestic law requires to contain effective deterrences to behaviour that would amount to a breach of the right to private life: *Stubbings* at para. 64.

[34] *Costello-Roberts* (*supra*; Z.v. United Kingdom, May 10, 2001 and *A. v. United Kingdom* (1998) 27 E.H.R.R. 611. In the latter case the European Court recognised that "children and other vulnerable individuals, in particular, are entitled to State protection, in the form of effective deterrence" against serious breaches of personal integrity.

[35] See, for example, *Cambell & Cosans v. United Kingdom* (1982) 4 E.H.R.R. 293; *Costello-Roberts v. United Kingdom, supra*; *A. v. United Kingdom, supra*; *Z. v. United Kingdom,* May 10, 2001.

of Human Rights is almost devoid of cases brought by children.[36] Care and protection cases are nevertheless common, but these have mostly arisen through challenges by parents, on the basis that states' actions, taken to protect children, have amounted to an unlawful interference with the parents' right under Article 8 of the European Convention to respect for their private and family life.[37] So the focus of the European Court's jurisprudence has been on the parents' right to be free from state interference rather than on the child's right to be protected by the state from the parent.[38] The problem is that both rights are contained in the same article and the task for both the European Court and domestic courts is to strike an appropriate balance in circumstances in which the two collide. The key to the balance under the European Convention is the justification, open to states which seek to protect children by compromising the freedom of parents, set out in Article 8(2): interference by a public authority in a person's private or family life is permitted only when this is "in accordance with the law" and is "necessary in a democratic society" for the protection of the health or of the rights and freedoms of others. So a child's protection is guaranteed by a side-wind, as it were—by a qualification to the right of the parents to be free from state interference with their private and family life.

In Accordance with the Law

This requirement contains in itself two distinct elements. First, the **8.9** removal of the child must be in accordance with legal provisions

---

[36] An unusual exception is *Johnstone v. Ireland* (1986) 9 E.H.R.R. 203 where the status of illegitimacy was successfully challenged by the child as an infringement of the right to respect for family life, notwithstanding that the parents' challenge to their inability to marry (due to non-availability of divorce in Ireland) was unsucccessful. And in *Andersson v. Sweden* (1992) 14 E.H.R.R. 615 both the mother and the child complained about restrictions on contact. It is interesting to note that, while family life must, by definition, be a mutual and two-way relationship, this is one of the very few cases in which the same interference in family life has been complained about by both members of the relationship. In *Eriksson v. Sweden* (1989) 12 E.H.R.R. 183 the mother complained on her own and on her daughter's behalf. After assessing in detail the mother's complaint, the European Court held in two short paragraphs (paras 88–89) that the daughter's claim raised the same issues. This emphasis is revealing of the Court's perception of family life as an issue of great importance for parents and, but as an afterthought too, for children too.

[37] Other cases involving the upbringing of children have been claims by parents alleging infringements of their rights: see for example *Hoffman v. Austria* (1993) 17 E.H.R.R. 293 (breach of parent's religious freedom); *da Silva Mouta v. Portugal* (2001) Fam. L.R. 2 (unjustified discrimination against parent). On Art. 8 generally, see O'Donnell, "Protection of Family Life: Positive Approaches and the ECHR" (1995) 17 J. Soc. Wel. Fam. L. 261; Connelly, "Problems of Interpretation of Article 8 of the ECHR" (1986) 35 I.C.L.Q. 567.

[38] See Van Beuren "Protecting Children's Rights in Europe" (1996) E.H.R.L.R. 171.

which are set out in a clear and accessible manner. As the European Court of Human Rights said in *Andersson v. Sweden:*[39]

> "the expression 'in accordance with the law' within the meaning of article 8(2) requires first that the impugned measures should have a basis in domestic law. It also refers to the quality of the law in question, requiring that it be accessible to the persons concerned and formulated with sufficient precision to enable them—if need be, with appropriate advice—to foresee, to a degree that is reasonable in the circumstances, the consequences which a given action may entail."

The Court has, however, also warned that,

> "Experience shows that absolute precision is unattainable and the need to avoid excessive rigidity and to keep pace with changing circumstances means that many laws are inevitably couched in terms which, to a greater or lesser extent, are vague."[40]

8.10 Secondly, the rules of law governing state interference in family life must conform to the Rule of Law, that is to say the law itself must contain sufficient protections against arbitrary action by the state.[41] This aspect of Article 8 overlaps to some extent with the requirement under Article 6 that, in the application of state measures, both the child and the parent receive a fair hearing. In this context a fair hearing requires, amongst other things, that the parents be fully involved in the decision-making process, to the extent that they are able effectively to take part and contribute their own point of view: this is as much an aspect of fairness in Article 6 as of procedural protection that is implicit in Article 8.[42] But the Article 8 protection is in fact broader since it covers administrative as well as judicial and quasi-judicial actions.[43]

---

[39] (1992) 14 E.H.R.R. 615 at para. 75.

[40] *Sunday Times v. United Kingdom* (1980) 2 E.H.R.R. 245 at para. 49; *Olsson v. Sweden (No. 1)* (1988) 11 E.H.R.R. 259 at para. 61.

[41] *Olsson sup. cit.* at para. 61; *Johansen v. Norway* (1997) 23 E.H.R.R. 33 at paras 53–59.

[42] *W. v. United Kingdom* (1987) 10 E.H.R.R. 29 at para. 64; *McMichael v. United Kingdom* (1995) 20 E.H.R.R. 205 at para. 91. See further, *infra*, at para. 8.21

[43] It is broader in other senses too. Grandparents, for example, have no "rights" in relation to their grandchildren and so they cannot access Art. 6 in demanding a "fair trial" for the determination of their rights; they can, however, claim protection under Art. 8 since grandparents and grandchildren can have "family life" as there protected: *Marckx v. Belgium* (1980) 2 E.H.R.R. 330 at para. 45.

Necessary in a Democratic Society

In order for a court to determine whether a particular action by the **8.11**
state is permitted as being "necessary in a democratic society",[44]
and so justified under Article 8(2), the court must follow a two-
stage process: first, a legitimate goal to the action must be identified
and, secondly, the measures taken in pursuit of that goal must be
shown to be proportionate, that is to say the minimum necessary to
achieve the goal and no more (for any "more" would be an infringement of a right without a legitimate goal).[45] In child protection cases, the issue of a legitimate goal is seldom in doubt. Respect
for family life[46] can be interfered with by the state if this is necessary
for the protection of health or is necessary for the protection of the
rights and freedoms of others. Abuse and neglect compromise a
child's physical and emotional health; and every child has a right to
physical integrity (as part of their own right to respect for their
private life). So any interference with a parent's right to respect for
family life that is motivated by the aim of protecting the child from
the parent's harmful acts or neglect clearly satisfies the requirement
for a legitimate goal.[46a] Indeed, if the parents' acts or neglects
amount to treatment that will infringe the child's Article 3 right to
be free from inhuman or degrading treatments, then the state is not
only entitled but is duty bound to interfere with the parents' right to
family life. The real issue for the court in most cases, and the thrust
of the discussion below, is whether or not the interference is proportionate to the goal identified.

Scottish Provisions for the Care and Protection of Children

This section will look at the extent to which Scots law, and in **8.12**
particular the provisions of Part II of the Children (Scotland) Act
1995, provide the protection from abuse and neglect that children in
Scotland are entitled, from the sources mentioned above, to expect.

---

[44] It may be noted that this concept justifies interference with rights protected by the
ECHR in a number of articles other than Art. 8, such as freedom of thought,
conscience and religion (Art. 9), freedom of expression (Art. 10), and freedom of
assembly and association (Art. 11). It also appears as a qualification to the
freedom of association and peaceable assembly in Art. 15 of the UN Convention.

[45] As the European Court has often said, "The notion of necessity implies that the
interference must be proportionate to the legitimate aim pursued": *Reime v.
Sweden* (1992) 16 E.H.R.R. 155 at para. 69.

[46] It is to be noted that the European Convention is not the only international treaty
giving protection to the "family". Art. 16(3) of the Universal Declaration on
Human Rights 1948, for example, provides as follows: "The family is the natural
and fundamental group unit within society and is entitled to protection by society
and the state".

[46a] *Z. v. United Kingdom*, May 10, 2001.

The legal mechanisms for care and protection of children differ according to whether the protection necessary is, first, emergency, that is to say designed to deal with a risk of imminent harm and essentially short-term; secondly, temporary protection which is designed to last for substantially longer than a number of days but with which the ultimate aim is the reunification of the child with his or her family; and thirdly permanent protection which is characterised by the intent to break the parent-child relationship and which is typified by, but not limited to, the process of adoption.

Emergency, or Short-term, Protection

8.13 It sometimes happens that a child is at risk of imminent harm and that the state has to step in immediately in order to obviate that risk. The emergency nature of such circumstances justifies a departure from the strict procedural requirements appropriate when time is not of the essence, but does not ever justify permitting the state to act in an uncontrolled, arbitrary or pernicious fashion. The legitimacy of states' actions is to be tested by the normal requirements of human rights law, as applied to and modified by the child's immediate need for summary protection. The methods by which a child in Scotland is given emergency protection is either through the medium of a Child Protection Order (a "CPO"), granted by a sheriff,[47] or of a warrant, granted by a sheriff or a children's hearing.[48] In most cases in which a CPO is made or a warrant granted, the order will authorise the immediate removal of the child from the alleged source of danger. Such removal is in all cases *prima facie* an interference with private and family life and so requires to be justified in accordance with the principles in Article 8(2) of the European Convention. Similarly, the sheriff may, as an alternative to a CPO, grant an exclusion order requiring a named adult to remove himself from the child's home.[49] If the adult to be excluded is a member of the child's family (which will frequently, though not invariably, be the case) there is again an interference with private and family life which requires to be justified on the same basis as the interference constituted by the CPO. Whether it is the child who is removed (in terms of a CPO) or the adult (in terms of an exclusion order) there is an interference in both the parent's and the child's family life, which is necessarily complementary: the issue under the European Convention is therefore essentially the same, though in justifying the interference the concept of welfare may be treated differently.

8.14   The circumstances in which a CPO can be granted[50] necessarily

---

Children (Scotland) Act 1995, s. 57.
1995 Act, ss. 45, 63, 66, 69 (for hearings) and s. 67 (for sheriffs).
1995 Act, s. 76. For an example, see *Russell v. W.*, 1998 Fam. L.R. 25.
1995 Act, s. 57(1) and (2).

are described in the Act with some vagueness: the applicant must show that there exist "reasonable grounds to believe" that the child is suffering or is likely to suffer "significant harm".[51] However, given that there are numerous provisions designed to avoid the order being granted (or at least maintained) arbitrarily, it is likely that the legislation governing CPOs is, as a whole, consistent with the rule of law, as required by Article 8(2) of the European Convention. In making an assessment of whether there are reasonable grounds to believe that the child is suffering or is likely to suffer significant harm, the sheriff is not bound by the three overarching principles in section 16 of the 1995 Act[52] but he is bound by them in determining whether to make the CPO when there are found to be such grounds. More important as a protection against arbitrary decision-making are the detailed provisions for review of the CPO contained in sections 59 and 60. In every case the matter must be looked at afresh very shortly after the implementation of the order, *i.e.* after removal of the child.[53] On the second working day after implementation either a sheriff or a children's hearing must examine the case in order to determine whether the grounds upon which the CPO was granted still exist and, if so, whether it remains in the interests of the child to be kept away from home[54] and failure to hold such a hearing brings the order to an end. A second review is possible after that held by the children's hearing: two working days therafter a sheriff, if requested, must examine the same issues again.[55] These provisions are primarily designed to ensure that if circumstances in a volatile situation change rapidly, the system can respond equally rapidly, but they also, importantly, protect the system itself from arbitrary application.

The real issue with CPOs, as it is in all child protection cases, is **8.15** whether the interference is proportionate to the legitimate aim of protecting the child, or, alternatively, whether it goes too far. [55a] The interference is often summary removal of a child on (as yet) unproven allegations and, as such, the interference is severe. So the goal must be important—which it is—and the means must go no further than is necessary to achieve that goal. There are a number of

---

[51] 1995 Act, s. 57(1)(a).

[52] These principles are applicable to discretionary decisions on how to respond to certain proved circumstances and not to the essentially factual question of whether these circumstances have been proved to exist: see, in relation to the welfare principle, *S. v. Miller*, 2001 S.L.T. 531, *per* Lord Macfadyen at p. 567.

[53] s. 57(4) permits other actions than the removal of the child from home, but removal is far and away the most common action authorised by a CPO.

[54] 1995 Act, ss. 59(4) and 60(7).

[55] 1995 Act, s. 60(8)(b).

[55a] The interference with family life will be "in accordance with the law" if the statutory provisions are followed, and it is not necessarily *not* in accordance with the law if an error of judgement is made, for example in assessing the reality of the risk the child faces: see *T.P. and K.M. v. United Kingdom*, May 10, 2001.

protections within the terms of the 1995 Act which aim to ensure
that a child is removed from home under a CPO only in circumstances that satisfy this requirement and only if these circumstances
continue to satisfy this requirement. First, the concept of "necessity" is inherent in the granting of the order. As well as establishing that there are reasonable grounds to believe that the child is
or may be suffering significant harm, the applicant for the order
must also show to the satisfaction of the sheriff that "an order
under [section 57] is necessary to protect the child from such
harm".[56] "Necessity" here has a rather stricter meaning than it does
within the concept of "necessity within a democratic society" in
article 8 itself and it thus provides greater protection from disproportionate interference. Wilkinson and Norrie interpret "necessity" in section 57 as follows:

> "this condition will be fulfilled when the child protection order
> is shown to be either the only, or the most efficacious, or in the
> circumstances the most appropriate, means of protecting the
> child. Necessity must be interpreted in the light of a continuing
> risk to the child, for the whole point of the order is to give
> immediate protection to the child from risk. So even when
> significant harm has been unquestionably caused, a child
> protection order will not be necessary unless there is a like-
> lihood of the harm continuing or being repeated".[57]

8.16 Second, there is an obligation on the reporter to keep the situation
under constant review and, during the currency of the child protection order if the reporter comes to the view that the order is no
longer "necessary", whether as a result of a change in the circumstances of the case or because he or she has received further information relating to the case, he or she must notify the person who
implemented the order: that notification has the effect of bringing
the order to an end.[58]

8.17   Third, ensuring that the order lasts only the minimum length of
time necessary to achieve its goal—the immediate protection of a
child from a potential source of risk until such time as the reality of
the risk can be properly established—a children's hearing will be
held on the eighth working day after the CPO has been implemented.[59] At that point, (i) the CPO comes to an end, (ii)
grounds of referral (*i.e.* the justification for longer-term protection)
must be prepared and put to the child and his or her parents[60] and

---

[56] 1995 Act, s.57(1)(b).
[57] Wilkinson & Norrie, *Parent and Child* (2nd ed., 1999) at para. 20.29.
[58] 1995 Act, s. 60(3). See also, to similar effect when a child has been taken to a place
of safety on the 24-hour authorisation of a justice of the peace or a constable,
s.61(8).
[59] 1995 Act, s. 65(2).
[60] "Relevant persons" as defined in s. 93(1), to be exactly accurate.

(iii) further interim protection, if it is to involve the keeping of the child away from home, is within the hands of the hearing with their powers to grant warrants to keep the child at a place of safety.

Warrants

Warrants to keep the child at a place of safety are permitted in **8.18** various provisions of the 1995 Act, in different circumstances, justified by different criteria and subject to different time-limits.[61] All warrants have clearly specified purposes, whether to ensure that the child attends a hearing[62] or to ensure the child's safety until a dispositive decision can be made.[63] Whether to grant a warrant, under whichever provision, is a decision to which the three over-arching principles apply, and the decision is always appealable. So long as hearings are clear in their reasons why the warrant is being granted and why it is necessary then the granting of warrants is likely to be both in accordance with the law and proportionate to the needs of the child.

Temporary, or Medium Term, Protection

Temporary protection of children in Scotland, beyond that char- **8.19** acterised by the emergency provisions discussed above, is by and large in the hands of the children's hearing,[64] which has the power to make supervision requirements over children,[65] including those with conditions that the child live elsewhere than in his or her family home.[66] The local authority has a duty to give effect to any supervision requirement made by a children's hearing.[67] Super-vision requirements can last for up to a year, and they may be continued within the year for a further year,[68] on satisfaction of the welfare test set out in section 16(1) of the 1995 Act.[69] Any super-vision requirement, because it obliges the local authority (re-presenting the state) to become involved in a child's life, is an interference with both the child's and the parent's family life as

---

[61] For an overview, see Wilkinson & Norrie, *sup. cit.* at paras 20.06–20.19.
[62] 1995 Act, s. 45.
[63] 1995 Act, ss. 66 and 69.
[64] 1995 Act, ss. 39–75, 85.
[65] 1995 Act, s. 70.
[66] 1995 Act, s. 70(3)(a).
[67] 1995 Act, s. 71(1).
[68] 1995 Act, s. 73(9)(e).
[69] Not only does s. 16 apply to this decision, but s. 3(1) provides that "no child shall continue to be subject to a supervision requirement for any period longer than is necessary in the interests of promoting or safeguarding his welfare". This means that, regarding the child's welfare as paramount, a hearing may continue a supervision requirement only when to do so will promote or safeguard the child's welfare.

protected by Article 8(1) of the European Convention and as such it requires to be justified under Article 8(2) as being both "in accordance with the law" and "necessary in a democratic society", as discussed above. Given the power to direct and review local authority actions that is vested in the children's hearing, and the power to review the decisions of the hearing that is vested in the sheriff, there is little doubt that interference in family life through the medium of supervision requirements is "in accordance with the law".[70] The more contentious issue, to be discussed shortly, is whether the interference is "necessary in a democratic society".

The Place of Welfare

8.20 As a public authority,[71] children's hearings must interpret the provisions of the 1995 Act in a way that is consistent with the European Convention,[72] even if that involves giving a strained or unexpected meaning to the words. So, for example, while the welfare test in section 16(1), which governs all decisions of a children's hearing, is not in its terms worded to require the striking of a balance between the welfare of the child and the rights of the parents—or indeed the right of the child—it can, and probably now must, be interpreted to require such a balance. That the welfare of the child is the children's hearing's paramount consideration does not necessarily mean that it is the determining nor even less the sole consideration.[73] To hold the child's interests to be in all cases determining would be to disapply the balance of rights and interests that is the hallmark of the European Convention and, as O'Donnell points out,[74] would ignore the fact that a child's different interests are sometimes in conflict *inter se* (*e.g.* the right to protection, the right to privacy and the right to non-interference in his or her own family life). Rather, giving paramount consideration to the child's welfare must now be taken to mean that the child's welfare is always relevant and is the single most important factor informing the

---

[70] The proceedings in *Olsson v. Sweden (No. 1)* (1988) 11 E.H.R.R. 259 were held by the European Court at para. 62 to be "in accordance with the law" because "safeguards against arbitrary interference are provided by the fact that the exercise of nearly all the statutory powers is either entrusted to or is subject to review by the administrative courts at several levels."

[71] Human Rights Act 1998, s. 6.

[72] Human Rights Act 1998, s. 3.

[73] In a private law case, *J. v. C.* [1970] A.C. 668, the House of Lords held, it is to be admitted, that the statutory paramountcy of welfare did indeed mean that consideration "rules upon or determines the course to be followed" (*per* Lord MacDermott at 710). But the point being made here is that this is not the only possible interpretation of the word "paramount" and courts today are obliged to interpret that word in a manner that is consistent with international conventions ratified and incorporated since 1970.

[74] "Protecting Family Life: Positive Approaches and the ECHR" (1995) 17 J. Soc. Wel. Fam. L. 261 at pp. 270–271.

decision, but it is not necessarily decisive[75]. This interpretation might be perceived by some as rather diluting the significance that Scots law has traditionally given to the child's welfare, but that would be a misunderstanding. In fact, the Children (Scotland) Act 1995 is but the latest attempt by domestic law to strike an appropriate balance between the competing interests of children's welfare, parents' rights, parents' responsibilities, and children's rights. Parents' responsibilities and rights have never been ignored in regarding the welfare of the child as paramount. That this is so is clear from the fact that Scots law has never permitted the state-instigated removal of a child from his or her parents merely because, on balance, the child's interests would be better served by alternative carers.[76] Judicial statements emphasising welfare[77] obscure but do not subvert this point. To hold "paramount" to mean "decisive", thereby ignoring parents' interests, or at best in every case allowing these interests to be overridden, would in fact be inconsistent with the UN Convention on the Rights of the Child, which is quite deliberately worded in terms of the welfare of the child being *a* rather than *the* paramount consideration.[78]

Rights of Participation

Any temporary interference by the state in a child's life is legitimate **8.21** only if a real opportunity has been given to the child and the parents to participate in both the decision to interfere and the determination of the nature and extent of the interference. This is an important principle in both the UN Convention and the European Convention. Under Article 9(2) of the UN Convention "all interested parties" must be given an opportunity to participate in protective proceedings and make their views known, and Article 12 of course, applying more widely, requires the child to be given an opportunity to make his or her views known. Participation by family members in the decision-making process is, under the Eur-

---

[75] In *L. v. United Kingdom* [2000] 2 F.L.R. 322 the European Court held (at p. 332H) that the importance which was rightly attached to the welfare of the child must not prevent a parent from being able effectively to participate in the decision-making process concerning his or her child. Again we see here the court consciously balancing the child's welfare with other legitimate interests. Similarly in Australia, where the child's welfare is statutorily declared to be paramount, the Full Court of the Family Court of Australia interpreted this to mean that it was the most important, but not the only, consideration: *A. & A.: Relocation Approach* [2000] Fam. CA 751.

[76] The European Court holds the same: *Olsson v. Sweden* (1988) 11 E.H.R.R. 259 at para. 72.

[77] The notorious statement of Lord Justice-Clerk Ross in *Kennedy v. A.*, 1986 S.L.T. 358 to the effect that the requirements of natural justice must in certain cases yield to the best interests of the child always was wrong and is now patently so.

[78] UN Convention, Art. 3(1).

opean Convention, an aspect both of the right to a fair trial (Article 6) and a right to respect for family life (Article 8).[79] Scots law gives effect to these requirements for participation by giving the right, and imposing the duty, on the child and "relevant persons" to attend the children's hearing.[80] And the child's right to effective participation is, to some extent at least, protected by provisions which (i) permit the exclusion from hearings of persons who inhibit the child from speaking freely[81] and (ii) permit the child to be accompanied by a representative whose function is to assist the person represented in the discussion of the child's case.[82] In addition, local authorities before making any decision with respect to a child subject to a supervision requirement must, so far as is reasonably practicable, ascertain the views of the child, his or her parents, anyone else who has parental rights in relation to the child and any other person whose views the local authority considers relevant,[83] and have regard to those views, so far as practicable.[84] The phrase "any other person" in this provision must, as a minimum, be interpreted to include any person who can claim "family life" under Article 8 of the European Convention[85] and who can be an "interested party" under Article 9(2) of the UN Convention. "Relevant person", being more precisely defined, is less open to interpretative extension but, at least in relation to the right to attend children's hearings, the position of "family members" and "other interested persons" who fall outwith the definition is to some degree ameliorated by the hearing chairman's power to permit

---

[79] *W. v. United Kingdom* (1987) 10 E.H.R.R. 29 at para. 64; *McMichael v. United Kingdom* (1995) 20 E.H.R.R. 205 at para. 87; *T.P. and K.M. v. United Kingdom*, May 10, 2001 at para. 82. See also *Olsson v. Sweden (No. 1)* (1988) 11 E.H.R.R. 259 at para. 71. Admittedly, both *W.* and *McMichael* involved parents' rights and the European Court has not yet expressly extended participation rights to children. But it is not conceivable that they would deny such rights, particularly given the existence of Art. 12 of the UN Convention. In any case the European Convention sets out minimum standards only and as can be seen from the text above Scots law, by involving the child, already goes further than the jurisprudence of the European Court.
[80] Though relevant persons can be excluded from any part of a hearing in certain circumstances (1995 Act, s. 46(1)), the chairman must, if a relevant person has been excluded, explain to that person the substance of what happened during the exclusion.
[81] See s. 43(4) (journalists) and s. 46(1) (relevant persons and their representatives).
[82] Children's Hearings (Scotland) Rules 1996, r. 11(2).
[83] 1995 Act, s. 17(3). This duty extends to the decision *whether* an order over the child should be sought as well as to decisions as to how to implement orders already made.
[84] 1995 Act, s. 17(4).
[85] See, on that issue, Kilkelly, *The Child and the European Convention* (1999) at pp. 187–197.

other persons to attend the hearing:[86] it must always be remembered that, as public authorities, hearings are not permitted to
exercise their power in a way that is inconsistent with the European
Convention.

The Child's Right of Privacy

In the determination of a child's civil rights and obligations, he or **8.22**
she is entitled under Article 6 of the European Convention to a "fair
and public hearing" at which judgment is pronounced publicly. The
press and public may, however, be excluded in the interests of the
child or the protection of the child's private life.[87] Similarly, under
the UN Convention, children have a right to privacy[88] and, if alleged to have committed a criminal offence, are further entitled to
have their privacy fully respected at all stages of the proceedings.[89]
Children's hearings are conducted in private[90] and while the
chairman has a discretion to permit the attendance of people
without a right or duty to attend[91] the exercise of that discretion is
circumscribed by the obligation to take all reasonable steps to ensure that the number of persons present at any one time is kept to a
minimum.[92] Bona fide representatives of the press have a right to
attend children's hearings[93] though they may be excluded if this is
necessary in order to obtain the views of the child, or if the presence
of the press representative is causing the child significant distress.[94]
The right of the press to be present may well indicate that the
children's hearing system is, in itself, a public system since the
purpose of publicity is to exclude the dangers of secret trials: this is
achieved without calling in aid the exception to publicity based on
the interests of the child. The child's right to privacy is further
protected by section 44(1) of the Children (Scotland) Act 1995,
under which it is a criminal offence for any person to publish any
matter in respect of proceedings at a children's hearing which is
intended to, or is likely to, identify the child or the address or school
of the child. This prohibition extends throughout the United
Kingdom and is not limited to publicity in Scotland.[95] The court

---

[86] Children's Hearings (Scotland) Rules 1996, r. 13. This merely permits attendance
and does not sanction full participation which would include, for example, the
right to accept or deny grounds of referral, and title to appeal.
[87] European Convention, Art. 6(1).
[88] UN Convention, Art. 16(1).
[89] *ibid.* Art. 40(2)(b)(vii) (referred to by the European Court in *T. v. United Kingdom*,
December 16, 1999 at para. 74).
[90] 1995 Act, s. 43(1).
[91] *ibid.* and Children's Hearings (Scotland) Rules 1996, r. 13.
[92] 1995 Act, s. 43(2).
[93] 1995 Act, s. 43(3)(b).
[94] 1995 Act, s. 43(4).
[95] 1995 Act, s. 105(8).

may permit publication if it is "in the interests of justice" to do so:[96] this decision is governed by the welfare principle in section 16(1) and so it must be in the interests of justice to the child. There are few circumstances in which this will be so, except, for example, when a child wishes publicly to clear his or her name from an accusation of, say, criminality which has been found not established.

Supervision at Home

8.23 The justification for imposing a supervision requirement under which the child remains at home is that the child needs "protection, guidance, treatment or control".[97] The Scottish system is essentially welfarist in philosophy[98] though that very element of the system means that it is also paternalistic and interventionist. But in order that paternalism does not compromise the child's freedom unwarrantably, intervention is justified only when an improvement of the child's welfare is a realistic possibility. A theory of welfare does not justify a practice of paternalism if the reality is that the child's welfare is not and cannot be advanced. This is illustrated by a case from the European Court of Human Rights, *Bouamer v. Belgium*.[99] In this case, a child was accused of having committed offences and was placed in protective custody under legislation which permitted this for educational purposes. The Belgian state tried to justify the pre-trial detention of the child, which was *prima facie* contrary to Article 5 of the European Convention, on the basis of Article 5(1)(d) which permits detention of minors for the purposes of "educational supervision". However, the reality was that the custodial placements the boy was sent to did not, in fact, provide any education and for that reason there was held to be a breach of Article 5. The lesson from this case for the Scottish system is this: invoking the welfare mantra is not in itself sufficient justification for the interference in private and family life that every supervision requirement constitutes[1]—it is the reality of the situation and in particular the likelihood that the terms and conditions of the supervision requirement will indeed do some good for the child that justifies interference. So hearings must be convinced when they make or continue supervision requirements that some benefit will accrue in fact. This proposition, extracted from European Human Rights law, is little different from the no-order presumption in

---

[96] 1995 Act, s. 44(5).
[97] 1995 Act, s. 52(3). It is important to note that the justification for imposing a supervision requirement is not the existence of a ground of referral but the child's needs.
[98] See Lockyer & Stone, *Juvenile Justice in Scotland* (1998) at pp. 17–18.
[99] (1987) 11 E.H.R.R. 1.
[1]   Similarly, as the European Court put it, "good faith in implementing the care decision ... does not suffice to render a measure necessary in Convention terms": *Olsson v. Sweden (No. 1)* (1988) 11 E.H.R.R. 259 at para. 82.

section 16(2) of the 1995 Act which directly governs hearings' decisions in any case.

Supervision Outwith the Home

A supervision requirement under which the child is required to **8.24** reside outwith the family home is a far greater interference with private and family life than a requirement with no residential condition, and under the UN Convention on the Rights of the Child such a requirement can be justified only when separation of parent and child is necessary in the best interests of the child.[2] The fact that the child is removed from his or her home and accommodated by the local authority, whether in a foster placement or an institutional setting, does not affect the existence of either the parent's or the child's right to respect for his or her family life. "The mutual enjoyment by parent and child of each other's company constitutes a fundamental element of family life; furthermore the natural family relationship is not terminated by reason of the fact that the child is taken into public care".[3] Removing a child from home may well have a legitimate aim, but actions are proportionate to that aim only if they are directed towards the ultimate goal of reunification of the family. It follows that a child has a right to have the terms of the supervision requirement, and its implementation, structured in such a way as assumes—and indeed furthers the possibility of—the child's return home. The removal of the child should be seen only in terms of giving an opportunity to ameliorate the situation that has led to his or her being taken into public care in the first place. It is only in exceptional circumstances that the child's welfare will require permanent removal from home, and only in exceptional circumstances, therefore, that the terms of a supervision requirement—or the manner in which it is implemented—can legitimately be directed towards permanent removal.[4]

> "The Court considers that taking a child into care should normally be regarded as a temporary measure to be discontinued as soon as circumstances permit and that any measure of implementation of temporary care should be consistent with the ultimate aim of reuniting the natural parent and the child ... [Permanent deprivation] should only be ap-

---

[2] UN Convention, Art. 9(1).

[3] *Olsson v. Sweden* (1988) 11 E.H.R.R. 259 at para. 59; *Reime v. Sweden* (1992) 16 E.H.R.R. 155 at para. 54; *Andersson v. Sweden* (1992) 14 E.H.R.R. 615 at para. 72 and *Eriksson v. Sweden* (1989) 12 E.H.R.R. 183 at para. 58.

[4] In *K. & T. v. Finland* [2000] 2 F.L.R. 79 the European Court held that there was a breach of Art. 8 when the state had failed to consider reunification as a serious option after having removed a child at birth from a mother who had a history of mental illness. That history was a significant factor but could not be regarded as decisive of the question of the mother's future fitness.

plied in exceptional circumstances and could only be justified if they were motivated by an overriding requirement pertaining to the child's best interests".[5]

8.25 While family reunification should nearly always be the aim of child protection measures which involve removal of the child, this does not require that the child be returned immediately, or even quickly.[6] His or her return must, in the interests of the child, be planned and sensitively handled. This might sometimes require the keeping of the child away from the parent even after a positive decision of return has been made. So in *Olsson v. Sweden (No. 2)*[7] there was no breach of Article 8 when a court decided that public care of two children should be terminated but at the same time prohibited the parents from removing the children immediately. The parents had not co-operated with efforts to prepare them and the children for reunification. "What will be decisive", said the European Court, "is whether the national authorities have made such efforts to arrange the necessary preparations for reunion as can reasonably be demanded under the special circumstances of each case".[8] There was, however, an infringement on the basis that the prohibition on the parents' removal of the children had no basis in law. It is interesting to compare this case with *L, Petitioners (No. 2)*[9] where the Inner House of the Court of Session, by exercise of the *nobile officium*, permitted a rehearing of grounds of referral when statute did not. When the grounds were subsequently found to be not established, the children were nevertheless kept in care since it would be contrary to their interests to return them to their parents immediately without preparation, given the length of time they had been separated. While few would deny that this was in the best interests of the children, the whole procedure suffered the same flaw as in *Olsson* by being not in accordance with the law: that flaw has since been remedied by section 85 of the Children (Scotland) Act 1995 which puts the process on a statutory footing and legislatively permits the child to be retained in care until preparations for return have been properly carried out. A parent who refuses to co-operate with such preparations could not complain of an infringement of their right since the provision is legitimately designed to protect children's interests rather than parents' rights.[10]

---

[5] *Johanssen v. Norway* (1997) 23 E.H.R.R. 33, at para. 78.
[6] "It is justified not to terminate public care unless the improvement in the circumstances that occasioned it appears with reasonable certainty to be stable; it would clearly be contrary to the interests of the child concerned to be restored to his parents only to be taken into care again shortly afterwards": *Olsson v. Sweden (No. 1)* (1988) 11 E.H.R.R. 259 at para. 76.
[7] (1992) 17 E.H.R.R. 134.
[8] *ibid.* at para. 90.
[9] 1993 S.L.T. 1342.
[10] See *Olsson* at para. 91.

Rights of Contact

It follows from the strong supposition that family reunification is **8.26**
the ultimate aim of child protection that local authorities have an
obligation to assist in the maintenance of family life to such extent
as is consistent with the protective purposes of the child's removal
from home. One practical consequence of this is that, if a child is
separated from his or her family in terms of a supervision requirement, contact between them should nearly always be permitted. Not only has the European Court held this on numerous
occasions but it is expressly stated in Article 9(3) of the UN Convention: "States parties shall respect the right of the child who is
separated from one or both parents to maintain personal relations
and *direct* contact with both parents on a regular basis, except if it is
contrary to the child's best interests".[11] Of course it may well be
inconsistent with the child's welfare to permit contact on particular
occasions, and "the parent cannot be entitled under Article 8 of the
[European] Convention to have such measures taken as would harm
the child's health and development",[12] but permanent termination
of contact is appropriate only when the child's welfare requires a
permanent destruction of the parent-child relationship. Given the
possibility of other protective mechanisms such as supervised contact it will seldom be necessary, in the sense of proportionate to the
child's needs, to prohibit contact completely.

Scots law contains two quite separate provisions which, taken **8.27**
together, create, at the very least, a strong supposition that contact
between the child and his or her parents is to be maintained. First,
children's hearings, whenever they make (or continue) a supervision
requirement, must consider the issue of contact and must include it
as part of the terms of a supervision requirement whenever the
welfare of the child so requires.[13] The minimum intervention
principle, together with the need for the terms of the supervision
requirement to be not inconsistent with the ultimate aim of re-
uniting the family, means that there is a fairly heavy presumption
against limiting the contact that the child is to have with his or her
family, and an exceptionally heavy presumption against the supervision requirement containing a term which prohibits contact
completely.[14] Hearings which do not apply these presumptions run
the risk of leaving their decisions vulnerable to appeal.

---

[11] Emphasis added.
[12] *Johanssen v. Norway* (1997) 23 E.H.R.R. 33 at para. 78.
[13] 1995 Act, s. 70(2). In its terms, this requires the hearing to consider contact
whenever a supervision requirement is made (or continued) and not just in cases
in which the requirement involves the child living away from home. But the
matter is of particular significance in the latter case.
[14] It is because decisions might, in practice though not in law, be irreversible that
there is a greater call than usual for protection against arbitrary interferences with
family life: *W. v. United Kingdom* (1981) 10 E.H.R.R. 29 at para. 62.

8.28   The second provision in Scots domestic law in favour of contact is contained in section 17(1)(c) of the 1995 Act.[15] This imposes a duty on local authorities, who are statutorily charged with giving effect to supervision requirements, to "take steps to promote, on a regular basis, personal relations and direct contact between the child and any person with parental responsibilities in relation to him as appear to them, having regard to their duty [to safeguard and promote the child's welfare] both practicable and appropriate." This obliges local authorities, who inevitably have a certain discretion in the matter, to encourage contact and, *a fortiori*, not to place obstacles in the way of the exercise of the right (on the child's part) and responsibility (on the parent's part) of contact. In *Olsson v. Sweden*[16] the state was held to be in breach of Article 8 of the European Convention when the local authority had no court or other order limiting contact but nevertheless placed the child at such a distance from the family home that the parents could not practically exercise any right of contact. As the court put it, reminding us that the ultimate aim of child protection should nearly always be family reunification,

> "The ties between members of a family and the prospects of their successful reunification will perforce be weakened if impediments are placed in the way of their having easy and regular access to each other".[17]

8.29 Interestingly, while the obligation on children's hearings to consider contact extends to that between the child and "any specified person or class of persons", the local authority's obligation is to encourage contact only between the child and "relevant persons". However, both children's hearings and local authorities are obliged under the terms of the Human Rights Act 1998 to interpret their statutory duties in such a way as is consistent with the European Convention, and so the hearing must consider contact in relation to the preservation of "family life" as understood in the jurisprudence of the European Court while the local authority must interpret the definition of "relevant person" (which includes persons with parental responsibilities and parental rights, and persons who ordinarily have charge of or control over the child[18]) in the same way. In order to keep the 1995 Act consistent with the European Convention the latter words in the definition may well require to be interpreted to include any person who has "family life" under Article 8 of the

---

[15] Applicable in respect of children "looked after" by the local authority, which all children subject to a supervision requirement are: 1995 Act, s. 17(6).

[16] (1988) 11 E.H.R.R. 259.

[17] *ibid.* at para. 81.

[18] 1995 Act, s. 93(2).

European Convention.[19] For it is a consequence of the right of family life recognised there that the members of the family have a right of contact with each other.

Deprivation of Liberty

It sometimes happens that the child is not only required to live away **8.30** from home but is required to submit to a deprivation of liberty. This can occur in Scotland with children who the law is trying to protect from neglect and abuse as readily as with children who have offended, because it is not the reason for the state intervention that justifies the deprivation of liberty but rather the need to prevent further harm. The criteria for requiring a child to reside in secure accommodation are set out in section 70(1) of the 1995 Act.[20] While *prima facie* this might be an infringement of the right to liberty recognised by Article 5(1) of the European Convention it will be justified under Article 5(1)(d) for the purposes of "educational supervision" if, but only if, as explained above, the reality of the detention does indeed provide education.[21] The UN Convention requires that no child shall be deprived of his or her liberty "unlawfully or arbitrarily":[22] "unlawfully" in the United Kingdom must now be taken to include "in a manner that is inconsistent with the European Convention". And it is here that one of the most significant shortcomings in Scots law can be identified. The right to a fair trial in Article 6 of the European Convention requires that decisions about a person's civil rights and obligations, such as their right to personal liberty, be taken by an independent and impartial tribunal. There is little doubt that a children's hearing is an independent and impartial tribunal[23]—but in relation to secure accommodation the hearing does not make the decision. The hearing merely authorises the child to be kept in secure accommodation,[24] while the actual (and unappealable) decision is taken by the person in charge of the establishment with the agreement of the chief social work officer of the relevant local authority.[25] The lack of a "tri-

---

[19] s. 3 of the Human Rights Act 1998 states that legislation must be interpreted consistently with the European Convention where it is possible to do so. The primary test for statutory interpretation is no longer, as it used to be, parliamentary intent, but consistency with the European Convention.
[20] The child must (a) have previously absconded, is likely to abscond again and is likely thereby to place his or her own physical, mental or moral welfare at risk, or (b) be likely to injure him or herself or some other person.
[21] *Bouamar v. Belgium* (1988) 11 E.H.R.R. 1.
[22] UN Convention, Art. 37(b).
[23] See Norrie *S. v. Miller*, 2001 S.L.T. 531, *per* Lord President Roger at p. 5415.
[24] 1995 Act, s. 70(9).
[25] *ibid.* This position was criticised by Sheriff Duncan at a Fatal Accident Inquiry in Glasgow, December 20, 2000, when a vulnerable young girl was not given secure accommodation notwithstanding the children's hearing's strong recommendation to that effect and, eight days later, she died in drugs-related circumstances.

bunal" making this most important of decisions is a glaring flaw in our system and is clearly a breach of Article 6[26] of the European Convention and, thereby, of Article 37(b) of the UN Convention.

Permanent Protection

8.31 The parent-child relationship can be permanently broken in legal terms only by the making of an adoption order, which has the effect of terminating one parent-child relationship and putting another one in its place.[27] This matter is explored more fully in Chapter 9.

8.32   But adoption is not the only method of permanent interference with family life. A child may be removed from his or her family environment and kept away until he or she is no longer a child: in other words, the provisions relating to temporary protection might, in fact though not in law, amount to permanency. This would be legitimate only if there were a continuing need throughout the person's childhood to keep him or her separate from his or her parents and when that application of the law were a proportionate response to that need. The only other method of permanent removal in Scots law is the making by a sheriff of a parental responsibilities order (a PRO), which has the effect of transferring parental responsibilities and parental rights (*i.e.* the power to bring up the child) from the parent to the local authority.[28] The parent is left with nothing, except the right to consent or refuse consent to the making of an adoption order.[29] This is the most extreme form of

---

[26] In *Bentham v. The Netherlands* (1985) 8 E.H.R.R. 1 the European Court said, at para. 40, "the power of decision is inherent in the very notion of "tribunal' within the meaning of the Convention". See further, K. Norrie, "Human Rights Challenges to the Children's Hearing System" (2000) 45 J.L.S.S. 19.

[27] A similar order is a parental order under s. 30 of the Human Fertilisation and Embryology Act 1990. Since this is available only with the consent of those who, without the order, are the child's parents the making of the order will not amount to an infringement of their right to respect for family life. *Quaere* whether the parents' consent, together with the conferral of parenthood on a couple at least one of whom must be the child's genetic parent, would in all cases obviate any infringement of the child's Art. 8 right to family life. That question might more aptly arise in the context of the child's right to identity, as recognised by Arts 7 and 8 of the UN Convention: see paras 5.8–5.12.

[28] Children (Scotland) Act 1995, s. 86. Under s. 86(5) it is competent for a sheriff to discharge the order on the application of the local authority, the child or the parent but in practice such orders are sought only when the intent is that the local authority takes over the parenting role on a long-term and probably permanent basis. Such orders are often a prelude to adoption.

[29] ibid., s. 86(3). This does not, however, mean to say that the parent has no right to family life: *W. v. United Kingdom* (1987) 10 E.H.R.R. 29 at para. 77.

interference with family life short of adoption and so is justified as being necessary in a democratic society only in exceptional circumstances. If the parent agrees to the making of the order[30] then the parent's right of family life can scarcely be said to have been interfered with—though that conclusion is not inevitable in relation to the child's right. [30a] If the parent does not agree, then the making of the PRO must not be such as is disproportionate to the legitimate goal of protecting the child. The grounds upon which the order can be made without the parent's consent are listed in section 86(2)(b) and are the same as those for dispensing with parental consent to adoption.[31] It is a peculiarity of section 86 that nowhere in its terms is there set out any test for the making of the order, other than that the order may be made if the parent consents or there is a ground for dispensing with parental consent. The only tests to be satisifed are the welfare test and the minimum intervention principle, but these are usually (and this is always so elsewhere in the 1995 Act) guidance for the court in exercising a discretion whether to grant an order once conditions-precedent for the granting of the order have been satisfied. There are no conditions precedent for the making of PROs and the welfare test, even taken with the minimum intervention principle, is entirely inadequate to describe when the court can—as opposed to when it should—grant the order.[32] For example, we cannot interpret the law as permitting a PRO to be made whenever the welfare of the child would be better served by making an order: this in no way takes account of the right of the parent (or indeed the right of the child) to maintain a family life with the child (or the parent).[33] To what extent, therefore, can any order made under section 86 be said to be "in accordance with the law", if that phrase means a law with such quality as to be "accessible to the persons concerned and formulated with sufficient precision to enable them—if need be, with appropriate advice—to foresee, to a degree that is reasonable in the circumstances, the consequence

---

[30] *ibid.* s. 86(2)(a).

[30a] See the interesting case of *City of Edinburgh Council v. H.*, 2001 S.L.T. (Sh.Ct) 51, where a mother did not oppose the making of a P.R.O., but the child, then aged ten-and-a-half, entered the process as a party minuter and did, strongly, oppose the order, The sheriff held that in such circumstances, it was not in the interests of the child.

[31] *i.e.* that the parent (i) is not known, cannot be found or is incapable of giving agreement, (ii) is withholding consent unreasonably, (iii) has persistently failed to fulfil parental responsibilities and (iv) has seriously ill-treated the child whose reintegration into the family is unlikely.

[32] See *H. v. Belgium* (1987) 10 E.H.R.R. 339 where, in a quite different context, a statutory provision allowing a certain decision to be made "in exceptional circumstances" was held to be entirely insufficient to allow parties to know whether the decision was likely.

[33] The European Court has long held that the state may not remove a child from a parent *merely* because the child's welfare would be better served with alternative carers: see n. 76 above.

which a given action may entail"?[34] It is tempting to find the conditions-precedent in the stated grounds for making the order in the absence of parental agreement, but while this might be satisfactory with some it is not with others. It would, for example, be a sufficiently precise ground to make a PRO that the parent has "seriously ill-treated the child, whose reintegration into the same household as that person is, because of the serious ill-treatment or for other reasons, unlikely".[35] But the same cannot be said from the mere fact that the parent is incapable of consenting to the making of a PRO:[36] that tells us nothing about the parent's capacity to bring up the child appropriately or the likelihood of the parent being able to resume care, or the child's need for the order to be made. The *quality* of the law in relation to PROs is therefore open to serious doubt. However, that is not to say that the application of the law cannot be defended. Children have a right to have a responsible person—or body— who will exercise upbringing functions in a way that safeguards and promotes their welfare. If it can be shown that their parents either do not or cannot exercise their responsibilities in this way then the children's right to be protected, and the local authority's duty to protect, may well be enough to justify the making of a PRO. But the permanency usually implicit in a PRO must reflect permanency in the parent's unwillingness or incapacity. Sheriffs must therefore be very clear as to their reasons for making such an order, specifying why it is necessary and how it is not going further than is needed to achieve its goal.

8.33   Once a PRO is made, there are some provisions in the Children (Scotland) Act 1995 that protect the existence of family life. For one thing, it is permitted for the local authority to allow the child to reside with the parent, where it appears to the authority that so to allow would be for the benefit of the child.[37] The interference with family life in this (admittedly unusual) situation is obviously far less than when the child is kept away from home, but since upbringing powers remain vested in the local authority, who can call for the return of the child to them at any time,[38] the interference is still significant and requires to be justified. Family life receives further protection under section 88, in terms of which the local authority must allow the child contact with any person who before the PRO was made had parental responsibilities.[39] The structure of this provision is significant, in that it is expressed in terms of an ob-

---

[34]   *Andersson v. Sweden* (1992) 14 E.H.R.R. 615 at para.75.
[35]   The ground under s. 86(2)(b)(iv).
[36]   The ground under s. 86(2)(b)(i).
[37]   1995 Act, s. 87(2).
[38]   1995 Act, s. 87(3).
[39]   1995 Act, s. 88(2). The sheriff may make such order as he thinks appropriate as to contact: s. 88(3).

ligation to allow the child contact rather than in terms of a parent's right to contact. As always there is a strong presumption in favour of contact, not only from the terms of the Act but from the requirements of the European Convention to maintain family life even when the child and parent are separated, and even when that separation is designed to be long-term or even permanent.

Conclusion

Children have a right to be protected even from their parents. The **8.34** state, therefore, has a duty to provide that protection. The welfare of the child, though a powerful and predominant consideration, is not the only consideration that the state must take into account in determining whether and how to exercise that paternalistic duty. The traditional approach to welfare, where different options are balanced in order to determine what is better, often marginally so, from the child's perspective is no longer sufficient. The law, particularly through the Human Rights Act 1998, now recognises that parents have a right to bring up their children in a manner which, from an objective rationalist point of view, is less of an ideal than another alternative; and indeed that children have a right to remain within the comfort of familiarity, though inadequate, rather than being removed to the alien environment that even the best foster care is often perceived by the child as being. The balancing task, inherent in applying the welfare test, is not new to Scottish courts, though the balance is no longer exclusively within the welfare test, but may now be between welfare factors and other considerations outwith, and sometimes placed in opposite to, welfare. There are few statutory provisions in the Scottish system of child protection that are a direct infringement of the European Convention, though there are some. Our legislature has made a conscious effort to be consistent with the UN Convention. But the system as a whole includes its operation as well as its statutory aspirations. The obligation remains on local authorities, children's hearings and the courts to ensure that in exercising their discretion in the application of the Scottish child protection provisions an appropriate balance is indeed struck between a child's indirect right to protection and his or her direct right to respect for private and family life.

CHAPTER 9

ADOPTION

JANYS M. SCOTT

The Nature of Adoption

Adoption gives a child a new legal identity. An adopted child ceases **9.1**
to be the child of the parents to whom that child was born and
becomes, in the eyes of the law, the child of the adopter or adopters.[1] Under the United Nations Convention on the Rights of the
Child (the "UN Convention"), a child has the right to respect for
his or her identity, including nationality, name and family relations.[2] Given that adoption takes away a child's original identity, it
should be an option only when there are cogent reasons why a child
cannot retain his or her original identity.

Not only does adoption cut across the child's right to his or her **9.2**
original identity, it also strikes at the heart of the child's right to be
cared for by his or her birth parents[3] and not to be separated from
them.[4] Following adoption, the parental responsibilities and rights
of a child's birth parent are extinguished and such responsibilities
and rights are vested in the adopters.[5] The child ceases to be a
member of the family of the birth parents and becomes a member of
the adoptive family. This is a radical change in family life and, as
such, constitutes an interference with the rights of birth parents and
child in terms of Article 8 of the European Convention on Human
Rights and Fundamental Freedoms (the "European Convention").
The right to respect for family life is not, however, absolute. There
are circumstances in which adoption may be justified.

Adoption in Scotland has changed over the last 40 years. **9.3**
Adoption in the mid-twentieth century was perceived as a solution
to the dilemma of unwanted parenthood on the part of birth parents and the infertility of persons who would like a baby. Contra-
ception and the acceptance of single parenthood leaves fewer babies

---

[1] Adoption (Scotland) Act 1978 (hereinafter "the 1978 Act"), s. 39.
[2] Art. 8
[3] UN Convention, Art. 7
[4] UN Convention, Art. 9
[5] 1978 Act, s. 12(1) and (3).

available for adoption. The trend towards children growing up with their birth parent or parents accords with the UN Convention. Indeed that Convention reinforces the trend by stating the obligation of the State to help birth parents meet their child-rearing responsibilities.[6] No child should be parted from parents unless necessary in his or her best interests.

9.4   The UN Convention regards separation as justifiable in cases where there has been abuse or neglect by the parents.[7] A child who cannot in his or her own best interests remain in his or her family environment is entitled under the Convention to special protection and assistance provided by the State. There should be alternative care available for such a child and one alternative form of care is adoption.[8] Again, this accords with current trends in Scotland where adoption is increasingly regarded as part of a range of care services for children.[9] The trend is confirmed by the rising age of children being adopted. By 1999, only 13 per cent of the children adopted were under two years old.[10]

9.5   As domestic adoption of very young children has declined, persons wishing to adopt babies have looked further afield. In the last decade of the twentieth century there were growing number of children brought into the United Kingdom for adoption. Most are of a different ethnic origin to the persons proposing to adopt. The trend seems likely to continue.

9.6   The last few years of the twentieth century have also seen other trends in adoption. Some adults adopted as children have sought out their original birth families. Research has suggested that children who know their birth families settle better into adoptive homes if they retain limited contact with their original family throughout childhood and adolescence.[11] The severance of all contact is no longer seen as a necessary concomitant of adoption.

9.7   These are, however, social trends. The structure of adoption law has remained largely unchanged from the days where most adoptions, other than by relatives, were baby adoptions. If a parent is determined to give up a child for adoption then there is no shortage of persons willing to adopt the child. These potential adopters are very likely to provide the child with a loving and secure home. The birth parent will consent to adoption and the child's identity will be changed. There is a level at which this does not accord with the child's rights under the UN Convention to retain his or her identity and not to be separated from birth parents, but by the time a court comes to consider the matter the child will probably be happily settled with the prospective adopters and it will not be in the child's

---

[6]   Art. 18
[7]   Art. 9
[8]   Art. 20
[9]   See *The Future of Adoption Law in Scotland* (Scottish Office, June 1993).
[10] Registrar General for Scotland *Annual Report 1999*, section 9.
[11] See also paras 5.1 and 5.14.

interests to disturb the arrangement.

The primary view of adoption under the UN Convention re- **9.8** mains, however, as a means of providing care for children who are unable in their own best interests to reside with their families of birth. It is a solution to be considered alongside foster care or care in an institution, having due regard to the desirability of continuity in the child's upbringing and to the child's ethnic, religious, cultural and linguistic background.[12] When children are separated from their families because they are in need of care and protection, then adoption designates the separation as permanent.[13]

Placement of Children for Adoption

The placement of children for adoption is subject to control. No **9.9** private person may place a child for adoption (save with a relative), nor may any body of persons other than an adoption agency make arrangements for a child to be placed for adoption.[14] Adoption agencies are local authorities and adoption societies which are approved by the Secretary of State.[15] Regulations govern the way that adoption agencies operate.[16] An agency is obliged to establish a panel to consider the case of each child and to make a recommendation as to whether adoption is in the best interests of the child. The panel also considers whether prospective adopters are suitable to be adoptive parents, and whether particular adopters are suitable to adopt particular children. The adoption agency considers the recommendations of the panel before placing the child for adoption. The framework is in place for careful scrutiny of adoption placements made in Scotland. There is however scope for express recognition of the rights of the child under the UN Convention within the regulations to reinforce respect for such rights.

An adoption agency reaching a decision relating to adoption of a **9.10** child is obliged to have regard to all the circumstances, giving paramount consideration to the need to safeguard and promote the welfare of the child throughout life.[17] The child's welfare thus predominates over all other considerations. Before the Children (Scotland) Act 1995, the welfare of the child was merely the "first" consideration, and could potentially be outweighed by a combination of other important factors. Under the UN Convention the best

---

[12] Art. 20

[13] For a detailed account of the law relating to adoption in Scotland, see P.G.B. McNeill Q.C., *Adoption of Children in Scotland* (3rd ed., 1998, W. Green).

[14] 1978 Act, s. 11.

[15] 1978 Act, ss. 1 and 3.

[16] Adoption Agencies (Scotland) Regulations 1996 (S.I. 1996 No. 3266) (hereinafter "the 1996 Regulations").

[17] 1978 Act, s. 6.

interests of the child are usually *a* primary consideration,[18] but, when the Convention deals with adoption, the best interests of the child become *the* paramount consideration.[19] The change introduced by the Children (Scotland) Act 1995 recognised the United Kingdom's obligations under the Convention and was a welcome recognition of the implications of adoption for the child.

9.11   It remains to be seen whether the emphasis in the UN Convention on the welfare of the child will survive the impact of the Human Rights Act 1998. The Adoption (Scotland) Act 1978 must now be read and given effect in a way which is compatible with European Convention[20] and, in the event that any statutory provision does not comply, the Court of Session or House of Lords may make a declaration of incompatibility.[21] Public authorities cannot lawfully act in a way which is incompatible with rights under the European Convention.[22] Local authorities acting as adoption agencies are undoubtedly public authorities, and adoption societies approved by the Secretary of State are public authorities in so far as they exercise functions of a public nature. Adoption agencies must have regard to the European Convention, and to the extent that there is conflict between the European Convention and the UN Convention, the former now has the effect conferred by the Human Rights Act 1998, whereas the latter is merely an aid to interpretation, on the assumption that the Scottish or Westminster Parliament may be assumed to have intended to comply with the ratification of the Convention.[23]

9.12   Article 8 of the European Convention permits interference with family life which is "in accordance with the law and is necessary in a democratic society..." The European Court of Human Rights has attached particular importance to the best interests of the child, and has recognised that there "may" override those of the parent. A parent is not entitled to insist on measures which would harm a child's health and development. However, the Court has only been prepared to endorse measures, such as adoption, which deprive a parent of family life with the child in exceptional circumstances, where justified by an overriding requirement pertaining to the child's best interests.[24]

9.13   Limiting potential adoption, as the European Court has, may not serve the welfare of children. In a strongly-worded dissenting judgment in an adoption case, one member of the European Court remarked, "Saying, as the majority did, that the child's adoption

[18] Art. 3.
[19] Art. 21.
[20] 1998 Act, s. 3.
[21] 1998 Act, s. 4.
[22] 1998 Act, s. 6.
[23] The Scotland Act 1998, s. 29(2)(d) prevents the Scottish Parliament from passing legislation which conflicts with the European Convention on Human Rights.
[24] *Johansen v. Norway* (1996) 23 E.H.H.R. 33.

was wrong is tantamount to saying that this particular child did not ... deserve a normal family life. The Court does not dispute that adoption is the next best thing to a family life with a natural parent. The conclusion that the majority underwrote was, in substance, that since the applicant's daughter could not have the best (the mother had manifestly failed to provide that), she was not entitled to the next best either. It seems that the mother's ability to wreck all the child's chances in life had to be total. In the Court's view, the fact that she was unable to give her child happiness conferred on her the right to ensure that no one else should." [25]

Where, however, a parent is given the opportunity to participate **9.14** in and influence the process of decision-making, the Court has been willing to intervene. In *Scott v. United Kingdom* [26] the Court refused to entertain a complaint by a mother with a history of alcoholism, who had been given the opportunity to show she could resume care of her child, but had failed. Proceedings to free the child for adoption were neither flawed nor premature. They were proportionate to the aim of protecting the child and therefore "necessary in a democratic society". The Court has also been prepared to endorse adoption where a child has in effect become a member of a new family. An adoption order may then confer benefits on the child which outweigh and potential advantages of retaining formal links with a birth parent.[27] If adoption is to remain an available solution to children's difficulties, adoption agencies must be aware of the new context of respect for the rights of parents. Parents must have a fair opportunity to care for children and should be involved in the process of making decisions, which should balance carefully the rights of all concerned.

The extreme implications of adoption for a child's identity and **9.15** family relationships are further recognised by the introduction in the 1995 Act of a new duty for adoption agencies under section 6A of the 1978 Act. The agency must, before making any arrangements for the adoption of a child, consider whether there is some better practicable alternative to adoption. It should not make arrangements for adoption where such an alternative exists.

Article 21 of the UN Convention provides that parents give in- **9.16** formed consent to the adoption of the child, on the basis of such counselling as may be necessary. Where children are placed for adoption by an adoption agency, parents should be supplied with written information about adoption.[28] There is, however, no obligation under the regulations to provide counselling. Local authorities are obliged to provide counselling services for persons with problems relating to adoption. [29] The Children (Scotland) Act

---

[25] *E.P. v. Italy* (November 16, 1999) *per* Judge Bonello.
[26] 2000 Fam. L.R. 102
[27] *Soderback v. Sweden,* 1999 Fam. L.R. 104.
[28] 1996 Regulations, reg. 14.

1995 was a missed opportunity to address in primary legislation the UN Convention emphasis on counselling for persons considering giving consent to adoption. There is a new express duty to counsel and assist adopted children and adopters. Counselling for other persons is required only if they have problems relating to adoption, rather than automatically provided at the point of considering consent.[30] The 1996 Regulations are similarly disappointing. They allow a parent to be dealt with at arms length, rather than coun- selled in relation to the sensitive and difficult issues raised by a potential adoption of his or her child.

9.17   By 1995, it was recognised that the placement for adoption was potentially the most significant step towards adoption. Once a placement had been made, children put down roots and parents had diminishing prospects of resisting adoption.[31] Prior to the 1995 Act, parents struggled to prevent placement taking place. In most cases, children were subject to supervision requirements made by the children's hearing and the hearing was responsible for deciding where the child should live. The struggles were therefore largely focused in proceedings relating to the child's supervision require- ment. It was said that the children's hearing should focus on the child's immediate future, and should not facilitate adoption.[32] The 1995 Act sought to address the issue in a number of ways. First, it gave the children's hearing an express role in relation to adoption. Where it is proposed to place a child for adoption, or to make an application to the court for a child to be declared free for adoption, or to petition the court for an adoption order, the children's hearing must be consulted.[33] The hearing considers the matter and reports to the court which ultimately comes to consider the issue of freeing or adoption. Second, the children's hearing is expressly required to consider the welfare of the child throughout childhood.[34] The hearing must, therefore, look beyond the immediate future when considering what is best for the child. The third way in which the 1995 Act changed the law was to allow regulations to make pro- vision for local authorities seeking to place a child with prospective adopters, against the wishes of birth parents, to apply to the court

---

[30] Children (Scotland) Act 1995 (hereinafter, "the 1995 Act") Sched. 2, para. 2, amending the 1978 Act, s. 1(2).
[31] See, *e.g. Re W.* (adoption: parental agreement) (1982) 3 F.L.R. 75; *Re R* (a minor (adoption (No.2)) [1987] F.C.R. 996; *Re H.* (infants) (adoption: parental consent) [1997] 2 All E.R. 339.
[32] See *A. v. Children's Hearing for Tayside Region*, 1987 SLT (Sh. Ct) 126; *M. v. Children's Hearing for Strathclyde Region*, 1988 S.C.L.R. 592; *D. v. Strathclyde Regional Council*, 1991 S.C.L.R. 185; *cf.* Adoption (Scotland) Act 1978 s. 65(3) (amended by Law Reform (Miscellaneous Provisions) (Scotland) Act 1985); *Kennedy v. M.*, 1995 S.L.T. 717.
[33] Children (Scotland) Act 1995, s. 73
[34] 1995 Act, s. 16(1).

for an order declaring the child free for adoption.[35] The intention behind this provision was to give an early opportunity for the issue of adoption to be brought before the court.

Freeing for Adoption

The procedure whereby children could be declared free for adoption **9.18** was originally conceived for the benefit of mothers who wished to surrender children for adoption, without waiting for the child to be placed in an adoptive family, and for an application to be made to the court for an adoption order.[36] Freeing was introduced on September 1, 1984 when section 18 of the 1978 Act came into force. It was welcomed by local authorities as an opportunity to seek the court's endorsement of the proposition that a child in care could not in his or her own interests be returned home, before the child was placed with prospective adopters.

This approach was reinforced by the changes introduced fol- **9.19** lowing the 1995 Act. The 1996 Regulations now require a local authority which determines that a child should be placed for adoption against the wishes of birth parents to make an application to the court for a freeing order, unless the child is already living with the prospective adopters and they have made an application for an adoption order.[37] The local authority is required to take action within strictly prescribed time limits, in order to ensure that the matter is placed before the court reasonably quickly. These limits cover the necessary referral to the children's hearing for a report on the question of adoption. The time limits were necessary as research had shown that there were extensive delays in bringing these matters before the court.[38]

The requirement to proceed by way of an application to free the **9.20** child for adoption may be theoretically sound. There is a clear procedure to consider whether the step of adoption is appropriate. The child's rights and those of the parents are reviewed at a relatively early stage. The early experience, in practice, is less encouraging. Research into the first few years of freeing showed delays in the court process.[39] Since the implementation of the 1995 Act, courts have been required to draw up timetables for procedure in disputed cases.[40] Experience of the requirement to timetable has

---

[35] 1978 Act, s. 9(3A)(a), and 1996 Regulations, regs 17 and 18.
[36] See Report of Houghton Committee (1972).
[37] 1996 Regulations, regs 17 and 18.
[38] L. Lambert *at al, Freeing Children for Adoption* (Scottish Office Central Research Unit, May 1989).
[39] *ibid.*
[40] 1978 Act. s. 25A; Child Care and Maintenance Rules 1997 2.4; Court of Session Rules 67.4A.

been mixed. Contested freeing cases frequently absorb a great deal of court time. There is no requirement for written pleadings. Evidence is often lengthy and diffuse. In practice, it is difficult for sheriff clerks to allocate scarce resources to these lengthy proceedings. Matters are not helped by delays in securing legal aid for parents.

9.21 Courts have wrestled with applications to free children for adoption partly because the process itself involves a child surrendering family ties with the birth family, before being assured of new relationships within an adoptive family. In the meantime, the local authority assume parental responsibilities and rights.[41] The child is entitled to respect for identity and family relations in terms of Article 8 of the UN Convention. Children and parents are entitled to respect for family life pursuant to Article 8 of the European Convention. Further, Article 21 of the UN Convention requires that parental consent to adoption is "informed". A parent whose child is subject to freeing will not have the reassurance of knowing that the child will be adopted into a particular family. Thus, there is justification for some ambivalence about freeing.

9.22 There are tensions between the modern movement towards contact after adoption and the process of freeing children for adoption.[42] A parent may not be unreasonable to take the view that the child requires some level of contact after adoption. If the child is declared free for adoption, then there is no means of assuring that contact will take place. A parent no longer has any locus to make an application for contact.[43] In contrast to an adoption order, the court cannot impose a condition of contact in a freeing order.[44] Sheriffs have in these circumstances refused to free children for adoption.[45] There is, however, a dilemma where a child's paramount requirement is for a family to which he or she can belong and in which to grow and develop. In such circumstances, Article 21 of the UN Convention may demand adoption. Refusal of freeing may deprive the child of the benefits of adoption which, in itself, may be a breach of human rights.[46] The issue of contact after adoption is not, in any event, a matter which should necessarily be regulated by court order. On one view, a birth parent with contact does not retain parental responsibilities or rights. Contact after adoption is a practical measure for the benefit of the child and is likely to vary over time. It may be best left in the control of the persons who are responsible for the child's welfare, namely the adoptive parents.[47] Where, however, the identity and attitude of the

---

[41] 1978 Act, s. 18(5)
[42] See also paras 5.1, 5.14 and 6.13.
[43] 1995 Act, s. 11.
[44] 1978 act, s. 12 (6); *B. v. C.*, 1996 S.L.T. 1370.
[45] *e.g. City of Edinburgh Council v. M.S.*, 2000 SCLR 605.
[46] *Barrett v. Enfield London Borough Council* [1993] 3 All E.R. 193.
[47] *F.B. and A.B., Petrs*, 1999 Fam. L.R. 2.

prospective adopters is unknown, then freeing may present a difficulty.

There is some limited but helpful mitigation of the finality of **9.23** separation of children from their birth families by freeing for adoption. The process is now more easily reversible in those cases where adoption cannot, in practice, be achieved. A parent who has made a declaration in the course of freeing proceedings that he or she prefers not to be involved in future questions concerning the adoption of the child may withdraw that declaration.[48] A parent who has made no declaration, or who has withdrawn a declaration, may apply for the freeing order to be revoked if the child has neither been adopted, nor placed for adoption. In appropriate cases an adoption agency will also be able to apply for revocation of an order declaring the child free for adoption. A court revoking a freeing order will be able to determine who will have parental responsibilities and rights on revocation.[49]

Step-parent Adoption

Over half of the adoptions in Scotland are adoptions by the step- **9.24** parent of a child.[50] The child in such an application will be living in a family with a parent and the spouse of that parent. No adoption agency will have been involved in the placement of the child.

Under the original adoption provisions, the child was adopted by **9.25** both the step-parent and the birth parent. The family no longer had access to the entry of the child's birth and a new certificate was issued from the Adopted Children Register. This caused unhappiness and confusion as the child remained related by birth to one parent but had no immediate certificate to show that this was the case. The Children (Scotland) Act 1995 amended the Adoption (Scotland) Act 1978 to allow a step-parent to adopt and to acquire parental responsibilities and rights together with the birth parent to whom he or she is married without the birth parent having to adopt as well.[51] The provision is helpful and recognises the right of the child to preserve identity as the recognised child of the birth parent in accordance with Article 8 of the UN Convention. The provisions would have been even more helpful had the provisions for registration of birth and adoption been amended.

The child will, however, lose his or her legal relationship with the **9.26** parent from whom there has been a separation. Article 9(3) of the UN Convention requires respect for the right of the child who is separated from one of his or her parents to maintain personal re-

---

[48] 1978 Act, s. 18(6); 1996 Act, Sched. 2, paras 12(a) and (d).
[49] 1978 Act, s. 20.
[50] Registrar General for Scotland, *Annual Report 1999*, section 9.1 and Table 9.2.
[51] 1978 Act, s.15(1)(aa) and s. 12(3A).

lations and direct contact with the separated parent on a regular basis, unless this is contrary to the child's best interests. The Convention therefore raises a question about the use of adoption to consolidate a step-family where the motive for adoption is to sever connections with the parent outside the new family. Step-parent adoption to this end is, however, already discouraged in Scots law.[52] Alternatives to adoption, such as an agreement whereby a step-parent may share responsibilities and rights with birth parents, are under discussion.[53]

Procedure in Applications for Adoption

9.27 Article 21 of the UN Convention requires adoption to be authorised only by competent authorities who determine, in accordance with applicable law and procedure and on the basis of all pertinent and reliable information, that adoption is permissible in view of the child's status concerning parents, relatives and legal guardians. In Scotland, adoption orders may be made only by the court. Both the sheriff court and the Court of Session have jurisdiction to make an adoption order.[54] Section 6 of the 1978 Act requires the court to have regard to all the circumstances, but to regard the need to safeguard and promote the welfare of the child throughout life as the paramount consideration. This conforms to article 21 of the UN Convention. Section 6, in its original form, provided that the need to safeguard and protect the welfare of the child throughout childhood was the first consideration for the court. Now, the child's welfare is the paramount consideration. Furthermore, the court is required to have regard to the child's welfare throughout life. A new restriction on adoption orders or orders declaring a child free for adoption will prevent the court making such an order unless it would be better for the child than if there were no such order.[55]

9.28 Under Article 12 of the UN Convention, adoption procedure should afford to a child capable of forming his or her own views the right to express those views freely. The child should have the opportunity to be heard either directly or through a representative. Adoption law does require that any adoption agency or court considering a question relating to the adoption of a child consider not only his or her welfare but also the child's views. Section 6 of the 1978 Act provided that the agency or court should, so far as practicable, ascertain the wishes and feelings of the child regarding the decision to be made and give due consideration to them, having

---

[52] *A. v. B*, 1987 S.L.T. (Sh.Ct) 121; *A. B and C.D v. E.F.*, 1991 G.W.D. 25-1420.
[53] *Parents and Children: A White Paper on Scottish Family Law* (Scottish Executive, 2000), paras 2.25–2.45. See, also para. 6.16, *supra*.
[54] 1978 Act, s. 56.
[55] 1978 Act, s. 24(3).

regard to the child's age and understanding. The 1995 Act amended the law to require consideration "so far as practicable to the views (if he wishes to express them) of the child concerned taking account of his age and maturity". The new terminology accords with the Convention and is consistent with the new duties imposed on those with parental responsibilities for children and on courts and children's hearings in other parts of the 1995 Act.

These provisions are, however, subject to the procedure and **9.29** practice of the courts which implement them. In theory, the mechanisms are in place to ensure compliance with the section 6 measures which accord with the convention. The practice however imposes limitations on the effectiveness of section 6.[56] In every adoption, the adoption agency which placed the child for adoption or the local authority for the area in which the prospective adopters are resident is required to investigate the case and submit a report to the court.[57] The report should deal with matters relevant to the operation of section 6. In the case of Mr. and Mrs. C,[58] the child who was the subject of an adoption petition was the natural child of one of the petitioners. The child was labouring under the misapprehension that the male petitioner was his father and had not been told of the adoption petition. The local authority did not submit a report because the applicants would not permit the child to be interviewed and the authority was therefore unable to investigate all matters relevant to section 6. The sheriff held that he could proceed without the local authority report and the child remained in ignorance of the adoption proceedings. Such an attitude on the part of the courts is inconsistent with the principle embodied in Article 12 of the Convention.[59]

A curator *ad litem* is appointed in every adoption in the sheriff **9.30** court and, where necessary to safeguard the interests of the child, in the Court of Session. The curator investigates matters relevant to the welfare of the child and ascertains the child's views about the adoption. Panels of curators *ad litem* were established pursuant to section 103 of the Children Act 1975. This section was repealed by the Children (Scotland) Act 1995. The current provision is found in the 1995 Act, section 101. There are, however, as yet no new regulations relating to curators. This has led to confusion in relation to the training and remuneration of curators. Training was formerly provided by the old regions, which ceased to exist when local government was reformed under the Local Government etc. (Scotland) Act 1994. The link to local authorities meant that curators were not perceived as truly independent. On the other

---

[56] For problems with attempts to comply with Art. 12, in other contexts, see Chap. 10 and paras 6.17–6.21, 7.22– 7.33, 8.21, 10.66–10.76 and 15.27–15.34.
[57] 1978 Act, ss. 22 and 23.
[58] 1993 S.C.L.R. 14.
[59] See also para. 5.1 for discussion of this case.

hand, training is important in undertaking a specialist professional role in relation to children. A minimal fee was paid by the local authority for the services of the curator on a case by case basis. [60] While many curators are dedicated to the welfare of children, the level of fee has not encouraged the use of professional time in fulfilling the role. The sheriff does, however, have the power to make an order relating to the expenses of the curator.[61] An order in respect of the curator's expenses may be made against any of the parties to the application before the court. In a freeing application the local authority may, as a party to the action, be ordered to pay a realistic fee.

9.31 For younger children, the new provisions in the Children (Scotland) Act 1995 may be found to fall short of the UN Convention. The Convention seeks the opportunity to be heard for all children capable of forming a view. The Act gives the opportunity only where "practicable". In the case of Mr. and Mrs. C, the court found that it was not practicable to ascertain the wishes and feelings of the child who did not know about the proceedings or their purpose. The sheriff nonetheless considered that an adoption order would safeguard and promote the child's welfare.

9.32 It is more difficult for the court to overlook the views of a child once he or she attains the age of 12. Such a child will be presumed under the new section 6 to be of sufficient age and maturity to form a view which should be taken into consideration by the court. Also, from the age of 12, a child can veto his or her own adoption or the making of an order declaring the child free for adoption,[62] unless the child is incapable of giving consent, in which case consent may be dispensed with.

9.33 Difficulties arise when children seek confidentiality for their views. The child must have the opportunity to be heard in terms of Article 12. The parent has the right to a fair and public hearing in terms of Article 6 of the European Convention. Balancing these competing interests is no easy task.[63] The House of Lords has given guidance in the case of *Re D. (minors) (Adoption Reports: Confidentiality)*.[64] The fundamental principle of fairness, that a party is entitled to the disclosure of all materials which might be taken into account by the court when reaching ad adverse decision, apply with particular force to adoption proceedings. The court should consider

[60] See Curators *ad litem* and Reporting Officers (Panels)(Scotland) Regulations 1984 (S.I. 1984 No. 566) as amended by Curators *ad litem* and Reporting Officers (Panels)(Scotland) Amendment Regulations 1985 (SI 1985 No. 1566). The regulations do not provide for payment by the local authority where a child was not placed by an adoption agency and an adoption order is not granted.
[61] Child Care and Maintenance Rules 1997 r.2.2, Court of Session r.67.7.
[62] 1978 Act, ss. 12 (8) and 18(8).
[63] A similar problem can occur in applications for parental responsibilities and rights, see paras 6.21 and 10.73–10.76.
[64] [1995] 4 All E.R. 385; followed in *McGrath v. McGrath*, 1999 S.L.T. (Sh. Ct) 90.

whether disclosure would involve a real possibility of significant harm to the child and should weigh the interests of the child in having the material properly tested against the magnitude and gravity of any harm. If the interests of the child pointed towards non-disclosure, then that should be weighed against the interests of the parent or other party in having an opportunity to see and respond to the material, taking into account its importance to the issues in the case. Non-disclosure should be the exception rather than the rule. The case of *Re D.* is significant not only for the approach to the question of confidentiality, but also as an illustration of the careful balancing of rights which is likely to be a feature of adoption in the future.

Parental Consent to Adoption

The UN Convention requires consent to adoption by a parent or **9.34** guardian to be "informed consent".[65] The person giving agreement must be aware of the implications of adoption. The 1978 Act, section 16(1), provides that parental agreement to adoption must be given freely and with full understanding of what is involved. The court appoints a reporting officer to ascertain that each parent or guardian whose consent to adoption is required understands the effect of an adoption order. If the parent or guardian is prepared to agree to adoption the reporting officer witnesses the form of consent.

Article 21 of the UN Convention is ambivalent about adoption **9.35** against the wishes of a parent or guardian. It proves that competent authorities may authorise adoption in accordance with applicable law and on the basis of all pertinent and reliable information and goes on to contemplate adoption where the persons concerned have "if required" given informed consent to adoption. However adoption is a solution for a child who cannot in his or her own best interests reside with his or her own family. [66] Adoption, if necessary without parental consent, is implicit in such a solution. In Scotland, the consent to adoption of a parent or guardian is usually required. Consent may, however, be dispensed with if a parent cannot be found; is withholding agreement unreasonably; has persistently failed without reasonable cause to fulfil parental responsibilities to the child; or has seriously ill-treated the child whose reintegration into the parent's household is unlikely.[67]

The UN Convention does not limit the court's consideration to **9.36** parents and guardians. It refers to "the child's status concerning

---

[65] Art. 21.
[66] Art. 20.
[67] 1978 Act, s. 16(2), as amended by the 1995 Act.

parents, relatives and legal guardians", and to consent of "the persons concerned".[68] One of the persons with the closest concern will be the father of a child, who will be a parent, unless he did not marry the child's mother. The UN Convention draws no distinction between a child born to married parents and the child of unmarried parents. The child has rights in respect of both parents. Scots law does not recognise these rights when agreement to adoption is required. Where a child's father has not been married to the mother, he has no parental responsibilities and rights, unless he has either entered into an agreement with the mother pursuant to section 4 of the Children (Scotland) Act 1995, or a court has conferred parental responsibilities or rights upon him. A father's agreement to adoption is only required where he has parental responsibilities or rights.[69] Where a father has any parental responsibilities or parental rights, however insignificant, this is sufficient to include him as a person whose agreement to adoption must be given or dispensed with.[70] Thus far, the United Kingdom has been able to justify the distinction in law between married and unmarried fathers, on the grounds that it is legitimate to differentiate between those sufficiently "meritorious" to participate in proceedings relating to children, and whose who are insufficiently committed to family life.[71] However, the European Court has also held that exclusion of unmarried father from participation in decisions relating to adoption is a violation of article 8.[72] Consideration is being given to a change in the law to allow unmarried fathers parental responsibilities and rights in some circumstances.[73] It is hoped that this will result in a change in the law relating to agreement to adoption.

9.37   The Children (Scotland) Act 1995 made no attempt to address the anomaly of the unmarried father who has no parental responsibilities or rights. His position falls to be considered before a child may be declared free for adoption. The court cannot grant a freeing order where such a father is likely to acquire any parental responsibilities or rights.[74] The unmarried father does not, however, have any automatic right to become a party to the court proceedings which consider this issue.

9.38   There is no question in Scotland of any more distant relative being given a right to consent or to withhold agreement to adoption. This does not however mean that a relative such as a grand-

---

[68] Art. 21(a).

[69] See definition of "parent" in 1978 Act, s. 65(1), combined with requirement for consent in s. 16(1).

[70] 1995 Act, s. 103 (1).

[71] *McMichael v. United Kingdom* (1995) 20 E.H.H.R. 205; *B. v. United Kingdom* [2000] 1 F.L.R. 1.

[72] *Keegan v. Ireland* (1994) 18 E.H.H.R. 342.

[73] *Parents and Children: A White Paper on Scottish Family Law* (Scottish Executive, 2000), paras 2.1–2.24. See also paras 5.2–5.7 and 6.8.

[74] 1978 Act, s. 18(7).

parent who has no immediate parental responsibilities or rights has no part to play in adoption proceedings. Where grandparents had applied for custody of a child, it was held that they could become parties to adoption proceedings.[75] The point was made that, if the court is to comply with section 6 of the Adoption (Scotland) Act 1978 and to consider all the circumstances having regard to the welfare of the child, then all persons able to assist the court in reaching an appropriate decision should participate in the proceedings. While the principle is admirable and accords with the UN Convention, there may be a practical difficulty in ascertaining whether there are relatives who should be given the opportunity to take part. The reporting officer under the current rules of court is required to identify such persons.[76]

Child's Identity after Adoption

Where adoption or an order declaring a child free for adoption have **9.39** extinguished parental responsibilities and parental rights, the birth parent can no longer make an application to the court for an order relating to parental responsibilities or rights.[77] This has benefits to the child whose security could be disrupted by applications after adoption, but the complete separation could be seen as inconsistent with Article 9 of the UN Convention. There has been no attempt to amend the law to accommodate the recognition that contact with members of a birth family after adoption may be in the child's interests.

Article 9, however, addresses the right of the child, not the right **9.40** of the parent, to maintain personal relations. A child may seek contact with a parent without the parent retaining a "right" in relation to the child. The child may even apply to the court for a contact order.[78] Scots law has traditionally respected the right of the adopted child to information about his or her original identity. Section 45 of the Adoption (Scotland) Act 1978 allows an adopted person access to details of the original entry in the register of birth which relates to his birth. The age at which an adopted person may seek these details was reduced from 17 to 16 by virtue of an amendment introduced by the 1995 Act. An adopted person who has attained the age of 16 may see the sheriff court process relating to his or her adoption.[79] The process is preserved for 100 years. An adoption agency may disclose information to an adopted person who has reached 16 years of age if in Scotland, or 18 in England

---

[75] *A.B. and C.D., Petrs*, 1992 S.L.T. 1064.
[76] Rule of Court 67.11(I)(I) and 67.24(1)(h).
[77] s. 11(4).
[78] 1995 Act, s. 11(5). See also paras 5.14 and 6.13.
[79] Child Care and Maintenance Rules rr 2.14(2) and 2.33(2), RC 67.32.

and Wales, and who has applied for counselling following receipt of birth records from the Registrar General for Scotland.[80] The agency's records are preserved for at least 75 years. When a child is placed for adoption by an adoption agency, the agency must advise prospective adopters of the need to tell the child about his or her adoption and origins.[81] These rights accord respect for the child's identity, pursuant to Article 8 of the UN Convention, despite the existence of an adoption order.

9.41   The question of a child's identity is raised particularly acutely where the proposed adopters and the child are of different ethnic or cultural origins. According to Article 30 of the UN Convention, children from ethnic, religious or linguistic minorities should not be denied the right in community with other members of their own group to enjoy their own culture; profess and practise their own religion; or use their own language. Transracial adoption is, at best, a limitation on such rights. It is a solution that is not consistent with the child's ethnic, religious, cultural and linguistic background. These aspects are not determinative, but are considerations to which due regard should be paid.[82] Section 7 of the 1978 Act requires an adoption agency placing a child for adoption to have regard to any wishes of the child's parents as to the religious upbringing of the child. In a case in the Court of Session,[83] there was attached to adoption orders in respect of two children a condition that the adopters use their best endeavours to secure that the children be made aware of their black identity and brought up with an understanding of their own ethnic origins and traditions. Consideration of a child's religious persuasion, racial origin and cultural linguistic background has been reinforced by the duty imposed on the court and an adoption agency to have regard to these matters in reaching any decision relating to adoption of a child.[84] These provisions are likely to be particularly relevant in the case of inter-country adoptions.

Inter-country Adoption

9.42 Adoption in Scotland has since its inception in 1930 been largely a domestic phenomenon. As the nature of adoption has changed, prospective adopters seeking babies have started to look abroad, to countries where babies are available for adoption. These have for

---

[80] 1996 Regulations, reg. 25.
[81] 1996 Regulations, reg. 19(1)(b).
[82] Art. 20(3).
[83] *A.H. and P.H., Petrs*, 1997 Fam. L.R. 84.
[84] 1978 Act, s. 6(1)(b)(ii).

the most part been less affluent parts of the world.[85] Article 21 of the UN Convention requires recognition of inter-country adoption as an alternative means of care for the child, if the child cannot be placed in a foster or adoptive family or cannot in any suitable manner be cared for in his or her country of origin. The Convention recognises that for some children the right to family life in an adoptive home may outweigh other rights such as those pertaining to nationality in Article 8 or culture in Article 30. Inter-country adoption should enjoy safeguards and standards equivalent to those existing in the case of national adoption.

This is not the case at present. The domestic legislation does not **9.43** regulate activities outwith Scotland. Any control over inter-country adoption is exercised via immigration controls. The Home Secretary admits children adopted in certain designated countries, or grants entry clearance where there is confirmation that persons seeking to bring in a child are suitable to adopt.[86] The first attempt of the Hague Conference, in 1965, to produce a Convention dealing with inter-country adoption was unsuccessful. That Convention was brought into force between only the United Kingdom, Austria and Switzerland.

In 1993, the Hague Conference looked again at inter-country **9.44** adoption. This time more than 65 countries took part in the preparation of a Convention on Protection of Children and Co-operation in respect of Inter-Country Adoption, which was concluded on May 29, 1993. The Convention is designed to secure implementation of the UN Convention in respect of inter-country adoption. The United Kingdom signed the Convention in January 1994. The Adoption (Inter Country Aspects) Act 1999 was passed to allow the United Kingdom to ratify the Adoption Convention. When the 1999 Act is brought into force, it will address deficiencies in Scottish provision for children involved in inter-country adoption.

The 1993 Convention sets out minimum standards for the process **9.45** of inter-country adoption. The child's state of origin is responsible for establishing that the child is adoptable; that inter-country adoption is in the child's best interests; and that there has been counselling and information given to persons whose consent to adoption is required, including the child where he or she has reached the age and degree of maturity to make his or her consent appropriate. The receiving state must determine that the prospective adoptive parents are eligible and suitable to adopt; that they have been counselled; and that the child is or will be authorised to enter and reside permanently in the receiving country. The details

---

[85] As the recent debacle surrounding the attempt by a couple from Wales to adopt American twins demonstrates, this is not always the case.
[86] Adoption (Designation of Overseas Adoptions) Order 1973 (S.I. 1973 No. 19) and Home Office leaflet RON 117.

of these provisions are to be found in regulations.[87] The adoption service provided by adoption agencies must include inter-country adoption.[88] Adoption societies may be approved to act as adoption agencies in relation to adoptions including inter-country adoptions.[89] Placements made under the Convention procedures will be treated as made by an adoption agency,[90] save that the child must reside with the prospective adopter for six months before an adoption order may be made.[91] Bringing children to the United Kingdom for adoption without complying with regulations is to be a criminal offence (unless the child is brought to the United Kingdom by a parent, guardian or relative).[92]

9.46   New regulations will provide for Convention adoption orders.[93] Convention orders made in other jurisdictions will be recognised in Scotland. Scottish adoption is irrevocable and severs legal links with a child's birth family. It is classified as "full" adoption. This is not the case in all overseas adoptions. The Court of Session may direct that a Convention adoption is not treated as if a full adoption had been made, where the order was not a full order in the child's country of origin; the child's parents have not consented to full adoption; and it would be more favourable for the child for a direction to be made.[94] A direction might be given where, for example, the child stands to receive a significant inheritance from the birth family, or there is contact with the birth family which could be prejudiced were the adoption treated as a full adoption.

9.47   The 1999 Act is clearly to be welcomed as a significant step in the implementation of the UN Convention. Scots law is already compliant in relation to other aspects of inter-country adoption which have in the past caused concern. Article 21 of the UN Convention expressly provides that states should take all appropriate measures to ensure that the adoption placement does not result in improper financial gain for those involved. Article 35 obliges states to take measures to prevent trafficking in children. There are dangers in parents and persons in less affluent countries supplying children for adoption to prospective adopters from a comparatively wealthy nation. Scots law does prohibit payments in connection with adoption of children.[95] Making or receiving such a payment is an offence. Contravention outside Scotland cannot be prosecuted within Scotland, but the court is obliged in all Scottish adoptions to satisfy itself that there have been no illegal payments, which failing

[87] 1999 Act, s. 1.
[88] 1999 Act, s. 9 amending 1978 Act, s. 1.
[89] 1978 Act, s. 3(3).
[90] 1998 Act, s. 13, amending 1978 Act, s. 65.
[91] 1999 Act, s. 11, amending 1978 Act, s. 13.
[92] 1999 Act, s. 14, introducing a new s. 50A to the 1978 Act.
[93] 1999 Act, s. 3, substituting a new s. 17 in the 1978 Act.
[94] 1999 Act, s. 25, amending ss. 38 and 39 of the 1978 Act.
[95] 1978 Act, s. 51.

there is at present a bar on an adoption order being made. If Scots law follows English law, then a payment may be authorised after the event under section 51(3) by the court which is considering the adoption and the court may grant authorisation to enable an adoption to proceed where this is demanded by the welfare of the child.[96] The Children (Scotland) Act 1995 removed the absolute bar on adoption following an illegal payment.[97] The effect is that the court can deal with cases on the basis of the paramount welfare of the child without having to authorise, after the event, an illegal payment. Sale of children must however remain abhorrent [98] and raise sharply the question of the welfare of such children.

Conclusion

Examined against the United Nations Convention on the Rights of **9.48** the Child, Scots law on adoption has a reasonable record. It has by tradition a respect for the child's identity and a recognition that adoption is an exceptional course. The Children (Scotland) Act 1995 reinforced compliance with the Convention by making the welfare of children paramount in adoption proceedings, and requiring adoption agencies and the court to have regard to the child's views, and to the child's religious persuasion, racial origin and cultural and linguistic background. The reform of step-parent adoption to preserve the child's formal relationship by birth with one parent was welcome. The participation of the United Kingdom government in the Hague Conference consideration of inter-country adoption and the passing of the Adoption (Inter Country Aspects) Act 1999 represents a significant commitment to children's convention rights.

There remains scope for further improvement. The UN Con- **9.49** vention emphasis on counselling for persons asked to give consent to adoption could be better reflected. The child's relationship with an unmarried father is not yet resolved in terms of the Convention. Further consideration should be given to whether any change in the law is necessary to support the child's right to identity by means of contact after adoption. The intentions behind the increased use of freeing for adoption are, on balance, sympathetic to children's rights, although the practice has resulted in delay and confusion over the issue of contact. Curators *ad litem* carry a significant responsibility for safeguarding the rights of children in adoption proceedings and their organisation, training, and remuneration

---

[96] *Re A.* (Adoption: Placement) [1988] 1 W.L.R. 229; *Re A.W.* (Adoption Application) [1993] 1 F.L.R. 87.
[97] Sched. 2, para. 16.
[98] Art. 35

must be addressed.

9.50   The most significant challenge to children's UN Convention
rights in adoption will be the rights of adults enshrined in the
European Convention, given effect by the Human Rights Act 1998.
It remains to be seen which will prevail over the coming years.

CHAPTER 10

THE CHILD'S RIGHT TO BE HEARD AND REPRESENTED IN LEGAL PROCEEDINGS

ALISON CLELAND

"A child's wishes are not to be discounted or dismissed simply **10.1** because he is a child. He should be free to express them and deci-sion-makers should listen".[1] This was stated in an English case in 1993, acknowledging the requirement under the Children Act 1989 that the court must have regard to "the ascertainable wishes and feelings of the child concerned.".[2]

Scottish legislation now contains a similar requirement that, in **10.2** family actions, the court shall have regard to the views of a child before deciding what order, if any, it is appropriate to make.[3] This chapter examines the extent to which Scots law relating to family and other court proceedings affecting children complies with the requirements of the UN Convention on the Rights of the Child ("the UN Convention") and the European Convention on Human Rights ("the European Convention"), in allowing children under 16 to be heard and represented in those proceedings. Those between 16 and 18 years old are not considered, since at that age of 16, young people acquire full legal capacity under Scots law.[4]

The UN Convention requires that children must be given an **10.3** opportunity to express views in all matters affecting them.[5] It is important to note, however, that the Convention does not merely say that children should be heard; it expects that, in appropriate cases, they will be represented: "The child, shall, in particular, be provided the opportunity to be heard in any judicial and adminis-trative proceedings affecting the child, either directly, or through a representative".[6] Criminal proceedings are specifically mentioned: "Every child alleged as or accused of having infringed the penal law

---

[1] Re S. (A Minor) (Independent Representation) [1993] 2 F.L.R. 437, at p. 448E, per Sir Thomas Bingham M.R.
[2] Children Act 1989, s. 1(3)(a).
[3] Children (Scotland) Act 1995, s. 11(7)(b).
[4] Age of Legal Capacity (Scotland) Act 1991, s. 1(1)(b).
[5] UN Convention on the Rights of the Child, Art. 12(1).
[6] ibid. Art. 12(2).

has...to have legal or other appropriate assistance in the preparation of his or her defence".[7]

10.4 The European Convention states that in the determination of his civil rights and of any criminal charge against him, everyone is entitled to a fair and public hearing within a reasonable time by an independent and impartial tribunal established by law.[8] Again, particular care is taken to stress that when someone faces a criminal charge, legal representation should be available: "Everyone charged with a criminal offence has [the right]...to defend himself in person or through legal assistance of his own choosing or, if he has not sufficient means to pay for legal assistance, to be given it free when the interests of justice so require".[9]

10.5 In addition, under the European Convention, parents and children have a right to private and family life and the state should not unduly interfere with that right.[10] When considering whether Scots law complies with the European Convention, it will therefore be important to bear in mind that children's hearings and family actions, in particular, may have outcomes which profoundly affect children's rights to family life and must be judged accordingly.

Formal Recognition of the Right to be Heard

10.6 The first essential step towards allowing children to be heard is for legislation to enshrine formal rights for children in the various processes that affect them.

10.7 In relation to prosecution for serious offences, a child under the age of 16 may be referred to the sheriff court or the High Court.[11] The child offender is entitled to separate legal representation to conduct his defence, with legal aid available.[12] In relation to the education process, children now have the right to appeal against their own exclusion from school.[13] In relation to abduction cases, the court is concerned with recognition and enforcement of adult rights in respect of children and it will be rare for a child to be party to such proceedings.[14]

10.8 Adoption law also has to concern itself with adult rights, particularly in relation to the dispensing with parents' consent to adoption; however, the court has a duty to ascertain the views of

---

[7]   *ibid.* Art. 40 (2)(b)(ii).
[8]   ECHR, Art. 6.1.
[9]   *ibid.* Art. 6.3(c).
[10] ECHR, Art. 8.
[11] Social Work (Scotland) Act 1968, s. 31(1).
[12] Advice and Assistance (Assistance by Way of Representation) (Scotland) Regulations 1988 (S.I. 1988 No. 2290).
[13] Standards in Scotland's Schools Act 2000, s. 41.
[14] See Chap. 7, paras 7.22–7.33.

the child[15] who is to be adopted, taking account of age and maturity, and the consent of a child aged 12 or over is required before the adoption can proceed.[16] Adoption legislation does not expressly provide for the child to become a party to the proceedings or to have separate representation.

Most children who have allegedly committed offences will be **10.9** referred to the children's hearing system. Children have a right to be accompanied by someone to a hearing "for the purposes of assisting them".[17] That representative need not be a lawyer and legal aid is not yet available for solicitors' attendance at hearings.[18] In practice, few children will obtain legal advice before or during a hearing. Most of those appearing on offence grounds of referral will therefore be unaware that acceptance of such grounds will be recorded as a conviction for certain purposes.[19] Children have the right to attend their own hearing[20] and cannot, therefore, be excluded from the hearing if they wish to attend—an important recognition of the child's place in the process. Children have a right to be represented by a legal representative, paid for by legal aid, at hearings before a sheriff to decide whether grounds of referral in respect of the child have been established[21] and in appeals against hearings' decisions.[22]

Since the UN Convention and the European Convention both **10.10** specifically mention legal representation, it may be argued that the non-availability of legal aid for hearings is a breach of the instruments' requirements. Certainly, the Inner House, in *S. v. Miller*,[23] found that Article 6(1) of the European Convention required that at least those children referred to hearings on offence grounds of referral should have legal aid available to them for representation. However, even after legal aid is made available for hearings, the important issue will remain whether the representation provided is appropriate to the child's needs.

In relation to emergency child protection, a child has a right to **10.11** apply for variation or recall of a Child Protection Order (CPO).[24] It should be noted, however, that a child's view need not be sought

---

[15] Adoption (Scotland) Act 1978, s. 6
[16] *ibid.* ss. 12(8) and 18(8).
[17] Children's Hearings (Scotland) Rules (S.I. 1996 No. 3261) 1996, r. 11(1).
[18] In *S. v. Miller*, 2001 S.L.T. 531, the Inner House decided that, in the case of a young person referred to a children's hearing on an offence ground, the young person's right to a fair hearing under Art. 6(1) of the European Convention might well require legal aid be made available to provide the young person with legal representation the hearing.
[19] Rehabilitation of Offenders Act 1974, s. 3.
[20] Children (Scotland) Act 1995, s. 45(2)(a).
[21] Children (Scotland) Act 1995, s. 68(4).
[22] Children (Scotland) Act 1995, s.51.
[23] 2001 S.L.T. 531.
[24] Children (Scotland) Act 1995, s. 60(7).

before a CPO is made.[25] The justification for this apparent breach of article 12 the UN Convention may be that the order is being sought in an emergency when there is little time to discuss matters with, or even explain intentions to, the child. It is suggested, however, that this is an unhelpful precedent to set. It is hoped that social work practice will fill the gap left by the legislators.

10.12   In relation to "relevant circumstances" in Sheriff Court or Court of Session proceedings,[26] the law provides that in reaching any decision relating to parental responsibilities and rights, the court must give a child the opportunity to express views if he or she wishes to, and have regard to those views.[27] This is a very strong recognition of the right to be heard. It is further underlined by the provision that a child aged 12 or over shall be presumed mature enough to form a view.[28] It is made clear that there is no necessity for the child to be legally represented in the proceedings—it is one option.[29]

10.13   It appears that in most proceedings affecting children, there is some formal legal recognition that children have a right to express views on the matters at issue, with the arguable exception of abduction cases. The question then becomes: what mechanisms exist to enable the child to turn those formal rights into reality?

Mechanisms for Enforcing the Right to be Heard

10.14   There are several key elements to consider, in deciding whether children are able to influence decisions which affect them. These are: methods of expressing views without entering the legal process; separate representation by a solicitor; availability of legal aid; and party status.

Expressing Views Without Entering the Legal Process

10.15   The UN Convention does not require legal representation in all cases, only that a child should be able to express views in all matters affecting him or her. The European Convention requires that everyone be given a fair and public hearing, which must include the right to express views, before a decision is made.

---

[25] Children (Scotland) Act 1995, s. 16(2) requires that the children's hearing or court should take account of child's views in the circumstances set out in s. 16(4): the subsection provides that a court, when considering variation or recall of CPO, shall have regard to such views, but not at initial stage of granting or refusing CPO.

[26] "Relevant circumstances" are defined in s. 11(3) of the 1995 Act and include applications by those who have and who do not have parental responsibilities and rights. The Act makes clear that an application may be made by a child—s. 11(5).

[27] Children (Scotland) Act 1995, s. 11(7)(b).

[28] *ibid.* s. 11(10).

[29] *ibid.* s. 11(9).

The question of influencing the case without entering the process **10.16** does not arise in criminal cases. When a child is accused of a crime and tried in respect of it, the method by which the court is influenced is through the giving of evidence and the presentation of a defence, with a lawyer's assistance.

In respect of education decisions, the right which a child has to **10.17** appeal his or her exclusion is an exception to the general rule, which is that pupils have no right to express views. The choice of school is a parental decision.[30] There is no provision for formal consultation with pupils when decisions as to their special educational needs are being taken.

In relation to abduction, a court does not require to ascertain a **10.18** child's view before taking a decision,[31] but, in contrast, there are detailed rules in adoption law to ensure that the reporting officer and the curator *ad litem* provide the court with information on the child's views.[32] This is not foolproof, since, where the child is very young, the requirement may be bypassed,[33] but it does provide a mechanism for some children's views to reach the court.

Children's hearings are intended to be child-centred. It has been **10.19** noted already that there is no legal aid to allow formal legal representation for a child at a hearing. Here, we are concerned with the informal contribution which may be made by the child to the proceedings.

Hearings are under a duty to give a child an opportunity to **10.20** express a view and to have regard, so far as practicable, to that view.[34] The rules governing the conduct of such hearings indicate the various ways by which children might express views to the members of the hearing. Any child whose case comes before a hearing may be accompanied by one person to assist him.[35] The rules also deal with situations where the child wishes to express a view other than through a representative. They provide that children may express views in writing, by audio or video tape, through a safeguarder, or simply by speaking directly to the members of the hearing.[36] Children 12 years old or more are presumed able to express a view.[37]

During the hearing, relevant persons may be excluded from the **10.21** hearing where it is regarded as necessary to obtain the child's views.[38] This provision in the Children (Scotland) Act 1995 was, in itself, something of a triumph for the principle of the child's right to

---

[30] Education (Scotland) Act 1980, s. 28A.
[31] See paras 7.22–7.33 for discussion of the issue.
[32] Children (Sc) Act 1995, s. 101.
[33] see, *e.g. C. Petrs,* 1993 S.C.L.R. 14.
[34] Children (Scotland) Act 1995, s. 16(2).
[35] Children's Hearing (Scotland) Rules, r. 11(1).
[36] Children's Hearing (Scotland) Rules, r. 15(4).
[37] *ibid.* r. 15(5).
[38] Children (Scotland) Act 1995, s. 46(1).

be heard. A consultation with young people on the government's
White Paper was carried out.[39] Those young people who had experience of children's hearings explained how difficult it was to
express views in front of their parents during a hearing: "nobody
seemed to see the pressure my mum and dad were putting on me
just by a movement or a look".[40] The provision to exclude relevant
persons cannot provide children with confidentiality,[41] but may
make it a little easier to explain their position to the hearing and
thus influence the decision.

10.22   One other way in which a child might advise a hearing of his or
her views would be through a safeguarder. A children's hearing,
and a sheriff considering a matter referred from a hearing, is under
an obligation in every case to consider whether a person should be
appointed to safeguard the child's interests.[42] Safeguarders may be
(but are not always) solicitors, but their role is entirely different
from that of a solicitor for a child. They are not appointed by the
child, cannot be dismissed by the child, and are under no obligation
to advocate the child's views.

10.23   The role of the safeguarder is set out in long-standing Scottish
Office guidance.[43] The guidance states that "the most important
requirement of the safeguarder's role is an ability to communicate
with the child and to determine what would be in the child's best
interests".[44] The child's views should be contained in the safeguarder's report.[45]

10.24   The children's hearing system has an admirable variety of
methods by which children may attempt to influence the hearing
decisions. However, despite this, research into the hearing system in
1998[46] suggested that children are rarely involved in the decision-
making process. It indicated that in 70 per cent of cases, the child
expressed no view or made a monosyllabic response to questions
posed.[47]

10.25   Given the limited contribution which children currently make at
hearings, the view expressed recently by the Lord President on the

[39] This consultation was carried out by ChildLine, Who Cares? Scotland and
Scottish Child Law Centre, published as *Scotland's Children: Speaking Out,
Young People's Views on Child Care in Scotland* (1995), HMSO.
[40] *ibid.* p. 4.
[41] Children (Scotland) Act 1995 s. 46(2) provides that the excluded person must be
informed of the substance of what took place during his or her absence. See also
para. 15.31
[42] Children (Scotland) Act 1995, s. 41(1).
[43] Social Work Services Group, Circular SW7/85.
[44] *ibid.* para. 16.
[45] *ibid.* para. 17.
[46] *C. Hallett and M. Murray; Evaluation of the Children's Hearing in Scotland—*
(Scottish Office Central Research Unit 1998).
[47] *ibid.*

assistance which could be given through legal representation are instructive. He said:

> "I find it quite impossible to conclude that all the children appearing before a hearing would be able to understand, far less to criticise and to elucidate, all the reports and other documents and all the factors which the hearing may be called upon to consider when deciding what measures are most appropriate to deal with their case".[48]

The Lord President went on to express doubt that lay representative would always be able to provide the necessary skilled assistance. The Court emphasised that, if the child was to contribute to the discussion, it was important that he or she should understand the reports and that a solicitor could aid this understanding. If, following this decision, legal aid is to be made available, while the existing powers remain, so that the role of any representative is to assist and not to disrupt the hearing, the representative may provide additional assistance in ensuring that the child's views are heard.

10.26 Sheriff Courts in family actions are obliged to ascertain whether a child wishes to express a view, and to take account of that view.[49] There are various mechanisms in the relevant court rules[50] and court procedures that attempt to support this obligation. These are: intimation on the child; appointment of reporter or curator to advise the court of the child's views; recording of the child's views; and the interviewing of the child by the Sheriff.

10.27 First, where a writ includes a crave for a section 11 order (residence order, contact order, parental responsibilities and rights, etc.), there should be intimation of the writ on the child[51] and that intimation must be in Form F9.[52]

10.28 A pursuer may crave that intimation of the child be dispensed with. This information is available in court records. A pilot study for the Scottish Executive, which examined 502 court processes[53] found that in 34 per cent of all cases (*i.e.* divorce and non-divorce cases) intimation to the child was craved and in 35 per cent of cases, dispensation was craved. It noted that the older the children, the higher the percentage of intimation.[54]

10.29 This study gives some indication of the level of intimation on children, at least in theory, although it does not tell us how many

[48] *S. v. Miller*, 2001 S.L.T. 531, p. 544, para. 36.
[49] Children (Scotland) Act 1995, s. 11(7)(b).
[50] Act of Sederunt Ordinary Cause Rules 1993 (S.I. 1993 No. 1956) for sheriff court cases; there are similar rules for the Court of Session.
[51] OCR r. 33.7(1)(h).
[52] The equivalent form in the Court of Session is Form 49.8N, RCS, r. 49.20.
[53] "Monitoring The Children (Scotland) Act 1995: Pilot Study", (2000) Scottish Executive Central Research Unit.
[54] *ibid.* para. 4.9.3–4. 84 per cent of 10–11-year-olds; 87 per cent of 12–14-year-olds; 93 per cent of 15–16-year-olds were to have intimation served on them.

children actually received the information personally. Information as to the level of return of the F9 forms would be helpful. The pilot study advised of a number of difficulties in data collection in respect of these forms. While some F9s may be in the court processes, some may be stored elsewhere and no record is made to advise whether an F9 was received. The pilot noted that in 26 per cent of cases where there was intimation to the child, a form F9 was attached to the court process.[55]

10.30   Second, the sheriff may appoint a reporter[56] or curator *ad litem* to investigate and report on the child's circumstances, including the child's views. In the pilot study, a reporter was appointed in 10 per cent of cases in the sample.[57] The tradition of appointing a curator *ad litem* to represent children's interests in civil cases has a long history. Stair makes reference to curators, who could be appointed to act on behalf of a child.[58] Case law notes that where an action was raised on behalf of pupils or minors, it was proper for the court to appoint a curator *ad litem* "for the purpose of protecting their interests, and of ascertaining and securing that they were not acting under any undue influence".[59]

10.31   Fraser, in the second edition of his book, *A Treatise on the Law of Scotland Relative to Parent and Child*, notes that the curator is not acting under the instructions of the pupil child, but has complete discretion as to how to proceed with the case: "If he thinks it unnecessary or improper to make appearance for pupils, he may refrain".[60]

10.32   The curator's role, like that of the safeguarder, may be contrasted sharply with that of a legal representative. The curator is appointed by the court, is an officer of the court, and is not bound to take instructions from the child or to advocate for the child's wishes. One experienced curator described the disappointment this could bring to a young person: "one girl in particular told me that she wanted to go home. I told her that I just could not conceive that this would be in her best interests for a whole variety of reasons. Her response was, 'But, I thought you were my lawyer and my Dad says your lawyer does what you tell him to'."[61]

10.33   Third, there are special rules for the recording of children's views, if these are expressed to the court. Where a child expresses a view (and the applicability of the rule is not limited to a particular method of expression, so could include information given to a re-

---

[55] *ibid.* para. 4.9.5.
[56] OCR r. 33.21.
[57] op cit. para. 4.9.6.
[58] Stair, I, v, 12 and I, vi, 31–35.
[59] *Harvey v. Harvey* (1860) 22 D. 1198 at p. 1207.
[60] Fraser, *A Treatise on the Law of Scotland relative to Parent and Child* (2nd ed., 1906), p. 213.
[61] *Children and Young People's Voices: The Law, legal Services, Systems and Processor in Scotland* (HMSO, 1999), p. 71.

porter or curator, to the sheriff in chambers, or in written form) the view must be recorded in a prescribed way.[62] Thereafter, the sheriff may decide that the views should be kept confidential and if she does so, may arrange for the views to be placed in a sealed envelope, marked "confidential—views of the child" and seen only be the sheriff.[63] There are no figures for the frequency with which this is done, but caselaw, examined below, indicates that the courts have struggled with the balance between the perceived right of the child to express views freely, and the right of the other parties to a fair hearing with knowledge of the case against them.

Fourth, there is the possibility that the sheriff may decide to **10.34** discharge her duty to take account of the child's views by speaking directly to the child in chambers. Informal discussions with some sheriffs have indicated that practice on this point may differ widely. Some take the view that, since views so expressed are evidence which has not been heard by the parties, if they give weight to the views they will simply guarantee that the decision will be appealed on procedural irregularity. Others are more comfortable with the idea of seeing and speaking to the child to assist their decision-making.

Separate Representation by a Solicitor

There is now no doubt that those under the age of 16 may instruct a **10.35** solicitor in civil proceedings. The amendments to the Age of Legal Capacity (Scotland) Act 1991 made by the 1995 Act read as follows:

> "(4A) A person under the age of 16 years shall have legal capacity to instruct a solicitor, in connection with any civil matter, where that person has a general understanding of what it means to do so; and without prejudice to the generality of this sub-section, a person 12 years of age or more shall be presumed to be of sufficient age and maturity to have such understanding.
>
> (4B) A person who by virtue of subsection (4A) above has legal capacity to instruct a solicitor shall also have legal capacity to sue, or to defend, in any civil proceedings."[64]

These provisions implement Article 12 of the UN Convention and **10.36** appear to meet the requirements of the European Convention.[65] Scots law places the responsibility for judging a child's capacity on the solicitor and the judiciary has made no move to interfere with the profession's decision-making. This contrasts markedly with the

---

[62] OCR, r.33. 20(2).
[63] *ibid.* r.33. 20(2).
[64] inserted by Children (Scotland) Act 1995, Sched. 4, para. 53.
[65] Art.6.

approach in English cases. English law states that a minor may
bring certain family proceedings without a guardian *ad litem* or next
friend, where a solicitor has satisfied herself that he can take instructions from the child. However, the English courts have insisted
that they may second-guess the solicitor: in *Re C.T.*,[66] it was emphasised that the court was the final arbiter on the child's competence.

10.37   The test of competence which the Scottish solicitor should apply,
i.e., whether or not the child has a "general understanding of what
it means" to instruct a solicitor may be regarded as a relatively low
test, certainly when compared to that applied by medical practitioners in respect of medical consent.[67] A solicitor may be able to
decide easily, on receiving answers to questions such as "what do
you want me to do for you?" whether the child can give instructions, although in difficult cases, it may be necessary to re-assess
capacity as matters progress.[68]

10.38   The formal provisions for children to instruct solicitors meet the
Conventions' requirements, therefore the important issue to address
is the extent to which children are able to take advantage of the
provisions. Research for the Scottish Office[69] into legal aid applications by and on behalf of children revealed some fascinating insights. First, 38 per cent of applications for under-16s were in
respect of reparation or damages actions, with 40 per cent being in
respect of family actions. This suggests that adults may be making
applications in damages cases, in their capacity as the child's legal
representative, and that the number of children actively instructing
solicitors for themselves may be limited. Second, the researcher
notes: "After speaking to solicitors the majority expressed their
preference of representing children as a curator".[70] While the
number of interviews with solicitors was very limited, this does raise
the question of whether the legal profession is geared up to the
demands of young clients.

10.39   It may be that many young people are not aware of their rights to
instruct solicitors (other than, perhaps, in respect of criminal
charges) and that those who are, still find the matter of approaching
a legal practice intimidating.

---

[66] *Re C.T. (A Minor) (Wardship: Representation)* [1993] 2 F.L.R. 278.
[67] They must be satisfied that the child understands the nature and possible
consequences of the treatment or examination", Age of Legal Capacity (Scotland)
Act 1991, s. 2(4).
[68] For more detailed discussion on the solicitor's role when instructed by child
clients, see Cleland, "Representing Young Clients: One Practitioner's Way",
1997, J.L.S.S. Vol. 42, No. 12, p. 495.
[69] Fiona Kean, "Research into the uptake of Civil Legal Aid by Children under 16
and its implications for Solicitors", unpublished Report for Scottish Office: Legal
Studies Research Branch.
[70] *ibid.* p. 11.

Availability of Legal Aid

In order to support the child's right to instruct a solicitor, it is **10.40** essential that the State is prepared to pay the solicitor's fees if necessary. Since April 1990 in Scotland, children under the age of 16 have been able to apply on their own behalf for advice and assistance under the civil legal aid scheme and have been assessed on their own resources.[71]

Legal Aid is automatically available to a child prosecuted in a **10.41** criminal case, and to those who wish to appeal against a children's hearing, or to challenge the grounds of referral in their case, before a sheriff.[72] Similarly, legal aid is available for a child to apply for a variation or recall of a Child Protection Order.[73]

As noted above, the Scottish Office commissioned some crucial **10.42** research into the uptake of civil legal aid by children.[74] The research indicated that the number of applications by children doubled, from 1995/6 to 1996/7, although the application still accounted for only three per cent of total applications, that is, 844 applications.[75] The increase in applications is important, in that some children are taking advantage of mechanisms available, but it may be suggested that on the figures, there must be many actions relating to parental responsibilities and rights where no application for legal aid is made by the child. Children affected by family actions may be expressing their views in other ways, but it is suggested that there may be a significant proportion of cases affecting children where those children have no direct input into the process.

There is no research presently available to indicate the rate of **10.43** refusal of legal aid applications by children, but a Legal Aid Board decision in England raised important matters in that regard. In *W. and Others v. The Legal Services Commission* [2000] 2 F.L.R. 821,[76] the Court of Appeal dealt with an application to set aside an LAB decision to refuse to allow legal aid in proceedings to terminate contact between the child and the parent. The Court of Appeal accepted that the LAB had discretion in the matter and refused to uphold the children's applications, since it was clear that to do so would result in delay while the decision was re-considered, which would be incompatible with the welfare of the child. However, Dame Butler-Sloss stated that the decision in this particular case was not to be taken as a precedent for further refusal of legal aid; she noted that a child litigant should not be deprived of the legal representation that she ought to receive.

The basis of the LAB decision to refuse was discussed in the case. **10.44**

---

[71] Legal Aid (Scotland) Act 1986, as amended by the Children (Scotland) Act s. 92.
[72] Legal Aid (Scotland) Act 1986, s. 29.
[73] *ibid.*
[74] Fiona Kean, *op. cit.*
[75] *ibid.* p. 6.
[76] [2000] 2 F.L.R. 821.

It was noted that there was a focus on multiple representation and the potential waste of public money. Anecdotal evidence and the writer's own experience tends to confirm that a similar position is being adopted by the Scottish Legal Aid Board. There are three tests which the Board will apply in deciding whether to grant an application: (1) financial; (2) is there *probabilis causa* and (3) is it reasonable in the interests of justice.

10.45   Most under-16s, unless they have trust funds in their names or an award from the Criminal Injuries Compensation Authority, will pass the financial test. Where an action has been raised, and defended, involving craves for section 11 orders, it is not difficult to show that the matter is appropriate for adjudication by the court. The difficulty appears to be with the "interests of justice" test. Refusals often make it clear that SLAB sees no need for separate representation where the child could speak to the sheriff or to a reporter or curator, or where the child wishes the same outcome as one of the adult parties. This is effectively the same approach as the LAB, concerned about potential waste of public funds.

10.46   The Scottish Legal Aid Board's position here appears to be a breach of the European Convention, Articles 6 and 8. In *Dombo Beheer v. Netherlands*[77] it was held that each party to a civil action should be able to present his case, including the evidence, in a manner which does not put him at a disadvantage as regards his opponent. A child cannot be left to rely on the possibility that a sheriff *may* consent to speak with her: the sheriff is under no obligation to do so, and, as has been noted above, may be reluctant to do so precisely because of the Article 6 principle that no-one should be disadvantaged and the other parties will not hear the evidence. Similarly, it is wholly inadequate to ask the child to rely on the reporter or curator to present her case, since neither has an obligation to do anything other than advise the court of the child's views and may, in some cases, advocate against them.

10.47   Article 8 states that there must be no undue interference by a public authority with the exercise of the right to private and family life.[78] A court is a public authority and in every action concerning parental responsibilities and rights, it may make a decision which interferes with family life, by, for example, stopping contact between a child and a parent or ordering that a child live in a particular place away from a parent or siblings. Courts can make such decisions as are necessary in a democratic society and this, of course, allows them to make decisions about children to protect the children's interests. However, a failure to ensure that the child is fully involved in the decision-making process affecting her future family life could, itself, be a violation of Article 8.

10.48   The Scottish Legal Aid Board's position also appears to breach

[77] 18 E.H.R.R. 213 (1994).
[78] ECHR, Art. 8(2).

Article 12 of the UN Convention. The Board has consistently adopted the position, as has its English equivalent, that a child who wants the same outcome as one of the adult parties requires no separate representation. Article 12 requires that children be respected as individuals capable of forming an independent view. In the writer's experience, a child may request the same outcome, but for entirely different reasons. The child has her own perspective and may have based her wish on information of which the parent is unaware. Without representation, the court will also remain unaware of the matters and the decision may be flawed.

The Board's position, regrettably, found some support from the **10.49** bench in the case of *Henderson v. Henderson.*[79] The action was raised by the father under the previous law[80] in 1990, seeking contact with his daughter. It came to court for proof in 1997, when the child of the parties was ten years old. The child was separately represented at the proof and gave evidence that she did not wish to see her father. The sheriff refused the father's crave for contact, but made the following comment in respect of legal aid for the child: "it is difficult to see what advantage a child being sisted as a party has in a situation where the child's views are exactly the same as the defender's...As all three parties were on legal aid, it also appears an unnecessary expense!"[81] The Sheriff's comments were reported under the banner headline "Sheriff attacks legal aid for divorce-case daughter".[82]

The Board appear less hostile to applications by children than **10.50** they were in the immediate wake of *Henderson*. It is likely that the incorporation of ECHR into Scots law will cause them to give more weight to the child's right to due process than might otherwise have been the case.

Party Status

It has been noted that there are several ways in which children may **10.51** seek to influence court cases affecting them, including being separately represented as parties to the actions. However, it is worth noting that, of the many different types of cases which may affect children, the children themselves are automatically party to the proceedings only when defendants in criminal cases and when their cases come before children's hearings.[83]

---

[79] 1997 Fam. L.R. 120.
[80] Law Reform (Parent and Child) (Scotland) Act 1986, s. 3(2).
[81] *Henderson v. Henderson,* 1997 Fam. L.R. 120 at p. 125.
[82] *The Scotsman*, July 15, 1997, p. 8.
[83] Kearney, *"Children's Hearings and the Sheriff Court"* (1st ed.), p. 186 took the view that, despite rules allowing children's presence to be dispensed with, the child was a party. Since that was written, the child has been given a right to attend the hearing, in addition to the duty to attend s. 45 Children (Scotland) Act 1995 and this makes the view even more compelling.

10.52　　As has been noted above, in family actions, while the child is not automatically a party, intimation must be sought or dispensed with, in respect of the child. Is this provision and the rule allowing anyone, including a child, to apply to be sisted as a third party[84] enough to satisfy the Conventions? Does the right to be heard necessarily require that children have party status in an action affecting them? To insist that it does would be to fall into the trap of equating children's rights with adults' rights without requiring that children's vulnerability be acknowledged. It cannot be denied that involvement in court cases is stressful for any client. If children can be enabled to express views without being subjected to the rigours of the court process, then this must happen and mechanisms must be flexible enough to allow it to happen.

Judicial Response to the Child's Right to be Heard and Represented

10.53　Is separate representation a good thing? So far in this chapter, it has been assumed that allowing children to become more directly involved in the processes that affect them is a desirable goal. There are some, however, who believe this is not at all self-evident.

10.54　　Some experienced family lawyers have explained to the writer how distressing it can be for children to hear the mud-slinging involved in many family actions. Others stress the damaging effects of the court process itself and feel it would be quite wrong to subject a child to it. "There is a world of difference between using the formal legal process to ensure that decisions about children are made according to procedures that are fair and just to the child and using that process regularly to determine what course of action would best promote that child's welfare and best interests".[85]

10.55　　Criticisms of the way the legal process handles cases involving children does not, however, negate the argument that any person whose future life is affected by a court's decision has the right to be heard before that decision is made. It is moreover an argument backed up by the requirements of the UN and European Conventions. In addition, if the court's goal is to make a decision which will promote a child's best interests, it must be the case that the court will be better able to identify that decision if it has an understanding of the issues from the child's perspective.

10.56　　It would, nonetheless, be irresponsible to insist on a civil liberties principle to the detriment of an individual child. The Scottish legal system must find ways of accommodating the child's right to be heard, without damaging those children whom it is trying to help. It is important to bear in mind that children are all different, that

---

[84]　OCR r. 13.1
[85]　King and Trowell, *Children's Welfare and the Law* (1992), p. 117.

cases vary in their circumstances and that the more ways there are for children to express views, the better. Christine Piper, discussing English family law proceedings, states: "The task is to open up a range of possibilities for children to receive information and to be consulted or represented, both inside and outside the family justice system".[86]

It is also important to bear in mind that children, whatever the **10.57** tabloids would have us believe, are not queuing up to sue their parents. Research with children of divorced parents[87] found that the children wanted there to be civility between the adults and to feel that they could help to shape arrangements. Crucially, the children made it clear that parenting styles and the quality of their relationships with their parents were more important than the actual residence and contact arrangements.[88]

This means that the concerns of Scottish solicitors about the **10.58** damaging effects of being involved in court cases must be given serious consideration. English courts have consistently expressed concern about children's presence in court. In *J. v. Lancashire County Council*,[89] a 15-year-old was ordered from the court at the appeal stage, despite having listened to the whole case in the family proceedings court. In *Re C. (a minor) (care: child's wishes)*[90] a judge reluctantly agreed that a 13-year-old girl could attend court but stated that children's presence "should not be encouraged to develop into settled practice"[91]. In *Re W. (secure accommodation order: attendance at court)*[92] the court refused to allow a ten year old boy to attend a hearing of an application to place him in secure accommodation and stated that children should only be allowed to attend if the court was "satisfied that attendance is in the best interests of the child".[93]

A requirement that it be in a child's best interests before they may **10.59** attend seems excessive paternalism, not to mention a clear breach of Article 6 of the European Convention, but the principle that the welfare of the child may be relevant to the issue of attendance at court is a sound one. However, rather than adopting the English approach that the court always knows best, it must be for the child's solicitor to consider these matters and to act accordingly. Only in an exceptional case might it be expected that the court would exercise its protective jurisdiction over the child.

---

[86] C. Piper, "Barriers to Seeing and Hearing Children in Private Law Proceedings", [1999] Fam. Law 394, at p. 398.
[87] Smart and Neale "It's My Life Too—Children's Perspectives on Post-Divorce Parenting" [2000] Fam. Law 163.
[88] *ibid.* p. 167.
[89] May 25, 1993, unreported but referred to in Children Act Advisory Committee Annual Report, 1992/93, p. 72.
[90] [1993] 1 F.L.R. 832.
[91] *ibid, per* Waite L.J. at p. 840.
[92] [1994] 2 F.L.R. 1092.
[93] *ibid. per* Ewbank, J. at p. 1095.

English Judicial Response

10.60 It has been noted that English courts are concerned that children's attendance at court will be detrimental to the children. English cases under the Children Act 1989 have raised other concerns about separate representation, which are worth considering before looking at the Scottish cases. Under the Children Act 1989, the courts, in deciding any question relating to a child's upbringing, must have regard to the ascertainable wishes and feelings of the child concerned, considered in the light of his age and understanding.[94] Children are automatically parties to English care proceedings[95] and a solicitor may be appointed to represent them[96]. Children are not parties to private law proceedings, and must apply to the court for leave to make an application; the court will grant this application when satisfied that the child has sufficient understanding.[97] Under the court rules, it is possible for the child to act alone[98] without a guardian *ad litem* or next friend.[99]

10.61 Some English judges have expressed approval of the principle of children's involvement in cases—such as Judge Booth who stated that a 15-year-old child's involvement in a case directed the parties and the evidence to the issues for the child.[1] However, the courts have, in many cases, shown discomfort at the notion of children having their own lawyers. The court decisions have produced barriers to children's representation.

10.62 The first barrier is that applications must go to the High Court. The now famous case of the 14-year-old Surrey girl who applied for a residence order to live with her boyfriend's parents[2] resulted in a practice direction[3] stating that because of the difficult issues raised in such cases, they should come to the High Court.

10.63 The second barrier is the limitation on the child's presence in court, which has been considered above. The third barrier is the view taken that justices should rarely interview children. In *Re M.,*[4] it was stated: "it should not be necessary, and it is not generally desirable, for justices to see the child. Any questions they may have as to the child's strength of feeling, or as to the reasons which he has

---

[94] Children Act 1989, s. 1(3)(a).
[95] Family Proceedings Courts (Children Act 1989) Rules 1991 (S.I. 1991 No. 1395), r. 7 and Family Proceedings Rules 1991 (S.I. 1991 No. 1247), r.4.7.
[96] Children Act 1989, s. 41(3).
[97] Children Act 1989, s. 10(8).
[98] Family Proceedings Rules 1991 (S.I. 1991 No. 1247), r.9.2A.
[99] For detailed discussion and analysis of English law on separate representation, see Fortin, "Children's Rights and the Developing Law"(1998) Butterworths, especially Chaps 7 and 8.
[1] *Re S.C. (A Minor) (Application for Leave by Child)* [1993] Fam. Law 553.
[2] *Re A.D. (A Minor)(Child's Wishes)*[1993] Fam. Law 405.
[3] See (1993) 143 N.L.J. 331 for Practice Direction.
[4] *Re M. (Child)(Ascertaining Wishes and Feelings)* [1993] 1 F.C.R. 721.

for the wishes he expresses, should properly be put...to the guardian *ad litem* or to the welfare officer concerned".[5] In *Re W.,* Wall, J, faced with the case of an eight year old whose parents were fighting about contact, said: "I find it difficult to conceive of circumstances in which any bench of Justices should see a child of W's age in relation to the issue of contact".[6]

The fourth barrier is the need to protect children. In *Re A.,*[7] a 14-year-old applied to discharge his care order. It was held that, while the starting point was that the boy was a party who would normally have a right to put his point of view, the court must balance this against the need to protect the child from exposure to potentially damaging material. In *Re S.,*[8] an 11-year-old child wished to be heard without a guardian *ad litem* in an extremely acrimonious and long-running custody battle. The court held that this would not be appropriate, given the emotionally complex and highly fraught nature of the proceedings. **10.64**

The fifth barrier is the role that the courts have taken upon themselves, to decide whether a child is capable of instructing a solicitor. It was confirmed in *Re C.T.*[9] that the court could override the solicitor's view that the child had sufficient understanding to give instructions. The courts appear to expect rather a high degree of sophistication from a child client: "Participation as a party, in my judgement, means much more than instructing a solicitor as to his own views...he must be able to give instructions on many different matters as the case goes through its stages and to make decisions as need arises".[10] Many family practitioners would be delighted if they could expect as much from their adult clients! **10.65**

Scottish Judicial Response

The barriers relating to the need to protect the child have been replicated in the Scottish cases under the 1995 Act. Other concerns have also emerged: manipulation of the child; appropriate procedure when the child is a third party; and confidentiality of the child's views. **10.66**

The Scottish judiciary has been concerned about children's welfare when they have become involved directly in court cases. In *Henderson v. Henderson,*[11] the Sheriff was clearly concerned about the effect on the ten-year old child who was a third party to the **10.67**

---

[5] *ibid. per* Booth, J. at p. 726.
[6] *Re W.(Child: Contact)*[1993] 2 F.C.R. 731, at p. 741.
[7] *Re A. (Care: Discharge Application by Child)* [1995] Fam. Law 291.
[8] *Re S. (A Minor) (Independent Representation)* [1993] 2 F.L.R.437.
[9] *Re C.T. (A Minor)(Wardship: Representation)*[1993] 2 F.L.R 278.
[10] *Re A. (A Minor) (Independent Representation)* [1993] 2 F.C.R. 437 *per* Mrs Justice Booth at p. 440.
[11] 1997 Fam. L.R. 120.

dispute about contact. He stated: " I do not regard the fact that the child entered the process as a party as of assistance. She was therefore entitled to remain while all the evidence, some of which would have been distressing to her, was heard. In fact, she chose not to do so, but I would have had some difficulty in excluding her".[12]

10.68   The Sheriff in *Henderson* has also expressed concern that the child appeared to have been influenced by the defender's opinions. In *Perendes v. Sim*.[13] two children, aged 11 and 10 at the date of the hearing before the Outer House, expressed views that they did not wish to see their father. It was clear that the mother had mis-represented facts to the children, due to her hostility to the father, and that she had manipulated them. The court took the decision that contact should, in principle, take place stating that while the children's wishes were important, they were of limited weight in the light of the mother's attitude. However, the court's overriding concern for the children's welfare is clear. It took the unusual step of ordering that the children should speak to a psychologist before any order was made, noting that the order would not be made if there were a risk of material psychological damage to the children.

10.69   The courts have not shown any great reluctance to take account of the views of children younger than aged 12, who do not benefit from the presumption of maturity at that age. In *Fairbairn v. Fairbairn*[14] the court heard a proof on residence of three children, aged 13, seven and five. At the end of the proof, the sheriff[15] sought the views of the two younger children, by appointing a curator *ad litem*. In his judgement he observed that the court was not pre-vented from seeking the views of children under 12 and that their views were to be taken into account.

10.70   Issues of appropriate procedures to be adopted when children seek to enter the process as third party minuters have been con-sidered judicially. *Fourman v. Fourman*[16] concerned an application by the mother of three children for a specific issue order, to allow her to take the children abroad to live with her. The application was opposed by the children's father. The eldest child, aged 14 at the time of the proof, wished to be heard in the process and was sisted as a third party to the action. The sheriff viewed that process as useful: "In this case PF has a view and a particular position to adopt, although she has not sided with either parent on the issue of going to Australia. Being represented has enabled her to take part in the proceedings as a party but not to be directly involved in the argument between her parents if she chose not to do so, which she

---

[12] *ibid. per* Sheriff Bell, at p. 125.
[13] 1998 G.W.D. 15-735.
[14] 1998 G.W.D 23-1149.
[15] Interestingly, the same sheriff who had conducted the *Henderson* proof.
[16] 1998 Fam. L.R. 98.

did not. Rather than give oral evidence she lodged an affidavit. It seems that the procedure adopted here of PF becoming a party minuter was entirely appropriate".[17]

The sheriff in *Fourman* also commented on procedural issues **10.71** relating to pleadings. He noted that there were no pleadings for the third party and no answers to these in the Record. He stressed that third party pleadings should be set out in the usual way and answered by the other parties. It is clear that, in terms of the parties" rights to due process under Article 6 of the European Convention, this is entirely justifiable. However, several sheriffs have dispensed with the need for the lodging of formal pleadings and answers in respect of a child party. They have accepted that the child's position can be set out in a Minute and is not relevant to many of the issues raised in the rest of the action, for example, divorce itself or financial provision. The matter of whether the court rules should be modified for child parties has yet to be formally addressed.

When children give evidence in criminal trials, the law provides **10.72** mechanisms to attempt to protect them from the damaging effects of the trial process.[18] There are no special rules to protect children in civil proofs, but the courts have attempted to make the experience less intimidating. In *Henderson*,[19] the sheriff's judgement described the procedure: "I removed my wig and gown and the child sat at a table. The solicitors and I sat round the table. There was some discussion whether the pursuer and the defender should remain in the court when [the child] gave evidence. They were not willing to leave, but both agreed to sit at the back of the court in the hope that this would remove some pressure from the child".

Confidentiality of the child's views, once they have been ex- **10.73** pressed, is the issue which has most concerned the Scottish judiciary to date and it is one that remains to be resolved. It was noted above that the sheriff court rules allow for the child's views to be placed in a confidential envelope, available only to the sheriff[20]. An examination of the cases reveals the dilemmas involved. In *Dosoo v. Dosoo*[21] two children aged 14 and 12 had been interviewed by a reporter. They had requested confidentiality and their views had been placed in a sealed envelope. The defender sought disclosure, arguing that refusal would be a breach of natural justice and of Articles 6 and 8 of the European Convention. The views were not disclosed and the court observed that for a child to feel able to express his views freely he had to feel confident in privacy if he wished, which the court should respect except in compelling circumstances.

---

[17] *ibid. per* Sheriff Morrison at p. 103.
[18] For discussion, see Chap. 15, paras 15.42 *et seq.*
[19] 1997 Fam. L.R. 120 at p. 123–4.
[20] OCR r. 33.20(2).
[21] 1999 G.W.D. 13-586.

10.74   The opposite view was taken in *McGrath v. McGrath*.[22] A case
was remitted for reconsideration where a Sheriff had taken account
of children's views as expressed to a curator *ad litem*, but had not
disclosed those views to the parties. It was stated that the welfare
principle did not apply to the question of whether a child's view
should be kept confidential. It was a fundamental principle that a
party was entitled to disclosure of all materials, although a court
could take into account whether disclosure would involve a real
possibility of significant harm to the child.

10.75   The case of *Oyeneyin v. Oyeneyin*[23] noted that the positions in
Dosoo and *McGrath* were irreconcilable. It did not resolve the
matter, but did agree that the welfare principle was not the deciding
factor in the matter of disclosure and that reporters should explain
to children that confidentiality could not be guaranteed. Similarly,
in *Grant v. Grant*[24], the court reserved its opinion as to whether the
1995 Act created a right of confidentiality for a child, but did refuse
to accept that there had been a breach of natural justice, since the
information in the curator's report had been explored at proof.

10.76   It may be suggested that it would be a clear breach of Article 6
routinely to cloak children's views in secrecy. Since Article 12 of the
UN Convention requires that children be able to express views
"freely", it might be that, in an exceptional case, concern for the
child's physical or mental wellbeing might override the right of
others to due process. Such a case, however, should be very rare
indeed.

Ensuring Quality Representation

10.77 The caselaw indicates that children's involvement in court cases
affecting them can give rise to ethical and legal dilemmas. It is
essential that the legal profession, which carries the bulk of the
responsibility for the conduct of the cases, ensures it is able to face
the challenges of children as clients.

10.78   Several writers have emphasised that solicitors must recognise
that children's needs as clients may differ from those of adults.
Liddle[25] outlines the importance of taking an interview at a child's
pace, being ready to explain in age-appropriate language about the
case, and having the skills to put the child at ease without being

---

[22] 1999 G.W.D. 20-915.
[23] 1999 G.W.D. 38-1836.
[24] 2000 G.W.D. 5-177.
[25] Liddle, *Acting for Children*, (English) Law Society's Handbook for Solicitors and
       Guardians *Ad Litem* Working with Children (1992).

patronising or clumsy. King and Young[26] suggest detailed preparation may be required before meeting a child client, to ensure an understanding of the child's family and his place in it.

The Law Society of Scotland has introduced a child law speci- **10.79** alism, but this is effectively meaningless. There is no requirement that an applicant has any training or experience in working with and communicating with children and young people. This being the case, what is the difference between the child and family law specialisms? There appears to be none, representing an abdication of the responsibilities which the Law Society should exercise in relation to child clients. The profession in Scotland must consider what training and experience it will demand of children's lawyers in the future, particularly in the light of the decision in *S. v Miller*.[27] It will be remembered that, there, the Inner House saw the role of the solicitor, before and during the hearing, as one of helping the child to understand reports and to take part in discussions about his or her future. Success in such a role will require the ability to communicate with children and to understand the pressures they face. It will also require an understanding of the unique procedures in the children's hearings system, to ensure that representation does not undermine the informality of the hearing, which is regarded as vital in promoting children's welfare.

The Family Law Association runs a "Working for Children" **10.80** course, to provide family practitioners with information about child psychology and development, in addition to exposing them to role-play scenarios where they are instructed by "children". It is to be hoped that such training is further developed, and eventually recognised by the Law Society of Scotland as a minimum requirement for anyone intending to assist children in the legal processes affecting them.

---

[26] King and Young, *The Child As Client: A Handbook for Solicitors Who Represent Children* (1992) especially Chaps 4–6.
[27] 2001 S.L.T. 531.

CHAPTER 11

MEDICAL TREATMENT

JOHN BLACKIE AND HILARY PATRICK

Children have more interactions with healthcare decision-making in **11.1**
Scotland, as in other parts of the developed world, than any other
group apart from the elderly. These interactions are not all about
medical treatment in the traditional narrow sense of diagnosis and
treatment by doctors supported by nurses. They may involve interactions with a wide range of other persons or bodies, extending
from the healthcare system through to social workers, teachers,
parents and other family members and even, for example in an
emergency, members of the public generally. In the healthcare
system itself, the context may be much broader than that of the
doctor patient relationship, as with the provision of various forms
of psychological therapy. It may take the form even of the provision
of a supportive environment, whether in a specific setting, such as a
school, or in the community generally. In considering the operation
of Scots law in the area of "medical treatment" against the background of both the United Nations Conventions on the Rights of
the Child (the UN Convention) and the European Convention on
Human Rights and Fundamental Freedoms (the European Convention), this wider reality of the interactions of children and young
persons with healthcare decision-making and the healthcare system
as, thus, broadly conceived, needs always to be borne in mind. In
some of the relevant legislation in Scotland, this wider background
is often not expressly reflected. In particular, the legislation[1] dealing
with the capacity of children and young persons to consent to
treatment or to refuse treatment makes provision for where a
"qualified medical practitioner" is treating a child under the age of
16, but only by implication covers a wider range of healthcare
providers.[2] Nor does that legislation define what is meant by

---

[1] Age of Legal Capacity (Scotland) Act 1991.
[2] s. 2 (4). How wide this phrase is is not completely clear: It has been commented:
"It is submitted that it will cover doctors, dentists, anaesthetists, nurses,
chiropodists, midwives, and all health professionals qualified to do that which
they are doing". (Wilkinson and Norrie, *Parent and Child* (2nd ed.) (1999) para.
15.09.) Whether is applies also to care workers, teachers, and so on, is doubtful.

"treatment".[3] Only the use of the word "any" in the descriptive phrase that it adopts[4] enables it to be applied to the full range of interactions of a child or young person with healthcare.[5]

11.2   It is not possible to cover the whole of the very wide scope of health and healthcare. Accordingly, the focus here is on what are the most significant issues at present, conscious that there are others that are interesting and of significance that we do not deal with.[6]

Rights to health and healthcare

11.3   The issue of whether there is a right of any meaningful sort to health is logically prior to the question as to whether there is a right to medical services. Articles 6 and 24 of the UN Convention, from different angles, overtly recognise this. Article 6 states that every child has the inherent right to life and to ensuring "to the maximum extent possible" the survival and development of the child. Article 24 refers to the right to "highest attainable standard of health". However, reflecting the fact that to realise any standard, and certainly an optimum standard, of health, rights to healthcare provision are also necessary, Article 24 of the UN Convention specifies the kind of measures which should be taken to achieve this. These include pre-natal care for mothers, attempts to reduce infant mortality, preventative health care and so on.

11.4   The starting point for consideration of the extent to which this is reflected in the law in Scotland is necessarily the legislation regulating the provision of the National Health Service in Scotland, as being by far the largest provider of healthcare in the country.[7] It imposes on the relevant government ministers a legal duty to ensure a comprehensive and integrated health service in Scotland,[8] free at

---

[3]   This has caused problems in being certain as to whether some children can take part in non-therapeutic research projects.

[4]   s. 2(4): "any procedure or treatment".

[5]   By contrast the definition of treatment that is relevant to compulsory detention and treatment under the Mental Health (Scotland) Act 1984 does reflect the wide range of interactions and has been held to be in accordance with the European Convention generally; *A. v. The Scottish Ministers*, 2000 S.L.T. 873.

[6]   In particular, issues which are at the antenatal stage.

[7]   The role of the private sector in Scotland (around six per cent, including nursing homes for the elder is even smaller than in England, and almost negligible with respect to the healthcare of children and young persons (See *Scotland—National Health Service Statistics* (published annually)). (A detailed analysis of the figures in 1996 can be found in J.W.G. Blackie, "England and Scotland" in G. Fischer and H. Lilie, *Medical Responsibility—The Comparative Law of Europe (Ärtzliche Verantwortung im Europäischen Recthsvergleich)* (1999) 195, at 198–201). A significant amount of dentistry for child and young persons, is, however, now carried out privately.

[8]   National Health Service (Scotland) Act 1978, s. 1 and Part III.

the point of use.[9] Specifically, it requires that arrangements are made for the prevention of illness and the provision of medical, nursing and rehabilitation services and hospital beds to meet all reasonable needs, bearing in mind the needs of the population. As the system in fact is structured in such a way that these functions are delegated to Health Boards, which cover various regions of the country,[10] and on which the legislation imposes duties to provide, [11] the reality is that there is a variation in the way these resources are deployed in different places in the country. This is further reflected in the practice that most hospital and community services are purchased by Health Boards from hospital and primary care trusts.

However, to determine whether this legislation means that the **11.5** provision of healthcare services in the National Health Service is in accordance with Article 24 of the UN Convention requires consideration of an issue which arises in considering the meaning of Article 24 itself. This is: does Article 24 impliedly mean that the question of the availability of resources to deliver healthcare is a factor that can be taken into account in satisfying its requirements, despite the apparently absolute form of words used in this Article? If the answer to that is in the affirmative, there is then a question as to whether our law has principles that appropriately reflect the way in which resource questions are impliedly relevant in Article 24. It seems inevitable that resources questions in some way are reflected in Article 24. Until recently it was clear that, whatever these principles are, our law did not give effect to them, since there were no principles in our law dealing with this, other than one that the matter was not justiciable, and solely political.[12] This was clear even though there was no Scottish case law directly in point. The approach was impliedly indicated, however, in two cases[13] on the associated question as to whether a government minister could ever be held liable on the grounds of negligent decision making in connexion with promoting the health of the population (through literature encouraging vaccination of children). The discretion of the government in effect, it was held, meant there could be no duty of care in this context.

The view that there are no principles applicable to deal with the **11.6** relevance of the distribution of resources to and within the healthcare system is no longer tenable in the light of incorporation into our law of the European Convention, and specifically of its Articles 2, 3 and 6. English case law considering the legal obliga-

---

[9] National Health Service (Scotland) Act 1978, s. 1(2).
[10] National Health Service (Scotland) Act 1978, s. 2.
[11] See Part III of the Act.
[12] For this in the first half of the 1990's, see John Blackie and Hilary Patrick, "Medical Treatment" in Alison Cleland and Elaine E. Sutherland, *Children's Rights in Scotland* (1996) at pp. 156–157.
[13] *Bonthrone v. Secretary of State for Scotland*, 1987 S.L.T. 34; *Ross v. Secretary of State for Scotland*, 1990 S.L.T. 13.

tions under the equivalent English legislation had already formulated some principles. These, however, make it almost impossible ever to challenge a decision that was based on resource
implications. The view developed through those cases is certainly
that the National Health Service is required to use resources sen-
sibly and reasonably.[14] But that is expressed in a form[15] that an
effective legal challenge on the question of distribution of resources
could only be sustained if the distribution was irrational, that is,
completely unreasonable in the public law sense of that word.[16] No
distinction, it may be noted further, is made in these cases between
children and young persons and adults. The approach has been
applied[17] as much where a baby, with a hole in the heart, actually
needed[18] the treatment as in a case where the treatment would
definitely not succeed,[19] and as in a case where parents wanted an
experimental treatment to be given to their ten-year-old child.[20]
What has been held challengeable in England is a blanket decision
taken as to the distribution of resources by classes of case without
consideration of the position of the individual patient.[21]

11.7   One case[22] from the European Court of Human Rights is equi-
vocal as to how far this is still the sole ground of challenge. The case
has been referred to, but without comment, in an English court.[23] It
establishes at least that having to rely on inadequate treatment
facilities can amount to "inhuman and degrading treatment" under
Article 3 of the European Convention. It may be argued, however,
that as the case was about whether a person suffering from an
illness (AIDS) should be deported to another country with inadequate treatment facilities for that condition, it goes no farther
than providing that the law must not deny a person healthcare

---

[14] See *R v. Secretary of State for Social Services ex parte Hincks* (1990) 1 B.M.L.R.
93(Court of Appeal).
[15] See also, in particular, *R v. Central Birmingham Health Authority, ex parte Walker*
*(*1987) 3 B.M.L.R. 32 *per* Sir John Donaldson.
[16] *i.e.* "Wednesbury" unreasonbleness (as first expounded in *Associated Provincial
Picture Houses v. Wednesbury Corporation* [1947] 2 All E.R. 680).
[17] *R v. Central Birmingham Health Authority, ex parte Walker (*1987) 3 B.M.L.R.
32.
[18] *per* Macpherson, J. (at first instance): "he needs an operation to repair his heart
that is all that need be said by way of a description of what is required".
[19] *R. (a minor) (medical treatment)* [1998] 1 F.L.R. 384 where the court refused to
order doctors to carry out treatment for a 16-month old boy suffering from
muscular atrophy where the medical evidence was that such treatment would be
futile.
[20] *R. v. Cambridge District Health Authority, ex parte B.* [1995] 2 All E.R. 129. (The
child, B., in fact later obtained the treatment through money being raised by an
appeal to the public though, sadly without it achieving a cure).
[21] See *R. v. North West Lancashire Health Authority, ex parte A. and Others* [1999]
Lloyd's Rep. Med.: a blanket policy of not providing gender reassignment
treatment for transsexuals successfully challenged.
[22] *D. v. United Kingdom* (1997) 24 E.H.H.R. 423.
[23] *NHS Trust A. v. M.; NHS Trust B. v H.* [2001] 1 All E.R. 801, *per* Dame Elizabeth
Butler-Sloss P. at 813.

resources that he or she already has access to, and also those that access would naturally lead to as his or her condition develops in the future. It is arguable, further, that Article 2 (right to life) of the European Convention is relevant.[24] If it is relevant that would mean that our law could reflect the additional support that Article 6 of the UN Convention gives to the rights to health and healthcare provided in Article 24 of that Convention. As we have a fairly sophisticated health, education and social welfare system that attempts to promote child health and welfare, in its essentials Article 2 of the European Convention is complied with in Scotland, and in that broad sense Article 6 of the UN Convention is appropriately reflected.

It is possible to argue that this, however, does not mean that our **11.8** law with respect to the provision and distribution of resources within the healthcare system is in accordance with Article 2 of the European Convention. This is controversial. One dictum in a decision of the European Commission on Human Rights[25] (considering police services) can be read as indicating that Article 2 of that convention adds nothing beyond the position reached in the recent English domestic case law which enables challenge of blanket decisions: "[Article 2] must be interpreted .. as requiring preventative steps to be taken to protect life from known and avoidable dangers .. the extent of the obligation varies ... there will be a range of policy decision relating *inter alia*, to the use of state resources". What is required is, then, that the states assesses aims and priorities, "subject to these being compatible with the values of a democratic society".[26] Controlling risk to life from disease factors was specified as a matter in the respect of which this arises. It would seem by analogy applicable also to the promotion of health more generally.

It might possibly be thought that Article 8 (right to private and **11.9** family life) of the European Convention could be used to consider the question of the right to health and healthcare since it promotes autonomy, and autonomy on one view is meaningless without health. However, such an extension of the concept has not been developed, and the only respect in which autonomy as guaranteed by Article 8 has been held to have a relevance in the field of medical treatment is to emphasise the right of a patient to refuse, as opposed to demand, treatment.[27]

---

[24] The European Court of Human Rights in *D. v. United Kingdom (supra)* did not find it necessary to consider that possibility, having decided in the plaintiff's favour under Art. 3 anyway.

[25] *Osman v. United Kingdom* (1999) 1 F.L.R. 193.

[26] at 321.

[27] See *NHS Trust A. v. M; NHS Trust B. v. H.* [2001] 1 All E.R. 801 per Dame Elizabeth Butler-Sloss P. at 812, following *X. and Y. v. Netherlands* (1985) 8 E.H.R.R. 235 and *Peters v. Netherlands* (1994) 77A DR 75.

Right to life in the narrow sense of not being deprived of life

11.10 Even if the right to life provided for in Article 2 of the European Convention does not have implications for the general question of access to healthcare and resources, it certainly does mean that our law now has principles that are capable of reflecting the narrower aspect of Article 6 of the UN Convention, namely that legal principles are required to determine end of life questions. Article 2 of the European Convention contains both a positive and a negative duty. The positive duty is to ensure that "everyone's right to life" is protected by national law. The negative duty is the prohibition on the taking of life.

11.11 *Law Hospital NHS Trust v. Lord Advocate*,[28] which determines that the taking of such a decision must be through asking what is in the "best interests of the patient" on that point implies a rule in essence identical to that applied in England. It has now been held in an English case[29] not to contravene Article 2 of the European Convention, for a number of reasons. The "negative obligation", not intentionally to deprive a person of life, is not infringed. The reason given for this view proceeds by making a distinction between acts of commission and acts of omission.[30] Another variant of this was also used in holding that it was not a breach of the negative obligation to part one conjoined twin from another surgically, knowing that one would die,[31] a distinction that has been widely criticised by commentators where it has been used in respect of other aspects of end of life decisions. The "positive obligation" under Article 2 was also seen as being complied with as the case law of the European Court of Human Rights[32] only requires that "reasonable steps be taken", and the use of the "best interests of the patient test" to determine the matter was considered to be a greater protection than the minimum which Article 2 required, which would be following the views of a competent body of medical opinion.[33] Finally, this was seen as confirmed in that the "best interests" approach was held to be itself implementing the auton-

---

[28] 1996 S.L.T. 848 (withdrawal of feeding from patient in persistent vegetative state).

[29] As laid down by the House of Lords in *Airedale NHS Trust v. Bland* [1993] A.C. 789.

[30] *per* Dame Elizabeth Butler-Sloss P. at 809.

[31] *Re A.* [2000] 4 All E.R. 961 at 1068 (the case of Jodie and Mary). That the point is the same is specifically stated by Dame Elizabeth Butler-Sloss P. at 808 referring to a passage in the judgement of Robert Walker L.J. in *Re A.* at 1068.

[32] *Widmer v. Switzerland*, European Court of Human Rights, February 10, 1993 (unreported), a case where the Swiss law, described as "passive euthanasia" was held compatible with Article 2 of the European Convention.

[33] *per* Dame Elizabeth Butler-Sloss P. at 809.

omy dimension of Article 8 of the European Convention.[34] This is an extended view of autonomy that autonomy exists even when a person, not any longer mentally capable of taking autonomous decisions, and the autonomy then becomes a right only to have things done to or for him or her that are in his or her best interests. This could not be applied directly in the case of the separation of conjoined twins, but essentially the positive obligation was complied with there through acting to safeguard the life of the viable twin.[35]

Two unresolved questions remain in Scotland. One is whether it **11.12** is ever possible to give treatment knowing that it will shorten life, and yet not infringe Article 2 of the European Convention.[36] The other question relates only to persons over 16, as below that age a court procedure can be initiated by anyone having an "interest" in terms of section 11(3) of the Children (Scotland) Act 1995.[37]

For those above that age, the rule in Scotland,[38] which contrasts **11.13** with that in England, is that the Court should not be used to take the decision[39] in withdrawal of treatment cases. It is submitted, however, that the positive obligation under Article 2 does not require such a further safeguard.[40] Nor does its absence result in blanket decision-making of the type that would be contrary to Article 6 of the European Convention (fair trial).[41]

Consent to and refusal of medical treatment

The law relating to consent to and refusal of medical treatment in **11.14** Scotland is based on three principles which can be abstracted from the common law, relevant statutory provisions, and the applicable provisions of the European Convention. These are the principle of

---

[34] *ibid.*
[35] Re A. [2000] 4 All E.R. 961, p. 1051. One judge (Brooke L.J.) expressed the view that other jurisdictions in Europe would take the same view, as it was inconceivable that such a procedure would be illegal everywhere in Europe.
[36] This point is expressly not dealt with in these recent English decisions. See in particular *NHS Trust A. v. M.; NHS Trust B. v H.* [2001] 1 All E.R. 801 *per* Dame Elizabeth Butler-Sloss P. at 810.
[37] There is the further question whether s. 11(3) and (4) is in all respects in accordance with Art. 12 of the UN Convention and Art. 10 of the European Convention.
[38] *Law Hospital NHS Trust v. Lord Advocate,* 1996 S.L.T. 848.
[39] Which will continue to be the position when the Adults with Incapacity (Scotland) Act comes into force in stages from the Spring of 2001.
[40] This can be argued to follow from the fact that the views of a competent body of medical opinion in favour of withdrawing treatment satisfies the requirement of Art. 2.
[41] Compare *Osman (op. cit).*

patient autonomy,[42] the principle that there may be proportionate limitations to the principle of autonomy, and the principle that healthcare professionals are required give a reasonable quantity and quality of information to patients.[43] The application of these three principles to children and young persons in Scots law is quite complex. There are rules relating to certain groups of children and young persons. But also relevant are rules that apply to particular groups of whatever age, notably those regulating the position where there is mental incapacity. Furthermore, an important dimension is the extent to which other people with a close relationship to the child should or should not be involved in the decision making process.

11.15   A young person who is 16 or older is an adult for these purposes.[44] By contrast to the position in England,[45] no one has the power to overrule his or her decision except in those limited situations where the decision of any adult can be overruled.[46] This is even more clearly the law than it was five years ago, and importantly means that the law in Scotland relating to treatment decisions with 16-and 17-year-olds better reflects both the UN Convention, and the European Convention, than does the law in England which fails properly to reflect the principle of autonomy in this connection.[47] The reasons our law is in this form are obvious. Firstly, the clear language giving the right to consent must also, by implication, give the right to refuse.[48] Secondly, the right in the Children (Scotland) Act to consent to any "transaction" on the child's behalf, which gives parents the authority to consent to medical treatment, is only available where the child is unable to consent themselves.[49] If the child can consent the parent does not

---

[42] For a clear statement of this principle in a Scottish case see *Law Hospital NHS Trust v. Lord Advocate,* 1996 S.L.T. 848 *per* Lord President Hope at 852: "the right of self determination provides the solution to all problems, at least so far as the court is concerned ... The patient's consent renders lawful that which would otherwise be unlawful".

[43] There is no reported appellate level decision in Scotland on this, but it is confirmed in two reported first instance cases (*Moyes v. Lothian Health Board,* 1990 S.L.T. 444; *Goorkani v. Tayside Health Board,* 1991 S.L.T. 94 following the English House of Lords case *Sidaway v. Board of Governors of the Bethlem Royal Hospital* [1985] A.C. 71).

[44] Age of Legal Capacity (Scotland) Act 1991 ss. 1(1)(b) and 2(7).

[45] *Re W.* [1992] 4 All E.R. 627, also *Re R. (A Minor) (Wardship: Consent to Treatment)* [1992] Fam. 11.

[46] This is different from the position in English law where it is thought parents have the right to overrule at least some decisions taken with respect to medical treatment by 16- and 17-year-olds.

[47] For the views of the present authors at that time see John Blackie and Hilary Patrick, "Medical Treatment" in Alison Cleland and Elaine E. Sutherland (eds.), *Children's Rights in Scotland* (1996) para. 9.10

[48] See Wilkinson and McK. Norrie, *Parent and Child* (2nd ed.,1999) para.15.09 and Sutherland, *Child and Family Law* (1999), para. 3.70.

[49] See Children (Scotland) Act 1995, s. 15(5)(b).

have any legal authority under that Act. Thirdly, where the 1995 Act deals with the making of supervision requirements containing a condition that a child submit to a medical examination or treatment, it is expressly stated that these can be carried out only if the child consents.[50] To maintain consistency, the power of the child to refuse must apply generally, not merely to these very specific circumstances. Finally, as the 1995 Act was intended to give effect to the UN Convention, and must be interpreted to reflect the European Convention, any ambiguity must be resolved to promote that, and hence to promote child autonomy and, accordingly, provide him or her the right to refuse. The application of this approach where a young person has mental health difficulties requires special attention.

Under the age of 16 the question whether the child or young **11.16** person has the capacity to take his or her own treatment decisions depends upon whether the "qualified medical practitioner"[51] attending the child is of the opinion that the individual child "is capable of understanding the nature and possible consequences of the procedure or treatment".[52] This test is not identical to the test that is to be applied in determining whether an adult has capacity to take treatment decisions.[53] In the absence of any Scottish caselaw, English[54] cases that have considered the matter as being whether the person can "sufficiently understand the nature, purpose and effects of the treatment" proposed.[55] This is approached by dividing the decision-making process into three stages: comprehension and retaining of information; believing it; and weighing it in the balance to arrive at a choice. This approach is reflected also in the relevant provisions of the Adults with Incapacity (Scotland) Act 2000,[56] which additionally points to five factors that should be considered: the person's capacity to make decisions, communicate them, understand them, retain them in memory, and act on them.[57] This approach is in line with the permitted limitations the principle of autonomy in the light of Article 8 of the European Convention.[58]

---

[50] Children (Scotland) Act 1995, s. 90.

[51] See (above) at fn. 2 for the extent of the meaning of this phrase.

[52] Age of Legal Capacity Scotland Act s. 2(4). An example of this being the case is in *Houston (Applicant)* 1996 S.C.L.R. 943 (For the special issues arising where the child or young person has mental health difficulties, as in this case see below at ...)

[53] It is, however, possibly less stringent than the English common law test in, which requires the child to have sufficient understanding and intelligence to enable him or her to understand fully what is proposed: *Gillick v. West Norfolk Wisbech Health Authority* [1986] A.C. 112 *per* Lord Scarman at 118.

[54] *Re T. (Adult: Refusal of Treatment)* [1993] Fam. 95.

[55] *Re C. (Adult: Refusal of Medical Treatment)* [1994] 1 W.L.R. 290, *per* Thorpe J. at 295.

[56] When brought into force in stages from 2001 on.

[57] These are definitely going to be the factors to consider in respect of whether an adult has capacity to take treatment decisions (Adults with Incapacity (Scotland) Act 2000 s. (1)(6)).

[58] See *per* Dame Elizabeth Butler-Sloss P. (*supra*)—at n. 30, *supra*.

The third aspect that is relevant with adults, the ability to weigh in the balance, is not part of the test the "qualified medical practitioner" has to apply in considering the question of child. For adults, the consideration of that ability to weigh in the balance does not relate to intellectual maturity, but to whether there is some feature present, as a mental disorder, that robs the person of the ability to make a valid decision in their own best interests. Another, more subtle difference relates to the significance of the fact that the decision the person is seeking to take appears to be irrational. Irrational decisions as such are not evidence of lack of capacity, as the case of a mental patient whose refusal of an amputation was upheld by an English court, even though the result meant that it was likely he would die of gangrene.[59] But an "irrational" decision of an adult that is not evidence of that adult's lacking capacity can, depending on its nature, be relevant to "qualified medical practitioner" deciding that a child lacked the necessary maturity. For example, if a child or young person under 16 were to seek to refuse treatment on the ground that all anaesthetics are too dangerous, it would follow that there is not understanding of the "nature" of the treatment. At the same time, for the principle of autonomy to be adequately reflected, a decision that a child of the same age would consider irrational does not entail that this child lacks the maturity to take the treatment decision.

The crucial decision of the "qualified medical practitioner as to maturity is, and was intended by parliament[60] in the legislation, to be final and not able to be appealed. Article 6 (1) of the European Convention, which provides that provides for access to the courts to determine civil rights and obligations may perhaps result in this provision in so far as it results in this as being contrary to the European Convention, particularly because the legislation provides not guidance to the "qualified medical practitioner" as to how to come to his or decision on the matter.[61]

Can a decision of a child under 16 who has capacity be overridden by a court?

11.18   If an adult with capacity refuses medical treatment, this must be respected, even if the person will die as a result. However, in the case of a child or young person under 16, any person with an interest can apply to the court for an order under section 11(e) of

---

[59]   *Re C (supra)*.

[60]   See the report of the Scottish Law Commission that led to the Act, *Report on theLegal Capacity and Responsibility of Minors and Pupils*, Scot. Law Com. No. 110, para. 3.74 for an explanation of why this was so.

[61]   See *Osman v. United Kingdom* (1999) 1 F.L.R. 193.

the 1995 Act to authorise the treatment.[62] A person with an interest would include the parents, but could also include a hospital or general practitioner. In such a case, the test would be not what the child or young person thought (although that would be taken into account, and if they were aged over 12 they would be presumed mature enough to have their views considered),[63] but what was in their best interests, in accordance with the welfare principle.[64]

Whilst it could be argued that it could never be in a person's best **11.19** interests to have a medical procedure which they did not want, there are also situations where it can be envisaged that, for example, a young Jehovah's Witness, should be given a blood transfusion despite her refusal.

The residual authority given to the court in such circumstances **11.20** reduces the young person's autonomy to take treatment decisions and could thus be seen as contrary to Article 12 of the UN Convention. This authority should not be used lightly and, in fact, there is no evidence that it is being so used. The young person's views will be taken into account in accordance with Article 12. It may seem acceptable that the welfare principle embodied in Scottish children's legislation should include provisions where, in a life or death situation, a young person can be protected even against themselves.

Treatment decisions for a child who lacks capacity

Where a child under the age of 16 does not, in the light of the above, **11.21** have the capacity to take treatment decisions, the parents (or those with parental responsibilities) can take these decisions and consent to treatment on his or her behalf.[65] Indeed, they must do so, since the parental right to take medical decisions is the corollary of the parent's responsibility to safeguard and promote the child's health, development and welfare.[66] Similar responsibilities and rights are given to the person who may have "care and control" of a child,

---

[62] Wilkinson and Norrie, argue (*op.cit.*, at para. 8.51,) that parents cannot ask for an order relating to parental responsibilities where a competent young person refuses treatment because they only have the right to take such decisions if the young person is unable to do so. See Children (Scotland) Act 1995, s. 15(5). However it could be argued that the application is not to allow the parents to give their consent but to substitute the decision of the court, in the child's best interests. The authors are not aware of a case in Scotland where this point has been raised. In any event, it would still be open to a hospital or doctor, as a person "with an interest" in the young person's welfare, to make an application under s. 11(3).

[63] Children (Scotland) Act 1995, s. 16(2).

[64] Children (Scotland) Act 1995, s. 16(1).

[65] The Children (Scotland) Act 1995, s. 2(1)(d) gives the parent the power to act as the child's legal representative, which includes giving consent to any transaction where the child is unable to consent (Children (Scotland) Act 1995, s.15(5)(b)). See Wilkinson and Norrie, *Parent and Child* (2nd ed., 1999) para. 8.48.

[66] Children (Scotland) Act 1995, s. 1(1)(a).

perhaps a childminder, foster parent or helper at a nursery,[67] provided they do not know of any reason those with parental responsibilities would refuse such treatment.[68] Any treatment
decision, whoever takes it, must, then, be "in the best interests of
the child". If it is not it can challenged by application to the
courts.[69] Accordingly, the question that we have considered under
Article 6 of the European Convention in connection with the
"qualified medical practitioner's decision" with regard to maturity,
not being in effect challengable, does not arise with the taking of the
treatment decision itself.

Children in care

11.22 Local authorities have a legal duty to "promote the welfare" of
children in care.[70] Article 6 of the UN Convention, which imposes
an obligations to "ensure to the maximum extent possible the survival and development of the child" would have been better reflected in the relevant legislation, if this primary statutory duty
expressly required the authority to safeguard the looked after
child's health.[71] However, it is clear by implication from the provisions that place on the local authority a duty to have the child's
health assessed and a plan of health care drawn up for the child.
The general rules that relate to the capacity of some children and
young persons to take their own treatment decisions are, for the
avoidance of doubt confirmed as applying in this context as much
as in any other.[72] In this an appropriate balance between the
principle of autonomy and the principle of proportionate limitations on it is preserved.

The role of the views of the child

11.23 In these situations, where treatment decisions must be taken not by
the child himself or herself but by someone else, consideration must
be given to the child's own views, if the child is mature enough to
express views, which is presumed if he or she is 12 or over.[73] This is

---

[67] But not teachers.
[68] Children (Scotland) Act 1995, s. 5.
[69] Children (Scotland) Act 1995, s. 1(1)(a). For this purpose a "child" means a
young person up to the age of 18. But a parent's right to take decisions on behalf
of the child terminates at 16 (s. 2(7)).
[70] Children (Scotland) Act 1995 s. 17(1).
[71] Contrast the duty on parents in s. 1(1)(a).
[72] The Arrangements to Look After Children (Scotland) Regulations (S.I. 1996 No.
3262, para. 13). This can cause serious problems in practice.
[73] Children (Scotland) Act 1995, s. 6.

just one aspect of the statutory law relating to the role of views of children. This statutory rule refers to "major decisions". For the law to reflect the provisions of Article 12 (1) of the UN Convention this phrase in the context of treatment decisions will have to be interpreted broadly, since that article refers to a child's right to express [his or her] "views freely in all matters affecting [him or her]". As the statutory rules, resulting in some children not being empowered to take their own treatment decisions, are exceptions to the general principle of autonomy, Article 8 of the European Convention (right to private and family life) can be seen as guaranteeing residual autonomy for such a child, in the same way as it has in England been held to do so for an adult lacking the necessary mental capacity to take treatment decisions. Accordingly, the view that in the context of treatment decisions, if a child is too immature to be able to form a serious view "little, if any, importance need be attached to his or her views on what treatment should be given"[74] no longer fully accurately represents the position. The view that there is still some role for the child's views in this context also would better reflect the Article 12(1) of the UN Convention, as it refers to maturity as only a factor relevant to the weight to be given to the child's views, while the requirement to take the child's views into account depends instead, but on the child being "capable of forming his or her own views".

How the views of a child in a situation where he or she cannot **11.24** take treatment decisions should be fed into decision-making in his or her best interests has hardly been explored. It is not, we submit, just a question of age, or of the hoped-for gain from treatment. That a child of three expresses his or her objection to necessary dental treatment by crying vigorously while it is being carried out would not mean that the decision-maker should follow the child's views. But if that child expressed those views in that way by refusing at the start, the exercise of responsible decision-making may require the decision-maker not to proceed, but, calm to the child. If a ten-year-old expresses a firmly held view that he or she does not want more painful therapy for a cancer known to be terminal, the best interests of that child may well be served by following those views, rather than rejecting them.

Children and young persons with mental health difficulties

There are special problems in this area. They apply only to children **11.25** and young persons under the age of 16. First, in assessing capacity, there is a difficulty in separating the test for maturity that the "qualified medical practitioner" should follow, from the test for

---

[74] Wilkinson and McK. Norrie, *Parent and Child*, at para. 8.49.

mental capacity. Secondly, there is a question of the relationship of the rules regulating treatment decisions and the special provisions of the Mental Health (Scotland) Act 1984, which enable compulsory detention and certain sorts of compulsory treatment to take place irrespective of consent of the patient. This second problem is not merely theoretical. Each year a small but significant number people under the age of 16 are detained under the provisions of the Mental Health (Scotland) Act 1984; in 1999–2000 19 children were detained under the emergency (72 hours) provisions, 14 under the short term (28 day) provisions and just three under long term (six month) provisions.[75]

11.26   It is clear with respect to the first problem that the principle of autonomy, and proportionate limitations on that principle, can only be satisfied by separating it from the question of whether the grounds for detention under the Mental Health (Scotland) Act arise, even if in reality it may be extremely difficult to separate out the two different tasks.

11.27   There is a convincing Sheriff Court decision supporting this approach.[76] It must be correct, because the Mental Health (Scotland) Act provisions are themselves only justified in the light of the European Convention, as proportionate limitations on the general principle of autonomy. If the child or young person under 16 has the maturity to take treatment decisions, a further question then follows as to whether he or she is at risk and treatment under the Mental Health (Scotland) Act 1984 is appropriate. Any other view would result in either an inappropriate failure to recognise the principle of autonomy through denying the ability to take treatment decisions at all, or a failure to recognise the principle of appropriate limitations on the principle of autonomy, because the Mental Health (Scotland) Act also contains safeguards against the arbitrary use of power, with rights of review and appeal and the oversight of the Mental Welfare Commission. These make the provisions reflect the principle of proportionate limitations on autonomy. To reflect the provisions of the UN Convention and the European Convention it is not enough just to ask the question: would it be in the interests of this child or young person to be cared for in hospital?[77] An earlier Sheriff Court decision,[78] dating from just before the Age of Legal Capacity (Scotland) Act 1991 codified the law relating to treatment decisions that proceeded on this basis, can be seen in the light of the law as it now is, as having failed in this way to reflect that the principles of autonomy and proportionate limitations on autonomy both have to be applied in a structured way so that they are seen to have been given effect to, even though the result of not

---

[75] Figures supplied by the Mental Welfare Commission.
[76] *Houston (Applicant)* 1996 S.C.L.R. 943.
[77] Our view also reflects the advice given now by the Mental Welfare Commission.
[78] *V. v. F.*, 1991 S.C.L.R. 225 (Sh. Ct).

doing this may in some cases be the same. The 15-year-old girl in that case was capable of understanding the court proceedings and the Sheriff's decision was solely on the grounds that detention and treatment under the provisions of the Mental Health (Scotland) Act was "unnecessary", because the parents could dictate that she stay in hospital and be treated. The Sheriff's view that this was a case where the provisions of the Mental Health (Scotland) Act did not apply because the role of the parents meant that it was not "necessary" that she be detained,[79] fails in the light of these wider issues to reflect the purpose of the legislation. There is, as the Sheriff recognised, the possibility of adding to any possible stigma associated with mental illness, by having her labelled as a patient who had had to be compulsorily detained. But, we submit, it is not a consideration of sufficient significance to justify a further and disproportionate reduction of limitation on the principle of autonomy.

The further considerations that then arise are the limitations on **11.28** autonomy of children and young persons that are contained in the compulsory detention and treatment provisions of the Mental Health (Scotland) Act 1984 themselves in accordance with the relevant provisions of the UN Convention and the European Convention. That Act itself contains an important provision reflecting autonomy that, even where the provisions would otherwise apply, they do not apply if the person is willing to be a voluntary patient.[80] Most young people needing psychiatric help will fall into this category. It follows, and this now reflects good practice, that a person should be compulsory detained in preference to exerting undue persuasion on him or her to become a voluntary patient.

There is still, however, a question as to whether the provisions in **11.29** the Mental Health (Scotland) Act 1984 are in accordance with the requirement of Article 12 of the UN Convention to permit the child or young person to express his or her views,[81] and further with Article 25 of that Convention (right to "a periodic review").

The Mental Health (Scotland) Act does not fully reflect the **11.30** provisions of Article 12 in that it is applicable to people of any age, and that there are no special provisions adjusted to the particular circumstances of children and young persons.[82] Additionally, it clearly fails to reflect Article 12, because there is no statutory requirement that professionals making decisions about the treatment or compulsory detention of the patient[83] should take into account

---

[79] Mental Health (Scotland) Act 1984, s. 17(1).
[80] See s.17(2).
[81] Art. 12(1).
[82] Other than a reference to local authorities with parental rights being treated as nearest relative, ss. 54, 55.
[83] Mental Health (Scotland) Act 1984, ss. 17 and Part V.

the wishes and feelings of the patient when deciding on treatment options, although this may happen as a matter of good practice. Nor is such an obligation imposed by the Mental Health Act Code of Practice. Further, it probably fails to accord with Article 12 of the UN Convention in the provisions that the child or young person's parents or the person with parental responsibility will generally be their "nearest relative" or next of kin for the purposes of the Act.[84] Further, in that there is no procedure whereby the young person can challenge an unsuitable relative, it is in breach of Article 8 of the European Convention.[85]

11.31 Neither the Act nor the procedural Act of Sederunt which supports it[86] contains any measures for making the detention procedures more appropriate to the needs of the young person. The procedures are generally regarded as intimidating for older persons. These shortcomings could make the procedures liable to challenge under the Article 3 and 8 of the European Convention.[87]

11.32 It may be that, even though the Mental Health (Scotland) Act does contain provisions for appeal against detention, these do not amount to the provision of a "period review of the treatment provided to [him or her] and all other circumstances relevant to his or her placement", as required under Article 25 of the UN Convention. This is because the right to appeal against detention (after the first six months for a long term detention) generally takes the form of a reconsideration of whether the patient needs to be detained. The Sheriff does not question treatment decisions made.[88]

Young people aged over 16

11.33 If the young person of 16 or 17 is under a mental incapacity which robs him or her of the ability to consent to treatment, he or she may fall to be treated under the provisions of the new Adults with Incapacity (Scotland) Act 2000 when it comes into force.[89] The new Act allows doctors to treat patients in the absence of consent, provided that this will benefit the patient.[90] The Adults with Incapacity Act accords more closely to Article 12 of the UN Convention than the Mental Health Act provisions, in particular in that it expressly stipulates that those carrying out interventions should

---

[84] Mental Health (Scotland) Act 1984, s. 53.
[85] See *J.T. v. The United Kingdom, The Times,* April 5, 2000.
[86] Act of Sederunt (Summary Applications, Statutory Applications and Appeals etc. Rules) (S.I. 1999 No. 929).
[87] *T. v. United Kingdom* and *V. v. United Kingdom* (2000) 30 E.H.R.R. 121.
[88] Mental Health (Scotland) Act 1984 s. 33 (4).
[89] In stages from Spring 2001 on.
[90] Adults with Incapacity (Scotland) Act 2000, s. 47.

take account of the wishes and feelings of the mentally disabled person.[91]

Access to information

Often, for a child or young person, what really matters to him or **11.34** her, more than taking a treatment decision, is access to information respecting his or her condition. This is so as much in situations where there is no capacity to take treatment decisions, as in those where there is. There is still a relationship of trust (in the lay person's sense of that word) between the child or young person and those responsible for his or her medical care.[92] That relationship cannot be optimised unless there a sufficient and appropriate amount of information about proposed treatment, alternatives, side effects and so on, expressed in language the young person can understand. The applicable principle is the third principle, that of a reasonable amount of information. Unfortunately, the current law essentially, despite some rhetorical gestures in favour of patient autonomy,[93] applies a test of what the reasonable doctor would decide to tell.[94] In the case of children, this may be particularly limiting. It is noticeable, however, that thinking in this area is still moving, at least in other jurisdictions, to a focus on "the skill in communicating the relevant information to the patient in terms which are reasonably adequate for that purpose having regard to the patient's apprehended capacity to understand that information".[95] It is to be hoped the law will eventually move in line with good practice. There are some small indications in the most recent English case that it will.[96]

Privacy and Confidentiality

"Privacy" is a word that requires elaboration. Scottish materials are **11.35** totally lacking. The view was expressed by the Scottish Law

---

[91] Adults with Incapacity (Scotland) Act 2000, s. 1(4).

[92] Anderson, *Choosing for Children, Parents' Consent to Surgery* (1990), pp. 184–185.

[93] *e.g.* in *Moyes v. Lothian Health Board,* 1990 S.L.T. 444, *per* Lord Caplan.

[94] *Sidaway v. Board of Governors of the Bethlem Royal Hospital and the Maudsley Hospital Hospital* [1985] A.C. 871.

[95] *Rogers v. Whittaker* [1993] 4 Med. L.R. 79 (High Court of Australia), *per* Mason C.J., Brennan, Dawson, Toohey and McHugh JJ. at p. 83.

[96] *Pearce v. United Bristol Healthcare NHS Trust* (1998) 48 B.M.L.R. 118 (Court of Appeal).

Commission some thirty years ago that the law recognises some sort of right to dignity.[97] But the case law relied on to support that view is limited in quantity, quite disparate, rather old and contains no discussion of what such an idea might mean.[98] The word "privacy", however, has more recently been used, though without elaboration, in a case where an adult had a remedy in respect of being required to remove her underclothing by the police.[99] In the only other case where it has appeared it is used as a synonym for "confidentiality" (a case where access to the health records of the birth mother of a foster child was sought by the foster mother seeking to prove that the local authority responsible for fostering had knowledge that the child had hepatitis).[1] It is thought that, against this background, a Scottish court in the future will follow the approach recently adopted by the English Court of Appeal,[2] directly inspired by consideration of Article 8 (right to private and family life) of the European Convention of developing a law of protection of privacy by broadening out from the concept of confidentiality. This follows naturally from the existing approach that what makes something confidential is not only the nature of the information, but the circumstances in which it is acquired.[3] In this way there is a right of privacy in the law, and the situations in the past seen as a breach of confidentiality become a sub-set of that. The law on that has been described as identical to the law in England, which will be an additional reason why Scots courts will take the lead to develop a concept of privacy.[4] The importance of this is that not only does it widen the range of the concept, but it gives a slightly fuller protection from breach by third parties. Medical confidentiality can affect third parties, but only if it comes into those third parties' hands in circumstances in which they have notice of its con-

---

[97] *Confidential Information*, Scottish Law Commission Memorandum No. 40, paras 48–60.

[98] *e.g. Conway v. Dalziel (1901)* 1 F. 918 (post-mortem not authorised by relatives). Unlike in continental European systems, although the idea was received from the common European tradition by at least 500 years ago, it was never developed. It can still be discerned in the late eighteenth century work on Scots law, Erskine, *Institute* IV.IV.80 and is mentioned in connection with Defamation, *e.g.* in Norrie, *Defamation and Related Actions in Scots Law* (1995). For the reasons why it did not develop properly as a concept in our law, see John Blackie, "Defamation" in (eds) R. Zimmermann and Kenneth Reid, *A History of Private Law in Scotland* (2000) Vol. 2, 633 at 665.

[99] *Henderson v. Chief Constable, Fife Police*, 1988 S.L.T. 61 *per* Lord Jauncey at 367.

[1] *Parks v. Tayside Regional Council*, 1989 S.L.T. 345.

[2] *Douglas v. Hello! Ltd* [2001] E.M.L.R. 9 especially *per* Sedley L.J.

[3] *A-G v. Guardian Newspapers (No. 2)* [1988] 3 All E.R. 545 at 658; *X. v. Y.* [1988] 2 All E.R. 648 at p. 661.

[4] *Lord Advocate v. The Scotsman Publications Ltd*, 1988 S.L.T. 490, *per* Lord Justice-Clerk Ross at p. 503.

fidentiality.[5] Moreover, in the case of some children, questions of the child's legal capacity are relevant to some issues that arise with confidentiality.

For the law to reflect appropriately the rights of the child in this now-recognised idea, "privacy" would, however, have to be fine-tuned to the context of children and healthcare. At present, there are various views even of the concept in general in the new English caselaw, which have arisen in looking at other contexts. It has been judicially recognised as difficult to define.[6] But the idea can be context-dependent.[7] A classic definition, "the right of the individual to be let alone",[8] is not meaningful in the context of children. Two other ideas in these cases are: "the "personal space in which the individual is free to be itself"[9] and "notions of what an individual might want to be kept "private", "secret" or "secluded'[which] are subjective to that individual".[10] The view of the European Court of Human Rights considering the context of healthcare has been expressed as "the sense of privacy of a patient".[11]   **11.36**

What is personal to a child may, of course, be different from what is personal to an adult. Many children have intense inward private lives, which they wish to keep secret.[12] It can, for example, be important to a child to lock his or her bedroom door at night.[13] A girl from an ethnic minority group might want to insist on being examined only by a female doctor or nurse. Even before the recent recognition in England of the concept "privacy", by extending the notion of "confidentiality", taking a photograph without permission in some contexts amount to a breach of that right.[14] In the light of the new developments, doubts that have been expressed about the legality of covert video surveillance in hospital to detect   **11.37**

---

[5] *Venables v. Newsgroup Newspapers* [2001] 1 All E.R. 908 per Dame Elizabeth Butler-Sloss P. at 933.

[6] See especially *R v. Broadcasting Standards Commission, ex parte British Broadcasting Corporation* [2000] 3 All E.R. 899 "a difficult word" (per Hale L.J. at 1000) "hard to grasp" (*per* Lord Mustill at 1002). Before the idea was recognised as part of the law some commentators took the view it. Some commentators think that the idea of privacy is not a very useful concept (see Wacks, *Personal Information, Privacy and the Law* (1988)).

[7] *per* Lord Woolf M.R. at 995.

[8] *Douglas v. Hello! Ltd per* Sedley L.J. quoting Warren and Brandeis, "The Right to Privacy" (1890) 4 Harvard L.R. 193.

[9] *R v. Broadcasting Standards Commission, ex parte British Broadcasting Corporation* [2000] 3 All E.R. 899 *per* Lord Mustill at 1002.

[10] *per* Hale L.J. at 100.

[11] *Z v. Finland* (1997) 25 E.H.R.R. 371.

[12] Bok, *Secrets: On the Ethics of Concealment and Revelation* (1986), p.36.

[13] Bok, *Secrets: On the Ethics of Concealment and Revelation* (1986), p.13, refers to a situation in a children's psychiatric ward in an American hospital where the policy was to observe any child at all times, even though he or she was not a suicide risk.

[14] *Adamson v. Martin*, 1916 S.C. 319 (Scotland); *Hellewell v. Chief Constable of Derbyshire* [1995] 1 W.L.R. 804 (England).

child abuse and Münchausen's syndrome by proxy may be correct.[15] However, again there is no guidance in the law as to what
contexts and what sorts of photographing or recording or filming
would now be potentially actionable as a breach of privacy in the
various contexts of healthcare. A very broad ground of action-
ability for any such photographing etc without consent, as supported by the Canadian Supreme Court where a teenage girl was
photographed by a journalist without permission in a public street,
and was not merely an "anonymous element in the scenery"[16]
would not be followed.[17] What is needed is some principle to determine for children where their sense of what they might wish to
keep secret is to be respected and where it can be disregarded. This
will require a balance which perhaps might draw on the welfare
principle. However, not only is there nothing in the former domestic
law of Scotland (nor England) that provides this, the case law of the
European Court of Human Rights likewise provides no material for
this.[18]

11.38   Both "confidentiality" and "privacy" are recognised throughout
the National Health Service in Scotland, in Codes of Practice and
patients' charters and in guidance from professional organisations.[19] The General Medical Council (the statutory disciplinary
body which is responsible for doctors throughout the United
Kingdom) in giving directions to the medical profession uses language wide enough to cover all information given by a patient to a
doctor or acquired about that patient by a doctor. This is reproduced in various leaflets advising health care professionals and
others.[20] This recognition may be seen as every bit as important in
reality as the rules of the law.

11.39   Even though "privacy" law will almost certainly now develop, in
the context of healthcare, "confidentiality" in the traditional sense
will still be an important part of the law for children as for adults.
Scottish law has long had a duty of confidentiality covering information on someone's medical condition and treatment, whether

---

[15] Thomas, *Child Protection, Privacy and Covert Video Surveillance* (1995) 17
J.S.W.L. 311.
[16] *L'Editions Vice-Versa Inc v. Aubry* [1998] 1 S.C.R. 591. See *per* Brooke L.J. in
Douglas v. Hello! Ltd on the difference between the relevant provisions in the
Quebec Charter and Art. 8 or the European Convention of Human Rights.
[17] *L'Editions Vice-Versa v. Aubry* [1998] 1 S.C.R. 591.
[18] Though note a person's "wedding photographs" have been held to be part of his
or her privacy, unless that person has already put them in the public sphere (*News
Verlags gmbh &cokg v. Austria,* January 11, 2000).
[19] See, for example, the *Code of Practice on Confidentiality of Personal Health
Information,* issued by the (former) Scottish Home and Health Department for
use throughout the NHS and Scotland.
[20] See, *e.g.* the leaflet, *Confidentiality and People Under 16,* issued and agreed on by
the profession and a number of other interested bodies, including the voluntary
body, the Brook Advisory Centres.

physical or mental,[21] and about a person's psychological state.[22] It also extends to cover information as to a person's sexual life,[23] certainly when that information is acquired in the context of medical advice or treatment.[24] Specifically, it has now been recognised (in an English case) that confidentiality applies as much to children as adults.[25] Further, it applies to all "health information", including information held by social workers and other carers, and would comprehend such things as records of any form of therapy, such as art therapy.[26] The only ground for breaching confidentiality is, as in England, where that is in the public interest.[27] This is consistent with the interpretation that has been given to Article 8 of the European Convention which requires "appropriate safeguards".[28] Cases in which it has been held to be in the public interest deal with physical risks to the public,[29] and with issues of press freedom generally[30] and certainly do not warrant a general breaking of the confidentiality of a young person.[31]

Whilst children and young people may, in general, have a right to confidentiality, there are certain circumstances where this may not be so clear cut. First there is the question of whether a child is legally competent to request that his or her information be kept confidential. The test is not necessarily the same as the test for consenting to medical treatment although, for all practical purposes, it might be argued that it should be. This distinction is recognised in the legislation giving patients access to health records. A parent is given access to the records of his or her child only if either the child is incapable of understanding the nature of the application for access and access would be in his or her "best interests" or if the child is capable and consents to the parent having access.[32] **11.40**

Guidance from the General Medical Council says that if a doctor considers that a young patient is incapable of giving consent to treatment or disclosure because he or she lacks the maturity to do **11.41**

---

[21] *Higgins v. Burton*, 1968 S.L.T. (Notes) 52; *Parks v. Tayside Regional Council, supra; A.B. v. Scottish National Blood Transfusion Service*, 1990 S.C.L.R. 263.

[22] *McBryde v. Strathclyde Regional Council*, Lord Dunpark, March 4, 1983, unreported.

[23] *X. v. Y.* [1988] 2 All E.R. 648.

[24] *A.B. v. C.D.* (1851) 14 D. 177; *A.B. v. C.D.* (1904) 7 F. 72, *sub nom. Watson v. McEwan* (1905) 7 F. (H.L.) 109.

[25] *Venables v. News Group Newspapers Ltd* [2001] 1 All E.R. 908 *per* Dame Elizabeth Butler-Sloss P. at 939.

[26] *ibid.*

[27] See *A-G v. Guardian Newspapers (No. 2)* [1988] 3 All E.R. 545 at 658 and *W. v. Edgell* [1990] 1 All E.R. 835.

[28] *Z. v. Finland (supra)*.

[29] As in *W. v. Edgell (supra)*.

[30] In which context rights under Art. 8 of the European Convention have to be balance with those under Article 10 ("Freedom of expression").

[31] See generally *Venables v. News Group Newspapers* [2001] 1 All E.R. 908.

[32] Access to Health Records Act 1990, s. 4.

so, the doctor should try to persuade him or her to allow an appropriate person to be involved in the consultation. If the young person refuses, the doctor may disclose relevant information to an appropriate person, if he or she considers it essential to do so in the patient's medical interests. For example, a parent may need information to fulfil his or her parental responsibilities for the health and welfare of the child. The doctor should inform the patient that he or she will be disclosing such information, and, if appropriate, should consider involving an advocate or carer.[33]

11.42   A young person may reveal to a doctor that he or she is at risk, perhaps of sexual abuse. The doctor may feel a duty to take action to protect the young person, particularly if the doctor considers the young person lacks the maturity to protect his or her own interests. Some commentators consider that this should only happen if a young person's life is threatened or they are exposed to a "demonstrable risk of serious harm".[34]

11.43   Many of the codes of practice in the health service recognise that the duty to respect confidentiality can be overridden in the best interests of the patient. The GMC advises that confidence can be broken in the public interest, particularly if someone is at risk of serious harm. Sexual abuse of children is particularly mentioned.[35] Unfortunately, some young people are unwilling to reveal abuse because they know that this may lead to further steps being taken against their will.

11.44   Another issue for children and young people is the information a parent should be given about their child. While the Children (Scotland) Act gives parents the responsibility of safeguarding their children's welfare,[36] parents are given no specific right by that legislation to have access to confidential health information. However if a child is at risk, perhaps of suicide or of abuse, and living at home, the doctor or social worker may have to consider whether parents need any information in order to help them care. The parent or guardian is entitled to such information[37] in so far, but only in so far, as he or she needs this to facilitate proper performance of their "parental responsibilities".[38]

11.45   Most codes of practice recognise that information can be shared on a "need to know" basis. However some families and carers claim that, while information is passed between professional agencies,

[33] *Confidentiality: Protecting and Providing Information*, para. 38, General Medical Council, June 2000.
[34] See, for example, *Re V. (A Minor) (Medical treatment)* [1992] 4 All E.R. 627.
[35] *Confidentiality: Protecting and Providing Information*, para. 37.
[36] Children (Scotland) Act 1995, s. 1(1)(a).
[37] Where it is a "person in care and control" who has the duty of consenting for a child they are in the same position as a person with parental responsibilities (Children (Scotland) Act 1995, s. 5).
[38] Children (Scotland) 1995, ss. 1–6.

their own need for information is often refused on grounds of patient confidentiality.

Access to records

Tied up with the right to privacy (including confidentiality) and **11.46** respect for family life is the right to see one's medical records, and the right to deny other people access to them. Although it is unlikely that there is any common law right to see one's records, there is now statutory provision in the Access to Health Records Act 1990 and the right is likely to be further strengthened by the incorporation of the European Convention into our law.[39]

The Access to Health Records Act gives patients the statutory **11.47** right to see health records made by a wide range of health professionals, including doctors, nurses, occupational therapists and dentists. However the right of access is limited in two ways. A health professional may withhold access if he or she believes access would cause "serious harm to the physical or mental health of the patient or of any other individual".[40] Access may also be denied if the record contains information about or provided by someone other than the patient who could be identified from the information, unless they have consented to the disclosure.[41]

Thus the person requiring access has no right to be told that any **11.48** part of his or her record has been held back. The patient may think he or she is seeing all of the relevant records whilst in fact seeing only a very restricted part. However the decision to withhold part of the records is only appropriate, if the doctor believes it would cause "serious" harm to do otherwise.[42]

A child[43] or young person may be granted access to his or her **11.49** records if he or she is capable of "understanding" the nature of the application.[44] His or her parent or person with parental responsibility may also see the records, provided that the young person consents. If the child is unable to understand the application, the

---

[39] See the important case of *Gaskin v UK* (1989) 12 EHHR 95, where a young man won the right to see social work records relating to his foster carers in order to enable him to make sense of his early life.

[40] s. 5(1)(a)(i).

[41] ss. 5(1)(a)(ii) and 5(2)(a).

[42] The BMA's guide to doctors, *Medical Ethics Today*, encourages doctors "to give patients access to all health information held about them" (i.e. including information recorded prior to the Act), and says that "refusing the patient access because the doctor believes the information would be harmful to the patient should be rare": para. 2.2.2.

[43] For this purpose, a young person under the age of 16. People over 16 years have the same rights as adults.

[44] Access to Health Records Act 1990, ss 3 and 4. This is probably not such a stringent test as the test of maturity to consent to medical treatment. See *Re K.* [1988] 1 All ER 358.

parent or person with parental responsibility may be granted access, if the health professional considers that access is in the child's best interests. Parents' rights to access are only granted, therefore, when in accordance with the welfare principle.

11.50   There is an overriding provision[45] that where a parent or person with parental responsibility applies for access, the record holder may withhold any information which the record holder believes the patient gave in confidence or which is the result of an examination or investigation which the patient believed was confidential.

11.51   These statutory provisions and the way they are approached have been designed with human rights law in mind. They are based on a balancing of factors and a proportionate response and as such have the detail that the common law still lacks and reflect with greater provision the approach of the UN Convention.

Conclusion

11.52 Health and healthcare is an area where human rights questions are particularly obvious. When it is the health and healthcare of children and young persons that has to be considered this is particularly marked, because it is central not only to their autonomy but to the development of their personhood. Some of the most important materials in our law governing issues relating to the health and healthcare of children were formulated with a conscious attempt to reflect human rights law is it was understood at that time. This was the case the Mental Health (Scotland) Act 1984, the Access to Health Records Act 1990 and the Children (Scotland) Act 1995. It was less overtly the case with the Age of Legal Capacity (Scotland) Act 1991. It is not surprising, therefore, that predominantly the relevant law does reflect both the provisions of the European Convention and the UN Convention. Further one central issue, which depends to a great extent on common law rules, privacy and confidentiality, has a flexibility that we consider will now result in its reflecting both of these Conventions, although that has not yet fully occurred. At the same time, however, there are significant points where the law does not yet reflect these Conventions or is not sufficiently fine-tuned to show how it would reflect them. Partly, this has because of inflexibilities in wider areas of law of which the area in question is a specialised part (as in the public law doctrines that affect the right to access resources in the healthcare system). In one case, the decision on the maturity of a child for the question of capacity, the inflexibility was a conscious legislative decision. In the field of mental health it was not. But where the problems we have identified arise because the legislation takes no special account of

---

[45] s. 5(3).

the position of children and young persons, it predates the UN Convention and has not yet been amended to reflect the more recent developments of the understanding of the European Convention. In some other contexts, particularly the involvement of children in decision-making, the problems relate to achieving an appropriate balance to reflect the developments in human rights law. Law reform work, however, is already being undertaken, through case law, and through the consideration of legislative reform. It is likely that over the next five years that the law will consequentially be further developed and fine-tuned to reflect even more generally both of the conventions.

CHAPTER 12

THE CHILD'S RIGHT TO EDUCATION

ALISON CLELAND

Scots law provides that education authorities have a duty to secure **12.1** "adequate and efficient provision of school education" for their area.[1] School education includes nursery education,[2] provision for special educational needs[3] and the teaching of Gaelic in Gaelic-speaking areas.[4] "School education" includes primary and secondary education[5] and school leaving age, for most pupils, is age 16.

To bolster education authorities' duties to provide education, **12.2** legislation also places parents under a duty to provide efficient education for their children[6] and recent legislation states that "it shall be the right of every child of school age to be provided with school education".[7] All this appears to reflect both the European Convention on Human Rights ("the European Convention") and the UN Convention on the Rights of the Child ("the UN Convention). The European Convention states "No person shall be denied the right to education".[8] The UN Convention provides that "States Parties recognise the right of the child to education", this right to be achieved "progressively and on the basis of equal opportunity".[9]

In addition to the basic right to education itself, both Conven- **12.3** tions address other matters. The European Convention provides that "the State shall respect the right of parents to ensure such education and teaching in conformity with their own religious and philosophical convictions".[10] It further states that "no-one shall be subjected to inhuman or degrading treatment or punishment".[11] The fundamental principle of the right to a fair and public hearing

---

[1] Education (Scotland) Act 1980, s. 1(1).
[2] *ibid.* s. 1 (5)(a)(i).
[3] *ibid.* s. 1 (5)(a)(ii).
[4] *ibid.* s. 1 (5)(a) (iii).
[5] *ibid.* s. 135 (2).
[6] *ibid.* s. 30.
[7] Standards in Scotland's Schools etc Act 2000, s. 1.
[8] ECHR, First Protocol, Art. 2.
[9] CRC, Art. 28.
[10] ECHR, First Protocol, Art. 2.
[11] ECHR, Art. 3.

of civil rights or of any criminal charge [12] may have implications for education decisions, as may the provisions that "Everyone has the right to respect for his private and family life".[13] The European Convention also provides that the rights in the Convention shall be enjoyed without discrimination of any kind.[14]

12.4   The UN Convention requires that "in all actions concerning children, whether undertaken by public or private social welfare institutions, courts of law, administrative authorities or legislative bodies, the best interests of the child shall be a primary consideration".[15] This is referred to in the chapter's discussion as "the welfare principle". The UN Convention also requires that children must have the right to express views in all matters affecting them,[16] which would include education matters.

12.5   This chapter looks at the development of Scots education law. Four specific matters are then considered: the fundamental right to education and whether existing law adequately provides for this; the curriculum; the welfare principle and its place in education law; discipline in schools and the extent to which its administration complies with Convention principles; and provision for special educational needs and the right to non-discrimination in education. As each matter is explored, existing law will be measured against the various articles of both Conventions. It will be argued that the law did not develop in a child-centred way and the result is provision that has needed considerable amendment to meet the basic requirements of the European Convention and the UN Convention. It will be suggested that further amendment will be necessary, if the law is to meet the spirit, rather than just the letter, of the Conventions.

The Historical Development of Education Law

Early Developments

12.6 Scrutiny of early parliamentary debates and statutes dealing with education reveals that those legislating for education were not at all concerned with the right to education: the focus was on the mechanics of provision. The preamble of the Education (Scotland) Act 1872 stated the aim to be "that the means of procuring efficient education for their children may be furnished and made available to the whole people of Scotland". Note the implication that children were not considered "people of Scotland"! That the Act was primarily concerned with the administration behind education was a

---

[12] *ibid.* Art. 6.
[13] *ibid.* Art. 8.
[14] *ibid.* Art. 14.
[15] CRC, Art. 3.
[16] *ibid.* Art. 12.

theme throughout the debates and is exemplified by one contribution: "we wish to interfere, not because Scotch children are running
about in the gutters, but because the present system is irregular,
uncertain and expensive".[17]

The Scottish education system had developed between the **12.7**
seventeenth and nineteenth centuries and consisted of parochial and
burgh schools, maintained and supervised by the Church. The debates around the 1872 Act considered the relative roles of the
Church and the State in education. In respect of religion, the Lord
Advocate, introducing the Bill, referred to the delay caused by
"fighting over the religious difficulty".[18] There were many passio-
nate contributions referring to religion, one such claiming that "a
mere secular education would only serve to perfect such little street
Arabs in the arts of knavery".[19]

Legislators were also concerned that education should provide **12.8**
technical skills to ensure the country's prosperity, and that it should
promote social stability: "The true object of education is not to
make men learned, but to make them good men and good subjects".[20] The parochial and burgh schools had met the needs of an
agrarian population, but industrialisation was taking place, and the
school system had to cope with population expansion and movement. The Government recognised that the State would have to
take more direct responsibility for education. The result was the
Elementary Education Act 1870 for England and Wales followed
by the equivalent Scottish legislation, in 1872.

The 1872 Act introduced a system of school boards, and ad- **12.9**
ministration of the parish and burgh schools was passed to these
boards. The next major Act was the Education (Scotland) Act 1918.
It too was concerned with administration of education, and in
particular, with the abolition of school boards. The Secretary for
Scotland said the Act was needed because the board system could
not support advances in education. Debates centred on the principle of boards, and on the boundaries for the proposed new authorities to administer the education system.

In debates on the 1872 and 1918 bills, many members of Par- **12.10**
liament were more concerned with employers' need for young
workers and parents' need for children's wages, rather than with
children's need to be educated. Referring to the clauses on compulsory education in the 1872 bill, Mr Orr Ewing said that he
"[w]ould much rather reward the parents who educated their children, by allowing them to be employed at an earlier age than other
children".[21] This view of children as their parents' property appears

[17] Mr Trevelyn, H.C. Deb., Vol. 209, ser. 3, col. 1541 (March 7, 1872).
[18] H.C. Deb., Vol. 209, ser. 3, col. 252 (February 6, 1872).
[19] Sir James Elphinstone, H.C. Deb., Vol. 211, ser. 3, col.322 (May 6, 1872).
[20] Mr Borthwick, H.C. Deb., Vol. 87, ser. 3, col .1254 (July 17, 1846).
[21] Mr Orr Ewing, H.C. Deb., Vol. 209, ser. 3, col. 1572 (March 7, 1872).

to have been commonplace at the time and arises again in the later debates. Indeed, concern for parents and employers was so common during the 1918 debate, that one member felt moved to express his wish to "impress upon this House the desirability of thinking more about the child and less about the employers, more of the child and less of the parent".[22] His was, however, very much a minority view.

12.11 In the debates on the 1972 bill, social stability had been linked to religious education. In the 1918 debates, education in a broader sense was seen as desirable to promote a stable society. The Government suggested that wider educational provision would increase democracy. Sir E. Parrott put it more colourfully, referring to "ill-educated voters" as " a danger to the state".[23]

Modern Developments

12.12 The modern Scots law of education has its roots in the Education (Scotland) Acts of 1945 and 1946. The 1945 Act dealt with primary education, the 1946 Act with secondary education. There were many debates and reports on education in the intervening years,[24] and for the first time the law showed more concern for the pupils themselves. Both Acts stated that education was to have regard to pupils' age, ability and aptitude.[25] Education remained, however, primarily concerned with administration. The then Secretary of State for Scotland, Tom Johnston, introducing the 1945 Bill, acknowledged this: "It is a machinery Bill...It does not touch the content or the substance of what is to be taught in the schools".[26]

12.13 Comparing the 1945 and 1946 Acts with the Scottish Advisory Council reports of the time, it appears that many progressive, child-centred suggestions about promoting children's rights to learn and develop were simply never translated into law—or even into guidance.

The Politicisation of Education Law

12.14 If the absence of concern for children was striking in the debates around education law, so, to a large extent, was party political

---

[22] Mr Tennant, 107 H.C. Deb., ser. 5, col. 1115.

[23] Sir E. Parrott, *ibid.* col. 1146.

[24] See, for example, "Report of the Committee of the Secondary Schools' Examination Council on Curriculum and Examinations in Secondary Schools" (Norwood) 1943 (England); SED, "Primary Education: A Report of the Advisory Council on Education in Scotland", Cmnd. 6973; SED, "Secondary Education: A Report of the Advisory Council on Education in Scotland", Cmnd. 7005.

[25] Education (Scotland) Act 1945, s. 1(2), and Education (Scotland) Act 1946, s. 1(2) and (3).

[26] H.C. Deb., Vol. 410, ser. 5, col. 1276.

ideology. Fundamental issues such as government support or otherwise for private schools and the value-base underlying the curriculum were not addressed. The rise of the Labour Party, however, meant comprehensive education, delivered through powerful local authorities, became a political goal in the 1970s. In answer to this, the "new right" criticised bureaucracy and suggested standards were in decline because of local authority control of education.[27]

The political belief in the desirability of diminishing local government power was translated into legislation under the Education Reform Act of 1988. The objectives of the 1988 Act were brought into the Scottish system by the Self-Governing Schools etc (Scotland) Act 1989 and the School Boards (Scotland) Act of 1988. These Acts allowed schools to "opt out" of local authority education department management, and provided for transfer of some local authority powers to school boards.[28]   **12.15**

Earlier, another important value of the Conservative Party, that of parental choice to decide which school their children attended, was enshrined in the "Parents' Charter". This theme was inserted into the Education (Scotland) Act of 1980,[29] and gave parents the right to make placing requests to the school of their choice. The introduction of schools boards gave parents further power within the system. The political motivations behind the changes were articulated by Mrs Thatcher who, referring to the 1987 Conservative election manifesto, said: "Just as we gained political support in the last election from people who have acquired their own homes and shares, so we shall secure still further our political base in 1991 and 1992 by giving people a real say in education and housing".[30]   **12.16**

Since the Labour Party returned to power in 1997 the pendulum has swung again towards local authority control, rather than parental choice, although it may be suggested that neither approach does a great deal to promote children's rights to quality education. "Opted out" schools have been returned to local authority control and the parental right to chose a school has been restricted by reform of the existing law made by the Standards in Scotland's Schools etc Act 2000.[31]   **12.17**

---

[27] For discussion, see Ranson, *The Role of Local Government in Education: Assuring Quality and Accountability* (1992).

[28] For more details of the1988 and 1989 Acts, see Marr and Marr, *Scots Education Law* (1995).

[29] Education (Scotland) Act 1980, s. 28A, inserted by the Education (Scotland) Act 1981, s. 1(1).

[30] Quoted in Simon, *Bending the Rules* (1988), p. 12.

[31] A parental placing request may be refused if, because of the child's admittance to the school, there would be a future need for additional staff to be employed— Education (Scotland) Act 1980, s. 28A (3)(a)(vi), as inserted by SSSA 2000, s. 44(4). Previously, local authorities could not anticipate future consequences of accepting placing requests and could refuse only if an additional teacher would immediately be required.

12.18   There has been a politicisation of education law, but an awareness of the European Convention can also be seen in recent reforms.
In particular, pupils now have the right to appeal against their own
exclusion from school,[32] a reform which the Scottish Executive finally agreed to, having previously insisted that it was not required
for ECHR compliance.[33] Most recent reform of Scots education
law has introduced what appears to be an additional tier for
monitoring of standards in schools,[34] by the Executive and by
school boards. It remains to be seen whether this will fulfil its aim,
which is clearly to improve the educational experience of children in
Scotland's schools.

The Right to Education

12.19 Article 2 of Protocol 1 of the European Convention is expressed
negatively: "No person shall be denied the right to education".
Despite this, it has been held that the Article does place a positive
duty on the contracting state.[35] The UN Convention is overtly
positive, requiring, in Article 28, that States Parties shall, with a
view to achieving the right of education progressively and on the
basis of equal opportunity, make primary education free and
compulsory, make higher education accessible to all and take
measures to encourage regular attendance.

12.20   Under Standards in Scotland's Schools etc Act 2000 (hereafter
"the 2000 Act"), it is stated , for the first time, that "It shall be the
right of every child of school age to be provided with school education...by an education authority".[36] Scottish education authorities have a duty to secure "adequate and efficient provision of
school education"[37] for their area. School education includes primary and secondary education[38]and, in general, a person is of
school age if he has attained the age of five years and has not
attained the age of sixteen years.[39] Parents, as defined in education
law,[40] have a duty to ensure that their children receive efficient
education by sending them to school "or by other means".[41]

---

[32] Education (Scotland) Act 1980, s. 28H(7).
[33] For further discussion on the Executive's approach to education reform, see
      Chap. 4, paras 4.53 *et seq.*
[34] Standards in Scotland's Schools etc Act 2000.
[35] *S.P. v. U.K.*, 23 E.H.R.R. C.D. 139.
[36] Standards in Scotland's Schools etc Act 2000, s. 1.
[37] Education (Scotland) Act 1980, s.1(1).
[38] *ibid.* s. 135(2) (a) and (b).
[39] *ibid.* s. 31.
[40] s. 135(1) of Education (Scotland) Act 1980 defines "parent" as "any person with
      parental responsibilities or rights in respect of, or with a duty to maintain, or who
      has care and control of, a child".
[41] Education (Scotland) Act 1980, s. 30.

To encourage regular attendance, a parent is guilty of an offence **12.21**
where a child of school age fails without reasonable excuse to attend
school regularly, unless the education authority has consented to
withdrawal of the child from the school.[42] In addition to prosecution, local authorities and courts may encourage attendance by the
making of attendance orders.[43]

Scots law appears to reflect the terms of both Conventions by **12.22**
giving children a right to education and placing education authorities and parents under duties to ensure that education is provided.
In particular, the UN Convention requirement that education be
provided on the basis of equal opportunity is addressed by
amendments to the law introduced by the 2000 Act. Scots law now
places education authorities under a duty to ensure that school
education is directed to development of pupils' abilities to their
fullest potential.[44] From 2001, the law will require education authorities to state, in their "annual statement of education improvement objectives",[45] the ways in which they will "in providing
school education, encourage equal opportunities".[46] Further, from
2001, there will be a requirement to provide mainstream schooling
for children, where possible.[47]

These recent reforms have brought Scots education law in line **12.23**
with the basic requirements of the Conventions.

The scope of the duty to provide education

To assess the extent to which Scots law delivers the right to edu- **12.24**
cation, it is necessary to consider the scope of the duty to provide
"adequate and efficient" school education. The duty has been held
to be qualified[48] and a local authority could seek to argue budgetary
constraints in the face of a claim that they were not providing
adequate and efficient education for a particular child. The scope of
this defence is clearly very wide and it may, in practical terms,
undermine the right of the child to education.

In an English case,[49] a local authority was held to be in breach of **12.25**
its duty to provide adequate education for a child with myalgic
encephalomyelitis (ME), by reducing home tuition from five to
three hours per week. It would be encouraging if a Scottish court
were to take a similar approach, but the word "efficient" does not

---

[42] *ibid.* s. 35(1).
[43] *ibid.* s. 36(2) and s. 44(2).
[44] SSSA 2000, s. 2(1).
[45] Required by SSSA 2000, s. 5(1).
[46] SSSA 2000, s. 5(2)(b).
[47] *ibid.* s. 15(1).
[48] *Walker v. Strathclyde Regional Council (No.1)* 1986 S.C. 1, 1986, S.L.T. 523 (O.H.).
[49] *R v. East Sussex County Council, ex parte Tandy* [1998] 2All E.R. 769 (H.L.).

appear in the equivalent English legislation and this may make such child-centred decisions less likely here.

12.26   It may be that children are, from time to time, unable to attend school. Scots law provides that where a pupil is unable to attend school, or it is unreasonable to expect attendance, due to prolonged illness, or any extraordinary circumstances, education authorities are required to make special arrangements for pupils to receive education elsewhere than at an educational establishment.[50] This is, again, child-centred, but does, of course, rely on the education authority's having resources available to make such alternative arrangements.

12.27   Scots law now attempts to define what might be regarded as "adequate and efficient" education. The 2000 Act provides that an education authority has a duty to ensure that education "is directed to the development of the personality, talents and mental and physical abilities of the child or young person to their fullest potential".[51] No caselaw has yet considered the matter, but it is suggested that since "talents" is mentioned, children with particular gifts could expect appropriate classes to be made available to them.[52] It is further suggested that the reference to "physical abilities" may require education authorities to ensure that all buildings and classrooms are accessible to children with physical disabilities.[53] The significance of the phrase "mental abilities" may be used to assist children who have, for example, mild learning difficulties.

The Curriculum

12.28   There is no statutory curriculum in Scotland and the law specifies only three matters that should be included in what is taught: physical education and training;[54] Gaelic in Gaelic-speaking areas;[55] and religious observance and instruction.[56]

12.29   The European Convention requirement that states ensure such education and teaching in conformity with parents' own religious and philosophical convictions is reflected in the right of parents to withdraw their children from religious observance and instruc-

---

[50] E(S)A 1980, s. 14(2).

[51] SSSA 2000, s. 2(1).

[52] This may be a forlorn hope if Scots law allowed education authorities the leeway shown in *R v. Secretary of State for Education, ex parte C.* [1996] 1E.L.R. 93 (Q.B.D.) in which the courts held that two contradictory decisions about a gifted child, both by the Secretary of State, did not indicate irrationality.

[53] For further discussion of legislation tackling discrimination against those with and affected by disability, see Chap. 4.

[54] E(S)A 1980, s. 1(5)(b)(iii).

[55] *ibid.* s. 1(5)(b)(iv).

[56] *ibid.* s. 8(1).

tion.[57] There is government guidance that stresses the importance of promoting understanding and respect for other beliefs.[58]

The question of sex education might be expected to give rise to **12.30** cases under the European Convention. Legislation that prohibited the promotion of homosexuality as a "pretended family lifestyle" has been repealed.[59] Section 56 of the 2000 Act provides that the Scottish Ministers may issue guidance to education authorities as to the manner in which such sex education should be conducted and education authorities are under a duty to have regard to such guidance. Previous legislation did not stop the teaching of sex education within schools, but, in some areas, restricted the information on same-sex relationships available to pupils.

In a Danish case under the European Convention, parents **12.31** challenged the compulsory teaching of sex education in state primary schools.[60] The Court held that a state was forbidden to pursue an aim of indoctrination that might be considered as not respecting parents' religious and philosophical convictions. The court looked at what was being taught and held that it was objectively conveying information. The case supports the teaching of sex education in state schools, but the court's reference to "indoctrination" could allow a challenge by parents, if they are unhappy with the way information on homosexuality is being presented.

The Welfare Principle

The UN Convention requires that administrative authorities (in- **12.32** cluding education authorities) regard the welfare of the child as the primary consideration, when taking actions affecting children.[61] Decisions relating to education should therefore put the pupils' welfare first.

No Statutory Welfare Principle in respect of state education

Article 3 of the UN Convention places "administrative authorities" **12.33** under a general welfare duty when making decisions affecting children. However, it is unfortunate that the article makes no specific mention of education authorities. "[I]nstitutions, services and facilities responsible for the care or protection of children" are to conform to established standards, especially in relation to safety

---

[57] *ibid.* s. 9.
[58] Scottish Office Education Department Circular, 6/91.
[59] Local Government (Scotland) Act 1973, s. 2A, repealed by Ethical Standards in Public Life etc (Scotland) Act 2000, s. 34.
[60] *Kjeldsen Busk Madsen and Pederson v. Denmark* (1976) 1 E.H.R.R. 711.
[61] CRC, Art. 3.

and supervision.[62] The UN Convention seems to view the welfare principle as relevant only to "care" settings and Scots law does the same.

12.34 The only specific reference to the welfare of pupils in education law is, ironically, in respect of independent schools. The state's responsibility in respect of the independent sector is limited to inspection and registration and there are several statutory grounds on which a complaint may be served on Independent School proprietors. The 2000 Act added a new ground, which is "that the welfare of a pupil attending the school is not adequately safeguarded and promoted".[63] There is no equivalent statutory duty on education authorities to safeguard and promote pupils' welfare in state schools, which is an illogical and indefensible omission.

12.35 Local authorities are under a duty to safeguard and promote the welfare of any child "looked after" by them.[64] They, and other bodies in charge of residential accommodation, also have a duty to safeguard and promote the welfare of any child sent to the accommodation "for the purposes of his being in attendance at a school".[65] In effect, where a child receives education somewhere other than at an ordinary state school, the welfare principle applies, but not otherwise. While child care legislation operates by acknowledging that services are being provided for the benefit of children and young people, education law appears to see pupils as the products, rather than the beneficiaries, of the system.

12.36 There is only one specific statutory reference to pupils' rights to safety. Every education authority "shall take reasonable care for the safety of pupils when under their charge".[66] Education authorities are required to ensure that premises and equipment conform to applicable standards and requirements and that they are maintained in such a condition as to conduce to the good health and safety of all persons occupying or frequenting the premises.[67] That duty, by implication, extends to pupils.

12.37 Those duties relating to safety that do exist are general. Local authorities, faced with this lack of specific legislation, often have detailed training and guidance packages for staff. These are, however, no substitute for clear statutory duties, not least because the latter would, in themselves, provide an avenue of recourse for an injured pupil. At present, such a pupil would require to pursue a claim under the ordinary law of delict. The incoherent range of provisions in Scots law intended to ensure children's safety in different settings is considered in chapter 14.

---

[62] *ibid.* Art. 3(3).
[63] E(S)A, s. 99, as inserted by SSSA 2000, s. 25.
[64] Children (Scotland) Act 1995, s. 17(1)(a).
[65] s. 125A E(S)A 1980.
[66] Schools (Safety and Supervision of Pupils)(Scotland) Regulations 1990 (S.I. 1990 No. 295), reg. 3a.
[67] E(S)A 1980, s. 19(2).

One English case dealing with a disabled child clearly illustrates **12.38** that relationship between the welfare duty and the content of education provision. The pupil had a congenital hip defect. Her mother had said she was not fit for games and this was on her file. The girl got into her shorts, told the teacher she could take part and the teacher did not check. The girl was injured and the court found the county council liable, stating: "[t]he school was under a duty to give effect to the mother's instructions".[68]

Analysis of this case in the light of the UN and European **12.39** Conventions may lead to conflicting conclusions. On the one hand, the UN Convention[69] requires that education should develop the child's abilities to their fullest potential, as does Scots law.[70] While there may be some circumstances in which there may be too great a risk in allowing a child affected by a disability to take part in certain activities, classes should be offered in such a way as to accommodate children with a wide range of abilities and needs. From the UN Convention perspective, the application of the law that placed the parent's wishes above the child's educational development is open to criticism.

On the other hand, the European Convention provides that "the **12.40** State shall respect the right of parents to ensure such education and teaching in conformity with their own religious and philosophical convictions".[71] It might be difficult to view a request that a child is excused from games as an exercise of a religious or philosophical conviction, but the European Convention clearly does accept the notion that parents' wishes should be followed in the provision of education. The above English case appears less offensive, viewed from a European Convention standpoint.

School Transport

In the 1980s, safety on school buses was the subject of public **12.41** concern, parental campaigns and media publicity. In July 1994, in answer to a Parliamentary question, it was announced that there would be a change to the law which allowed three children in a seat for two, and that all new minibuses and coaches were to be supplied with seatbelts.[72] It is highly unsatisfactory that public service vehicles are not required to have seatbelts and many children will travel to and from school in such vehicles.

Other than these minor changes to the law, there have been no **12.42**

---

[68] *Moore v. Hampshire County Council* (1980) 80 L.G.R. 481.
[69] CRC Art. 29.
[70] SSSA 2000, s. 2(1).
[71] ECHR, First Protocol, Art. 2.
[72] Road Vehicle (Construction and Use) (Amendment) (No. 2) Regulations 1996, brought into force in 1997 (for coaches registered after Oct. 1988) and 1998 (for coaches registered before 1988).

major safety initiatives in respect of school transport[73] and there are no special rules about supervision on such transport. Education authorities are required to make such arrangements as they consider necessary to convey pupils, without charge, between home and school.[74] There is a "reasonable excuse" for a pupil's non-attendance where the child would have to walk more than two miles (for under eight years) or three miles (eight years and over) to get to school.[75] This may still leave many children to walk to school—an activity fraught with potential dangers. Where they do qualify for a place on the school bus, the standards of the transport will be a matter for the providers. It may be speculated that if the law does not require special protective measures, they are unlikely to appear.

12.43   Safety of transport arrangements has been discussed in some school attendance cases. In *Sinclair*[76] an attendance order was made in respect of a particular school. The child's parents appealed since they wanted her to go to a different school in order to avoid crossing a busy road and to avoid being taken by bus to a temporary building while repairs to the designated school were ongoing. The issue for the court was whether the local authority had to comply with the parent's wishes. After considering *Huckstep*[77] and *Kidd*,[78] the court decided that the local authority could insist on the designated school. Interestingly, bearing in mind the terms of the European Convention Article 2 of Protocol 1, the court based its decision on the wording of the local authority duty, which was to "have regard to", rather than to "give effect to" parents' wishes.

12.44   In *Buchanan v Price*[79], parents were prosecuted for failing to ensure their child's school attendance. The parents had not sent their teenage daughter, who suffered from cystic fibrosis, to school because of medical advice that exposure to wet, damp of cold conditions would exacerbate her condition. The transport arrangements for returning her from school involved a possibility of her being left at the end of a private road, over a mile from her home. The parents were initially acquitted, but convicted on appeal and the case illustrates the narrow focus of the law. In non-attendance cases, the courts have been unable to deal with the real issue for the child: the safety of school transport.

12.45   In civil cases concerned with local authority powers and duties to provide transport, there is little scope for a child-centred approach.

---

[73] The Review of Scottish "Safer Routes to School" Projects are discussed in Chap. 14; these promote walking and cycling and do not directly address school transport itself.

[74] E(S)A 1980, s. 1(1).

[75] *ibid*. s. 42 (1), (4).

[76] *Sinclair v. Lothian Regional Council*, 1978 S.L.T. (Sh. Ct.) 56.

[77] *Huckstep v. Dunfermline District Education Sub-Committee*, 1954 S.L.T. (Sh. Ct.) 109.

[78] *Kidd v. New Kilpatrick School Council*, 1978 S.L.T. (Sh. Ct.) 56.

[79] 1982 S.C.C.R. 534.

The English case of *Jacques*[80] held that local education authorities operating school buses had a common law responsibility for the safety of pupils. On judicial review of the authority decision not to provide transport for a nine year old who was technically "within walking distance", the court upheld the council's decision, despite the fact that the route to school was rural, unlit and used by farm vehicles.

In the Scottish case of *Steele*,[81] the local authority refused to **12.46** continue transport for four children over the age of eight, despite letters from police and the headteacher advising that the decision would put the children at risk; there was no public transport and traffic on the road was heavy. The refusal to allow interim transport until a final decision was made was reduced by the Outer House, but again, the Court did not consider safety, only the appropriateness of the decision-making process adopted by the Council.

Bullying

The European Convention provides that "no-one shall be subjected **12.47** to humiliating or degrading treatment or punishment"[82] and the UN Convention provides that children have the right to be protected from all forms of abuse.[83] It is worth noting that the UN Convention makes specific reference[84] to education in placing states parties under a duty to take "appropriate legislative, administrative, social and educational measures to protect the child from all forms of physical or mental violence". There can be no doubt that bullying in school may harm a pupil mentally and physically and in extreme cases, may prevent a pupil from taking advantage of educational provision all together.

Research into bullying in Scottish secondary schools[85] showed **12.48** that, out of 942 pupils, half had been bullied at some time and six per cent were victims of "long-standing violence". In an analysis of telephone calls about bullying to ChildLine in England and Wales, children said that felt isolated, lonely and powerless. Victims saw themselves as the cause of bullying and thought there was something the matter with them.[86]

Existing law makes no specific mention of bullying. Regulations **12.49** require there to be a minimum of supervision by one adult in the playgrounds of primary schools of over 50 pupils and of special

---

[80] *Jacques v .Oxfordshire County Council* (1967) 66 L.G.R. 440.
[81] *Steele v. Western Islands Council* 1994 G.W.D. 14-885.
[82] ECHR, Art. 3.
[83] CRC, Art. 19.
[84] *ibid.* Art. 19.1.
[85] Mellor, "Bullying in Scottish Secondary Schools", SCRE Spotlight No.23 (1990).
[86] "Bullying: The Child's View", Calouste Gulbenkian Foundation (London, 1991).

schools.[87] It is, however, unlikely that such limited supervision would act as an effective deterrent to a determined bully. During the 1990s, all schools were issues with anti-bullying packs.[88] While these measures can be seen as a first step towards tackling the problem of bullying, they do not go far enough to guarantee that, as required by both Conventions, children will not be subjected to inhuman or degrading treatment, or to mental or physical violence.

12.50   Cases in which bullying has been an issue do not give grounds for optimism. It is not uncommon for children to refuse to go to school, through fear of bullying. The law has taken an unsympathetic approach to such fear. In *Montgomery v Cumming*,[89] a child was being bullied and refused to go to school. The school had been unable to take action against the bullies since the child had refused to name them and the court's decision was that the fear did not afford a "reasonable excuse" for non-attendance.

12.51   Courts have also been reluctant to award damages, where it has been claimed that local authorities failed to tackle bullying within schools. In *Walker v. Derbyshire County Council*,[90] a girl with cerebral palsy claimed damages for intimidation and bullying by pupils which her secondary school had never tackled and which left her psychologically scarred. The county court found against the girl on the facts. In *Scott v. Lothian Regional Council*,[91] a Scottish court also refused to make a finding of negligence in a school bullying case.

Discipline in Schools

Corporal Punishment

12.52   Scotland had a long history, not only of permitting corporal punishment in schools but—one suspects—of seeing it as part of the educational process. In *Gray v. Hawthorn*,[92] Lord Guthrie stated that "a school teacher is vested with disciplinary powers to enable him to do his educational work".

12.53   The UN Convention Article 28 states that children have a right to expect that "school discipline is administered in a manner consistent with the child's human dignity", but it is European provision that has significantly influenced law reform in this area. The Eur-

---

[87]   Schools (Safety and Supervision of Pupils)(Scotland) Regulations 1990 (S.I. 1990 No. 295).

[88]   SCRE, "Action Against Bullying" (1991), and SCRE, "Supporting Schools Against Bullying: The Second Anti-Bullying Pack" (1993).

[89]   1999 G.W.D. 5-258, available on the internet at http://www.scotcourts.gov.uk/opinions/Ljg2112a.html.

[90]   Unreported, discussed in Childright 1994, No. 108, p. 3 and No. 109, p. 6.

[91]   1998 G.W.D. 33-1719.

[92]   1964 J.C. 69, at p. 75.

opean Convention Article 3 states that "No-one shall be subjected to inhuman or degrading treatment or punishment". In *Campbell and Cosans v. United Kingdom*,[93] the United Kingdom was held to be in breach of the European Convention by allowing corporal punishment in schools.

The decision led to the amendment of Scottish legislation to re- **12.54** move, as a defence to legal action resulting from the use of corporal punishment, the teacher's educational position in state schools. Present legislation, under the clear heading "No justification for corporal punishment", makes it clear that no-one may use the position of teacher as a defence in civil or criminal proceedings,[94] bringing Scots law in line with the European Convention.

Exclusion from School

Exclusion from school, by its very nature, significantly affects a **12.55** child's right to education. Headteachers had, under common law, power to "suspend" pupils. There are now, however, only two legal grounds for exclusion: (a) the parent refuses to comply, or to allow the child to comply, with school rules; or (b) the pupil's continued attendance would be seriously detrimental to order and discipline in the school or the educational well-being of other pupils.[95]

Research has raised many questions about the use of exclu- **12.56** sions.[96] Racism and the erosion of black children's rights through exclusion were identified in Nottingham research[97] and in an Institute of Race Relations study.[98] Research into exclusion in Scottish schools has been undertaken and indicates varied practice throughout local authority areas.[99]

The European Convention provides that in determination of civil **12.57** rights, everyone is entitled to a fair and public hearing within a reasonable time by an independent and impartial tribunal established by law.[1] The crucial question is whether existing appeal procedures for exclusions are likely to satisfy the European Convention.

If a pupil is not to be re-admitted to the school within eight days **12.58** of the decision to exclude, a parent must be given written reasons

---

[93] (1982) 4 E.H.R.R. 293.
[94] SSSA 2000, s. 13.
[95] Schools General (Scotland) Regulations 1975, SI 1975/1135, reg. 4A, as amended by S.I. 1982 No. 56 and S.I. 1982 No. 1735.
[96] For further discussion of the issues, particularly in the context of equal opportunity issues, see Chap. 4, para. 4.43 *et seq.*
[97] Nottingham County Council, "Pupil Exclusions from Nottingham secondary Schools" (1989).
[98] Bourne, Searle, *Outcast England: How Schools Exclude Black Children*, Institute of Race Relations (1994).
[99] See P. Munn, M.A.Cullen, M. Johnstone, G. Lloyd (1997) *Exclusions and In-School Alternatives*, the Scottish Office.
[1] ECHR, Art. 6.

for the decision, details of any conditions placed on the pupil's re-entry to the school, and information about the right to appeal.[2] Two preliminary questions arise: first, what happens where a child is excluded for less than eight days?; second, what sort of conditions may be attached to re-entry and might these jeopardise the right to education?

12.59 Any decision to exclude a child may be appealed, either by the parent,[3] or by the child, where that child has legal capacity.[4] It is possible to appeal against an exclusion of less than eight days, but the reality is that, by the time an education committee has been convened to consider the appeal, the child will have been re-admitted to school. This is because an appeal must be made within 28 days of the exclusion decision.[5] There is, therefore, no effective appeal against short-term exclusions from school, a clear violation of the European Convention.

12.60 Conditions may be attached to re-entry and in *Wyatt v. Wilson,*[6] a court considered these. A father appealed against his conviction for failure to ensure his son's school attendance. He argued that he was justified in keeping his son at home because the undertaking he was asked to sign, stating his son "would comply with rules, regulations and disciplinary requirements of the school", was unreasonable. The court upheld the conviction noting that the condition, while not happily phrased, had been legitimately attached to re-entry. A future condition might be successfully challenged under Article 2, Protocol 1 of the European Convention if it were to be shown to be too wide, or in some way conflicting with a parent's religious or philosophical convictions.

12.61 In relation to longer-term exclusions (*i.e.* more than eight days) there is a two step process, first to an appeal committee of the local authority, second, to the sheriff court, by way of summary application.[7] In respect of an appeal committee, it might be argued that it cannot be regarded as "an independent and impartial tribunal". If such a challenge were made, the European Court would look to guidance available to education authorities, and to the subordinate legislation governing committee procedures.[8] Scottish Office guidance advises that a pupil facing exclusion should always be given the opportunity to express a view and have that view taken into account.[9] It does not, however, deal with fairness and disclosure of

---

[2] Schools General (Scotland) Regulations 1975, S.I. 1975 No. 1153, reg. 4A.
[3] E(S)A 1980, s. 28H(1).
[4] SSSA 2000, s. 41.
[5] E(S)A 1980, s. 28H.
[6] 1992 S.C.C.R. 747.
[7] E(S)A 1980, s. 28H(6).
[8] Relevant subordinate legislation is Education (Appeal Committee Procedures) (Scotland) Regulations 1982, S.I. 1982 No. 1736.
[9] Scottish Office circular No.2/98 "Guidance on Issues Concerning Exclusion from School", para. 57.

information in committee hearings themselves. One obvious problem is that any information which appellants wish the committee to see must be sent to the education authority for distribution. The hearing will be arranged by education authority officials and the chair of the committee considering the appeal may be someone who previously worked for the local authority.

The relevant regulations provide that "the procedures of an appeal **12.62** committee prior to, at, or subsequent to a hearing on a reference, shall be such as the education authority setting up and maintaining the committee or the chairman of the committee may determine".[10] This is a clear violation of Article 6 of the European Convention, as the decision-maker has control of the forum to scrutinise the decision and therefore the forum cannot be independent.

In respect of a sheriff court appeal, there cannot be said to be the **12.63** same problem with independence. However, there is a potential problem in respect of the nature of such appeals and the breadth of issues that may be raised. There are no criteria in law for such appeals.[11] This has led to conflicting approaches by different courts. In one case, the court regarded its role as limited to consideration of the reasonableness of the appeal committee's decision.[12] In another, a full re-hearing of the circumstances leading to the exclusion took place.[13] It may be argued that where the sheriff's powers on appeal are uncertain, the appellant is disadvantaged by not knowing the extent of the case to be prepared; and second, as with an appeal committee hearing, it is possible that an exclusion will have run its course long before the matter gets to the sheriff, denying a hearing within a reasonable time.

One case illustrates the unsatisfactory state of the present law. In **12.64** *Kelly v. Dumfries & Galloway Regional Council,*[14] a parent argued that a decision to exclude had been taken by someone to whom the power could not competently be delegated. Despite accepting the parent's argument, the court held that the application was incompetent. The reason given was that it did not have the power to declare an exclusion *ultra vires* as that would require determination of whether a directive was competent and such a decision was beyond its powers in an appeal against exclusion. The result is that pupils and their parents have no remedy[15] against arbitrary and unlawful exclusions. It is hard to imagine a more glaring breach of Article 6.

---

[10] Education (Appeal Committee Procedures) (Scotland) Regulations 1982 (S.I. 1982 No. 1736), reg. 4.
[11] E(S) Act 1981, s. 28H (6) provides for appeal to the sheriff and s. 28H(7) provides simply that the sheriff may confirm or annul the decision.
[12] *Crawford v. Strathclyde Regional Council,* 1999 Fam. L.R. 120.
[13] *Mackie v. Grampian Regional Council,* 1999 Fam. L.R. 122.
[14] 1994 G.W.D. 12-763, 1999 Fam. L.R. 122.
[15] With the possible exception of a petition to the *nobile officium.*

12.65   Successful challenges to existing exclusion law would depend on the European Court's being prepared to rule that Article 6 were applicable to education issues, *i.e.* that these were "civil rights". This is a matter yet to be decided, but where a child is excluded from school on the basis of an alleged offence, there can be no doubt that Article 6 will be applicable to his case. Scots law has, so far, failed to appreciate the relevance of the European Convention to such appeals.

12.66   In *Wallace v. Dundee City Council*,[16] a pupil was excluded from school. It was alleged that he had been involved in setting fire to the school. Three pupils were implicated, and the Headteacher had been advised by the police that it was not clear who had done what. The pupil was excluded without being given an opportunity to state his position. The sheriff upheld the exclusion and in doing so, stated that he was not convinced that the presumption of innocence was unequivocally relevant to decisions on exclusion. No arguments based on the European Convention were put to the sheriff. To avoid repeating the clear breach of Article 6, these matters will require to be considered in any future case.

Special Education Provision

12.67   The European Convention Article 2 Protocol 1 states that "No person shall be denied the right to education". Article 14 states that "The enjoyment of the rights and freedoms set forth in this Convention shall be secured without discrimination on any ground...". Article 23 of the UN Convention states that disabled children should have effective access to education and the law of special educational needs should, essentially, be about providing equality of opportunity for children.

12.68   In relation to meeting special educational needs, two key documents had a major impact on policy and provision for children with learning difficulties in Scotland. The first was the Warnock Report.[17] This argued against the use of the statutory categories of handicap that existed in the previous legislation, stating that these stigmatised children unnecessarily. The second was an HMI Progress report[18] that pointed out the dangers of withdrawal of pupils for individual tuition by remedial teachers, leading to problems with re-integration of the pupils.

---

[16]   2000 G.W.D. 2-52, available on the internet at http://www.scotcourts.gov.uk/opinions/B295_99.html.

[17]   "Special Education Needs" Warnock Report, 1978, DES.

[18]   "The Education of Pupils with Learning Difficulties in Primary and Secondary Schools in Scotland", 1978 HMI.

Narrow Definition of Special Educational Needs

The response to these reports was the Education (Scotland) Act **12.69**
1981. This amended existing legislation to provide that, following a
multi-disciplinary assessment, a Record of Needs would be opened
for a child whose needs were regarded as pronounced, specific or
complex, were of a continuing nature, and which could not be met
by the class teacher unaided.[19]

The law is concerned with those children who have the most **12.70**
complex difficulties. There are few provisions for children who may
have mild or moderate difficulties. It is questionable whether,
without significant amendment to its existing structure, the law has
mechanisms in place to allow it to recognise a wider range of
children with learning difficulties. This places a question mark over
the fulfilment of the new duty on authorities to ensure that school
education is directed to development of pupils" abilities to their
fullest potential.[20]

Assessment Procedures

If a child is assessed as having special educational needs in the sense **12.71**
specified in the legislation, a Record of Needs may be opened for
him.[21] That Record is a legal document, which describes the child's
special educational needs and the measures proposed to meet those
needs. A parent has a right to request an assessment for special
educational needs and the education authority must normally
comply with such a request.[22] This right to request an assessment is
important, since without the assessment and the opening of a Record of Needs, a child may have no hope of having his needs recognised and met by the education authority.

On rare occasions, parents themselves may be reluctant to accept **12.72**
that their child has special needs. If parents could refuse to submit a
child for assessment, a child's right to measures to meet his needs
would be severely compromised. It is therefore in line with the UN
Convention Article 23 and Article 2, Protocol 1 of the European
Convention that an education authority may issue a written notice
requiring a parent to allow the child to be assessed, and that a
parent who does not comply with the notice commits an offence.[23]

The right to express views and have those views taken into ac- **12.73**
count is absent from assessment processes, a clear violation of
Article 12 of the UN Convention. Notice of assessment is served on
parents,[24] there is no requirement for children to be consulted or

---

[19] E(S)Act 1980, s. 60 (2).
[20] SSSA 2000, s. 2(1).
[21] E(S)A 1980, s. 61.
[22] *ibid.*, s. 61 (6).
[23] *ibid.*, s. 61(1), (4).
[24] *ibid.*, s. 61(1)(a).

even informed, and parents are even given a right to be present at a child's medical examination[25], breaching the child's right to privacy.[26] Children, unless they have reached school leaving age, have no right to appeal against any special educational needs decision,[27] including the school they are to attend.

Provision for Special Educational Needs

12.74 The "provision" for those children who are judged to have special educational needs in terms of the legislation is not really provision at all: it is a system of assessment, with no guarantee of support. This is because it is possible to appeal only against those parts of the Record of Needs which describe the child's impairments and special educational needs, not against the part which states the measures proposed to meet those needs.[28] An authority could accurately record a child's needs, then provide woefully inadequate measures which failed to allow the child to develop educationally. Without wider appeal provisions, the child's right to education could, in some cases, be meaningless.

12.75 Since the legislation provides no remedy against inadequate local authority provision, it is important to consider how the courts have dealt with special educational needs cases. There are very few Scottish cases, which is a cause for concern. The lack of an independent tribunal may be the reason for this. Parents may appeal to the sheriff in respect of a decision as to the school their child should attend.[29] Their only remedies in the face of any other decision on provision for their child's special educational needs are referral to the Scottish Ministers[30] and judicial review. The latter is costly,[31] the remit of the court narrow[32] and a successful outcome will not guarantee the required provision.

12.76 By contrast, parents and pupils unhappy with provision in England may refer the matter first to a Special Educational Needs Tribunal, which can take a decision about the appropriateness of provision, then to the court. To translate the statement of the child's special educational needs in the Record of Needs (equivalent to the Statement in England) into reality, the education authority's

---

[25] *ibid.* s. 61(2).
[26] CRC Art. 16.
[27] E(S)A 1980, s. 63(1) and (2).
[28] *ibid.* s. 63(1)(b).
[29] *ibid.* s. 65(1).
[30] *ibid.* s. 64(1).
[31] The case must be raised in the Court of Session, where the services of an advocate will be required
[32] The court will consider whether a public authority has acted reasonably, see *Associated Provincial Picture Houses v. Wednesbury Corporation* [1947] 2All E.R. 680 (C.A.) and not whether the decision was the right one in the circumstances.

duties in framing and acting upon the Record must be clear. *In R v. Secretary of State for Education and Science, ex parte E.*[33] the court held that authorities had a clear duty to specify all the special educational needs and the provision required and to make arrangements for appropriate provision. In *L v. Clarke and Somerset CC*[34] the court held that the test was whether the statement was so specific as to leave no room for doubt as to what had been decided was necessary for the individual child.

The duty of English local education authorities in compiling the statement of a child's needs has been clarified. There has been no such clarification in Scotland. The result, based on the writer's experience, is Records of Needs that are so vague about provision as to be meaningless, leaving children without the educational support to which they should be entitled, if the right to education were being taken seriously. **12.77**

The courts have also had to look at the extent of local authorities' duties to children with special educational needs, in the light of scarce resources and many client groups requiring support. A decision fully in tune with the spirit of the Conventions was taken in *R v. East Sussex CC, ex parte Tandy*[35]. The House of Lords decided that the duty to provide "suitable education" was owed to the individual child. A Scottish case would be likely to come to the same view, particularly in the light of the new duty to ensure that school education is directed to development of pupils'' abilities to their fullest potential.[36] The court also held that there was no reason to treat resources as a relevant consideration in decisions about provision. Were this to be applied in Scotland, the child with learning difficulties might have a real right to education. As suggested above however, the existence of the word "efficient" in the Scottish legislation[37] would allow a court to limit a child's right depending on the resources available in their particular authority. **12.78**

It is a sad fact that legal rights are more likely to be delivered to clients of local authorities after one authority has been successfully sued.[38] It is therefore a great cause for concern that in *Phelps v. Hillingdon LBC*[39] it was held that the local authority was not liable for the negligence of its educational psychologist who failed to identify dyslexia and instead diagnosed emotional difficulties. The **12.79**

---

[33] [1992]1 F.L.R. 377 (C.A.).
[34] [1998]E.L.R. 129 (Q.B.D.).
[35] [1998]2 All ER 769 (H.L.)
[36] SSSA 2000 s. 2(1).
[37] E(S)A 1980, s. 1(1) provides "it shall be the duty of every education authority to ensure that there is made for their area adequate and efficient provision of school education".
[38] e.g. after the decision in *R v.Lancashire County Council, ex parte M.* [1989] 2 F.R.279 (C.A.) in which the court decided that speech therapy could be an educational need, local authorities in both Scotland and England could no longer refuse to provide this for children with special educational needs.
[39] [1998] E.R.587 (CA).

message this gives—that mistakes in relation to children with special educational needs will not result in liability—is a dangerous and highly unsatisfactory one.

Conclusion

12.80 Scots education law began by all but ignoring children. Recent developments state that children have a right to education and give them some limited rights to appeal against their own exclusion, and to an education that allows them to develop to their fullest potential. This, along with the duty on local authorities to provide education, including provision for special education, and the parental duty to ensure that children attend school, amounts to a fulfilment of the most basic requirements of the Conventions.

12.81 Fundamental reform is required, however, to meet the spirit of the Conventions. There is no welfare duty in respect of state education, a breach of the UN Convention. There are no protective measures relating to school transport, a deficiency affecting tens of thousands of children every day throughout Scotland. There is no independent tribunal to which decisions on exclusion and on special educational needs may be referred, a breach of the European Convention Article 6. Most unacceptably of all, children with special educational needs continue to be treated as third class citizens (after their parents, who are treated as second class). They have no right to be consulted about, or express views in relation to, decisions affecting them, and no guarantee that the law is behind them, when a local authority fails in its duty to them.

CHAPTER 13

THE SCHOOL OF HARD KNOCKS: EMPLOYMENT OF CHILDREN

PETER HUNTER

Most children work. They may drift in and out of jobs, and few are **13.1** employed for more than a few hours per week, but research consistently shows that "somewhere between two thirds and three quarters of children have some experience of paid employment before they reach the minimum school leaving age".[1] Despite the fact the work is clearly a common childhood experience, there is little apparent consensus on a variety of issues. For example, is paid employment an appropriate activity for children? If it is appropriate, does it require special regulation and is such regulation a priority? And, if there is to be some form of legal control, is this to be achieved by giving children rights, or should the state assume a protective role and deliver safety through public law rather than individual, private remedies? As this chapter reveals, there is little consistency or coherence in the answers to these questions and, consequently, despite regular public displays of anxiety about the fate of child workers, little continues to be done to protect children at work. This chapter summarises the nature of child employment before analysing the policy and legal framework for regulation by public authorities, before closing with a comment on the private remedies available to Scottish children.

The Nature and Extent of Child Employment

The group of researchers centred based at the University of Paisley **13.2** probably represent the leading researchers on child employment in the United Kingdom. The largest of their surveys covered around 1,400 children in 11 schools in southern Scotland and Northern England. In findings that echo the results of previous studies, they found that 43 per cent of the sample were "currently employed" and 71 per cent had been employed at some time in the past. Drawing

[1] Sandy Hobbs, Sandra Lindsay, Jim McKechnie, *The Extent of Child Employment in Britain*, British Journal of Education and Work, vol. 9 no.1 1996 pp. 5–18.

on estimates of the school population the research suggests that at any given time between 1.1 and 1.7 million children are in paid employment in the United Kingdom.[2] Given the consistency in employment patterns for children north and south of the border it is probably safe to assume that the child workforce in Scotland numbers around 100,000 to 150,000.

13.3   To give some impression of the scale of child employment it is worth drawing a comparison with part time employment in the adult labour market. Women dominate the world of part time work, but at 1,074,000 the number of adult men employed part time is increasing steadily.[3] If we assume that the University of Paisley estimate is reliable, then it is quite likely that the number of child workers in the economy exceeds the number of men employed on a part time basis and is second only to part time women.

13.4   In theory, the employment of children is limited to workers aged 13 or over and employment before 7.00 a.m. and after 7.00 p.m. is unlawful. The failings of this system will be discussed more fully below, but, while plotting the extent of child employment, it is worth exploring working patterns in more detail. In 1997 the TUC commissioned a MORI survey of over 4,000 children aged 11–16. This research found that 20 per cent of 11-year-olds and 23 per cent of 12-year-olds had been employed in breach of the age restriction in their local bye laws. Furthermore, 36 per cent of all children had worked before 7.00 a.m. and over 50 per cent had worked after 7.00 p.m.[4]

13.5   The question of working hours is also interesting. Those commentators who oppose attempts to regulate child employment commonly cite the fact that most children only work for relatively few hours per week. This pattern is borne out in Department of Employment research which shows that most children work comparatively few hours, although 10 per cent were employed for over 15 hours per week.[5] What tends to be overlooked is the fact that children spend around 35 hours per week at school in addition to any commitment they have to paid employment.

13.6   Finally, in this brief picture of the extent of child employment, we must turn to health and safety. Much of the legislation is drafted from the viewpoint that children are especially vulnerable at work and regulation is required to protect the health and welfare of children. From this standpoint it could be argued that health and safety is the most important marker against which we can measure the regulation of child employment. Precise records are hard to obtain, but the Low Pay Unit asserts that there were four deaths and 193 serious injuries between 1993 and 1999.[6]

---

[2]   *ibid.* pp. 5–18.
[3]   *Labour Market Trends*, January 2001, Table B1 pp. S18–S19.
[4]   *Working Classes: A TUC Report on School Age Labour*, January 1997.
[5]   Employment Gazette, April 1995, "Young People at Work".
[6]   *The Guardian*, February 14, 1999, *"Lessons of the Sweatshop"*.

International Obligations

The need for special protection for children and young people has **13.7** been identified in both international and European contexts. The United Nations (UN) Convention on the Rights of the Child contains several articles which are relevant to employment—Articles 13 (the right of access to information); 26 (the right to benefit from social security); 28 (the right to education including vocational education on the basis of equality of opportunity); 31 (the right to rest, leisure and play opportunities); and 32 (the right to be protected from economic exploitation).[7]

The United Kingdom Government signed the UN Convention **13.8** and ratified the document on December 16, 1991. Although it adopted most other articles of the Convention without qualification, the Government entered a reservation on Article 32. This Article covers the right of the child (defined in the Convention as below the age of 18 years) to be "protected from economic exploitation and from performing any work that is likely to be hazardous or to interfere with the child's education, or to be harmful to the child's health or physical, mental, spiritual, moral or social development", and that appropriate measures should be taken to ensure "effective enforcement".

The United Kingdom reservation stated that "Employment leg- **13.9** islation in the United Kingdom does not treat persons under 18, but over the school leaving age as children, but as "young people". Accordingly the United Kingdom reserves the right to continue to apply Article 32 subject to such employment legislation".[8] However, the United Kingdom Government did ratify Article 3—one of the fundamental principles of the Convention which states that "In all actions concerning children, ... the best interests of the child shall be a primary consideration." The government should, therefore, have regard to the intentions of Article 3 and ensure that "in all decisions about legislation on children's employment, the best interests of young people up to eighteen is a factor which is taken into account."[9]

In August 1999 the United Kingdom withdrew its reservation **13.10** against Article 32. Long awaited implementation of the E.C. Directive[10] would fulfil the requirement to protect the welfare of under 18-year-olds. But what about protection against economic exploitation? All workers under 18 are excluded from the minimum

---

[7] Children's Rights Development Unit, *U.K. Agenda For Children*, 1994, p. 230.
[8] Quoted in Children's Rights Development Unit, *op. cit.* p. 230.
[9] Cleland and Gillespie, *A Response to the Employment Department Consultation Document: European Commission Draft Directive on the Protection of Young People at Work* , p. 2.
[10] Council Directive 94/33/E.C. on the Protection of Young People at Work.

wage and it is arguable that in the absence of a reservation on economic exploitation, the lack of pay protection for young workers is in breach of the UN Convention.

13.11.   Also, at an international level, the United Kingdom has ratified, in 1999, the ILO Convention on the Worst Forms of Child Labour.[11] At a political or philosophical level it is interesting to note the reference to the "worst" forms of child labour. The obvious suggestion is that some child labour is unacceptable, but other forms are at least tolerable. Does this reflect a sense of unease within the industrialised world about the nature of child employment in developing countries? Alternatively, is it a pragmatic acknowledgement that some children would starve but for the income they derive from child employment? Or is it simply an acknowledgement that exploitation of children is the problem rather than child employment *per se*? In any event the convention is unlikely to have much effect on child employment in Scotland.

13.12   Despite two private member bills in 1973 and 1997,[12] and the best efforts of the European Union and the United Nations, the regulation of child employment in Scotland still relies on the dated provisions of the Children and Young Persons (Scotland) Act 1937. In 1973 a private members bill which became the Employment of Children Act 1973 was designed to standardise the rules throughout the country, but it has never been brought into force. Following the general election in 1997 Chris Pond M.P., the former Director of the Low Pay Unit, introduced another private members bill on Child Employment. But prior to its second reading on February 13, the Bill was withdrawn in response to a Government commitment to review child employment legislation.

13.13   The review was due to report at the end of 1998. Although it is understood that the review was completed some time ago there has been no Government comment on its content or any possible policy response. Recent legislative developments have instead centred around the EC Directive on the protection of young people at work.[13] Although the directive was due to be implemented by the June 22, 1996, it was only with the passage of regulations in 1997,[14] 1998[15] and 2000[16] that the United Kingdom Government started to address the question of compliance with E.U. law.

---

[11] C182, Worst Forms of Child Labour Convention, Internal Labour Organisation 1999.
[12] On May 22, 1997, Chris Pond M.P. came seventh in the ballot for Private Member's bills and introduced a bill to modernise, standardise and strengthen the law on the employment of children. The Bill was withdrawn in response to a commitment by the Government to review child employment law.
[13] E.C. Directive (94/33/E.C.-O.J. L216/12, August 20, 1994).
[14] The Health and Safety (Young Persons) Regulations 1997 (S.I. 1997 No. 135).
[15] The Children (Protection at Work) Regulations 1998 (S.I. 1998 No. 276).
[16] The Children (Protection at Work) (Scotland) Regulations 2000 (S.S.I. 2000 No. 149).

Public Opinion & the Policy Response

There are apparent contradictions in the public and policy response **13.14**
to child employment. On the one hand, public opinion is quite
quick to criticise organisations or agencies perceived to be connected to child employment. On the other hand, statistics suggest
that most parents permit their children to work while still at school.

In publicity terms, the price of association with child employment **13.15**
can be high and various multinationals have had their fingers burnt
by unwitting association with suppliers who use child workers. In
September 2000, the BBC reported allegations by the Hong Kong
based Christian Industrial Committee that child workers were
locked in toilets and dormitories while monitors investigated a firm
sub contracting to fast food giant McDonalds.[17] No evidence of
child labour was reported but, conscious of their public image,
McDonalds applied a strict code of conduct and withdrew the
contract from the suppliers.

Closer to home, the press and media devoted extensive coverage **13.16**
to the fact that Glasgow was home to around 3,000 child workers,[18]
some working as late as 2.00 a.m.[19] Employers' groups, charities
and the trade unions were united in their concern at the widespread
evasion of local bylaws, yet Strathclyde Police indicated that it was
not an issue which attracted complaints from the public.

Even at ministerial level there is a mixed message over the status **13.17**
of child employment. When questioned about his Department's
efforts to protect child workers, President of the Board of Trade,
Stephen Byers, is reported to have said that part time employment
can be an important addition to a pupils National Record of
Achievement.[20] But when later asked whether their status as part
time workers would attract paid holidays under the working time
directive, Stephen Byers is reported to have reacted with fury to the
suggestion that individual legal rights might extent to children at
work.[21] Of course the application of working time rules is a matter
for the judicial process and the views of the Department of Trade
and Industry are of little consequence once the legislation is passed.
However the perception of child workers as people with lesser legal
status tells us something of the Government's attitude to child
employment.

---

[17] BBC News, September 8, 2000, "MacDonalds Sack Chinese Toy Maker".
[18] BBC News, February 17, 2000, *"Child Labour Campaign Launched"*.
[19] BBC News, January 27, 2000, *"Children's Role In Street Industry"*.
[20] *The Guardian*, February 14, 1999, *"Lessons of the Sweatshop"*.
[21] BBC News, February 11, 1999, *"Paper boys could get paid holidays"*.

13.18 Without developing a comprehensive view of the philosophical underpinnings of public policy, it is possible to speculate on the forces that shape the rights of children at work. On the one hand there seems to be a view that a little bit of work never did anyone any harm and that children should show some initiative and make their own way in the world. This is the apparent tone of Stephen Byers' position where children at work should be seen but not heard. At the other end of the spectrum there is an identifiable and strong welfare view which assumes that children require protection from exploitation in the labour market. On occasion this view goes as far as to encompass calls for an outright ban on child employment.

13.19 There is, of course, no reason that these views cannot be accommodated within a balanced system. In fact, there is research evidence which suggests that, while long working hours may be detrimental to children, moderate involvement in part-time work is beneficial. In one study those working a small number of hours had better school attendance and academic performance than those children who had never worked.[22]

13.20 The question, therefore, is how to obtain a balanced system within which children can accelerate their development through moderate involvement in safe work without being exposed to the dangerous conditions or long working hours that make the experience exploitative and counter productive from an educational and developmental perspective. As in many areas the Government turns to the law and administrative systems in an attempt to achieve that balance. The question is whether this approach is effective.

The Regulatory System

13.21 The domestic law on child employment draws on many different sources: the UN declaration, EC directives, Westminster legislation, devolved regulations and local authority bylaws. Rarely, however, has so much legislative effort combined to achieve so little practical effect. The actions of children, parents and employers control the pattern of child employment with little apparent regard for child employment laws. In addition to various elements of public law, there are the private law remedies available to child workers. This second strand of law is considered separately.

13.22 The law that seeks to regulate the employment of children applies to people below the minimum School Leaving Age (MSLA). In Scotland there are two school leaving dates: the "summer leaving

<hr>

[22] S. Hobbs and J. McKechnie, *Child Employment in Britain: A Social and Psychological Analysis*, 1997.

date" which is the last day of May and the "winter leaving date" which is the earlier of December 21 or the first day of the Christmas Holiday period.[23] In mainstream employment law a classic source of ambiguity is whether a person is engaged under a form of contract that falls within the scope of the law. The law limits the capacity to contract to those aged 16 or over[24] with an exception for contracts "commonly entered into by a child of his age and circumstances". Employment contracts arguably fulfil the requirements of that exception and it is almost certain that children have the capacity to form contracts of employment.[25]

If any doubt were to arise on this point a child might use the **13.23** Human Rights Act 1998 and seek to rely on the European Convention as an aid to the interpretation and application of the law on capacity to contract. Taking Articles 6 and 14 of the European Convention on Human Rights together, it can be argued that everyone is entitled to a determination of their civil rights and obligations and to receive this determination without discrimination. Age is not referred to specifically in Article 14 but the list of grounds contained is not exhaustive and age difference has been the subject of successful arguments in previous cases.

Although proof of a contractual relationship is a pre-requisite for **13.24** the enforcement of individual employment rights[26] it is not a requirement for the application of child employment regulations. The Children and Young Persons (Scotland) Act 1937 defines an employed child as "a person who assists in a trade or occupation carried on for profit shall be deemed to be employed notwithstanding that he receives no reward for his labour".[27] This has the effect of removing many "traditional" child tasks such as babysitting and car washing from the scope of the law. However, there are other relevant legal obligations on adults when they are deemed to be responsible for a child in their care.[28]

Returning to the world of commerce, the rules on child em- **13.25** ployment will therefore cover a wide range of relationships whether or not they comply with the definition of an employment contract. For example, a child assisting a parent in a family business will be covered even if there is no contractual nexus between the parent and child and no payment of wages.

---

[23] Education (Scotland) Act 1980, s. 31.
[24] Age of Legal Capacity (Scotland) Act 1991, s. 1.
[25] *ibid.* s. 2(4).
[26] See paras 13.28 *et seq.*
[27] s. 37(e) Children and Young Persons (Scotland) Act 1937.
[28] *e.g.* Children (Scotland) Act 1995, s. 5, which provides that someone over 16 who has care and control of a child but does not have parental responsibilities and rights must do what is reasonable in the circumstances to promote the child's welfare.

13.26 Although the 1937 Act has been amended on various occasions, the current provisions are as follows: the general minimum age for lawful employment of a child has been raised from 13 to 14;[29] children aged 13 or over may still be employed in light work where express provision for such employment is contained in revised local authority bylaws;[30] light work is defined as: not likely to be harmful to the safety, health or development of children; and not likely to harm their attendance at school or involvement in work experience;[31] it is unlawful to require children to work during normal school hours on a normal school day;[32] it is unlawful to employ a child before 7.00 a.m. or after 7.00 p.m.;[33] and it is unlawful for a child to work for more than two hours on a school day or on a Sunday.[34]

Working Time

13.27 There are new and complex limits on the daily, weekly and annual working hours of school age children.[35] In addition to this series of limits there is a requirement that any child employed for four or more hours per day must have a rest break of at least one hour.

Type of Restriction	Age Band	Maximum Working Hours
Daily Limits		
Normal School Day	All children	2 hours
Any Sunday	All Children	2 hours
Saturdays and Holidays (excluding Sundays)	Under 15 years	7 hours
	15 years and over	8 hours
Weekly Limits		
Term time	Under 15 years	12 hours
	15 years and over	18 hours
School Holidays	Under 15 years	35 hours
	15 years and over	40 hours

---

[29] Children & Young Person's (Scotland) Act 1937, s. 28(1)(a).
[30] See The Children (Protection at Work) Regulations 1998 (S.I. 1998 No. 2761).
[31] Children & Young Person's (Scotland) Act, 1937, s. 28(2)(a) (I).
[32] *ibid.* s. 28 (1)(b).
[33] *ibid.* s. 28(1)(c).
[34] *ibid.* s. 28(1)(e).
[35] E.C. Directive on the Protection of Young People at Work (94/33/EC).

The EC Directive was introduced within the EU Treaty[36] and **13.28** various specific safety requirements are laid out in the new law. All employers have a general duty to protect the health, safety and welfare of employees. This duty is both delictual and contractual. However, the regulations on child employment fit into a greatly expanded framework of statutory safety provisions. For example, the new law starts by revisiting the general duty on employers to promote health and safety, but from a child's perspective. The EC directive points out that children can face additional risk because they lack experience or awareness and may not have matured fully. Employers now have a statutory duty to take these factors into account.[37]

In addition to creating a stronger general duty, the directive sets **13.29** out various grounds upon which work is to be prohibited by member states. These grounds describe a range of potential hazards from which children are to be protected. But perhaps more importantly the directive requires employers to conduct a risk assessment targeted specifically at hazards that might affect young people. This assessment is required prior to a young person starting work and should be revised when there is a major change in working conditions.[38] Key features of the assessment process include the layout of the workstation, the type of equipment used and the duration of its use, the way in which work tasks are organised and the level of training given to young people. Although the directive was implemented by regulations in 1998,[39] it is hard to imagine that any significant number of children are employed in circumstances where such a detailed assessment has been carried out.

In health and safety cases there are two potential remedies avail- **13.30** able to children, both resulting in similar awards: a standard personal injury claim is one option; an action for breach of statutory duty is another. Other than that, the regulatory scheme relies on action by the statutory authorities. Given that children are banned from industrial undertakings, their chances of an encounter with the Health and Safety Executive should be slim.[40] Children are more heavily reliant on local enforcement of health and safety by the Environmental Health Department within each local authority. Additionally there are various criminal offences within the regulatory system that could be more rigorously enforced by the police.

---

[36] Health and Safety provisions.
[37] Art. 7.1 E.C. Directive 94/33/E.C.
[38] Art. 6.2 E.C. Directive 94/33/E.C.
[39] The Children (Protection at Work) Regulations 1998 (S.I. 1998 No. 276).
[40] s. 1 and s. 3(2) of the Employment of Women, Young Persons and Children Act 1920.

Enforcement Processes

13.31 Prior to the implementation of the E.C. Directive, the enforcement
of child employment rules had fallen into disrepute. In 1998 the
Scottish Low Pay Unit surveyed Scottish Local Authorities to establish the level of activity; the results were quite worrying. Of the
32 questionnaires distributed 16 were not returned or not completed
because the councils were unable to identify an official with responsibility for child employment. Of the 16 authorities that gave a
reply, only nine were aware that local authorities had responsibility
for maintaining and enforcing bylaws on child employment. Additional information from those Councils that took part demonstrated that many bylaws had not been updated since the 1930s or
1940s.

13.32   The granting of permits for child employment is a central part of
the regulatory system, and although three quarters of respondents
were aware of a permit system, only four councils were able to give
information on the distribution of permits. One comparatively
small council had over 400 permits in circulation, while others had
far fewer. The SLPU research uncovered one Council with only 23
permits, but later investigation by the media revealed one fairly
large local authority with only nine children working under a lawful
permit.[41] Helpfully the respondents gave information on the system
they would prefer to see in place. Most opted to retain the permit
system but with a higher level of pubic awareness and participation
from employers, parents, teachers and police. Thankfully, this is the
direction in which the system has turned since the publication of
this research in January 1999.

Recent Developments

13.33 Following the implementation of the E.C. Directive there has been
a flurry of activity. Although the E.C. Directive was implemented at
a United Kingdom level by the Department of Health, the issue of
child employment appears to have been included within the devo-
lution package despite the fact that general employment matters are
reserved to Westminster. Although child employment cuts across a
number of policy areas it has come to rest in the Children & Families Division within the Children & Young People's Group of the
Scottish Executive's Education Department.[42] When local authorities make or revise bylaws on the employment of children they
must be submitted to the Scottish Executive for confirmation. Re-

---

[41] "Half of Pupils Have Jobs", *The Herald,* April 21, 1999.
[42] Scottish Executive Correspondence February 6, 2001.

sponsibility for enforcing bylaws rests with individual local authorities. The Executive issues advice to local authorities from time to time—usually to inform them of a change in legislation. They do not, however, offer an interpretation of the statute as this is a matter for individual local authorities but do deal with enquiries from local authorities on an ad-hoc basis.

Following the 1998 Regulations, 20 of the 32 local authorities **13.34** have had revised bylaws confirmed and nine have submitted draft bylaws and are currently involved in a process of dialogue with the Scottish Executive and revision of these draft rules prior to confirmation.[43] However, the Scottish Executive were unable to respond fully to a question in the Scottish Parliament in June 2000 by Duncan McNeil MSP when he sought to establish whether local authorities had dedicated child employment officers and whether there had been any recent prosecutions under the 1937Act.[44]

These administrative changes are beginning to be matched by **13.35** action on the ground, but it has to be stressed that improved enforcement efforts are starting from a low base. In Edinburgh new bylaws were accompanied by what is possibly the first inter-departmental campaign by any council in Scotland. Social Work, Education, Corporate Services and Environmental Health were united in a combined strategy to enforce child employment rules in the city.[45] Similarly in Glasgow a publicity drive was launched to draw the attention of parents and employers to the impact of new bylaws. In addition the permit application process in Glasgow has been streamlined and centralised within the education authority.[46]

All this does herald the beginnings of a system that might bring **13.36** child employment patterns within the boundaries set by the law. Having said that, a recent enquiry to the Scottish Executive's Justice Department revealed that there had still been no recorded prosecutions of employers as recently as 1999.[47] Without detailed permits and adequate enforcement strategies the United Kingdom will undoubtedly be in breach of various elements of the E.C. Directive. On the question of compliance the Scottish Executive are quick to indicate that enforcement of the regulations rests with local authorities. However, the obligation on central government in the United Kingdom is a strict liability. Whether devolved or centralised in terms of delivery, ultimate responsibility for the protection of children rests with national government.

---

[43] *ibid.*
[44] Scottish Parliament Official Report, Written Answers, June 21, 2000.
[45] Minute of the General Purposes Committee, City of Edinburgh Council, August 20, 1998.
[46] BBC News, February 17, 2000, "Child Labour Campaign Launched".
[47] Scottish Executive Correspondence February 14, 2001.

Individual Employment Rights

13.37 Much of the law discussed above relates to various public authorities and their statutory duty to protect children. But what about
the individual statutory and contractual rights of child workers?
The media report that the Secretary of State for Trade and Industry
was furious at the suggestion that children should receive paid
holidays was noted above. Notwithstanding the fact that interpretation of the law is a matter for the judiciary, there is a strong
case to argue in opposition to Mr Byers.

13.38   The range of possible rights for children is set out below. The
series of columns reflect the fact that the extent of entitlement tends
to depend on two factors: contractual status and length of service.
There are only two age restrictions that exclude children: both the
minimum wage and redundancy pay require a worker to be at least
18 years of age. A requirement for a minimum number of working
hours previously excluded many part time workers from legal
protection. This obviously excluded many children, but the requirements relating to hours were, however, discriminatory on
grounds of gender and were abolished some time ago.[48]

13.39   Of the remaining rights, some require a certain amount of con-
tinuous service. Whether a child can meet this requirement will
obviously vary from case to case, but service requirements will not
exclude every child from legal protection. The key issue, therefore,
is whether the relationship between a child worker and an employer
is contractual and, if it is, whether the contract is an employment
contract or a worker's contract.

13.40   The Scottish law on contract is broad in scope. In England, a
worker would have to show that the arrangement was based on a
mutual agreement, that both parties intended it to be enforceable,
and that the obligation is balanced by some form of consideration
such as payment of wages. In Scotland, no consideration is required. Evidence of a pattern of payments in return for work will
support the existence of an agreement whether expressed or implied.
The issue is whether the parties intended the agreement to be enforceable. Given all the international treaties, declarations and directives to which the UK is a signatory, it is inconceivable that a
court or tribunal would prevent a child from recovering payment
due from an employer under an agreement to perform work. The
only valid interpretation of the law indicates that child employment
agreements are enforceable contracts. The true question is: what
type of contract are we dealing with?

13.41   A worker's contract is defined in the Employment Rights Act
1996 as "a contract of employment, or any other contract, whether

---

[48] Employment Protection (Part-time Employees) Regulations 1995 (S.I. 1995
No.31).

express or implied and (if it is express) whether oral or in writing, whereby the individual undertakes to do or perform personally any work or services for another party to the contract whose status is not by virtue of the contract that of a client or customer of any profession or business undertaking carried on by the individual".[49] The definition is cumbersome, but the key phrase is the description of "any other contract whereby the individual undertakes to perform work". The terms of the contract need not be discussed in advance, far less recorded in writing. The position of children is clear, work performed under a contract brings at least some legal protection.

Statutory Protection	People Covered	Qualifying Period
Right to receive the minimum wage	Workers	None
Protection against unlawful wage deductions	Workers	None
Dismissal for asserting a statutory right	Workers	None
Health and safety dismissal	Workers	None
Dismissal linked to holidays or working time	Workers	None
Dismissal linked to minimum wage	Workers	None
Maternity Allowance	Workers	26 weeks
Protection against sex discrimination	Workers	None
Protection against race discrimination	Workers	None
Protection against disability discrimination	Workers	None
Right to daily and weekly rest breaks	Workers	None
Right to receive holidays with pay	Workers	13 weeks
Accrued holiday pay on termination	Workers	13 weeks
Right to receive a pay slip	Employees	None
Receive a written statement of conditions	Employees	4 weeks
Unfair Dismissal	Employees	One year

---

[49] s. 230 Employment Rights Act 1996.

Protection against pregnancy dismissal	Employees	None
Dismissal linked to maternity leave	Employees	None
Protection during business takeover	Employees	One year
Time off for ante natal care	Employees	None
14 week maternity leave	Employees	None
Extended maternity leave of up to 40 weeks	Employees	Two years
Maternity Pay	Employees	26 weeks
Sick Pay	Employees	None
Right to join a union	Employees	None
Redundancy Pay	Employees	Two years
Collective consultation on redundancies	Employees	None
Collective consultation on business transfers	Employees	None

13.42 Access to full legal protection requires proof that the relationship is an employment contract rather than a broader worker's contract. The key difference is that employers and employees share a mutual obligation to supply and perform work on an ongoing basis whereas workers contracts can be quite casual. Individual cases will turn on their facts, but even without the benefit of employee status, children clearly enjoy greater legal protection than many observers might expect.

Conclusion

13.43 Many children clearly want to work and, by and large, society is willing to endorse that choice. The question is the nature of the arrangements under which children are employed and the relationship with more fundamental issues such as health, development and education. If a balance has been struck, the balance point still has little connection with the law, public or private, which fails to deliver for children much of what it promises.

CHAPTER 14

THE RIGHT TO A SAFE ENVIRONMENT

Dr David Stone and Colin Moodie

The right to a safe, risk-free environment in which to live, learn, **14.1**
play and grow is a very fundamental right of a child, and was
recognised by the UN Convention on the Rights of the Child in
several Articles. Article 3(3) states that those responsible for children's care "shall conform with the standards established by competent authorities, particularly in the areas of safety, health and
competent supervision". Article 24 makes the connection between
safety and health-care issues, Article 6 declares the right of the child
to survive and develop, and Article 32 says children must be protected from hazardous employment. A right to a safe environment
is also a necessary prerequisite to the right of children to play recognised in Article 31. The Convention reflects the realities of
children's lives—that there are many factors that may adversely
impact on their right to be safe.

This chapter considers two issues: the public policy aspects of the **14.2**
child's right to be safe; and the legal safeguards which presently
exist which may be regarded as upholding children's rights to be
safe.

Public Policy Considerations

Safety and Child Health

Article 24 of the UN Convention asserts that all children and young **14.3**
people have a right to "the enjoyment of the highest attainable
standard of health". The World Health Organisation[1] defines
health as "a state of complete physical, mental and social well-being
and not merely the absence of disease or infirmity". The protection
of children from injury, therefore, clearly lies fully within the remit
of the Convention, even in the absence of explicit references to child
safety, of which there are several, as noted above.

Threats to the health of children arise either from intrinsic **14.4**

---

[1]   Constitution of the World Health Organisation, W.H.O., New York (1946).

sources (such as genetic, endocrine or intellectual disorders) or extrinsic factors (such as micro-organisms, extreme temperatures or poor nutrition). Children are especially vulnerable to injury because they are developmentally immature and have not yet learned how to avoid the multiplicity of extrinsic hazards to which they are exposed.

14.5   Newborn infants are largely protected from their surroundings by their parents who feed, clothe, bathe and transport their children within an artificially contrived "safe" micro-environment. After the first year, toddlers have a powerful exploratory instinct that enables them to assess and cope with the world around them—a process that is essential to physiological, intellectual and social development. This relentless curiosity, when combined with increasing physical strength and mobility, brings young children into direct contact with inanimate objects (such as doors, walls and furniture), with mechanical and electric devices, with the elements (particularly fire and water), with animals, insects and plants, and with other human beings. All of this is enormously stimulating, enjoyable and important to the growing child. At the same time, the risk of injury—from the most trivial to the most lethal—is ubiquitous. The result is that children are injured in vast numbers throughout the world every year.

14.6   The injuries suffered by children may be accidental or non-accidental—and intent cannot always be determined. The damage is caused by the acute exposure of the child to physical, chemical or other harmful agents. As well as the immediate effects, there are often adverse longer-term consequences in the form of disability, educational disruption, emotional disturbance and financial cost. These can affect not only the child, but also the family, peer group and the wider community.

14.7   In an influential paper, Haddon[2] described the "natural history" of an injury in terms of classical epidemiological triad of host, agent and environment. Haddon's formulation emphasised both the complexity of the phenomenon of injury and its dynamic nature. An injury is the outcome of a process rather than a single event. Moreover, the nature and determinants of that process are amenable to investigation and, ultimately, modification. This view of injury causation as potentially predictable and therefore avoidable has profound implications for the development of public health strategies designed to promote child safety.

---

[2]   W. Haddon, "The Changing Approach to the Epidemiology, Prevention and Amelioration of Trauma. The Transition to Approaches, Etiologically Rather than Descriptively, Based", 1968, Amercian Journal of Public Health, Vol. 58, pp. 1431–1438.

The Epidemiology of Injury in Childhood

Trauma is the single largest contributor to death in childhood after **14.8** the age of one year. Younger (pre-school) children are most at risk of being killed in their homes, while school-age children are most at risk of road accidents. An analysis of data published by the Scottish Office Home and Health Department (1994) showed that, over the period 1980–1991, the home accident fatality rate for those under the age of five in Scotland was higher than the road accident fatality rate for the five–15 year age group[3]. Of the various causes of home accident deaths, the most frequent are fire and flames, and choking. Amongst road accident fatalities, the largest proportion involves pedestrians. Indeed, the child pedestrian fatal accident rate in Scotland is higher than that of England and Wales, and one of the highest in Western Europe[4]. Injury mortality rates in childhood have been falling over the past 30 years, but this trend should be viewed in the context of declining child death rates generally. Moreover, there is some evidence that the decline in child injury rates in Scotland has reached a plateau or may even be increasing.[5]

The epidemiology of injury varies with severity.[6] There is a clear **14.9** social class gradient in childhood injuries which is more marked in fatalities than in non-fatal injuries (which are the vast majority)—or in childhood mortality from other causes. This striking social patterning suggests that environmental factors play an important role in causing childhood injuries. While in England and Wales, socio-economic inequalities in injury risk appear to be widening, this has not yet been reported from Scotland. In addition to occurring at home and on the roads, injuries to children can occur during leisure activities, such as sport or while playing, at school, or as a result of inter-personal violence. Data on the relative frequency of the various locations, circumstances and causes of childhood injury in Scotland are scant, simply because there is no mechanism for collecting and analysing, on a routine basis, the appropriate data .[7]

---

[3] C.J Smith and A.M. MacKintosh, "A Review of Child Accident Prevention in Scotland", Glasgow, Centre for Social Marketing (University of Strathclyde, 1994).

[4] Scottish Development Department (1989), "Must Do Better—a Study of Child Pedestrian Accidents and Road Crossing Behaviour in Scotland". Report by MVA Consultancy, Edinburgh, Scottish Office.

[5] The Scottish Executive Health Department, "Health in Scotland 1998", (1999, HMSO, Edinburgh).

[6] S.S.Walsh and S.N. Jarvis, "Measuring the frequency of "severe" accidental injury in childhood," (1992) Journal of Epidemiology and Community Health 46, 26–32.

[7] The need to collect data on child accidents has been recognised: Scottish Office: "Towards a Healthier Scotland", (1999, HMSO, Edinburgh) paras 73–74.

14.10   The consequences of injury are equally poorly documented. In economic terms, the health care and social support costs are enormous.[8] More importantly, the effects on the quality of life of victims, who may be severely physically or mentally disabled (or both), and their families can be devastating.[9]

14.11   Scottish children suffer a higher injury mortality rate than their counterparts in the rest of the United Kingdom. Possible reasons for this higher level of risk include the high concentration of areas of multiple deprivation in Scotland's cities, adverse weather conditions, an unusually hazardous environment, and a high prevalence of alcohol and drug abuse. Academic researchers, the health service and governmental departments have tended to neglect the subject of childhood injury, despite its public health importance. The most obvious manifestation of this phenomenon is the lack of comprehensive national or regional strategies for the prevention of childhood injury or for the promotion of child safety.

Levels of Prevention

14.12 In conventional medical terms, the aim of a preventive measure is to interrupt the natural history of a disease so that progression to the next stage is halted. The UN Convention, in Article 24 dealing with health and health services, acknowledges the importance of preventative measures. Article 24(2) deals with the State's responsibility to take appropriate measures to diminish infant mortality, combat disease, and specifically, at 24(2) (f) "to develop preventive health care, guidance for parents and family planning education and services".

14.13   There are three levels of prevention: primary, secondary, and tertiary. Primary prevention seeks to pre-empt the occurrence of an injury by interrupting the chain of events leading to it. This can be achieved by deploying strategies often referred to under the headings of the three Es—education, engineering and enforcement. Of these, education is probably the least effective, yet the most widely used. Pedestrian injuries will serve to illustrate this. Children as young as five or six are inculcated with the Green Cross Code, despite their being unequipped, physiologically, to translate its principles into action. Their sensory systems, reaction times and musculature are too immature to identify and avoid potentially hazardous vehicles. Enforcement of speed limits to slow traffic passing in close proximity to child pedestrians is intermittent at

---

[8]   D.H. Stone, "Costs and Benefits of Accident Prevention", in Popey and Young (eds), *Reducing Accidental Death and injury in Children* (1993 Manchester Public Health Research and Resume Centre).

[9]   Research Institute for Consumer Affairs. "Knocked Down—a study of the personal and family consequences of road accidents involving pedestrians and pedal cyclists" (London, Consumers Association, 1990).

best, being dependent on the allocation of scarce police resources to the task. Environmental engineering, such as traffic calming schemes and, ideally, the complete separation of traffic from pedestrians, is by far the most effective approach, but requires a major investment of resources.

Secondary prevention is designed to ensure that the energy **14.14** transfer from the agent to the victim is dissipated as rapidly as possible, thereby avoiding or minimising pathological effects to the victim. Early disease detection (screening) and treatment, intended to try to reduce mortality and morbidity associated with diseases, is part of a secondary prevention strategy. Similarly, the wearing of car seat restraints by children, does nothing to reduce the risks of a motor vehicle accident, but can protect the occupants from severe injury.

Tertiary prevention aims to minimise the harmful consequences **14.15** of injuries. The physical, mental and social rehabilitation of children who have sustained serious injury is part of tertiary prevention. Such intervention consumes substantial time, energy and resources, but is of critical importance in ensuring a return to "normal" living and learning for those children and young people.

Need for a Strategic Approach

Several reports[10] have drawn attention to the need to develop a **14.16** comprehensive, multi-agency strategy for child injury prevention. A major difficulty is the lack of a single organisation with overall responsibility for injury prevention in the United Kingdom, despite the topic being accorded key area status in the government's health promotion policy statements, "Saving Lives: Our Healthier Nation,[11] "Scotland's Health—A Challenge to Us All"[12] and most recently "Towards a Healthier Scotland".[13] The National Health Service can contribute relatively little to the promotion of children's safety because virtually all of the key factors lie outside of its control. Local authorities, police forces, civil engineers, architects, trading standards officers, consumer safety organisations, politicians and civil servants are all better placed to protect children from hazardous environments than are doctors, nurses or other health professionals. The health service could, however, make crucial contributions to preventing child injury in three areas. One is the

---

[10] see, *e.g.* H. Ward, "Preventing Road Accidents to Children : the Role of the NHS", London Health Authority (1991); and L. Schelp, "Community intervention and changed in accident pattern in a rural Swedish municipality", (1987) Health Promotion 2, 109–25.

[11] Department of Health, "Saving Lives: Our Healthier Nation", (1999, HMSO, Edinburgh).

[12] Scottish Office, "Scotland's Health—A Challenge to us All", (1992, HMSO, Edinburgh).

[13] The Scottish Office Department of Health, "Towards a Healthier Scotland" White Paper on Health, (1999, HMSO, Edinburgh).

collection, analysis and dissemination of good quality data on the causes, clinical presentations and consequences of injury. Without adequate data, the development and monitoring of injury prevention programmes are severely hampered.

14.17   The second role of the health service is advocacy. By constantly highlighting the huge burden of avoidable childhood death, disability and unhappiness attributable to injuries, those sectors of society which are in a position to implement safety measures will be more likely to react than if a "softly, softly" approach is adopted. Pless[14] has called upon United Kingdom public health department to take a lead in informing their local communities of the scale—and avoidability—of the problem of injuries. Most have responded by attempting to document the frequency and causes of accidents in their populations as the first step towards the formulation of a strategy. It is too early to judge the success or otherwise of their efforts.

14.18   The third unfulfilled role of the health service is the co-ordination of the numerous professional and voluntary agencies concerned with the same objective. The formation of "healthy alliances" is one means of achieving this, but success has proved elusive, mainly because insufficient resources have been invested in the task. Effective inter-agency co-ordination depends less on good will than on the existence of appropriate administrative structures to ensure that the rhetoric of co-operation is translated into practical action.

14.19   As has been noted above, agencies other than the health service have a crucial role to play in implementing policies and practices which will tackle the causes of child accidents and promote children's rights to a safe environment. Repeated complaints about the "lack of data" tend to disguise how much is already known about the prevention of injuries in children. While there is undoubtedly scope for further research, the widespread application of existing knowledge by local authorities, central government and others could potentially prevent between a third and a half of all childhood injuries. Key safety measures of proven efficacy which remain inconsistently deployed include the use of car passenger restraints (front and rear), the wearing of cycle helmets, the fitting and regular maintenance of smoke detectors to all households, the appropriate setting of domestic hot water thermostats, traffic calming in densely populated areas, and the laying of absorbent surfaces in playgrounds. None of these lies beyond the scope of a moderately sophisticated industrialised society and all would pay handsome dividends in terms of deaths and injuries avoided for relatively little financial outlay. In 1998, a special conference of injury prevention professionals called for the creation of national agencies for injury prevention throughout the United Kingdom.[15]

---

[14] I.B Pless, "Accident Prevention", British Medical Journal 303, 462–4.
[15] Supplement to Injury Prevention, December 1998, Vol. 4, No. 4.

Legal Measures

Legal safeguards in Scots law, which promote such safety measures, **14.20** are examined below, to determine to what extent existing law can be regarded as promoting a child's right to a safe environment.

Common Law Duty

Until the Industrial Revolution there was little distinction in the law **14.21** between what we now look on as civil wrongs, and crime. During the 19th Century the Scottish courts developed the law of delict to protect persons from unjustifiable wrongs inflicted on them by others. Such a wrong might be to a person, to business interests, to property, to reputation or to liberty. To protect persons from unjustifiable wrongs, the concept of negligence was refined and developed. As far as wrongs to the person are concerned, it reached its most succinct expression in the famous and much quoted case of *Donoghue v. Stevenson*: "You must take reasonable care to avoid acts or omissions which you can reasonably foresee would be likely to injure your neighbour. Who, then, in law, is my neighbour? The answer seems to be: persons who are so closely and directly affected by my acts that I ought to have them in contemplation as being so affected when I am directing my mind to the acts or omissions which are called in question".[16]

Negligence therefore arises when there is an act or omission **14.22** causing unintentional but reasonably foreseeable harm, and that harm is caused or permitted by the wrongdoer, whom the law recognises as having a legal duty not to cause or permit such harm. The standard of care required is that which a reasonable man would consider he had a duty to take. The harm has to be reasonably foreseeable, that is harm that the victim should have guarded against, with reasonable steps and precautions, where there was a material risk (and not a remote possibility) of that harm occurring.

The breach of the duty to take care must have caused harm to the **14.23** person. This is known as causation. There must be a direct link between the injury and the breach of duties. Causation is often an important element, and area of controversy, in medical negligence cases. For example, in cases of brain damaged or cerebral palsic children, it has to be shown that not only were the medical staff negligent at the birth, but also that negligence caused the brain damage to the child. These are always tragic cases, and it is not uncommon to find that there was negligence at the birth, but it made no difference because the child was already brain damaged from other causes prior to the negligence.

---

[16] 1932 S.C. (H.L.) 31, *per* Lord Atkin at p. 44.

14.24 Lastly, the injured person must be in the area of risk and within the classes of person that the law recognises as able to claim. There are legal restrictions placed on classes of claimants as a matter of public policy and practicality, to avoid multiplicity of claims. Two examples of this may be found in decisions of the House of Lords in claims relating to children. In *McFarlane v. Tayside Health Board*,[17] a woman became pregnant following negligent medical advice after her husband's vasectomy. Overturning the Inner House of the Court of Session, it was held that the claim for the costs of the upbringing of the child were not recoverable on, broadly, public policy considerations. A clear example of the public policy exclusion of claims is found in *X. (Minors) v. Bedfordshire County Council*.[18] In this case, children who had been severely neglected at home attempted to sue the responsible local authority for failing to act to protect them. It was decided that no action lay against a local authority in negligence or breach of statutory duty under the Children Act 1989.[19]

14.25 The duty of care that a person owes towards children will in most circumstances be greater than the duty of care that the person owes to an adult. This is because the law recognises that children, because of their age and lack of reasoning powers, will not have the same capacity to appreciate danger as will adults. A child's curiosity and sense of adventure will take him or her into a situation where injury might occur, and if it is reasonably foreseeable that a child will find him or herself in such a situation and might foreseeably come to harm, there is a duty to take reasonable precautions against this.[20]

14.26 The law also recognises that people can contribute to their own downfall and be partly to blame for an accident. This has led to the development of the doctrine of contributory negligence. Where a defender is negligent, but the injured person has also been negligent, the court will apportion the blame between them. Children can be contributorily negligent,[21] but again, their age and powers of reasoning are factors affecting whether, and to what extent, it will be held that they should have appreciated the risk involved in their conduct. If an accident occurs while a child is in the care of an adult, the child's claim is not compromised or reduced by the fact that the adult was also negligent. As well as being contributorily

---

[17] 2000 S.L.T. 154.

[18] 1995 3 All E.R. 353.

[19] The public policy considerations included the potential inhibiting effect which the possibility of claims might have on the actions of local authorities. The question of whether this exclusion breached the human rights of the children concerned has subsequently been considered by the European Court. See *Z and Others v. United Kingdom*, Strasbourg, May 10, 2001, judgment available on the European Court of Human Rights website at *www.echr.coeint.*

[20] For a reminder that the duty is only to do what is reasonable see *Ahmed v. City of Glasgow Council*, 2000 S.L.T. (Sh. Ct) 153 (no liability for injury to child in school).

[21] *McKinnel v. White*, 1971 S.L.T. (Notes) 61.

negligent, children may in some circumstances be regarded as wholly responsible for the harm which befalls them.[22]

Statute Law

In addition to the common law duty to take care, Acts of Parlia- **14.27** ment and Statutory Regulations impose on persons some statutory duties in relation to safety. There are two important Acts which protect the public in general. These are the Occupiers Liability (Scotland) Act 1960 and the Consumer Protection Act 1987.

The Occupiers Liability (Scotland) Act 1960, as its title implies, concerns dangers on premises. The Act imposes a duty of care on the occupier of premises to show to a person entering onto those premises, in respect of dangers which are due to the state of the premises, such care as—in the circumstances—is reasonable. An occupier of premises has to show reasonable care towards all persons on the premises in respect of dangers there, although it is still material whether the injured person was on the premises with permission or was a trespasser.

The duty owed by an occupier towards children is again higher **14.28** than towards adults, if it is foreseeable that children might be on the premises and might foreseeably be harmed by dangers therein, such as hidden traps, objects of curiosity and so on. Children have therefore succeeded in claims for damages when they have wandered onto railway lines and been injured,[23] fallen down inadequately guarded holes,[24] played with machinery on a building site,[25] eaten poisonous berries[26] and been injured using play equipment such as climbing frames.[27]

The Consumer Protection Act 1987 is a very important piece of safety legislation passed as a result of the Product Liability Directive from the European Community. The act imposes strict liability on manufacturers and producers of products, for injury caused by defective products; a pursuer's claim does not therefore depend on proving negligence. A product is defective if it does not meet the standard of safety which consumers are entitled to expect. In deciding what consumers are entitled to expect, all the circumstances are to be taken into account, including the manner in which and the purpose for which a product has been marketed and any instructions or warnings for its use and what might reasonably be expected to be done with it.

---

[22] *Devlin v. Strathclyde Regional Council,* 1993 S.L.T. 699.
[23] e.g. *Haughton v. North British Railway,* (1892) 20 R. 113.
[24] *Hughes v. Lord Advocate,* 1963 S.C. (H.L.) 31.
[25] *Shields v. Smith,* 1948 S.L.T. (Notes) 24.
[26] *Taylor v. Glasgow Corporation,* 1922 S.C. (H.L.) 1.
[27] e.g. *Bates v. Stone Parish Council,* 1954 1 W.L.R. 1249 (chute), and *Imrie v. Dumfries and Galloway Regional Council,* unreported, 1993, at Dumfries (fall from playground climbing frame onto concrete).

14.29   Product liability under the Act is in its early days and as yet there is no case law. However, it is known that claims have been brought and successful settlements achieved, in respect of exploding hair-dryers, bottles and kitchen equipment, wooden spales in packets of sweets,[28] surgical scissors breaking during an operation, food poisoning at restaurants and holiday camps,[29] defective bolts on a climbing frame,[30] a dressing gown which caught fire and at least one case involving the defective design of a vehicle. The types of cases involved show the importance of the legislation for the protection of all persons, and, in particular, children.

14.30   One of the most useful applications of the Act could be in relation to defective vehicle design. There are considerable concerns amongst transport experts and lawyers involved in this field about several aspects of current vehicle design. These centre on the provision of lap seatbelts, air bags, mirrors and child safety seats, and the lack of front under-run bars on lorries and proper three point seatbelts for bus passengers. Lap seatbelts exist in many cars and are often used by children in the back seat. Their use—because of the bio-mechanics involved—can lead, in an accident, to horrific injuries to the lower spine or the lower internal organs. Many experts in the field believe they should not be fitted to cars and should be replaced by the normal three point seatbelts. As a result of extensive litigation in the USA, they are no longer fitted to cars there. Air bags can prevent serious injury but are only fitted to a few vehicles here, while fitting is standard in the USA.

14.31   Drivers of lorries or buses have two dangerous blind spots, but mirrors are not fitted to assist the drivers. The result is that children who cross the road in front of such vehicles cannot be seen by the drivers. This has led to fatalities. Both problems could easily be solved at modest expense by the provision of adequate mirrors. Such mirrors are standard on school buses in British Columbia and should be here. Child safety or restraint seats are subject to regulation under the BSI Standards, but concerns remain about the ways in which they are attached to cars.

14.32   There is considerable concern about the failure of motor manufacturers to provide front under-run bars on lorries over 3.5 ton in weight, to prevent a car going under the lorry in a head-on collision. When the car goes under the lorry, the front of the lorry enters the passenger space, leading in many cases to the deaths of the occupants. Studies by the Transport Research Laboratory[31] have esti-

---

[28] National Consumer Council, "Unsafe Products", November 1995.
[29] *e.g.* outbreak of salmonella at a Lancashire holiday camp in July 1995 and see N.C.C. Report *supra* at p. 12.
[30] N.C.C. Report *supra* at p. 9.
[31] Analysis of Fatalities in Heavy Goods Vehicle Accidents, Department of Transport, TRRL Contractor Report C.R. 289, 1991 and see B.S. Riley and B.J. Robinson, "Protecting Car Occupants in Frontal Collisions with Heavy Goods Vehicles", paper from 27 ISATA conference 1994.

mated that around 70 per cent of fatalities in head-on collisions between cars and lorries could be prevented by the provision of such under-run bars. In these situations, it is not only the driver and the front seat passengers who are killed, but also those in the rear, who are, in many cases, children.

Unfortunately, the power to introduce regulations to combat **14.33** these problems no longer lies with the United Kingdom Government. Under the E.C. Treaties and Rules on Harmonisation of Legislation, regulations in the area of transport have to be done on an E.C. basis by the issuing of an appropriate Directive for member Governments to implement. The United Kingdom Government, to its credit, is pressing for appropriate regulations in some of the areas identified, but it is thought that a Directive is some way off. The Government should be urged to consider introducing the said regulations unilaterally, under the exception rules, to prevent unnecessary fatalities and serious injury.

Legal Measures in Specific Settings

Apart from the general protection of the child's safety under **14.34** common law and statutory provisions already mentioned, there are certain specific settings where a child is likely to be exposed to danger, and therefore requires protection.

Home

At home, the child is protected by negligence and product liability **14.35** laws, but also requires protection against abuse and neglect by parents, and against the negligence of third parties. There are mechanisms for the state to intervene where child abuse or neglect is suspected, discussed in Chapter 8. Criminal sanctions may be used against carers, for assault or sexual abuse.[32] The Children and Young Persons (Scotland) Act 1937 may also be used to prosecute where a child has been exposed to ill-treatment or neglect.[33]

House fires lead to many fatalities amongst children, the majority **14.36** of which could have been avoided with better fire prevention and detection. The fitting of smoke alarms is now mandatory in new houses[34] and both they and house fire fighting equipment should be in every house. Many Local Authorities are recognising this problem and installing smoke alarms in existing housing stock. Those

---

[32] The statutory offences relating to sexual abuse of children are now largely found in the Criminal Law Consolidation (Scotland) Act 1995.

[33] s. 12, Children and Young Persons (Scotland) Act 1937.

[34] Building Standards (Scotland) Regulations 1990, and BS 5839, Part 1:1988 Fire Detection and Alarm Systems for Buildings.

who do not do so could successfully be sued if it were shown that the provision of a smoke alarm might have prevented a fatal tragedy. It would, in any event, be sensible (and in line with the requirements of Article 3 of the Convention), to install smoke alarms and fire fighting equipment.

School

14.37 In relation to school, the Local Authority at common law must provide reasonably safe premises, and is responsible for any negligence which teachers or other employees commit, in the course of their employment. When in charge of school children, a teacher owes the same duty of care to each child as does a reasonably careful parent. Many accidents to pupils occur in school gyms, while playing sports, in the playground and on school trips. The standard of care required by teachers in such circumstances is one of reasonable supervision, through taking reasonable precautions to prevent foreseeable injury. This duty also applies to school buses.

14.38   One of the major recent concerns has been bullying, in school or on school buses.[35]Education departments and teachers have a responsibility to prevent bullying, and to protect pupils from it. If they know it is occurring and take no reasonable steps (including providing adequate supervision) to prevent it, they could successfully be sued for that failure.[36]

Education departments also have a statutory duty to secure that premises and equipment conform to applicable standards and requirements, and that they are maintained in such a condition as to conduce to the good health and safety of all persons on the premises or using the equipment. This duty is owed as much to pupils as to local authority employees.[37]

Breach of this general duty has been held not to give rise to any claim against the authority, as was seen in *Johanneson v. Lothian Regional Council*.[38]It is important to recall that general duties in the Health and Safety at Work Act 1974 apply to schools and other work premises that accommodate children. This creates responsibilities not just to children but also to the children on the premises (section 3 of the 1974 Act).

There is also a statutory duty, in respect of special schools and primary schools of more than 50 pupils, to secure supervision by at least one adult, during break times.[39]

---

[35] see Chap. 12, paras 12.47–12.51.
[36] The difficulties of succeeding in such a case on the facts is shown by the decisions in *Scott v. Lothian Regional Council*, Court of Session, September 29, 1998 and *McPherson v. Perth and Kinross Council*, January 26, 2001.
[37] Education (Scotland) Act 1980, s. 19(2).
[38] 1996 S.L.T. (Sh. Ct) 74.
[39] Schools (Safety and Supervision of Pupils)(Scotland) Regulations 1990 reg. 3. (S.I. 1990, No. 295).

Play

Play equipment may be sited in local authority housing areas, in **14.39**
school grounds or as part of commercial enterprises. Wherever
located, defects such as the lack of soft surfaces, and individual
components being too large for the size of the child likely to use
them, result in serious injuries through falls. There are no Regulations governing the provision, siting and construction of such
equipment, but concerns have been such that the British Standards
Institute has since 1978 published standards on impact-absorbing
surfaces and construction standards. These are very thorough, and
provide, as far as possible, reasonable safety for children. It is
thought that most manufacturers of play equipment follow the
standards, but there are still many play parks and school playgrounds for which local authorities are responsible, which do not
conform to the standards. Successful court actions have been
brought against local authorities for failure to comply with such
standards.[40]

Although there is no direct statutory requirement to ensure that **14.40**
all play equipment conforms to these standards, where organised
play or nursery care requires to be registered under Part X of the
Children Act 1989 (which requires some services for children under
eight to be registered), the registering authority will require equipment to be safe as a condition of registration.[41]

Adults Suitable to Work With Children

As well as ensuring the physical safety of children those who pro- **14.41**
vide services for children need to ensure that employees and volunteers are suitable to work with children. In the provision of
substitute family care, the law makes extensive provision to ensure
that those approved as adoptive and foster carers are fit to do
so.[42]Provision is also made in relation to carers who are not approved by the local authority, *i.e.* private foster carers.[43]

Where childminding and day care services for children under **14.42**
eight require to be registered, the local authority requires to be
satisfied that those working with the children are fit persons. In all
of these cases and, more broadly where an employee has substantial
access to children, the authority will seek a printout of previous

---

[40] *Imrie v. Dumfries and Galloway Regional Council, supra.*
[41] The provisions of Part X are shortly to be repealed and superseded by the
Registration of Care (Scotland) Act 2001. The local authority registration
function will be transferred to the Scottish Commission for the Regulation of
Care.
[42] Adoption Agencies (Scotland) Regulations 1996 (S.I. 1996, No. 3266), and the
Fostering of Children (Scotland) Regulations 1996. (S.I. 1996 No. 3263).
[43] Fostering of Children (Scotland) Act 1984 and the Foster Children (Private
Fostering) (Scotland) Regulations 1985 (S.I. 1995 No. 1798).

criminal conviction from the Scottish Criminal Records Office. Arrangements are currently non-statutory and rest on circulars issued by the Scottish Office.[44] The system for checking the criminal record of those seeking to work with children was placed on a firmer footing by the provisions of Part V of the Police Act 1997. The Act provides a statutory basis for the provision of conviction information in relation to the assessment of prospective employees and volunteers with substantial access to children and, for instance, the registration of childminders.[45] In England and Wales, the Protection of Children Act 1999 provides for the maintenance of a register of those dismissed or who have resigned in circumstances where a child has been harmed or placed at risk of harm. Where such a person is registered it is unlawful to offer them a post in a child care situation. The Scottish Executive have announced that they propose to submit similar legislation to the Scottish Parliament.[46]

On the Road

14.43 Drivers have a duty to drive carefully, to keep a good look out, and to take reasonable care to avoid a known hazard. If children are around, their presence should therefore be noted and a driver should take appropriate action and be ready for the possibility of a child to rush into the road. Children can, of course, appear from behind vehicles without warning, and in such circumstances, a driver will not be blamed unless s/he was, for example, speeding. Speed is a major factor in most accidents, and therefore in areas where children are numerous, such as housing schemes and near schools, local authorities should take appropriate safety steps, such as traffic calming measures, safety islands and barriers and controlled pedestrian crossings. Local authorities are now encouraged to do so as an aspect of the government's road safety strategy.[47]

Conclusion

14.44 The law promotes children's rights to a safe environment by criminalising certain behaviour injurious to children's health, and

---

[44] Protection of Children: Disclosure of Criminal Convictions of those with Access to Children SOED circular 5/89 and SWSG circular 9/89.

[45] s. 115. This part of the Act is not yet in force.

[46] Just a press release at the moment but there should be a parliamentary answer or statement to refer to shortly.

[47] Department of Environment, Transport and the Regions/Scottish Executive: "Tomorrow's Roads", (2000 HMSO, Edinburgh). Local authorities now have the power to impose 20 mph limits without the consent of the Scottish Ministers— see Road Traffic Regulation Act 1984 (Amendment) Order 1999 (S.I. 1999 No. 1608).

by providing civil remedies against individuals and agencies who fail to take reasonable care for children's safety. The law further provides some specific safeguards that may be used to benefit children, such as occupiers and product liability statutes and regulations requiring supervision in school playgrounds.

However, it is clear that many of the measures which could prevent childhood accidents, such as traffic calming schemes, legally enforceable standards for play parks and equipment, protective helmets for cyclists and special safety seats and belts in all cars and buses, are not subject to specific regulation. These gaps in legal provision leave Scots law some way short of full compliance with the UN Convention's requirement that children should be brought up in a safe environment.

CHAPTER 15

THE CHILD IN CONFLICT WITH THE LAW

ELAINE E. SUTHERLAND

The vast majority of children who infringe the criminal law in **15.1**
Scotland are dealt with through the children's hearings system, a
system which deals also with children in need of protection.[1] Given
the praise heaped on the hearings system, both internationally[2] and
at home,[3] it would be all too easy to assume Scots law deals well
with juvenile offending. However, offending continues to be a significant problem and it is in the interests of the young offenders
themselves and the community as a whole that we remain vigilant in
finding effective responses and have in place a system which cor-
responds with the various preventive, constructive and protective
international standards. In addition, it must be remembered that
the children's hearings system does not deal with all children and
young people who offend. It remains possible for a child as young
as eight years old to be prosecuted before an ordinary (adult)
criminal court,[4] albeit there is provision for involving the hearings
system in advising on disposal.[5] Once a young person reaches sixteen years old, he or she will usually be beyond the embrace of the

---

[1] Child protection is discussed in Chap. 8. The children's hearings system, founded
on the Kilbrandon philosophy, is predicated, at least in theory, on treating
"children who do wrong" along with "children who are wronged". While they
may be facets of similar underlying problems, child protection and juvenile
offending sometimes raise separate issues and are often governed by different
international provisions. Thus, each merits separate consideration.
[2] The late Professor Sanford Fox of Boston College School of Law described it as
"a model for restructuring juvenile justice systems"; S. Fox, *Children's Hearings
and the International Community*, 1991 Kilbrandon Child Care Lecture (Scottish
Office, 1991), at p. 17. See also, W.S. Geimer, "Ready to Take the High Road?
The Case for Importing Scotland's Juvenile Justice System" 35 *Cath. U. L. Rev.*
358 (1986), which, as the title suggests, advocates importing the hearings system
into the U.S.
[3] It has been variously described as "remarkable and unique"(George Younger,
then Secretary of State for Scotland, in the Foreword to F.M. Martin and K.
Murray (eds), *The Scottish Juvenile Justice System* (Scottish Academic Press,
1982)); "this reform which has earned so much praise" (*Sloan* v. *B*, 1991 S.L.T.
530, *per* Lord President Hope at p. 548); and "a vastly superior way of dealing
with children and their problems than ever the old courts were" (*Twenty one years
of children's hearings* (The Scottish Office, 1993)), at p. 24).
[4] See Chap. 15, *infra*.
[5] Criminal Procedure (Scotland) Act 1995, s. 49.

hearings system altogether[6]. Adult responsibility for misdeeds can come early to young people in Scotland.

15.2   There is something of a fear of young people in our society. Perhaps it is no more than the old refrain "things are getting worse", that the public perception is of more children and young people offending than ever before and of them committing more serious offences. The media bears some responsibility for this in the attention it gives to both serious and persistent offenders, sometimes failing to distinguish between the two. Undoubtedly, this perception is fuelled by events outside Scotland, including the murder of James Bulger, in England, and the series of school shootings, in the USA. If we are to address juvenile offending effectively, it is essential that we are clear about facts rather than perceptions.

15.3   Assessing the incidence of offending is aided by the fact that statistical returns on the operation of the children's hearings system have been available since its earliest days, as have statistics on the prosecution of 16-and 17-year-olds. What do these figures tell us? Since its early days there has been a, very substantial, shift in the work of children's hearings, from offenders to child protection cases. Between 1989 and 1999/2000, offence referrals increased from 24,210 to 30,633, an increase of 26.45 per cent.[7] While, "[t]he number of convictions of 16-year-old and 17- year-old males *per* 1,000 population fell by about two fifths and a fifth respectively between 1988 and 1998",[8] the statistics in respect of females are less encouraging.

15.4   While the hearings system has been subject to research and evaluation, the early research focussed on the process.[9] The relative dearth of research in Scotland into the causes and subtleties of, and effectiveness of responses to, juvenile offending has long been a concern. This forced reliance on research from other jurisdictions and the danger is that one never really knows how accurately findings from one country translate into another. In the mid-1990s,

---

[6]   See para. 15.46, *infra.*

[7]   The Scottish Children's Reporters Administration (SCRA) assumed responsibility for the relevant statistics from April 1997 and the *Statistical Bulletin: Referrals of Children to Reporters and Children's Hearings 1999/2000* No. 24 (SCRA, 2001) is the most recent at the time of writing. During the period 1989 to 1999/2000, it should be noted that referrals overall increased by 71 per cent, with non-offence referrals increasing by 167 per cent and the number of children under 16 referred *per* 1,000 population increased by 50.7 per cent.

[8]   *Statistical Bulletin: Criminal Proceedings in Scottish Courts 1998* (CrJ/1999/8), para. 7.1. The *Statistical Bulletin: Criminal Proceedings in Scottish Courts 1999* (CrJ/2000/9) does not provide details of 16-and 17-year-old offenders, since it groups persons under the age of 21 together. It notes that "convictions *per* 1,000 population has generally followed a downward trend for all age groups except females aged under 21"; para. 7.1.

[9]   See, for example, F. Martin, S. Fox and K. Murray, *Children Out of Court* (1981) and J. Grant & S. McLean, "Police Contact with Children under Eight Years of Age" 1981 J. Soc. Welf. L. 140.

the Scottish Office responded to this concern and commissioned research into what information was available on youth offending in Scotland with the intention that it should form a base line for future research.[10] Subsequently, an impressive range of research was commissioned by the Central Research Unit.[11] The Scottish Executive turned its attention to juvenile offending in November 1999 and commissioned a Review of Youth Crime.[12] The Advisory Group[13] set up to conduct the Review produced its First Report[14] in June 2000, the Executive responded[15] and engaged in further consultation. It should be noted that the Advisory Group's first Report concentrated on the issue of persistent young offenders, although its recommendations have fundamental implications for juvenile justice generally. In particular, its suggestion that children's hearings might deal with 16 and 17 year-old offenders, while refreshing, appears not to have been thought through. It also recommended renaming the children's hearings system by deleting the reference to children altogether[16] and that the age of criminal responsibility should be examined further.[17] With government, all the main research organisations, and countless academics engaged in research into juvenile offending and juvenile justice in Scotland, it can no longer be said that there is (or will be) a shortage of local data. The next step is to ensure that we put this effort to good effect in developing a constructive and coherent plan for the future.

---

[10] S. Asquith, M. Buist, N. Loughran, C. Macaulay & M. Montgomery, *Children and Young People Offending in Scotland* (CRU, 1998).

[11] Reports are usually available on the CRU website at www.scotland.gov.uk/cru which also provides information on publications pending and research in progress.

[12] The background to, relevant documents of, and latest news on, the *Youth Crime Review* can be found on the web at www.scotland.gov.uk/youth/crimereview.

[13] The Advisory Group comprised individuals from a wide range of agencies involved in juvenile justice including, the judiciary, the children's hearings system, government, social work, education, the police and children's, offenders support and victims support groups. A notable omission from the Working Group was representation of academia, despite the fact that research and commentary on juvenile justice comes, most frequently, from that quarter.

[14] *Report of Advisory Group on Youth Crime* (2000).

[15] *Scottish Executive Response to the Advisory Group Report on Youth Crime Review* (2000).

[16] It is submitted that this would be a mistake. Granted, if it is to deal with 16-and 17-year-olds, the word "children" is inappropriate. "Children's and Young People's Hearings System" is rather inelegant. Perhaps the solution lies in renaming the system "Young People's Hearings System", thus, emphasising the non-adult nature of the focus, recognising the humanity of those who come into the system, and avoiding the, sometimes negatively perceived, word "youth".

[17] This matter has now been referred to the Scottish Law Commission; see para.15.14, *infra*.

International instruments

15.5 The hearings system had already felt the impact of the European
Convention on Human Rights long before the Human Rights Act
1998 was passed.[18] However, with the coming into force of the 1998
Act imminent, it was hardly surprising that the system should be
subject to further scrutiny from an European Convention perspective.[19] As we have seen, while the European Convention is not
generally child-specific, the human rights guaranteed, including the
prohibition on torture (Article 3), the right to liberty and security
(Article 5), the right to a fair trial (Article 6) and the right to respect
for private and family life (Article 8), apply to children.[20]

15.6   The European Court had the opportunity to elaborate on the
particular application of the principles to children tried in a court
setting in *T. v. United Kingdom* and *V. v. United Kingdom*,[21] which
followed the much-publicised trial and sentencing of two ten year-
olds, convicted of the murder of a two-year-old in England in 1993.
It found that there had been various breaches of the Convention, in
particular: Article 6(1), since the children's inability to participate
effectively in the proceedings resulted in them being denied a fair
hearing; Article 6(1), in respect of the Home Secretary's role in
setting the tariff; and Article 5(4), in respect of sentencing as it
impacted on the lawfulness of detention. T. and V. were each
awarded damages in respect of these breaches of their Convention
rights. There is no doubt that these cases will have an impact on
juvenile justice, not only in England, but in all states which are
parties to the European Convention.

15.7   In *S. v. Miller*[22] the Inner House had the opportunity to consider
what will probably be the first of many European Convention
challenges to the children's hearings system. We will return to the
case throughout this chapter but, briefly, it concerned a 15-year-old
boy referred to a hearing in respect of his allegedly having committed the offence of assault to severe injury. S. was alleged to have

---

[18]   The most notable example is *McMichael v. United Kingdom* (1995) 20 E.H.R.R.
205. While this case was concerned with child protection, the European Court was
critical of a number of aspects of the hearings system generally, including the fact
that, while reports of social workers and others were available to panel members,
only the "substance" of the reports was made known to the child and the family.
As a result, the Children's Hearings Rules now provide for reports being made
available to the relevant persons, although they are still not given to the child, see,
para. 15.26–15.29 *infra*.

[19]   The Scottish Children's Reporter Administration (SCRA) set up a working group
to examine to possible impact of the ECHR; *1st Report by the SCRA Human
Rights Working Group: The European Convention on Human Rights and the
Children's Hearings System* (SCRA, September 1999).

[20]   See, paras 3.20–3.22 and U. Kilkelly, *The Child and the European Convention on
Human Rights* (Ashgate, 1999).

[21]   (2000) 30 E.H.R.R. 121.

[22]   2001 S.L.T. 531.

assaulted a third party, L., in the course of what appears to have been a fracas involving S., his father, and L., with S.'s father dying some months later as a result of injuries sustained during the incident.[23] In many ways, the decision is a disappointment, in part because the Court concluded the children's hearings proceedings were not the "determination of a criminal charge" and the child was not a person "charged with a criminal offence"[24]. However, more generally, it is regrettable that the Court failed to address the issue of juvenile justice in a wider international context since neither the UN Convention, nor a wealth of other international material, was addressed. On a more positive note, the case illustrates attempts by both the legislature and the Scottish Children's Reporter Administration to make the hearings system more Convention compliant,[25] albeit cynics might observe that these were simply pre-emptive defensive strikes on matters that should have been addressed long ago.

The UN Convention, being child-specific, addresses juvenile **15.8** justice directly in Articles 37 and 40 and, of course, other provisions are relevant. In addition, several other international instruments address juvenile justice issues. The International Covenant on Civil and Political Rights 1966 addresses certain narrow areas of the administration of juvenile justice, requiring: the separation of juveniles and adults; speedy adjudication; and that trial procedures should take account of the age of juveniles and the desirability of promoting their rehabilitation.[26] The United Nations Standard Minimum Rules for the Administration of Juvenile Justice, known as the Beijing Rules and adopted in 1985, address the administration of juvenile justice from the perspectives of the child's rights and child development. While the Beijing Rules predate the UN Convention, a number of the Rules find expression in Article 40, thus making them binding, at least in international law terms. In 1990, the United Nations adopted two further instruments, the United Nations Guidelines for the Prevention of Juvenile Delinquency, also known as the Riyadh Guidelines, and the United Nations Rules for the Protection of Juveniles Deprived of their Liberty, known as the JDL Rules. Unless incorporated into the UN Convention, these "rules" or "guidelines" are of similar, non-binding, effect.[27] However, the European Court and courts in other jur-

---

[23] The possibility that S. may have been attempting to defend his father is hinted at; see Lord Penrose at p. 562.

[24] See para.15.16, *infra.*

[25] In respect of legal aid being made available to fund representation prior to and at hearings and in the plan to make documents available to children; see paras 15.31–15.34 and 15.26–15.29, respectively, *infra.*

[26] Arts 10(2)(b) and 14(4).

[27] For a discussion of the various forms of international regulation and their interaction, see G. Van Bueren, *The International Law on the Rights of the Child* (Martinus Nijhoff, 1995), Chap. 7. See also, Kilkelly, *supra*, Chap. 3.

isdictions[28] have cited them and they should be seen as a part of the general regime of international regulation of juvenile justice, albeit they were not mentioned in *S v. Miller.*

15.9　　Lest we run ahead of ourselves, it must be remembered that fundamental to any system of juvenile justice system is prevention and this is recognised both specifically, through the Riyadh Guidelines and, more generally, through the UN Convention, when it seeks to promote the welfare and inclusion of children. International regulation has several strands but fundamental is the importance of recognising the child's age, both in the context of ascribing responsibility and in the conduct of proceedings[29]. Respect for human rights, including the presumption of innocence, information of the charges, decision by an independent and impartial body in a fair hearing, and legal or other assistance, is stressed.[30] In addition, the child's well-being is a concern, with continuity of family relationships being an integral part of that well-being.[31] The child's reintegration into society is also viewed as an important goal and Van Bueren explains the shift in emphasis from "rehabilitation" to "reintegration" as reflecting the greater responsibility placed on society, rather than the individual, in the latter.[32] That is not to suggest that the child is absolved of developing a sense of responsibility for his or her actions, although the focus is on helping the child to do so by promoting his or her sense of belonging in society.[33] Having a suitably wide-ranging and effective variety of dispositions is inherent in this process.[34]

15.10　　Article 37(3) of the UN Convention encourages diversion of children from formal trial, provided that "human rights and legal safeguards are fully respected". In the light of this and the fact that the emphasis in the hearings system on the paramountcy of the child's welfare,[35] and on the participation of the child[36] and the family[37] in the process, one might expect that the children's hearings system would be seen as one of the United Kingdom's showpiece institutions. Any such expectation was shown to be illusory when the United Kingdom ratified the UN Convention subject to a specific reservation in respect of the children's hearings system, principally due to the lack of legal representation offered, at least in

---

[28] See, for example, *McKerry v. Teesdale and Wear Valley Justices*, Queen's Bench Division, February 7, 2000, unreported, where reference was made to the Beijing Rules.

[29] See, for example, UN Convention, Art. 40 (3) and Beijing Rules, r.14.

[30] Art. 37(2).

[31] UN Convention, Art. 5 and 9; Beijing Rules, r.19; and JDL Rules, r.59.

[32] *supra*, at pp.172–173.

[33] Beijing Rules, rr.10 and 11.

[34] UN Convention, Art. 40(4).

[35] 1995 Act, s. 16(1).

[36] 1995 Act, ss. 16(2) and 45(1).

[37] 1995 Act, s. 45(8) and the 1996 Rules, r.7.

the early stages of intake into the system.[38] In its *First Report on the United Kingdom,*[39] the UN Committee on the Rights of the Child identified juvenile justice as one of its "Principal subjects of concern". It stated:

> "The administration of the juvenile justice system in the State party is a matter of general concern to the Committee. The low age of criminal responsibility and the national legislation relating to the administration of juvenile justice seem not to be compatible with the provisions of the Convention, namely Articles 37 and 40."[40]

Given that the *First Report of the UK to the Committee on the Rights of the Child* focussed on the position in England and Wales, with only passing reference to Scotland, it may be that the Committee did not understand the nature and fundamental welfare-based philosophy of the children's hearings system.[41] Nonetheless, we cannot assume that the Committee had no knowledge of the hearings system which, as we shall see, is open to objection on a number of grounds. Due to legislative changes implemented in the Children (Scotland) Act 1995, the United Kingdom Government felt able to withdraw the reservation on April 18, 1997. It may have been premature and over-optimistic in so doing. The United Kingdom's *Second Report* to the UN Committee on the Rights of the Child, which has a separate section devoted to Scotland, is very much more upbeat and confident on the issue of juvenile justice.[42] Whether the carefully-crafted account will blind the Committee to some of the system's patent shortcomings will only be known when the Committee's *Second Report on the United Kingdom* is published. **15.11**

---

[38] The Reservation was in the following terms: "In Scotland there are tribunals (known as 'children's hearings') which consider the welfare of the child and deal with the majority of offences which a child is alleged to have committed. In some cases, mainly of a welfare nature, the child is temporarily deprived of its liberty for up to seven days prior to attending the hearing. The child and its family are, however, allowed access to a lawyer during this period. Although the decisions of the hearings are subject to appeal to the courts, legal representation is not permitted at the proceedings of the children's hearings themselves. Children's hearings have proved over the years to be a very effective way of dealing with the problems of children in a less formal, non-adversarial manner. Accordingly, the United Kingdom, in respect of article 37(d), reserves its right to continue the present operation of children's hearings."

[39] For a full discussion of the reporting process under the UN Convention, see Chap. 16.

[40] *ibid.,* at para. 17.

[41] For a discussion of the Anglo-centric nature of the United Kingdom's First Report, see paras. 16.27–16.30 and 16.38.

[42] *Convention on the Rights of the Child: Second Report to the UN Committee on the Rights of the Child by the United Kingdom 1999,* paras 2.9 and 2.11–2.12. Strictly speaking this is the *First Periodic Report* but, since it is the U.K.'s second actual report, that term is used here.

The age of criminal responsibility

15.12 It is little wonder that people abroad, and possibly some in Scotland, are astonished to learn that the criminal responsibility can attach from the time a child is eight years old.[43] Scotland has one of the lowest ages of criminal responsibility in the world.[44] Where a child is below eight years old, he or she has no criminal capacity and cannot commit an offence. Usually, the child's chronological age at the time of the alleged offence is used in establishing criminal responsibility, but where it can be demonstrated that a child's actual mental capacity is less than the chronological age, the former will govern responsibility.[45]

15.13   While the European Convention is silent on the issue of age of criminal responsibility, Article 6(1) requires that the accused should be given a fair hearing, one element of which is the opportunity to participate in the proceedings. In *T. v. United Kingdom* and *V. v. United Kingdom*, the European Court recognised that, despite the provision of legal representation and special arrangements made in the way the court proceedings were conducted, the accused, by virtue of their ages and states of mind, were unable to participate effectively in the proceedings and, thus, had been denied the right to a fair hearing, in breach of Article 6(1).[46]

15.14   While the UN Convention requires that *an age* of criminal responsibility should be identified, it does not attempt to specify *what that age should be*.[47] This is a failing of the Convention continued from the Beijing Rules and, combined with the lack of consensus among member states of the Council of Europe, led the European Court to conclude that there had been no violation of Article 3 in *T. v. United Kingdom* and *V. v. United Kingdom*. However, in its *First*

---

[43] Criminal Procedure (Scotland) Act 1995, s. 41. In 1925, the Morton Committee recommended raising the age of criminal responsibility from seven to eight; *Report of the Departmental Committee on Protection and Training* (HMSO, 1928), p. 48. The Report gives only a brief explanation for this very minor change and one is left with the impression that the Committee would have liked to raise the age further. It may have been that the Committee, like so many since, was conscious of what would be politically acceptable.

[44] H. Johnson, "Age of Criminal Proceedings in Europe" in *Child Offenders: U.K. and International Practice* (Howard League for Penal Reform, 1995), p.14 cites the relevant ages provided in a Parliamentary Answer from February 27, 1995. A. Lockyer and F.H. Stone (eds), *Juvenile Justice in Scotland: Twenty-Five Years of the Welfare Approach* (T&T Clark, 1999), at p. 245, provides a table of the age of criminal responsibility in other European countries. Both illustrate that most European countries have an age of criminal responsibility considerably higher than 8, with many countries opting for 14, 15 or 16.

[45] Various national newspapers reported a case of an 11-year-old boy who was originally charged with attempted murder having allegedly stabbed a nine-year-old girl, the charges being dropped when psychologists found that the boy had a mental age below 8; see, *The Times*, January 22, 2001, p. 1.

[46] *ibid.* at para. 89.

[47] Art. 40(3)(a).

Report on the United Kingdom,[48] the UN Committee on the Rights of the Child expressed concern over the low age of criminal responsibility in the various parts of the United Kingdom. In addition, it must be remembered that the UN Convention applies to all persons below the age of 18.[49] The Scottish Law Commisssion has examined the age of criminal responsibility and its proposals are currently the subject of consultation.[50]

The Children's Hearings System

The Philosophy

The children's hearings system is predicated upon treating the **15.15** child's needs not punishing his or her deeds.[51] How does this approach measure up to international standards? As we have seen, the UN Convention favours procedures specially designed for children who have fallen foul of the criminal law "providing that human rights and legal safeguards are fully respected".[52] It then proceeds to list particular safeguards[53] and these are, not surprisingly, very similar to the fair hearing requirements found in Article 6 of the European Convention. Can these requirements be met in a system premised on the welfare approach? The problem lies, not in the welfare approach itself, but the danger that, in the course of applying it, the fundamental guarantees inherent in natural justice can be lost sight of.[54] Since the earliest days of the hearings system, warnings have been given that it might not pass muster when subjected to scrutiny in the light of these human rights require-

---

[48] CRC/C/15/Add. 34, discussed at para. 16.33, *supra.*
[49] Art. 1 defines a child as being "below the age of 18 years of age".
[50] (Scot. Law Com. Discussion Paper. No. 115, 2001): While the discussion paper contains interesting arguments, the tentative proposal, essentially, to address criminal responsibility through prosecutional policy rather than an age of capacity, may fall short of the requirements of the UN Convention.
[51] *Report of the Committee on Children and Young Persons* (Cmnd. 2306, 1964), known as the "Kilbrandon Report", at para. 15. For a discussion of the Kilbrandon philosophy, see, Lockyer & Stone, *supra,* Chaps 1 and 2, and Sutherland, *Child and Family Law* (T&T Clark, 1999), paras 9.5–9.7.
[52] Art. 40(3)(b).
[53] Art. 40(2).
[54] This was the thrust of the reasoning of the U.S. Supreme Court in *In re Gault,* 387 U.S. 1 (1967) where it criticised the lack of due process protection afforded to a juvenile in the system operating at the time. That case is often seen as signalling the end of a separate system of juvenile justice in the US but, as the Court made clear in a later decision, *Gault* did not "spell the doom of the juvenile justice system or ... deprive it of its "informality, flexibility or speed'"; *McKiever v Pennsylvania,* 404 U.S. 528 (1971) at p.533. In the U.S., the movement away from what was perceived by some as a "liberal" model of juvenile justice was prompted, at least in part, by a desire for more punitive responses to juvenile offending.

ments.[55] Respecting the child's rights to a fair trial does not necessarily mean that juveniles can never be treated differently to adults and, indeed, the limited capacity of juveniles may, itself, mandate different treatment. However, in the name of taking a welfare approach in respect of a juvenile offender, we must not forget that he or she has rights.

15.16   Until the recent decision of the Inner House in *S. v. Miller*,[56] it was widely assumed that the whole parcel of rights found in Article 6 of the European Convention and Article s. 37 and 40 of the UN Convention applied to children's hearings proceedings where the child was referred to the hearing under section 52(2)(i) of the 1995 Act on the basis of his or her alleged commission of an offence. The First Division unanimously rejected that approach when it concluded that, despite a referral under that provision having its roots in an allegation of criminal conduct by the child, the referral did not amount to "determination of a criminal charge" and the child was not a person "charged with a criminal offence".[57] Without wishing to over-simplify the numerous factors which influenced the decision, the *sui generis* nature of hearings[58] and the lack of any penalty being levelled against the child appear to have been particularly influential. The Court relied on the fact that the child's welfare substantially determines what, if any, compulsory measures of supervision may be ordered in respect of the child. With respect, this approach fails to address the fundamental tension which exists between welfare and rights; a matter on which there is extensive caselaw and literature, not least from the U.S.[59] and in relation to the UN Convention. The decision is all the more regrettable since the Court was presented with persuasive examples of the criminal nature of referrals under section 52(2)(i).[60]

15.17   It was accepted, however, that the decision of a hearing could affect the child's civil rights and obligations, both in respect of his or her liberty and in respect of freedom of family life.[61] The distinction is important since the European Convention affords

---

[55] See, for example, J.P. Grant, "The legal safeguards for the rights of the child and the parents in children's hearings" (1975) J.R. 209.

[56] 2001 S.L.T. 531.

[57] The Court considered this issue at length and each of the judgments warrants reading in full; see pp. 537–540 (The Lord President), pp. 522–557 (Lord Penrose) and pp. 568–576 (Lord Macfadyen).

[58] *McGregor v. T.*, 1975 S.L.T. 76; *Kennedy v. O.*, 1975 S.L.T. 235; *McGregor v. D.*, 1977 S.C. 330.

[59] See fn. 54, *supra.* Unlike the U.S. Supreme Court, the Inner House has not clarified which rights extend to children and which do not.

[60] Unlike all the other grounds of referral, the criminal, rather than the civil, standard of proof applies to this ground of referral; the civil rules of evidence in respect of corroboration and hearsay evidence do not; and the Rehabilitation of Offenders Act 1974 applies.

[61] See pp. 40 (The Lord President), pp. 557–558 (Lord Penrose) and pp. 576 (Lord Macfadyen).

greater protection to the individual in the context of criminal, as opposed to civil, proceedings. Indeed, it was the Court's finding in this respect, combined with eleventh-hour responses by the legislature and the Principal Reporter,[62] that saved the hearings system from the damning criticism it might otherwise have attracted.[63] Assuming that the Inner House decision survives any appeal, this means that future challenges to children's hearings proceedings under the European Convention will have to be based on the civil protections offered to an individual rather than the more extensive protection offered by Article 6(2) and (3), albeit the individual is guaranteed substantial rights under Article 6(1).

Where does this leave the UN Convention requirements? While **15.18** some of its provisions refer to a child being deprived of his or her liberty,[64] other provisions regulate the rights of the child "alleged as or accused of"[65] and, sometimes, "recognized as",[66] "having infringed the penal law". No mention was made of the UN Convention in the course of *S. v. Miller* but it is possible that these phrases might be subject to the same narrow interpretation as was Article 6 of the European Convention. Indeed, it might be that the UN Convention's emphasis on the paramountcy of the child's welfare would again be used to distinguish children's hearings proceedings from criminal proceedings. On the other hand, it must be remembered that Article 40(3)(b) of the UN Convention stresses the need to respect the child's "human rights and legal safeguards" in any special procedures for dealing with children diverted from the criminal justice system. In the light of the European Court's willingness to use the UN Convention to flesh out its own, rather adult-centred, provisions, it is regrettable that this point was not made to the Inner House. One can only speculate on how the European Court would have treated the matter until it is given the opportunity to do so.

The welfare approach to juvenile justice raises a second issue. In **15.19** the name of attempting to serve the child's welfare, the legal system may intrude more in the child's life than it would were it simply seeking to punish a wrongdoer. We must examine whether the particular disposal employed actually does anything effective to serve or promote the child's welfare. Perhaps what is really being stressed here is that "welfare" is more than just good intentions. Essentially, the question is "Are the measures taken effective?"

---

[62] See the issues of legal aid and documents being made available to children, at paras 5.31–5.34 and 5.26–5.29, respectively, *infra*.
[63] In the words of Lord Penrose at p. 557, "Had I been of the opinion that the proceedings were criminal in the relevant sense, there would, in my view, have been a substantial issue whether the system was structurally defective in failing to provide adequate guarantees for the purposes of Article 6".
[64] Art. 37(b)–(d).
[65] Art. 40(2)(b).
[66] Art. 40(1) and (2)(a).

15.20   The procedure for children's hearings is governed by Part II of the Children (Scotland) Act 1995 (the "1995 Act") and detailed description of it can be found elsewhere.[67] Here, some of the concerns in relation to children's hearings in the light of the international instruments will be explored.

A fair hearing and public hearing within a reasonable time before an independent and impartial tribunal?

15.21   Article 6(1) of the European Convention requires that, in the determination of civil rights and obligations, an individual is entitled to a "fair and public hearing within a reasonable time by an independent and impartial tribunal established by law".[68] That a children's hearing is a tribunal established by law[69] appears uncontentious and the issue of delay is one which the system itself has addressed.[70] The independence of panel members, in terms of their mode of appointment, [71] appears unobjectionable, given that the European Court relies on such factors as "the existence of guarantees against outside pressures and the question whether the body presents an appearance of independence".[72] "Impartiality" denotes a lack of prejudice or bias[73] and requires compliance with both a subjective and an objective test. Harris *et al* find it unsurprising that a breach of the subjective test has never been established before the European Court, since it requires a showing of actual personal bias

---

[67] The Act is supplemented by the Children's Hearings (Scotland) Rules 1996 (S.I. 1996 No. 3261) ('the Children's Hearings Rules'). See B. Kearney, *Children's Hearings and the Sheriff Court* (2nd ed., 2000, W. Green); K. McK. Norrie, *Children's Hearings in Scotland* (1997, W. Green); and E.E. Sutherland, *Child and Family Law* (T & T Clark, 1999), Chap. 9.

[68] The right applies also to criminal proceedings and Art. 40(2)(b)(iii) of the UN Convention is couched in similar terms.

[69] A "tribunal" has been defined by the European Court as "determining matters within its competence on the basis of rules of law and after proceedings conducted in a prescribed manner"; *Belilos v. Switzerland* (1988) 10 E.H.R.R. 466, para. 64. Appeal lies to a court where a children's hearing is not conducted in the prescribed manner, something which recent research has found remains a problem; C. Hallett and C. Murray with J. Jamieson and B. Veitch, *The Evaluation of Children's Hearings in Scotland: Volume I: Deciding in Children's Interests* (CRU, 1998). Of course, in the absence of legal representation, families may not be aware of breaches in procedure.

[70] The *Blueprint for the Processing of Children's Hearings Cases—Inter-agency Code of Practice and National Standards* (Scottish Office Social Work Services Group, 1999) provides guidance on how cases can be dealt with timeously.

[71] The fact that they are appointed by the Scottish Ministers, sometimes on the advice of the local Children's Panel Advisory Committee, and can only be dismissed by the Scottish Ministers with the consent of the Lord President protects against the kind of challenge made successfully to the mode of appointment of temporary sheriffs in *Starrs v. Ruxton*, 2000 S.L.T. 42; *S. v. Miller, supra, per* the Lord President at pp. 504–541.

[72] *Campbell and Fell v. United Kingdom* (1984) 7 E.H.R.R. 165, para.78.

[73] *Piersack v. Belgium* (1982) 5 E.H.R.R. 169, para. 30.

by the particular judge.[74] Demonstrating a breach of the objective test may be slightly easier to satisfy, since that test requires, essentially, that justice should "be seen to be done". Most of the European caselaw here relates to trial judges who have been involved in earlier stages of the cases disposed of by them.[75] The real concern for the hearings system, in terms of independence and impartiality, relates to the role of the reporter in assisting panel members in their deliberations; a matter to which we will return presently.

However, in order to satisfy the European and UN Conventions, **15.22** it is not enough that the tribunal should be independent and impartial. The individual must also be given a "fair hearing". While in civil cases, the right to be present at the hearing is not absolute, it has been supported where the individual's "personal character and manner of life" are at issue.[76] Provided it is "established in an unequivocal manner and ... attended by minimum safeguards commensurate to its importance", a person may waive his or her right to be present.[77] The child has both a right and a duty to attend the hearing[78], albeit he or she can be freed from the obligation to attend, where such presence would be detrimental to his or her interests. It is difficult to imagine circumstances in which it would be detrimental to a child accused of having committed an offence to be present and, in any event, the child cannot be prevented from attending the hearing if he or she wishes to do so.[79]

Yet another aspect of a "fair hearing" is the concept of "equality **15.23** of arms". This requires that "each party must be afforded a reasonable opportunity to present his case—including his evidence— under conditions that do not place him at a substantial disadvantage vis-a-vis his opponent".[80] As we saw in respect of the requirement of an "independent and impartial tribunal", the notion of justice being seen to be done is important. In *Borgers v. Bel-*

---

[74] D.J. Harris, M. O'Boyle and C. Warbrick, *Law of the European Convention on Human Rights* (Butterworths, 1995), p. 237.

[75] See, for example, *Piersack v Belgium, supra,* (presiding judge had previously been head of the department of the public prosecutor's office that had investigated the case against the accused: breach of the objective test established). See also, *Hauschildt v. Denmark* (1989) 12 E.H.R.R. 266. Not every involvement of the judge in an earlier stage of the case which will give rise to a breach of the objective test; *Sainte Marie v France* (1992) A 253-A (1992) (two members of the appeal court which sentenced the accused had been involved in refusing him bail at an earlier hearing; no breach of Art. 6(1)).

[76] *X. v. Sweden* No. 434/58, 2 YB 354 at 370 (1958). In criminal cases, the right to be present at one's own trial is a matter of general principle; *Ekbatani v. Sweden* (1988) 13 E.H.R.R. 504, para. 25.

[77] *Poitrimol v. France* (1993) 18 E.H.R.R. 130, para.31 (concerning the conviction of the accused for absconding with his children in breach of a custody order).

[78] 1995 Act, s. 45(1).

[79] 1995, s. 45(2).

[80] *Dombo Beheer v. The Netherlands* (1993) 18 E.H.R.R. 213, para. 33.

gium,[81] a case which may come to have particular importance in the context of children's hearings, the European Court reiterated this notion of the appearance of justice being done in respect of "equality of arms". There, the Belgian practice of permitting the Procureur General to state his opinion in open court on whether the accused's appeal should be allowed and then to retire with the judges to advise on their opinion, when no such opportunity was afforded to the accused or his legal representative, was found to be in breach of Article 6(1).

15.24 Aside from the fact that the child is not given the documents available to other parties at the hearing and the role of the reporter advising the hearing, to which we will return presently, at least one other part of the children's hearings process requires mention in the context of "equality of arms". There is the possibility of a "business meeting" to discuss procedural and other matters which may take place between panel members and the reporter, but without the child or the relevant persons being present[82]. It is unlikely that the requirements to let the family know that the meeting will take place, for the reporter to make any views they wish to express known, and to report back to them on what happened, will save the practice from successful challenge under Article 6(1).

What information is given to whom?

15.25 More specifically, there is a problem over what information is given to whom prior to the hearing. While the panel members and the relevant persons[83] must receive copies of a whole range of documents, including a statement of the conditions for referral and any background reports[84], the child is entitled to receive only a copy of the statement of the conditions for referral[85] and not the other documents available to everyone else. Given that the hearing reaches its decision on the basis of the child's welfare, presumably as assessed in the light of all the circumstances of the case, including factors addressed in reports, how can the child exercise his or her rights under Article 6(1) in the absence of knowing what that information is?

15.26 In addition, how can a child exercise his or her right to express views, as required by Article 12 of the UN Convention and the 1995

---

[81] (1991)15 E.H.R.R. 92, effectively reversing *Delcourt v. Belgium* (1970) 1 E.H.R.R 355.

[82] 1995 Act, s. 64(1) and 1996 Rules, r.4(1), giving statutory effect to the decision in *Sloan v. B.,* 1991 S.L.T. 530.

[83] Prior to the 1995 Act, relevant persons were not given copies of reports and simply had the substance of them disclosed by the hearing chair, a practice the European Court found to be in breach of Article 6(1) in *McMichael v. United Kingdom, supra.* See also the European Court's decision in *T.P. and K.M. v. United Kingdom,* May 10, 2001.

[84] 1996 Rules, r.5(1).

[85] 1996 Rules, r.18(1)(b).

Act,[86] since a person can hardly fully express views on a situation in the absence of all the relevant information? Of course, that old chestnut "good practice" requires that any relevant issues arising from reports should be addressed in the hearing, thus giving the child the opportunity to respond to them, but "good practice" is not always observed. Indeed, in *S. v. Miller* Lord Penrose questioned whether, in the absence of legal assistance, a lay chairman would necessarily be up to the task of communicating "the intricacies of the legal issues which arise" and appreciating "the nature and degree of lack of understanding of the child" in every possible case[87].

It might be argued, on the basis of Article 3 of the UN Convention, that the child's welfare would not be served by having, sometimes sensitive, information about other family members that is in a particular report disclosed in this stark manner. However, the tension between Articles 3 and 12 is not unique to the hearings system and it falls to the system to find a way to respect the child's rights under both the European and UN Conventions. A further difficult exists in reconciling an adult family member's right to respect for his or her private and family life, under Article 8 of the European Convention, and the child's rights under Article 6. **15.27**

This was the subject of one of the pre-emptive defensive strikes in *S. v. Miller* since the Principal Reporter presented the Court with the guidance he had issued to all reporters requiring that the child would, in future, receive the same documents as the panel members and the relevant persons, save in exceptional circumstances[88]. This, in the Court's view, rendered the point moot. Nonetheless, the Lord President took the opportunity to issue a clear warning that "a blanket policy that documents should not be supplied to the child" would pose problems under Article 6(1) of the European Convention.[89] **15.28**

The lack of legal representation

The European Court has interpreted Article 6(1) as meaning that an individual must have a meaningful right of access to a court in respect of civil rights and obligations.[90] While this does not man- **15.29**

---

[86] s. 16(2).

[87] *op. cit.*, at p. 562.

[88] Lord President at pp. 541–542. The exceptions would include the situation "where the information would cause significant harm to the child or any other person or where it would significantly prejudice the prevention or detection of crime or the apprehension or prosecution of an offender'.'

[89] *ibid.* He may have felt the need to issue this warning since the Solicitor General, on behalf of the Scottish Ministers, had continued to argue that Article 6(1) did not require that documents be given to children.

[90] *Golder v. United Kingdom* (1975) 1 E.H.R.R. 524. While a person accused of an offence must be provided with the essential elements of a "fair hearing", including the opportunity to defend himself or herself, legal representation need only be provided free of charge "where the interests of justice so require"; Art. 6(3)(c).

date the provision of free legal representation in all cases, a failure to do so may constitute a breach of Article 6(1) where the individual would be unable to put forward his or her case effectively without such representation.[91] The UN Convention is rather more explicit in requiring that the child shall have "legal or other appropriate assistance in the preparation and presentation of his or her defence"[92] and that "the matter" [guilt or otherwise] shall be determined "in the presence of legal or other appropriate assistance".[93] Of course, this brings us back to the question of whether Article 40 applies to proceedings before a children's hearing. In any event, no further guidance is given on what is meant by "other appropriate assistance", but the obvious inference is that lay assistance is envisaged as being adequate in some cases.

15.30 At present, the child and the relevant persons[94] may receive a certain amount of legal advice under the Legal Advice and Assistance Scheme,[95] but Legal Aid is not available to provide the child or the relevant persons with pre-hearing advice nor for representation at hearings. As Kearney points out "a number of solicitors are prepared to represent children for no or minimal remuneration".[96] However, relying on the charity of public-spirited lawyers is no way to run a legal system and, in any event, many children do not receive this largesse. It might be thought that the gap, in terms of representation or assistance, could be filled by the appointment of a safeguarder but, as the Lord President accepted in *S. v. Miller*[97] there are a number of reasons why this is not the solution. First, while the hearing is obliged to consider whether it is necessary to appoint a safeguarder, the decision on appointment is discretionary.[98] Secondly, to date, the appointment of safeguarders has been comparatively rare and uneven across the country.[99]

---

[91] *Airey v. Ireland* (1979) 2 E.H.R.R. 305.
[92] Art. 40(2)(b)(ii).
[93] Art. 40(2)(b)(iii).
[94] A "relevant person" is anyone, including a parents, who has parental responsibilities or rights in respect of the child, or who appears ordinarily (other than by reason of employment) to have charge of, or control over, the child; 1995 Act, s. 93(2). The invidious position of the non-marital father in Scots law has been discussed at length elsewhere; see paras 5.2–5.6, and 6.8. Again, he faces discrimination in the hearings system. If he has not acquired parental responsibilities or rights and is not caring for the child he is not a relevant person, a position which the European Court found unobjectionable in *McMichael v. United Kingdom, supra*. He is permitted to attend a hearing if he qualifies as the genetic father, but not on equal terms with relevant persons.
[95] Legal Aid (Scotland) Act, Part II.
[96] B. Kearney, *Children's Hearings and the Sheriff Court*, above, para. 22.18.
[97] *Op. cit.*, at p. 545.
[98] 1995 Act, s. 41(1).
[99] In 1999/2000, a safeguarder was appointed in only 477 (or 9.3 per cent) of cases. This is less than in the previous two years, albeit the number of appointments has always been small. See, *Referral of Children to Reporters and Children's Hearings 1999/2000, supra*, at section 8.

Thirdly, the safeguarder's obligation is to "safeguard the interests of the child".[1] The present author is on record as expressing the view that, provided he or she is vigilant to the responsibilities inherent in the dual task, a safeguarder can represent both the child's interests and the child's views.[2] That position was taken in respect of safeguarders in the child protection context. However, on further reflection, it now appears both unreasonable and dangerous to expect one person to discharge both functions simultaneously. If that is the case in the context of child protection, then a safeguarder is even less suited to the task of taking instructions and acting as a legal representative for a person accused of having committed an offence.

Legal representation was the subject-matter of the second pre- **15.31** emptive defensive strike in *S. v. Miller* when the Court was given a copy of the Convention Rights (Compliance) (Scotland) Bill, which the Minister of Justice has presented to the Scottish Parliament. Clause 6(2) of the Bill includes children's hearings with the extended list of courts and tribunals for which legal aid might be made available. Despite the fact that change was in the air, counsel sought to argue that the failure to provide legal aid for representation at hearings was a matter of policy, rather than financial pressure. In the words of the Lord President, "The view was taken that the introduction of legal representation would detrimentally affect the informal and flexible nature of the proceedings".[3] The transparency and illogicality of this contention was demolished swiftly by the Lord President, not least because lawyers were not presently prohibited from representing children at hearings. Their Lordships expressed real concerns over the lack of legal aid, due to the range of complexity of proceedings, the fact that panel members are lay persons, the youth and inexperience of many of the children involved, and, in particular, where a child faces deprivation of liberty[4]. The matter was continued to allow for intimation to the Advocate General.[5]

Thus, at the time of writing, it appears that Legal Aid will be **15.32** available in the future to allow for legal representation of the child at hearings in at least some cases. Should it be available to every child or, at least, every child referred under section 52(2)(i)? What is the position of the accused child and his or her family who do not have a legal representative? Aside from any assistance they receive from friends, spiritual advisers and other lay person, they are on their own. This creates a fundamental problem for the children's

---

[1] 1995 Act, s. 41(1)(a).
[2] "The Role of the Safeguarder" in *Representing Children: Listening to the Voice of the Child* (Scottish Child Law Centre, 1995), at pp. 32–33.
[3] *op. cit.*, at p. 543
[4] See the Lord President at pp. 542–546, Lord Penrose at pp. 559–563 and Lord Macfadyen at pp. 577–579.
[5] Human Rights Act 1998, s. 5(1).

hearings system at a variety of stages. When one considers that children will be facing decisions about whether to accept the allegation of criminal conduct and what, if any, defences may be available, it cannot be suggested, with the slightest degree of conviction, that they are on an equal footing with the reporter who will either be legally qualified or will have access to legal advice. In the hearing itself, in the absence of a legal representative, how is the family to judge whether the appropriate procedure has been followed and, thus, whether they have any right to appeal against the hearing's decision? It is hard to see how fundamental fairness could require anything other than full legal representation provided free of charge where the family resources are insufficient to secure such representation. If anything, this position is reinforced by the fact that, assuming the conditions for financial eligibility are met, Legal Aid is available for court proceedings associated with the hearing, whether in the context of establishing the conditions for referral, the introduction of new evidence, or to appeal against a hearing's decision.[6]

15.33   It has been asserted, on behalf of the Principal Reporter, that reporters "offer their views to members of the children's hearing on any legal issues that arise".[7] This poses a fundamental challenge to the independence and impartiality of children's hearings. What of equality of arms? Remember, the reporter decides whether to convene a hearing, arranges the hearing, and makes a record of the proceedings,[8] all with the benefit of legal advice or on the basis of his or her own legal training. The child and the relevant persons may have no legal advice. At the very least, a reporter who has taken a good faith decision that a child is in need of compulsory measures of supervision can be seen as having a stake in the outcome of the case. It is entirely human to want to be proved right and, to use modern management jargon, it would be all to easy for the reporter to have "ownership" of his or her original decision. If he or she then plays any significant role in helping the panel members to arrive at their decision, can that decision be regarded as being taken by an independent tribunal? It is submitted that it cannot, particularly in the light of the decision of the European Court in *Borgers v. Belgium*.[9] It has been suggested by Norrie that "at the hearing itself the Reporter has an entirely disinterested position as far as the outcome is concerned".[10] This author begs to differ with a respected colleague on this point. Given the reliance

---

[6]   Legal Aid (Scotland) Act 1986, s. 29, as substituted by the Children (Scotland) Act 1995, s. 92.
[7]   In *Miller v. Council of the Law Society of Scotland*, 2000 S.L.T. 513, at p.516L.
[8]   An argument might be made that, the reporter's role as record maker is a breach of Art. 6(1).
[9]   (1991)15 E.H.R.R. 92, discussed at para. 15.23, *supra*.
[10] K. McK. Norrie, "Human Rights Challenges to the Children's Hearings System" (2000) 45 J.L.S.S. 19, p. 21.

that some panel members appear to have placed on advice from reporters in the past, it is questionable that simply emphasising the need for independence to panel members in training will suffice.[11]

Publicity and children's hearings

What of the "public" nature of the hearing to which the accused is entitled under both the European and UN Conventions? Article 6(1) of the European Convention contains a whole range of exceptions to the requirement of "public" justice permitting the exclusion of the public and the press from proceedings. The most significant of these, in the context of children, is the power to exclude "from all or part of the trial . . . . . where the interests of juveniles or the private lives of the parties so require". In addition, Article 8(1) guarantees individuals respect for private and family life. The UN Convention requires full respect for the child's privacy "at all stages of the proceedings"[12] and does not provide for derogation. **15.34**

While bona fide representatives of the media have the right to be present at hearings[13] and at associated court proceedings, they may be excluded by the hearing where exclusion is necessary in the child's interests or in order to obtain the child's views, or where their presence is causing distress to the child or may have this effect.[14] In addition, there are strict restrictions on what may be reported in respect of children's hearings and related court proceedings,[15] albeit the penalty for infringement is probably little deterrent.[16] Reporting restrictions may be lifted by the sheriff, the Court of Session in an appeal, or the Scottish Executive "in the interests of justice", but only to the extent "considered appropriate".[17] Norrie argues that the lifting of reporting restrictions is subject to the welfare test by reading "in the interests of justice" as **15.35**

---

[11] This option is suggested in J. Rose, "The ECHR and the Children's Hearings System" (August 2000) SCOLAG 11, at 11.

[12] Art. 40(2)(b)(vii).

[13] 1995 Act, s. 43(3)(b).

[14] 1995 Act, s. 43(4). Where a journalist has been excluded, the chairperson of the hearing may inform him or her of the substance of what has taken place during the period of exclusion but does not appear to be obliged to do so; 1995 Act, s. 43(5).

[15] There must be no publication of information which is intended or is likely to identify any child concerned in the proceedings or the address or school of such a child; 1995 Act, s. 44(1). The prohibition extends not only to the child accused of the offence but also to any other children involved, including child witnesses.

[16] The penalty is a fine up to level 4; 1995 Act, s. 44(2). At present, this means the maximum fine which can be imposed is £2,500, arguably, a sum of no real significance to a major newspaper or television company.

[17] 1995 Act, s. 43(5).

meaning "interests of justice *to the child*".[18] While the present author sympathises with this ingenious and desirable approach, it is
submitted that the view of Kearney, that "interests of justice"
should be given its ordinary meaning, being general rather than
child-centred, is to be preferred.[19]

15.36 In the light of the extensive restrictions on reporting, the hearings
system would appear to meet the standards of the European Convention. However, the possibility of reporting restrictions being
lifted, albeit this has never been done in respect of a case dealt with
under the hearings system, fails to meet the rather more exacting
standard of the UN Convention. Given the UN Convention's emphasis on "the promotion of the child's sense of dignity and worth",
"the child's reintegration into society", and "the child's assuming a
constructive role in society"[20] —all goals entirely consistent with
the Kilbrandon philosophy—it is submitted that the 1995 Act must
be amended to ensure respect for the accused child's privacy in all
cases dealt with by hearings and in associated proceedings.

Secure accommodation

15.37 A child can be detained in secure accommodation pending a children's hearing, during a continuation or after the hearing has
reached its final decision.[21] While, in *S. v. Miller* it was accepted
that this amounts to "deprivation of liberty" under Article 5(1) of
the European Convention, the Inner House simply followed a recent Court of Appeal decision[22] in holding that such deprivation of
liberty came within the permitted exception under Article 5(1)(d).
That allows for deprivation of liberty of a minor "for the purpose of
educational supervision or his lawful detention for the purpose of
bringing him before the competent legal authority". The point does
not appear to have been argued with any great rigour and, it must
be admitted that the Court of Appeal was itself following a recent
European Court decision which gave a very wide interpretation to
the term "educational supervision".[23] Nonetheless, the criteria for
ordering secure accommodation are not limited to the child's education, nor even the child's welfare, since they include the possibility

---

[18] K. McK. Norrie, *Children (Scotland) Act 1995* (Revised edition, 1998, W. Green), p. 77.

[19] B. Kearney, *Children's Hearings and the Sheriff Court* (2nd. ed., 2000, Butter-worths), para. 28.08.

[20] Art. 40(1).

[21] 1995 Act, ss. 66(10), 68(10), 69(11) and 70(9). See futher, para. 8.30, *supra.*

[22] Cited by the Inner House as *W Borough Council v. D.K.* , November 15, 2000, reported as *Re K. (a child) (secure accommodation: right to liberty)* [2001] 1 F.L.R. 526.

[23] *Koniarska v. United Kingdom,* October 12, 2000.

of the child injuring a third party[24]. In addition, once secure accommodation has been authorised, the decision to implement the authorisation is highly discretionary.[25] It can be anticipated that this issue will be revisited in the future.

What if?

Much has been made of the Inner House's refusal, in *S. v. Miller* to **15.38** accept that a referral under section 52(2)(i) might be criminal proceedings. Had it done so, what difference would this have made for the rights of the child? Since the European Court has not yet had the opportunity to consider the matter[26] and, in any event, the law is not static, it is worth taking a little time to explore this question. In criminal proceedings, the accused would have all the rights spelled out more explicitly in Article 6(2) and (3) of the European Convention are; to be informed promptly, in a language the accused understands and fully of the nature and cause of the accusation; to have adequate time and facilities to prepare a defence; to defend oneself in person or through legal assistance of one's own choosing, that legal assistance be provided free where the interests of justice so require; to have the opportunity to examine prosecution witnesses and to lead defence witnesses, under the same conditions as prosecution witnesses; and to have free assistance of an interpreter if the accused cannot understand the language used in court.

In addition, the accused has protection from self incrimination,[27] **15.39** a requirement spelt out explicitly in the UN Convention.[28] Freedom from self incrimination is also linked to the express right, set out in Article 6(2) of the European Convention and Article 40(2)(b)(i) of the UN Convention, to be presumed innocent in criminal proceedings. While both the Beijing Rules[29] and the UN Convention[30] favour diversion from formal trial, the danger that a child might feel a degree of coercion to "confess" has long been appreciated and

---

[24] 1995 Act, s. 70(10).
[25] The child's detention in secure accommodation may be "during such period as the person in charge of the establishment, with the agreement of the chief social work officer of the relevant local authority, considers necessary"; 1995 Act, s. 70(9)(b).
[26] That the European Court is free to reach a different conclusion to even the highest domestic court is illustrated very recently in *Z. and others v. United Kingdom*, May 10, 2001, where the decision of the House of Lords in *X. v. Bedfordshire County Council* [1995] 3 All E.R. 353 was dealt a serious blow.
[27] *Funke v. France* (1993) 16 E.H.R.R. 297; *Sanders v. United Kingdom* (1996) 23 E.H.R.R. 313. The High Court had the opportunity to consider this requirement in respect of the obligation to give information about who was driving a car at a particular time and the use of that information in prosecuting a person accused of driving after consuming excess alcohol, albeit its decision was overturned by the Privy Council; *Brown v. Scott*, 2000 S.L.T. 379 (High Ct); 2001 S.L.T. 59 (P.C.).
[28] Art. 37(2)(iv).
[29] r.11.1.
[30] Art. 40(3)(b).

the Beijing Rules suggest that consent to diversion should be subject to review by a competent authority.[31] At the earliest stage of the hearing, whether the child accepts the conditions for referral dictates what will happen next. There is serious doubt that an (at present) unrepresented child who does accept the truth of allegations made is afforded adequate protection. It is not enough to hope that this objection can be met by requiring simply that panel members will observe "good practice" in explaining the options to the child and ensuring that he or she is under no pressure to accept the grounds of referral simply in order "to get the whole thing over with" or, indeed, for any number of other invalid reasons. In respect of failure to attend school, the child faces a "reverse onus of proof" since it falls on him or her to establish a reasonable excuse. This appears to be a clear violation of the presumption of innocence.

15.40 A further point is worth noting under the "what if" category. Other jurisdictions recognise "status offences"; that is offences which can only be committed by young people, there being no adult equivalent. A number of other conditions for referral, including, the child being "beyond the control of any relevant person"; "falling into bad associations or [being] exposed to moral danger"; having "failed to attend school regularly without a reasonable excuse", having misused alcohol or any drug, or a volatile substance, look remarkably like status offences.[32] Do status offences pose a problem under either the European or UN Conventions? Failure to attend school without a reasonable excuse can probably be dealt with fairly swiftly, since the European Convention provides that a minor may be deprived of his or her liberty "by lawful order for the purpose of educational supervision", always providing that the deprivation of liberty is "in accordance with a procedure prescribed by law".[33] What of the other grounds? It might be thought that status offences amount to discrimination on the basis of age, but neither the European nor the UN Convention specifies age as one of the prohibited categories of discrimination although each prohibits discrimination on the ground of "other status".[34] It could be argued that status offences pass international muster since they indicate a need for protection of the child and, thus, serve the promotion of the child's welfare,[35] or that they serve a preventive function in diverting the child from future, clearly criminal, conduct. On the

---

[31] r.11.3.
[32] These are set our in the 1995 Act, s. 52(2)(a), (b), (h), (j) and (k), respectively.
[33] Art. 5(1)(d). In addition, the importance of education is reinforced in the First Protocol, Art. 2. For a full discussion of the child's right to education, see Chap. 11.
[34] European Convention, Art. 14; UN Convention, Art. 2.
[35] UN Convention, Art. 3, See also: the duty to protect the child from abuse, neglect and exploitation (Art. 19); and the obligation to protect the child from sexual exploitation (Art. 34).

other hand, status offences may stigmatise a child unnecessarily. The Beijing Rules allow for status offences,[36] the Riyadh Guidelines counsel against penalising children for conduct which would not be considered criminal in an adult,[37] and the UN Convention is silent on the matter. Given the lack of international consensus, it seems unlikely that the European Court would be persuaded that status offences are discrimination *per se*. One further argument against status offences might be considered. While proof beyond reasonable doubt is required in respect of ordinary offences, these status offences can be established by proof on the balance of probabilities.[38]

Prosecution of children under the age of 16

Despite the creation of the children's hearings system, it has always been possible for a child below the age of 16 to be prosecuted in court, albeit such prosecution must be "at the instance of the Lord Advocate". Successive Lords Advocate have addressed their responsibility by issuing guidelines, indicating which offences should be considered for prosecution, with the most recent dating from 1996.[39] There are three categories of offences covered. First are offences which require prosecution on indictment, including the pleas of the Crown, certain statutory offences, and other serious offences like assault to severe injury and possession of a class A drug with intent to supply. The second category is restricted to persons over the age of 15 years where disqualification from driving is either a mandatory or optional sentence upon conviction, not being a disposal available to a children's hearing. The third category covers children over the age of 16 who are subject to a supervision requirement and will be considered presently.[40] It should be noted that a reporter's decision not to refer a child to a hearing does not preclude prosecution.[41]   **15.41**

While the European Convention does not prohibit the prosecution of children under the age of 16, the European Court found that, due to their ages and states of mind, two ten-year-olds were unable to participate effectively in the proceedings, and, thus, were   **15.42**

---

[36] rr. 3.1.

[37] Guideline 56.

[38] This argument might be developed further in the light of *Merrin v. S.*, 1987 S.L.T. 193 (circumstances which would have indicated an offence, had the child been at least eight years old cannot be used to refer the child to a hearing on other grounds, like being beyond parental control) and *Constanda v. M.*, 1997 S.C.L.R. 510 (a child over the age of eight cannot be referred on a non-offence ground, where proof would be on the balance of probabilities, where the facts relied upon indicate an offence).

[39] For ease of reference, these, along with "Explanatory Notes" can be found in Kearney, above, at paras 1.25–1.26.

[40] See para. 15.46, *infra*.

[41] *Mackinnon v. Dempsey*, (High Court), November 9, 1984, unreported.

denied a fair hearing under Article 6(1).[42] This does not mean that
every child under 16 would necessarily be in the same position, but
it is a clear signal that the prosecution of such children must be
approached with great caution. It is imperative that lawyers defending children should utilise all the professional services at their
disposal in addressing the issue of the child's competence in respect
of both the commission of the offence and instructing a defence.[43]
The UN Convention applies to all person under the age of 18 and,
thus, both its general provisions and its specific provisions on juvenile justice apply to all persons below that age. While these do not
necessarily preclude subjecting children to trial, they certainly discourage the practice, particularly when all the considerations in
Articles 37 and 40 are taken into account.

15.43   The publicity associated with the trial and what happens to a
child thereafter, particularly after release from prison, pose further
dangers to respect for children's rights. It is worth remembering
that, while the UN Convention requirement on respect for the
child's privacy "at all stages of the proceedings"[44] probably does
not cover post-conviction publicity, this aspect is covered by the
injunction that child-offenders should be "treated in a manner
consistent with the promotion of the child's sense of dignity and
worth" and that account should be taken of their "age and the
desirability of promoting the child's reintegration and the child's
assuming a constructive role in society".[45] In Scotland, the prohibition on disclosing the identity of any child involved is automatic[46]: that is, it applies unless it is dispensed with, in whole or in
part, by the court where it is satisfied that to do so "is in the public
interest".[47] It was particularly unfortunate that this was done in one
case prior to the accused's appeal against conviction being heard,
since her conviction was overturned on appeal.[48] Once the proceedings are completed (*i.e.* after any appeal has been heard) the
Scottish Ministers may dispense with reporting restrictions, again,
either in whole or in part, and if such dispensation is in the public
interest.[49] A proposal was mooted to amend the legislation to

---

[42] *T. v. United Kingdom, V. v. United Kingdom, supra.*
[43] In the U.S., where, sadly, the prosecution of juveniles is more commonplace,
many attorneys have developed expertise in which issues to address; how to locate
and enlist appropriate professional assistance, particularly from developmental
psychologists; and how best to present this evidence to juries and judges. For
excellent discussions of the various aspects of challenging the child's competence
and in working with other professionals, see, T. Grisso & R.G. Schwartz (eds),
Youth on Trial: A Developmental Perspective on Juvenile Justice (University of
Chicago Press, 2000).
[44] Art. 40(2)(vii).
[45] Art. 40(1).
[46] Criminal Procedure (Scotland) Act 1995, s. 47(1).
[47] 1995 Act, s. 47(3)(b).
[48] *Cordona v. H.M. Advocate,* 1996 S.L.T. 1100.
[49] 1995 Act, s. 47(3)(c).

remove the automatic reporting restrictions where an under-16-year-old was convicted of a serious offence[50] but, happily, nothing seems to have come of this proposal. A particularly enlightened view of the need to protect the privacy of children convicted of a very serious offence can be found in the decision in England to protect the identity of Robert Thompson and Jon Venables after their release and to prevent reporting in respect of their new identities and whereabouts.[51]

The sentencing of persons under the age of 16 raises further **15.44** questions although, at present Scots law appears to comply with the letter, if not necessarily the spirit, of international regulation. While the European Convention prohibits "torture or inhuman or degrading treatment or punishment",[52] the UN Convention goes further in also providing that detention "shall be used only as a measure of last resort and for the shortest appropriate period of time"[53] and that "neither capital punishment nor imprisonment for life without the possibility of release shall be imposed for offences committed by persons below the age of eighteen years of age".[54] Turning first to non-life sentences, the European Court found it unobjectionable that a 15-year-old convicted of attempted murder was ineligible for remission of sentence when an adult in the same position would have been.[55] The sentencing of persons under 16 is probably further protected in Scotland by the various ways in which the children's hearing can be involved in non-mandatory sentence cases. Where a child is already subject to a supervision requirement, the High Court may, and other courts must, remit the case to the reporter to obtain the advice of a children's hearing on sentencing.[56] Where the child is not subject to a supervision requirement, the court may refer for such advice.[57] In respect of the imposition of a "life sentence" the European Court found no violation of Article 3 or 5 in *T. v. United Kingdom* and *V. v. United Kingdom*. Several points should be emphasised in respect of the Court's decision. First, a "life sentence", in the United Kingdom context, does not mean "imprisonment for life without the possibility of release" as prohibited by Article 37(a) of the UN

---

[50] *Consultation Paper on Identification of Children: Proposals to Amend section 47 of the Criminal Procedure (Scotland) Act 1995* (Scottish Office, 1996).
[51] *Venables and another v. News Group Newspapers Ltd* [2001] 1 All E.R. 908. See also, *McKerry v. Teesdale and Wear Valley Justices, supra*, where the court criticised the lifting of reporting restrictions in respect of a 15-year-old persistent offender charged with theft.
[52] Art. 3.
[53] Art. 37(b).
[54] Art. 37(a).
[55] *Nelson v. United Kingdom* (1986). This case was brought under Art. 14.
[56] Criminal Procedure (Scotland) Act 1995, s. 49(3) and the Crime and Disorder Act 1998, Sched 8, para.118.
[57] Criminal Procedure (Scotland) Act 1995, s. 307(1) and Children (Scotland) Act 1995, s. 93(2)(b).

Convention, since the boys would be eligible for parole having served the "tariff" portion of their sentences. This possibility applies in Scotland.[58] Secondly, at the time of the European Court's decision, the House of Lords had ruled that the decision in relation to the tariff should be determined by the a court rather than the Home Secretary.[59] Thirdly, the Court appears to have accepted the United Kingdom Government's submission that Thompson and Venables each "was held in conditions appropriate to his age and needs".[60]

16 and 17-year-old offenders

15.45 Many of the concerns expressed in relation to the prosecution of children under 16 apply to the prosecution of 16-and 17-year-olds who are, in terms of the UN Convention, still children. Of course, the young person's ability to participate effectively in the proceedings will increase as he or she matures but practitioners should remain vigilant to the possibility of a young client's capacity in this respect. Given that the various international instruments do not prohibit the prosecution of person below the age of 16, prosecution of a person above that age is competent.

It is encouraging to note that the Scottish Executive is prepared to give further thought to the recommendations of the Advisory Group and suggests that a more constructive approach may be taken in dealing with young offenders in the future.[61]

---

[58] The Crime and Punishment (Scotland) Act 1997. See, for example the press release relating to the release on licence of Barbara Glover, who had been convicted, in 1991, of the murder of a fellow pupil in a school playground when she was 15 years old; < http://www.scotland.gov.uk/news/press2000_01/se0164.asp >.

[59] *R v. Secretary of State for the Home Department, ex parte Venables; R v. Secretary of State for the Home Department, ex parte Thompson* [1998] A.C. 407. The trial judge had set the tariff at 10 years and the Home Secretary had sought to raise it to 15 years. In the wake of the House of Lords decision, the Lord Chief Justice, Lord Woolf, set the tariff at eight years, making release a possibility from February 21, 2001; *Re Thompson and Venables (Tariff recommendations)* (2000) 150 N.L.J. 1626.

[60] (2000) 30 E.H.R.R. 121, para. 117.

[61] The recommendations of the Advisory Group included: examining the possibility of a bridging project, to transfer as many 16–17-year-old offenders from the courts to the hearings system; developing a broader range of interventions and programmes to be available to procurators fiscal and the courts in dealing with this group, reducing the use of custody and fines (and consequent fine default) in respect of 16–17-year-olds; improving multi-agency co-ordination; broadening the training of those involved in delivery; and increasing dissemination of information about the system: *Report of the Advisory Group on Youth Crime, supra*, s. 2, para. 7.

Conclusions

Since the passing of the Human Rights Act, the question on the **15.46** minds of everyone involved in the hearings system has been "Can the children's hearings system survive European Convention scrutiny?". Given the European Court's willingness to use the UN Convention and other instruments, like the Beijing Rules and the Riyadh Guidelines, to flesh out its provisions with respect to children, a supplementary question should be "Can the hearings system survive scrutiny under these instruments as well?". It is submitted that the answer to both questions is "Yes, but only after significant reform".

The fundamental problem with the hearings system when viewed **15.47** from a children's rights perspective is the very thing that has been seen by many as its great strength—its lack of "legalism". Of course, it would be possible simply to abandon the hearings system and return to juvenile courts. This option has been adopted in many jurisdictions across the US where "liberal" models of juvenile justice came under a pincer attack from civil libertarians and the "hang them, birch them" lobby. The result has been transfer of juveniles to adult courts, mandatory sentencing, and the proliferation of juvenile curfews, boot camps and parental responsibility laws. These options largely fail to measure up to international standards; they do not "work", in the sense of deterrence or reducing recidivism; and they should not be considered in Scotland.[62]

Instead, it is submitted, we must approach each of the problems **15.48** with the hearings system and find answers, since answers undoubtedly exist. The process is already underway, as the proposals to give full information to children prior to hearings, and in respect of Legal Aid for representation at hearings, illustrate. Of course, these proposals themselves must be subject to rigorous scrutiny. Other issues still require to be addressed. The role of the reporter in deciding a hearing should be arranged, then acting as clerk and adviser to the hearing, cannot be dealt with adequately simply through changes in "good practice". If hearings had a legally qualified chair, then the reporter would not be put in this compromised position and hearings would be able to determine matters of procedure and law from within their own number. All of this would, perhaps inevitably, bring about a change to the fundamental nature of hearings as envisaged by Lord Kilbrandon, but the greater involvement of lawyers in the hearings system should not be

---

[62] The Advisory Group on Youth Crime's proposals are somewhat unclear on its perceptions of the approach which should be taken. It appeared to adhere to the Kilbrandon philosophy; Annex C, para. 14. However, it also appeared to anticipate incorporating of elements of a "justice" model into the hearings system alongside the "welfare" model; paras 11 and 12.

seem as a cause for gloom. Lawyers are already involved in the hearings system; as panel members, as reporters, in providing free representation, as safeguarders, in panel training, and, of course, as commentators. While some panel members share what is probably a more general, societal, wariness of lawyers, it should not be assumed that lawyers are incapable of appreciating how a children's hearing differs from the more adversarial procedures often found in courts. In the, perhaps tactless, words of the Lord President, "skilled lawyers are chameleons who readily adapt their approach and techniques to the particular tribunal in which they appear".[63] The point here is that, if the accused child's rights are to be protected and, thus, the hearings system is to be freed from a myriad of legal challenges, change is imperative. Of course, these changes would involve additional expenditure but, if that is what it takes to respect the rights of children accused of infringing the criminal law, so be it.

15.49   Other, more minor changes to the hearings system, like the abolition of business meetings as presently arranged, create no real problem since they only received official sanction comparatively recently. The outcome of the Scottish Law Commission's consultation on the age of criminal responsibility is awaited.[63a] The Commission is not proposing that the issue should be addressed by raising the age of capacity but, rather, that prosecution policy and practice should, at first instance, determine the matter. It has left open the question of whether there should be a statutory rule preventing prosecution of children below a specified age.

As we have seen, while the international instruments do not prohibit the prosecution of children, it would be more in keeping with the thrust of both the UN Convention and the Beijing Rules if as few children as possilble were taken down this formal route, assuming always that adequate disposals are available at the end. Further consideration might also be given to the, albeit bare and unexplained, recommendation of the Review of Youth Crime that consideration be given to children's hearings dealing with at least some 16 and 17-year-old offenders, something which, again, would be in line wiht the spirit of the various international instruments.

15.50   These changes might well make the hearings system better able to deal with a broader range of under 16-year-old offenders. As we have seen, while the international instruments do not prohibit the prosecution of children, it would be more in keeping with the thrust of both the UN Convention and the Beijing Rules if as few children as possible were taken down this formal route, assuming always that adequate disposals are available at the end. It might also make more realistic the, albeit bare and unexplained, recommendation of the Review of Youth Crime that consideration be given to chil-

---

[63] *S. v. Miller, supra*, at p. 543.
[63a] Discussion Paper on the Age of Criminal Responsibility, *op. cit.*

dren's hearings dealing with at least some 16 and 17-year-old offenders, something which, again, would be in line with the spirit of the various international instruments.

Two messages for the hearings system seems clear. First, it must adapt if it is to survive. Secondly, it must take a more proactive approach to children's rights than it has taken so far. Rather than defending itself from challenges as they arise, it must embrace children's rights and the various international instruments that protect them so that it may, once again, rightly be described as "this reform which has earned so much praise".[64]

---

[64] *Sloan v. B*, 1991 S.L.T. 530, *per* Lord President Hope at p. 548.

CHAPTER 16

MONITORING AND ENFORCING CHILDREN'S INTERNATIONAL HUMAN RIGHTS

JOHN P. GRANT

The UN Convention on the Rights of the Child, adopted by **16.1** the General Assembly in November 1989,[1] is, without question, the paramount articulation of the international human rights of children. It has rightly been hailed as "a definitive body of international law on human rights" [2] and as a "turning point in the international law of children's rights".[3] The Convention was generally considered to be a positive step forward for the human rights movement as it encompassed not only civil and political rights, but also economic, social and cultural rights for one group, children;[4] and, additionally, included a comprehensive range of rights for this particular group in times of peace and armed conflict.[5]

That said, the final text of the Convention failed to live up to the **16.2** expectations of many. The principal cause of this dissatisfaction is easy to identify: the haste to complete the drafting process in 1989. That year was regarded as especially significant for children's rights, being 65 years after the Declaration of Geneva, the first international instrument recognising the rights and protection owed to children,[6] 30 years from the adoption of the UN Declaration of the Rights of the Child[7] and the tenth anniversary of the UN International Year of the Child. The result was, in the words of one commentator, "a rush to completion at the expense of clarity, consistency, and a great deal of substance".[8]

---

[1] 1577 UNTS 3; (1989) 28 I.L.M. 1448.
[2] M. Jupp, "The UN Convention on the Rights of the Child: An Opportunity for Advocates", (1990) 12 Human Rights Quarterly 130, at p.135.
[3] C.P. Cohen in the Introduction to Saulle, *The Rights of the Child* (1995), p. xix.
[4] J.S. Cerda, "The Draft Convention on the Rights of the Child: New Rights," (1990) 12 Human Rights Quarterly 115, at p. 115.
[5] G. Van Bueren, *The International Law on the Rights of the Child* (1996), p. 16.
[6] For the early history of the rights of children, see C.P. Cohen, *The Human Rights of Children* (1983) 12 Cap.L.R. 369.
[7] G.A. Res. 1386 (XIV).
[8] R.L. Barsh, "The Convention on the Rights of the Child: A Re-Assessment of the Final Text" (1989) 7 N.Y.L.S.J.H.R. 142, at p. 160.

16.3   It would be comforting to think that haste in some way also contributed to the deficiencies in the international mechanisms and procedures for enforcing and monitoring the compliance of states with their obligations under the Convention, Sadly, however, the Convention is no worse, and no better, than other human rights instruments in its enforcement and monitoring provisions. It is generally accepted that enforcement and monitoring measures are the most imperfect and least developed aspect of the entire UN human rights structure.[9] It has been said that "for human rights to be a reality in law, they have to be governed by a system of law",[10] a reference to the perceived need for some judicial or quasi-judicial enforcement mechanism. The UN Convention has provided no strict system of law, and certainly no new system of law, but has instead relied upon a tried and tested—though somewhat improved—monitoring mechanism and procedure.[11]

16.4   Before examining the machinery and procedures used for gauging compliance with human rights instruments generally, and assessing the operation and efficacy of the system used under the UN Convention, a cautionary note on terminology is needed. The process of gauging compliance is frequently, and rather uncritically, referred to as enforcement. That term can be properly applied to the process as it operates in the European Convention: the task of the European Court of Human Rights is to "ensure ... observance";[12] it is, in its composition[13] and procedure[14], clearly a judicial tribunal; its decisions are final[15] and binding,[16] with the supervision of execution assigned to the Committee of Ministers.[17]

16.5   The term "enforcement" cannot be readily extended to the UN Convention on the Rights of the Child. The Committee on the Rights of the Child (CRC) is not a judicial tribunal;[18] it does not operate any kind of judicial procedure; and its task is essentially to consider and comment on reports by states on the progress they

---

[9]   Van Bueren, *supra*, at p. 378.

[10]   K. Vasak, Human Rights: As Legal Reality in *The International Dimensions of Human Rights* (ed. Vasak, 1982), at p. 7. See also L. Sohn, Human Rights: Their Implementation and Supervision by the United Nations, in T. Meron, *Human Rights in International Law* (1984) 368 at 368.

[11]   M. Barsch, "The Convention on the Rights of the Child: A Re-Assessment of the Final Text" (1989) 7 N.Y.L.S.J.H.R. 142 at 152, expresses disappointment that the Convention "did not envisage any innovative implementation mechanisms."

[12]   European Convention of Human Rights and Fundamental Freedoms 1950, ETS No. 5, Art. 19.

[13]   *ibid.*, Art. 21.

[14]   *ibid.*, Arts 26–49.

[15]   *ibid.*, Art. 44.

[16]   *ibid.*, Art 46(1).

[17]   *ibid.*, Art. 46(2).

[18]   The members of the CRC are "experts of high moral standing and recognised competence in the field covered by this Convention": UN Convention on the Rights of the Child, Art. 43(2).

have made in giving effect to the rights set out in the Convention.[19] For these reasons, some commentators have preferred the term "implementation" to describe this process.[20] The difficulty is that implementation can be seen as a term of art, referring to the incorporation of the terms of a treaty into municipal law. Thus, Article 4 of the UN Convention requires states to "undertake all appropriate legislative, administrative and other measures for the implementation of the rights recognised" in the Convention.

A term which more accurately reflects the nature of the task **16.6** undertaken by the CRC is "monitoring".[21] The whole thrust of Part II of the UN Convention, which deals with the CRC and its functions, is towards overseeing and supervising the progress of states in giving effect to the rights in the Convention. This is hardly enforcement, and it is only implementation in the sense that the process is designed to induce states to implement in their own law and practice the obligations they have accepted under the Convention.

Governments have proved generally reluctant to adopt effective **16.7** measures for the internal implementation of human rights treaties that they have ratified. Experience proves that, for a variety of reasons, states do not always incorporate into their own law, much less enforce, the terms of international instruments to which they have subscribed. Given the simple fact that these same states are likely to be the direct or indirect violators of human rights norms, there is a clear need for some international mechanism to ensure, or at least induce, compliance.

Human Rights Monitoring and Enforcement Models

Essentially, there are two mechanisms in international human rights **16.8** instruments At the most basic level, provision may be made for periodic reports by states as to the progress they have made in giving effect to the rights contained in an instrument. These reports will then be examined by some international body of experts, which

---

[19] The CRC's task comprised "examining the progress made by State Parties in achieving the realisation of the obligations" in the Convention (*ibid.* Art. 43(1)) on the basis of reports made by these states (Art. 44(1)) and thereafter making "suggestions and general recommendations" (Art. 45(d). The CRC itself refers to this exercise as being "meaningful dialogue" (General guidelines for periodic reports (1996) CRC/C/58), though a more usual and accurate term for what happens in practice is "constructive dialogue".

[20] Van Bueren, *supra*, at Chap. 14; L.J. LeBlanc, *The Convention on the Rights of the Child* (1995) at p. x, xxi and 285.

[21] It has to be admitted that the term "monitoring" is also used to describe the process whereby states, prior to becoming bound by a convention, assess the compatibility of their law and practice with the obligations contained in the convention; and the process whereby states, prior to reporting on their progress towards the standards of a convention, assess that progress internally.

might receive additional information, particularly from Non-Governmental Organisations (NGOs), and might question re-presentatives of the reporting state, and which will ultimately issue concluding observations. This process, the very essence of the monitoring regime in the Convention on the Rights of the Child, posits that the self-evaluation inherent in preparing a report, followed by dialogue with the relevant monitoring committee, will induce states to enhance their compliance with the standards set by the instrument. There is clearly no sanction in any technical sense, reliance instead being placed on states' desire for approbation and against criticism.

16.9 At a more advanced level, the instrument may allow for complaints or petitions (in UN parlance, communications) to be received by some international body which will then undertake the judicial, or at least quasi-judicial, task of weighing the acts complained of against the standards set by the instrument. The complaints or petitions may be made by other states or, at the most sophisticated level, by aggrieved individuals. The international body receiving these complaints or petitions may, by composition and function, be quasi-judicial, particularly in being mandated to seek a friendly settlement, or it may, again by composition and function, be a court, with power to determine infractions and remedies. The model thus described is the model of the European Convention on Human Rights, the most sophisticated and arguably most successful human rights enforcement regime in existence.

16.10 Within the United Nations corpus of human rights treaties, two have opted exclusively for a reporting mechanism: the International Covenant on Economic, Social and Cultural Rights of 1966[22] and the Convention on the Rights of the Child[23] All the other UN human rights treaties in this corpus include both a reporting and complaints mechanism. The International Covenant on Civil and Political Rights of 1966,[24] provides for reports[25] and, after separate (and additional) agreement, inter-state complaints;[26] and, subject to further separate agreement under Protocol 1,[27] individuals communications. The Convention on the Elimination of All Forms of Racial Discrimination of 1965,[28] mandates reports[29] and inter-state complaints[30] and allows, following separate agreement, individual complaints.[31] The International Convention on the Elimination of

---

[22] 999 UNTS 3; (1967) 6 I.L.M. 360, Art. 18. 143 parties, including the U.K.
[23] Discussed in more detail *infra*.
[24] 999 UNTS 171; (1967) 6 I.L.M. 368. 147 parties, including the U.K. Art. 41 deals with periodic reporting, Art. 42 with inter-state complaints.
[25] *ibid.*, Art. 40.
[26] *ibid.*, Art. 41.
[27] 999 UNTS 171 (1967) 6 I.L.M. 368, Art. 1. 97 parties, but not the U.K.
[28] 660 UNTS 195; (1966) 5 I.L.M. 350. 156 parties, including the U.K.
[29] *ibid.*, Art. 9.
[30] *ibid.*, Art. 11.
[31] *ibid.*, Art. 14.

All Forms of Discrimination Against Women of 1979[32] began with a reporting regime[33] and, with the entry into effect of the Optional Protocol of 1999[34], has now been extended to include individual complaints.[35] The Convention Against Torture and Other Cruel, Inhuman or Degrading Treatment or Punishment of 1984[36] also operates both mechanisms, requiring reports [37] and allowing, following separate agreement to each, complaints by states[38] and individuals.[39] Finally, the International Convention on the Protection of the Rights of All Migrant Workers and Members of Their Families of 1990[40] mandates reports[41] and allows, following separate agreement for each, complaints by states[42] and individuals.[43]

Conventional wisdom dictates that complaints regimes are **16.11** effective and efficient, though the experience of the European Convention on Human Rights would hardly support any real claim to efficiency,[44] while reporting regimes are woefully ineffective. The same thundering common sense suggests that complaints regimes are best suited for instruments in which civil and political rights ("hard rights") predominate, while reporting regimes are all that can be expected for instruments in which economic and social rights ("soft rights") predominate. The hard rights, we are told, are to be subject to "immediate application",[45] and hence require complaints; the soft rights, dependent as they are on the state of development of the parties, are to be subject to "progressive realization",[46] and hence can accommodate no more than periodic reports. The reality lies somewhere between these extremes.

Both complaints and reporting regimes suffer from inherent and **16.12** practical defects—both are flawed to some extent—but neither is inherently better than the other. The drafters of international human rights agreements, at the UN and regional levels, realised that

---

[32] 1249 UNTS 13; (1980) 19 I.L.M. 33. 166 parties, including the U.K.
[33] *ibid.*, Art. 18.
[34] GA Res. 54/4; (2000) 39 I.L.M. 281. 11 parties, but not the U.K.
[35] *ibid.*, Art. 2.
[36] 1465 UNTS 85; (1984) 23 I.L.M. 1027. 118 parties, including the U.K.
[37] *ibid.*, Art 19.
[38] *ibid.*, Art. 21.
[39] *ibid.*, Art. 22. The Committee on Torture has an additional power of investigation where it receives "reliable information which appears to it to contain well-founded indications that torture is being systematically practised...": Art. 20.
[40] GA Res. 45/158: (1991) 30 I.L.M. 157. 12 parties, but not the U.K. This Convention has not entered into force.
[41] *ibid.*, Art. 73.
[42] *ibid.*, Art. 76.
[43] *ibid.*, Art. 77.
[44] It has been estimated it takes five years to get a case to the European Court of Human Rights and costs £30,000: Rights Brought Home: The Human Rights Bill (1997), Cm. 3782, para. 1.14.
[45] *United Nations Manual of Human Rights Reporting*, UN Doc. HR/PUB/91/1 (1997) at 4.
[46] *ibid.*

enforcement through complaints better suits civil and political rights and that constructive dialogue based upon periodic progress reports better suits economic and social rights. There is no reason, other than conventional wisdom and adherence to the status quo, that treaties containing both soft and hard rights could not be subject to a complaints regime. That is, after all, what has happened to CEDAW, which entered into force in 1981 with only a reporting mechanism, and which, through an optional protocol, has had a complaints system from December 2000. The Convention on the Rights of the Child, like CEDAW, contains a mixture of civil and political and economic and social rights, and steps may be taken in the near future, presumably through an optional protocol, for a complaints regime to supplement the existing reporting regime.[47]

Critique of Monitoring and Enforcement

16.13 In a devastating critique of the enforcement and monitoring of universal agreements, one authority,[48] Anne Bayefsky, essentially rejects the effectiveness of both regimes. She identifies a total of seven shortcomings in the present arrangements and suggests nine steps towards a better system. Although her analysis serves as a convenient point of departure for any assessment of enforcement and monitoring regimes, it is not necessary, or even sensible, to adopt all her criticisms and all her remedies. Her assertions[49] that, underlying the difficulties, is a front of rejectionism within the United Nations, coupled with machinery rooted in outdated beliefs about state sovereignty and domestic jurisdiction and a lack of shared democratic values, are overstated and simplistic.[50] The difficulties she identifies may be real, but at the same time unavoidable in a world community with 190+ members with diverse political and economic structures seeking to make common cause in the pursuit of some universal fundamental rights. And her remedies range from the trite (minimum qualification for members of treaty bodies[51]) to the bizarre (expulsion of states which do not meet minimum standards, discontinuation of periodic reporting[52]).

16.14 The Bayesfsky critique in relation to reporting regimes are reducible to three principal areas: late or no reports; a backlog of reports awaiting examination; and ineffectual working methods in

---

[47] Report of the CRC to the General Assembly, 2000, A/55/41. Para. 1558(j).
[48] A. Bayefsky, "Making the Human Rights Treaties Work", in L. Henkin and J.L. Hargrove, *Human Rights: An Agenda for the Next Century* (1994), 229.
[49] *ibid.* 231.
[50] See P. Alston, Looking to the Future, in Alston and Crawford, *supra*, 501 at 503ff.
[51] *ibid.* 264.
[52] *ibid.*

the treaty bodies. There is no doubt that states submit their periodic reports late or not at all.

As Table 1 demonstrates, reporting under the Convention on the Rights of the Child is far from a model of success. Most reports, when they are submitted, are submitted late. Perhaps most disconcerting is the overwhelming number of states that have never submitted a report. As of July 2000, 46 states out of 192 (about 25 per cent) had not returned an initial report. Of those that did submit an initial report, 49 (again about 25 per cent of the states parties) were between three and five years late.

Table 1[53]   16.15

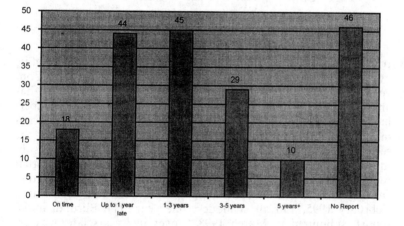

Initial Report

As Table 2 demonstrates, the situation appears to be getting worse. **16.16**
Of the 142 states that were due a second periodic report,[54] 105 have not done so. Additionally, of those states that have not submitted a second report, many are two (27) and three (57) years late. Only eight states submitted their second report on time. The inescapable conclusion is that non-submission and late submission are the norm.

---

[53] Source: CRC/C/99 (2000).
[54] The language is confusing. The first report is due two years after a state has ratified the Convention, subsequent reports being due five years thereafter: Convention, Art. 44(1)(a) and (b). The first report is referred to as the initial report: see General guidelines regarding the form and content of initial reports... (1991), CRC/C/5. The next report, strictly the first periodic report is, in the practice of the Committee, called the second periodic report. It will be referred to as the second report.

16.16 Table 2[55]

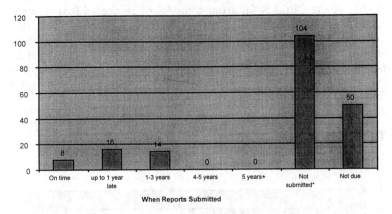

Second Periodic Report

When Reports Submitted

16.18 It seems almost carping to criticize the CRC for being a victim of its own success in having secured so many states parties to the Convention so quickly, but it, along with the other treaty bodies, has amassed a formidable backlog of reports to examine. One expert has estimated that the backlog in examining initial reports is running at up to two years, with a greater backlog projected for the second reports.[56] As concrete examples, the United Kingdom submitted its initial report in March 1994[57], four months late; that report was examined and government representatives questioned in January 1995[58]; and the concluding observations were published in February 1995;[59] in all, a modest one year. The Burundi initial report, submitted in March 1998[60], over five years late, was examined in September 2000[61] and the concluding observations published one month later[62] — in all, two and a half years. If this rate of slippage were to increase, then the possibility exists of a state's report not being examined and commented upon before the next periodic report is due. At the very least, a state may have very little time between receipt of concluding observations suggesting changes in law and practice and its next periodic report indicating

[55] Source: CRC/C/99 (2000).
[56] G. Lansdown, "The Reporting Process under the Convention on the Rights of the Child", in P. Alston & J. Crawford, *The Future of UN Human Rights Treaty Monitoring* (2000) 113 at 125.
[57] CRC/C/11/Add.1.
[58] CRC/C/SR.204-205.
[59] CRC/C/15/Add.34.
[60] CRC/C/3/Add.58.
[61] CRC/C/SR.645-646.
[62] CRC/C/15/Add.133.

how it has given effect to these changes. Ironically, it is only the late submission of reports which enables the CRC to keep the turn-round time for concluding observations within manageable bounds. If *all* the outstanding initial and second reports were to be submitted immediately, the Committee would be completely swamped.

Bayesfski also suggests that there are flaws the working methods **16.19** of UN treaty bodies. Essentially, these relate to a general lack of criticism on the part of treaty bodies[63]—on the lateness and inadequacy of reports, on the inadequacy of further written comments and oral presentations, on the limited role of NGOs, on the lack of follow-up and on failure to foster relations with the world's press. Much of this criticism does not, in the words of one authority,[64] "provide an accurate and balanced picture" and "is based on a fundamental misunderstanding of the nature and objectives of the system."

The real problem, admittedly acknowledged also by Bayefski,[65] is **16.20** the persistent and lamentable under-funding of the entire UN human rights system. Recognising the difficulties in monitoring the Convention on the Rights of the Child, the Vienna Declaration and Programme of Action of 1993 demanded that the CRC "should be enabled expeditiously and effectively to meet its mandate, especially in view of the unprecedented number of ratifications and subsequent submission of country reports."[66] This demand for adequate resources to be made available to allow the CRC to fulfil its function resulted in the establishment of a Plan of Action between the CRC and the Office of the High Commissioner for Human Rights (OHCHR) to enhance the capacity of the Committee to perform its monitoring function.[67] This programme, itself limited in resources, has achieved limited success, though it has refined and improved some of the CRC's practices.

Yet, in many other respects, the working methods of the CRC **16.21** seem well suited to its task. Reports are to be submitted in conformity with guidelines established by the Committee. Its General Guidelines on initial reports of 1991[68] run to some 24 paragraphs and specify what are the reporting obligations under Article 44(1)(a) of the Convention.[69] The 1996 General Guidelines for

---

[63] A. Bayefski, *supra*, at 246–249.
[64] P. Alston, "Looking to the Future", in Alston and Crawford, *supra*, 503.
[65] A. Bayefski, *supra*, 249.
[66] A/CONF.157/24; (1993) 32 I.L.M. 166.
[67] See CRC/SP/26, CRC/C/38, CRC/C/SR.288, CRC/C/SR.616 and CRC/SP/31.
[68] CRC/C/5.
[69] Thus, the Guidelines require information under a number of heads: definition of the child; general principles, including non-discrimination, best interests, the right to life, survival and development and respect for the child's views; civil rights and freedoms; family environment and alternative care; basic health and welfare; education, leisure and cultural activities; and special protection measures, including refugee children, children in armed conflict, juvenile justice and exploited children.

Periodic Reports,[70] running to some 165 paragraphs, provide further detail on the required information, and emphasise the importance of reporting on the steps taken to give effect to follow up previous CRC suggestions and recommendations.[71] In the event of reports containing insufficient information to provide the CRC "with a comprehensive understanding of the implementation of the Convention"[72], the Committee has the power to request further information.[73] The Committee has the assistance of, and information from, relevant Specialized Agencies.[74] In this respect, the work of the CRC, as of all the treaty bodies, benefits enormously from the input of Non-Governmental Organizations. NGOs have been deemed to be "other competent bodies" to which the CRC can turn for "expert advice" under Article 44(a) of the Convention.[75] NGOs are indeed central to the monitoring process in this and all the other UN human rights treaties.[76]

16.22   The CRC undertakes a pre-examination of a state's report and the other information available to it before the session at which the report is due to be examined through pre-sessional working groups.[77] This pre-examination identifies issues which are then communicated to the reporting state and which form the basis of the oral discussions with state representatives. The Committee finally agrees and publishes its concluding observation,[78] invariably expressed in relatively mild terms. By and large, states are not directly condemned for their failings; rather, the language used is that

---

[70] CRC/C/58.
[71] *ibid.*, para. 6.
[72] Convention on the Rights of the Child, Art. 44(2).
[73] *ibid.*, Art. 44(4).
[74] *ibid.*, Art. 45(a).
[75] See Rules 34 and 37(2) of the Provisional [and only] Rules of Procedure 1991: CRC/C/4. Thus, in attendance at the 24th session of the CRC, in the spring of 2000, were two UN bodies (UNICEF, OHCHR), three Specialized Agencies (ILO, UNESCO and WHO), three general NGOs, 13 international NGOs and three domestic NGOs: CRC/C/97, paras 5–7. The formal recognition of the role of NGOs is possibly the result of the contribution that they made in the drafting of the Convention: C.P. Cohen, "The Role of Non-Governmental Organizations in the Drafting of the Convention on the Rights of the Child" (1990) 12 Hum.Rts.Q. 137 at 142. This role was ensigaged during the drafting process: see E/CN.4/1988/28 at para. 182.
[76] Vienna Declaration of Programme of Action, 1993, *supra*, Part I, para. 38, Part II, para. 52; L. Wiseberg, "Human Rights Information and Documentation", in *United Nations Manual on Human Rights Reporting*, UN Doc HR/PUB/91/1 (1997), 45; A. Clapham, "UN Human Rights Reporting Procedures: An NGO Perspective", in Alston & Crawford, *supra*, 175; F. Gaer, "Reality Check: Human Rights NGOs Confront Governments in the UN", in T.G. Weiss & L. Gordenker, NGOs, *The UN and Global Governance,* (1996) 51; S.N. Hart & L. Thetaz-Bergman, "The Role of NGOs in Implementaing the Convention on the Rights of the Child", (1996) 6 Trans'l. L & Contemp.Probs. 373.
[77] See, *e.g.*, CRC/C/97, paras 9–11.
[78] Concluding observations are divided into four sections: A. Introduction; B. Positive aspects; C. Principal subjects of concern; D. Suggestions and recommendations.

of "concern" (and not condemnation), and that concern is invariably at apparent "inconsistencies" or "incompatibilities" with the Convention (and not clear breaches or violations). This terminology is important if the CRC is to engage in constructive dialogue. The Committee also has the power,[79] which it has used frequently,[80] to recommend technical advice and assistance from appropriate governmental and non-governmental organisations. Indeed, the entire monitoring procedure is "couched in terms of assisting States Parties with their treaty compliance, rather than penalizing or pressuring States Parties that fail to comply".[81]

While the members of the CRC are undoubtedly " experts of high **16.23** moral standing and recognised competence in the field",[82] they are appointed on a part-time basis. The CRC now meets for three sessions of four weeks each year.[83] To the end of 2000 the CRC has held only 25 sessions. The Committee has decided to increase the country reports considered at each session to nine,[84] thus allowing 27 reports to be considered and commented on in each calendar year. In an attempt to meet even this quite modest goal, the membership of the CRC will be increased from 10 to 18 when an amendment to the Convention[85] eventually enters into force. In addition, the Office of the UN High Commissioner for Human Rights, responsible for servicing this and the other treaty bodies, has created five new posts.[86]

There can be little doubt that the problems confronting the **16.24** CRC—and indeed all the treaty-monitoring bodies—are well known within the international community. These problems are only more acute in the CRC because of the large number of states parties, almost 50 more than any other UN human rights treaty, and the fact that within ten years of the Convention entering into force two sets of reports fall to be examined, the initial reports, due two years after ratification,[87] and the first periodic report, due five years later.[88] There may be no quick fixes.

Is it conceivable that the UN, already strapped for cash, will **16.25**

---

[79] Convention on the Rights of the Child, Art. 45(b).
[80] CRC/C/40/Rev.16 outlines the advisory services and technical assistance suggested in respect of the reports of 84 states.
[81] C.P. Cohen, "United Nations Convention on the Rights of the Child—Introductory Note" (1989) 28 I.L.M. 1448 at 1452.
[82] Convention on the Rights of the Child, Art. 43.
[83] Although one week of each session is devoted to the pre-consideration of the next session's countries' reports.
[84] CRC/C/94.
[85] Proposed by Costa Rica to a Conference of States Parties and endorsed by the General Assembly in Res. 50/155 on February 28 1996. The amendment, will enter into effect when accepted by two-thirds of the states parties to the Convention: Art. 50(2). It may be a sign of states' commitment to the CRC and effective monitoring that the amendment is not in force after five years.
[86] Lansdow, *The Reporting Process etc.*, *supra*, 125.
[87] Convention on the Rights of the Child, Art. 44(1)(a).
[88] *ibid.* Art. 44(1)(b).

allocate more resources to its human rights functions?[89] Is it conceivable that states will agree to additional subventions to support human rights in general or the Committee on the Rights of the Child in particular?[90] Without more funding, additional commitments in time from committee members or additional OHCHR staff to service the CRC just will not happen. The suggestion that periodic reports should fall due five years from the submission of the previous report, and not five years from the date on which the previous report was due[91], might well ease the strain for the CRC, but would also reward the states who submit late and thereby potentially subvert the entire monitoring system.

The Acid Test: Effectiveness

16.26 There is another way of examining the efficacy of the CRC's reporting system and that is to assess whether the process impels any change in the law and practice of the states parties. In a very real sense, this is the acid test, whatever defects and difficulties exist within the system. The United Kingdom's experience provides some insights into the system in operation.

16.27 The United Kingdom's initial report was submitted in March 1994.[92] Running to some 625 paragraphs over 100 pages, it is striking in two respects. The first is the air of complacency that pervades the entire document. If the CRC reporting process is initially about rigorous self-analysis, that is not apparent from this report. The United Kingdom, we are told, "while not complacent, can claim with some confidence to have a good record in general on its treatment of children."[93] That said, the report valiantly attempts to provide information and data in line with the Committee on the Rights of the Child's guidelines. Equally striking, from a Scottish

---

[89] The World Conference on Human Rights 1993 call for adequate resources has hardly had a significant impact: A/CONF.157/24; (1993) 32 I.L.M. 1661, Part I, para. 35 and Part II, paras 9–12. See Clark & Gaer, "The Committee on the Rights of the Child: Who Pays?" (1989) 7 N.Y.L.Sch.J.Hum.Rts. 123; E. Evatt, "Ensuring Effective Supervisory Procedures: The Need for Resources", in Alston & Crawford, *supra*, 461; and M. Schmidt, "Servicing and Financing Human Rights Supervisory Bodies", *ibid.*, 481. Funding for the Committee comes from the regular UN budget (art. 43(11)), infinitely preferable than direct state funding. The regular budget allocated through the OHCHR for the work of the Committee on the Rights of the Child for 2000 and 2001 (a UN biennium) totals only $1,116,800 (OHCHR, *Annual Appeal 2000*, (2000), 10) and the Office is seeking more than half as much again for the Committee from voluntary contributions (*ibid.*, 95).
[90] Though it has to be submitted that a number of states have made voluntary contributions, amounting to some $2m, to support the CRC's examination process and technical assistance programmes: CRC/SP/26, paras 5–6 and Annex.
[91] Lansdown, *supra*, at 126.
[92] CRC/C/11/Add.1.
[93] *ibid.* para. 3.

point of view, is that very little reference is made to Scotland.[94] Such references as there are essentially "tag" Scotland on to the main, *i.e.* English and Welsh, law and practice. One must have a certain sympathy for those charged with the task of drawing together the material for a report to a human rights treaty body, considering that the material must embrace three jurisdictions, at least seven government departments and innumerable local authorities. The United Kingdom's second report,[95] submitted in August 1999, obliquely acknowledges the limited regional diversity in the initial report when it adopted "a different approach ... in distinguishing material related to the different parts of the United Kingdom,"[96] an aim achieved by the report itself. But if Scotland (and Northern Ireland) did not have sufficient input into the United Kingdom's initial report, no more did children, perhaps astonishing in the light of Article 12 of the Convention; the second report professes to having expanded the "very limited" participation of children in the initial report.[97]

The nine hours during which the Committee on the Rights of the Child discussed the United Kingdom's initial report with senior civil servants[98] offer some insights into the Committee's concerns, which in turn were replicated in the concluding observations.[99] The UK's representatives were compelled to respond about, inter alia, the extent of the United Kingdom's reservations,[1] corporal punishment and chastisement of children,[2] discrimination, particularly in relation to unmarried fathers,[3] rights in education[4] and the age of criminal responsibility.[5]   **16.28**

In conformity with its normal practice, the Committee's Concluding Observations are divided into three categories: "positive aspects"; "principal subjects of concern"; and "suggestions and recommendations". Given the lack of specific reference in the United Kingdom's report to Scotland, it is necessary to separate out those comments which apply in a Scottish context. The positive aspects included initiatives taken to combat bullying in schools,[6] the attempts to address the issue of child sexual abuse;[7]   **16.29**

---

[94] See *ibid.*, paras 9, 14, 23, 38, 76, 89, 119, 138, 158, 193, 221, 323, 325, 369, 371, 380, 386, 387, 517, 523, 552, 569-572, 576-578, 604, 619; and Annex, para. 6.
[95] *United Nations Convention on the Rights of the Child. Second Report by the United Kingdom* (1999). Not yet published by The Committee on the Rights of the Child.
[96] *ibid.*, para. 1.2.4.
[97] *ibid.*, para. 1.6.1.
[98] On January 24 and 25 1995: CRC/C/SR.204-206.
[99] CRC/C/15/Add.34.
[1] CRC/C/SR.204, paras 6 and 22.
[2] CRC/C/SR.205, paras 59 and 70; CRC/C/SR.206, paras 9 and 10.
[3] CRC/C/SR.205, paras 35 and 37.
[4] CRC/C/SR.206, para. 29.
[5] CRC/C/SR.206, paras. 51–52.
[6] CRC/C/15/Add.34, para. 4.
[7] *ibid.*

the government's commitment to legislation on adoption[8] and the commitment to extending pre-school education.[9] While commending the United Kingdom for its intention to consider withdrawing some of its reservations to the Convention,[10] it later expressed concern about the broad nature of the existing reservations[11] and recommended a review of these reservations in prospect of their withdrawal.[12]

16.30 Indeed, the first, and most general, of the principal subjects of concern raised by the Committee was the very broad ambit of the United Kingdom's reservations to the Convention and their compatibility with its object and purpose. One of these reservations related to the children's hearings system (and has now been withdrawn), although there is no specific mention of the system in the concluding observations. This is particularly interesting since the Committee went on to express concern about low age of criminal responsibility in the United Kingdom[13] and recommended raising it.[14] Given the silence of the role of children's hearings in the initial report and the scant oral explanation of the system by United Kingdom representatives,[15] one wonders whether, had the Committee understood the non-punitive philosophy underlying the hearings system, it might have been prompted to make a positive comment.

16.31 Other areas of concern included insufficient expenditure in the social sector to meet the demands of Article 4;[16] insufficient attention being given to the child's right under Article 12 to express his or her opinion;[17] the physical and sexual abuse of children, particularly the "imprecise nature" of reasonable chastisement;[18] and the situation of Gypsy and travelling children.[19] Given the centrality of internal monitoring to the Convention system, the Committee expressed concern about the apparent absence of any

---

[8] *ibid.*, para. 5.
[9] *ibid.*, para. 6.
[10] *ibid.*, para. 3.
[11] *ibid.*, para. 7.
[12] *ibid.*, para. 22.
[13] *ibid.*, para. 17. The age of criminal responsibility is 10 years in England and Wales, while in Scotland and Northern Ireland it is eight. In Scotland, the matter has been referred to the Scottish Law Commission for consideration and the possibility of raising the age of criminal responsibility to 12 has been mooted.
[14] *ibid.*, para. 36.
[15] "In Scotland, there were children's hearings in which the well-being of the child was taken into consideration. The bodies concerned were competent to hear most of the offences that might be committed by or against a child": CRC/C/SR.204, para. 5. "...[i]n Scotland, ...the vast majority of child offenders were brought before relatively informal bodies known as Children's Hearings": CRC/C/SR.206, para. 51.
[16] CRC/C/15/Add.34, para. 9.
[17] *ibid.*, paras 11 and 14.
[18] *ibid.*, para. 16.
[19] *ibid.*, para. 21.

coordinating—and independent—mechanism,[20] a theme it returned to in its suggestions and recommendations.[21]

The final section of the Committee's concluding observations, the **16.32** suggestions and recommendations, essentially carries forward those areas over which it had already expressed concern. Thus, the Committee suggested that the United Kingdom have regard to the best interests test of Aricle 3 in allocating resources in the social sector;[22] that greater priority be given to ensuring respect for the principles in Article 3 and Article 12 in policy and administrative matters, as well as in decisions in the community and the family;[23] that consideration be given to lowering the age of criminal responsibility;[24] and that more pro-active steps be taken for Gypsy and travelling children.[25] It recommended the adoption of measures to ensure that the administration of juvenile justice was more "child-oriented".[26] Again, one wonders what the Committee might have said if it had known something (anything?) of the children's hearings system.

On the subject of the physical punishment of children, the **16.33** Committee on the Rights of the Child, for the first and only time, does not pull any punches. It all but declared in terms that physical punishment of children is prohibited through the operation of Articles 3 to 19 of the Convention.[27] One assumes that this statement would have been stronger but for the singular view of the United Kingdom representatives who attended the oral hearing that corporal punishment at private schools and reasonable chastisement within the family were permissible.[28] The Committee also stressed the application of the Convention to education, recommending in particular that there should be an effective appeal against any exclusion from school and that children be afforded an opportunity to express their views on educational matters.[29]

The logic of the reporting regime of the Convention on the **16.34** Rights of the Child dictates that the concerns, suggestions and re-

---

[20] *ibid.*, para. 8.
[21] *ibid.*, para. 23.
[22] *ibid.*, para. 24. See also para. 25.
[23] *ibid.*, para. 27.
[24] *ibid.*, para. 36. A representative of the Government had already told the Committee that there were "no plans to raise the age of criminal responsibility": CRC/C/SR.206, para. 52.
[25] *ibid.*, para. 40.
[26] *ibid.*, para. 35.
[27] *ibid.*, para. 31.
[28] "The United Kingdom had taken advice on the question; the advice had consistently been that its position was in keeping with the Convention": CRC/C/SR.205, para. 70. The same representative later became bolder when pressed further on the issue: the Government "which had carefully examined all the articles of the Convention that dealt with the matter and had taken legal advice, was convinced that its position was wholly in keeping with the Convention": CRC/C/SR.206, para. 9.
[29] *ibid.*, para. 32.

commendations made by the Committee in 1995 should be reflected in the state's ensuing periodic report, properly title the Second Periodic Report.[30] Certainly, this report is an improvement upon its predecessor in a number of respects, with separate sections being devoted to particular developments in different parts of the United Kingdom,[31] a clear attempt to involve children in an ambitious and commendable programme,[32] and input from NGOs.[33]

16.35   It might be thought that it starts well, when it purports to list the UN Committee's areas of concern[34] and suggestions and recommendations.[35] That would have been a good, if somewhat obvious, start, had the list been expressed in other than the barest outlines of the concerns and of the suggested and recommended action to be taken. One has to turn to Annex A to find the full text of the concluding observations of the Committee on the Rights of the Child. That would have been an even better start had the report then immediately addressed the concerns and suggestions and recommendations in detail. That is not the approach taken; instead, there merely appears the tantalizing promise that "[p]rogress on a number of these matters is set out in the report".[36]

Other contributors to this volume have analysed the veracity of this statement. Only three, controversial areas of concern will be discussed here: the criticism of the breadth and nature of the United Kingdom reservations to the Convention, of corporal punishment and family chastisement and of the age of criminal responsibility.

16.36   As it had promised, the Government conducted a review of the reservations it had entered and, again as it had trailed in 1995,[37] the reservation concerning the children's hearing system has been

---

[30] Second Report to the UN Committee on the Rights of the Child by the United Kingdom, HMSO, August 1999; not yet published by the Committee. Hereinafter referred to as the *Second Report*.

[31] Sections are devoted to developments in Scotland, Northern Ireland and Wales, before the Report moves on to the particular themes required by the Committee, in which progress and regional differences are noted.

[32] Consultation with children was conducted through NGOs and, in Scotland, Save the Children was commissioned to undertake the 'Our Lives' project which sought the views of children and young people on the main themes of the Convention, see *Second Report*, paras 1.6.1–1.6.7.

[33] *ibid.*, paras 1.5.1. and 1.6.2–1.6.5, and Annex C. Government departments in the various parts of the United Kingdom were encouraged to involve local NGOs. The *Report to the Government on Progress towards Implementing the Convention on the Rights of the Child* (February 1998) was produced by a group of non-governmental organizations which work with and for children, including the Scottish Child Law Centre and the Scottish Children's Rights Alliance. It highlighted out a number of deficiencies in the U.K.'s compliance with the Convention.

[34] *ibid.*, paras 1.3.2–1.3.3.

[35] *ibid.*, paras 1.3.5.

[36] *ibid.*, para. 1.3.6.

[37] CRC/C/SR.204, paras 6 and 22.

withdrawn.[38] This concession is, of course, more the result of the ruling of the European Court of Human Rights in *McMichael v. United Kingdom*,[39] and the remedial measures taken in the Children (Scotland) Act 1995. Another reservation, concerning employment legislation for persons under 18, has been withdrawn because of the implementation of two European Community Directives.[40] The definitions in the reservation relating to live births and parents are, we are now told, not reservations *stricto sensu*, but rather "interpretative declarations".[41] In respect of the reservation on citizenship and nationality, the response is that the United Kingdom has no plans to shift its position because of its "particular circumstances.[42]

The issue of physical punishment of children is identified in the **16.37** abbreviated list of concerns at the beginning of the report as "judicial interpretation of the present law permitting the reasonable chastisement of children within the family context",[43] a somewhat euphemistic paraphrase of the Committee's expressed concerns. Later, the report smugly relates that, in an unnamed case under the European Convention on Human Rights, in fact *A. v United Kingdom*,[44] the Commission had found that a state was not required to enact legislation to punish any form of physical rebuke.[45] As the report acknowledges, the United Kingdom did not prevail in the European Court of Human Rights. However, this misses the point— and presumably not by accident. Article 3 of the European Convention, under which this case was brought, contains a prohibition on "inhuman or degrading treatment or punishment", any breach of which, in the jurisprudence under the Convention and the holding of the Court in *A*. requires a minimum threshold degree of severity. That is clearly not the position under the UN Convention, in which the prohibition on physical chastisement is drawn from "the provisions and principles of the Convention, including those of its Articles 3, 19 and 37".[46] What may not be illegal under the

---

[38] The reservation sought to exclude the children's hearings system from the application of art. 37 of the Convention, guaranteeing prompt access to legal and other assistance on the deprivation of liberty. The reservation was withdrawn on 18 April 1997. *Second Report*, paras 1.8.1–2 and 2.12.1.

[39] (1995) Series A. No. 308; 20 E.H.R.R. 205.

[40] *Second Report*, paras 1.8.2.d and 10.68.1. The Directives are 94/33/EC and 93/104/EC.

[41] *ibid.*, paras 1.8.2.a–b.

[42] *ibid.*, para. 1.8.2.c. Somewhat inconsistently, the report later states: "The Government believes that the United Kingdom's immigration and nationality law is entirely consistent with the Convention. In fact the United Kingdom makes generous provision both for the admission of foreign children to join their parents settled here, and for the acquisition of citizenship": para. 7.31.2.

[43] *ibid.*, para. 1,3,3,g.

[44] (1998) 27 E.H.R.R. 611.

[45] *Second Report*, para. 7.12.1.

[46] CRC/C/15/Add.34, para. 11.

European Convention may yet be illegal under the different standard of the UN Convention. After this startling piece of non-
information, the report simply indicates that consultation on the
matter is underway, records that physical punishment is no longer
permitted in respect of a child in state care and notes the opposition
of some NGOs to all physical punishment of children.[47]

16.38   While the section of the report dealing with Scotland mentions
the age of criminal responsibility—indeed, describing it as one of
the UN Committee's main criticisms[48]—the remainder of the report
is silent on the entire issue. The Scottish section relates the fact that
the vast majority of children are dealt with by children's hearings
and not by the courts and that prosecution is reserved for only the
most serious crimes. It seems clear that, for all of the United
Kingdom apart from Scotland, there is no intention on the part of
the government to reconsider the age of criminal responsibility.[49]
On the other hand, the Scottish Executive, to its credit, has referred
the age of criminal responsibility to the Scottish Law Commission.

Conclusions

16.39   It is perhaps exaggeration to describe the system as in crisis, but it
has run into a short- to medium-term problem of some magnitude.
This problem undermines the essential logic of reporting, which
requires regular, timely and thorough reports and regular, timely
and thorough responses to these reports, so that a state may eval-
uate its progress, have that progress checked and then progress
further before it has to report again. Without timely reports and
timely responses the CRC will be unable to engage in the kind of
meaningful and constructive monitoring envisaged by the Convention and so readily accepted by the Committee. However, that
does not, and cannot, mean that monitoring the Convention on the
Rights of the Child is not worth the candle. As one observer correctly says, "[t]he success of the CRC has exceeded all expectations
and the role of the Committee in contributing to the understanding
and implementation of children's rights has not been insignificant."[50]

16.40   It is commonly accepted that the right of an individual to petition
some international body concerning violation of a human rights
norm is "the cornerstone of any efficient system of international
protection of human rights."[51] As has been seen,[52] this is clearly the

---

[47]   *Second Report*, paras 7.12.2–7.13.3.
[48]   *ibid.*, para. 2.11.1.
[49]   CRC/C/SR.206, para. 52.
[50]   *ibid.*,
[51]   Mahoney & Mahoney, *Human Rights in the 21ˢᵗ Century: A Global Challenge*,
        (1993), at 49.
[52]   *supra.*

UN preference, with five of the seven core human rights agreements already providing, albeit at one remove, a right of individual petition. Only the International Covenant on Economic, Social and Cultural Rights, an agreement whose object and terms militate against anything other than monitoring by state reports, and the Convention on the Rights of the Child abjure any system of enforcement through complaints. There have been calls for the addition of a complaints mechanism to the Convention.[53] The Committee on the Rights of the Child has recently flagged up its intention to consider a protocol to the Convention to allow for the right of individual petition.[54]

Within the next few years, there will probably exist a right of **16.41** individual petition similar in terms to that just established in a Protocol to the Discrimination Against Women Convention.[55] Certainly, many of the "hard' rights contained in the Convention would be capable of this level of quasi-judicial enforcement, e.g. the right to life under Article 6(1), to freedom from exploitation (Articles 19(1) and 32(1)) and to education (Article 28(1)); but can the same be said of many of the economic and social rights, *e.g.* the right of access to information via the media (Article 17(1)), to an adequate standard of living (Article 27 (1)) and to engage in play (Article 31(1)). The Convention contains many such "soft" rights, the implementation of which depends on the level of economic development of the state. It is expressly recognised that, for economic and social rights, states are required to provide guarantees only "to the maximum extent of their available resources".[56]

There is also a significant difference in the way rights are **16.42** expressed in this Convention and in, for example, the International Covenant on Civil and Political Rights. Rights for children are expressed as obligations on states, rather than as rights vested in the individual. So, in the former instrument, Article 14 states that the "States Parties shall respect the right of the child to freedom of thought, conscience and religion", while in the latter the equivalent provision is: "Everyone shall have the right to freedom of thought, conscience and religion".[57] Too much should not be read into this difference, for in most cases the intent and result will be the same, but it is worth remarking that the rights in the CRC are expressed in the same way as the manifestly non-justiciable International Covenant on Economic, Social and Cultural Rights. The solution may lie in a bifurcation of the Convention's rights, with only the

---

[53] Van Bueren, *supra*, 410–411.
[54] Report of the CRC to the General Assembly, 2000, A/55/41, para. 1558(j): "The Committee will consider initiating discussions on an Optional Protocol to the Convention providing a mechanism for individual communications, to ensure the availability of legal remedies at the international level..."
[55] GA Res. 54/4; (2000) 39 I.L.M. 281.
[56] Convention on the Right of the Child, Art. 4.
[57] International Covenant on Civil and Political Rights, Art. 18(1).

civil and political rights, insofar as they can be separately identified, subject to the right of individual petition.

16.43 If an optional protocol providing for a complaints regime is inevitable, some pause for consideration should be made lest a complaints mechanism is drafted which secures virtually no ratifications.[58] Also, and critically, any moves towards a complaints system will have to be accompanied by recognition that the Committee on the Rights of the Child is inadequately resourced for its present task.[59] Further, it is possible that, by requiring the Committee on the Rights of the Child to act as both a benevolent monitor and an adjudicating tribunal, the constructive dialogue so carefully crafted by the Committee over the last decade is destroyed.

---

[58] McSweeney, "The Potential for Enforcement of the UN Convention on the Rights of the Child: The Need to Improve the Information Base", (1993) 16 Bos. Co. Int. & Comp. L. R. 467 at 487. In the drafting process, fears were expressed about individual petitions producing confrontations with states: Van Bueren, *supra*, 411. It cannot now be true that states are politically daunted by a human rights "judiciary", given that they have accepted so many other human rights "judiciaries: *cf.* Schmidt, "Individual Human Rights Complaints Procedures Based on UN Treaties and the Need for Reform" (1992) 41 I.C.L.Q. 645 at 648.

[59] Van Bueren, *supra*, 411.

APPENDIX 1

EUROPEAN CONVENTION ON HUMAN RIGHTS

(As incorporated into U.K. Law by section 1 and Schedule 1 of the Human Rights Act 1998.)

THE CONVENTION
RIGHTS AND FREEDOMS
Article 2
Right to life

1. Everyone's right to life shall be protected by law. No one shall be deprived of his life intentionally save in the execution of a sentence of a court following his conviction of a crime for which this penalty is provided by law.
2. Deprivation of life shall not be regarded as inflicted in contravention of this Article when it results from the use of force which is no more than absolutely necessary:
(a) in defence of any person from unlawful violence;
(b) in order to effect a lawful arrest or to prevent the escape of a person lawfully detained;
(c) in action lawfully taken for the purpose of quelling a riot or insurrection.

Article 3
Prohibition of torture

No one shall be subjected to torture or to inhuman or degrading treatment or punishment.

Article 4
Prohibition of slavery and forced labour

1. No one shall be held in slavery or servitude.
2. No one shall be required to perform forced or compulsory labour.
3. For the purpose of this Article the term "forced or compulsory labour" shall not include:
(a) any work required to be done in the ordinary course of detention imposed according to the provisions of Article 5 of this Convention or during conditional release from such detention;

(b) any service of a military character or, in case of conscientious objectors in countries where they are recognised, service exacted instead of compulsory military service;

(c) any service exacted in case of an emergency or calamity threatening the life or well-being of the community;

(d) any work or service which forms part of normal civic obligations.

Article 5
Right to liberty and security

1. Everyone has the right to liberty and security of person. No one shall be deprived of his liberty save in the following cases and in accordance with a procedure prescribed by law:

(a) the lawful detention of a person after conviction by a competent court;

(b) the lawful arrest or detention of a person for non-compliance with the lawful order of a court or in order to secure the fulfilment of any obligation prescribed by law;

(c) the lawful arrest or detention of a person effected for the purpose of bringing him before the competent legal authority on reasonable suspicion of having committed an offence or when it is reasonably considered necessary to prevent his committing an offence or fleeing after having done so;

(d) the detention of a minor by lawful order for the purpose of educational supervision or his lawful detention for the purpose of bringing him before the competent legal authority;

(e) the lawful detention of persons for the prevention of the spreading of infectious diseases, of persons of unsound mind, alcoholics or drug addicts or vagrants;

(f) the lawful arrest or detention of a person to prevent his effecting an unauthorised entry into the country or of a person against whom action is being taken with a view to deportation or extradition.

2. Everyone who is arrested shall be informed promptly, in a language which he understands, of the reasons for his arrest and of any charge against him.

3. Everyone arrested or detained in accordance with the provisions of paragraph 1(c) of this Article shall be brought promptly before a judge or other officer authorised by law to exercise judicial power and shall be entitled to trial within a reasonable time or to release pending trial. Release may be conditioned by guarantees to appear for trial.

4. Everyone who is deprived of his liberty by arrest or detention shall be entitled to take proceedings by which the lawfulness of his detention shall be decided speedily by a court and his release ordered if the detention is not lawful.

5. Everyone who has been the victim of arrest or detention in contravention of the provisions of this Article shall have an en-

forceable right to compensation.

Article 6
Right to a fair trial

1. In the determination of his civil rights and obligations or of any criminal charge against him, everyone is entitled to a fair and public hearing within a reasonable time by an independent and impartial tribunal established by law. Judgment shall be pronounced publicly but the press and public may be excluded from all or part of the trial in the interest of morals, public order or national security in a democratic society, where the interests of juveniles or the protection of the private life of the parties so require, or to the extent strictly necessary in the opinion of the court in special circumstances where publicity would prejudice the interests of justice.

2. Everyone charged with a criminal offence shall be presumed innocent until proved guilty according to law.

3. Everyone charged with a criminal offence has the following minimum rights:

(a) to be informed promptly, in a language which he understands and in detail, of the nature and cause of the accusation against him;

(b) to have adequate time and facilities for the preparation of his defence;

(c) to defend himself in person or through legal assistance of his own choosing or, if he has not sufficient means to pay for legal assistance, to be given it free when the interests of justice so require;

(d) to examine or have examined witnesses against him and to obtain the attendance and examination of witnesses on his behalf under the same conditions as witnesses against him;

(e) to have the free assistance of an interpreter if he cannot understand or speak the language used in court.

Article 7
No punishment without law

1. No one shall be held guilty of any criminal offence on account of any act or omission which did not constitute a criminal offence under national or international law at the time when it was committed. Nor shall a heavier penalty be imposed than the one that was applicable at the time the criminal offence was committed.

2. This Article shall not prejudice the trial and punishment of any person for any act or omission which, at the time when it was committed, was criminal according to the general principles of law recognised by civilised nations.

Article 8
Right to respect for private and family life

1. Everyone has the right to respect for his private and family life, his home and his correspondence.
2. There shall be no interference by a public authority with the exercise of this right except such as is in accordance with the law and is necessary in a democratic society in the interests of national security, public safety or the economic well-being of the country, for the prevention of disorder or crime, for the protection of health or morals, or for the protection of the rights and freedoms of others.

Article 9
Freedom of thought, conscience and religion

1. Everyone has the right to freedom of thought, conscience and religion, this right includes freedom to change his religion or belief and freedom, either alone or in community with others and in public or private, to manifest his religion or belief, in worship, teaching, practice and observance.
2. Freedom to manifest one's religion or beliefs shall be subject only to such limitations as are prescribed by law and are necessary in a democratic society in the interests of public safety, for the protection of public order, health or morals, or for the protection of the rights and freedoms of others.

Article 10
Freedom of expression

1. Everyone has the right to freedom of expression. This right shall include freedom to hold opinions and to receive and impart information and ideas without interference by public authority and regardless of frontiers. This Article shall not prevent States from requiring the licensing of broadcasting, television or cinema enterprises.
2. The exercise of these freedoms, since it carries with it duties and responsibilities, may be subject to such formalities, conditions, restrictions or penalties as are prescribed by law and are necessary in a democratic society, in the interests of national security, territorial integrity or public safety, for the prevention of disorder or crime, for the protection of health or morals, for the protection of the reputation or rights of others, for preventing the disclosure of information received in confidence, or for maintaining the authority and impartiality of the judiciary.

Article 11
Freedom of assembly and association

1. Everyone has the right to freedom of peaceful assembly and to freedom of association with others, including the right to form and to join trade unions for the protection of his interests.
2. No restrictions shall be placed on the exercise of these rights other than such as are prescribed by law and are necessary in a democratic society in the interests of national security or public safety, for the prevention of disorder or crime, for the protection of health or morals or for the protection of the rights and freedoms of others. This Article shall not prevent the imposition of lawful restrictions on the exercise of these rights by members of the armed forces, of the police or of the administration of the State.

Article 12
Right to marry

Men and women of marriageable age have the right to marry and to found a family, according to the national laws governing the exercise of this right.

Article 14
Prohibition of discrimination

The enjoyment of the rights and freedoms set forth in this Convention shall be secured without discrimination on any ground such as sex, race, colour, language, religion, political or other opinion, national or social origin, association with a national minority, property, birth or other status.

Article 16
Restrictions on political activity of aliens

Nothing in Articles 10, 11 and 14 shall be regarded as preventing the High Contracting Parties from imposing restrictions on the political activity of aliens.

Article 17
Prohibition of abuse of rights

Nothing in this Convention may be interpreted as implying for any State, group or person any right to engage in any activity or perform any act aimed at the destruction of any of the rights and freedoms set forth herein or at their limitation to a greater extent than is provided for in the Convention.

Article 18
Limitation on use of restrictions on rights

The restrictions permitted under this Convention to the said rights and freedoms shall not be applied for any purpose other than those for which they have been prescribed.

PART II
THE FIRST PROTOCOL
Article 1
Protection of property

Every natural or legal person is entitled to the peaceful enjoyment of his possessions. No shall be deprived of his possessions except in the public interest and subject to the conditions provided for by law and by the general principles of international law.

The preceding provisions shall not, however, in any way impair the right of a State to enforce such laws as it deems necessary to control the use of property in accordance with the general interest or to secure the payment of taxes or other contributions or penalties.

Article 2
Right to education

No person shall be denied the right to education. In the exercise of any functions which it assumes in relation to education and to teaching, the State shall respect the right of parents to ensure such education and teaching in conformity with their own religious and philosophical convictions.

Article 3
Right to free elections

The High Contracting Parties undertake to hold free elections at reasonable intervals by secret ballot, under conditions which will ensure the free expression of the opinion of the people in the choice of the legislature.

PART III
THE SIXTH PROTOCOL
Article 1
Abolition of the death penalty

The death penalty shall be abolished. No one shall be condemned to such penalty or executed.

Article 2
Death penalty in time of war

A State may make provision in its law for the death penalty in respect of acts committed in time of war or of imminent threat of war; such penalty shall be applied only in the instances laid down in the law and in accordance with its provisions. The State shall communicate to the Secretary General of the Council of Europe the relevant provisions of that law.

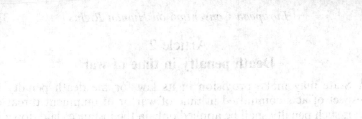

APPENDIX 2

CONVENTION ON THE RIGHTS OF THE CHILD

PREAMBLE

The States Parties to the present Convention,

Considering that, in accordance with the principles proclaimed in the Charter of the United Nations, recognition of the inherent dignity and of the equal and inalienable rights of all members of the human family is the foundation of freedom, justice and peace in the world,

Bearing in mind that the peoples of the United Nations have, in the Charter, reaffirmed their faith in fundamental human rights and in the dignity and worth of the human person, and have determined to promote social progress and better standards of life in larger freedom,

Recognizing that the United Nations has, in the Universal Declaration of Human Rights and in the International Covenants on Human Rights, proclaimed and agreed that everyone is entitled to all the rights and freedoms set forth therein, without distinction of any kind, such as race, colour, sex, language, religion, political or other opinion, national or social origin, property, birth or other status,

Recalling that, in the Universal Declaration of Human Rights, the United Nations has proclaimed that childhood is entitled to special care and assistance,

Convinced that the family, as the fundamental group of society and the natural enviromnent for the growth and wellbeing of all its members and particularly children, should be afforded the necessary protection and assistance so that it can fully assume its responsibilities within the community,

Recognizing that the child, for the full and harmonious development of his or her personality, should grow up in a family environment, in an atmosphere of happiness, love and understanding

Considering that the child should be fully prepared to live an individual life in society, and brought up in the spirit of the ideals proclaimed in the Charter of the United Nations, and in particular in the spirit of peace, dignity, tolerance, freedom, equality and solidarity,

Bearing in mind that the need to extend particular care to the child has been stated in the Geneva Declaration of the Rights of the Child of 1924 and in the Declaration of the Rights of the Child adopted by the General Assembly on 20 November 1959 and recognized in the Universal Declaration of Human Rights, in the International Covenant on Civil and Political Rights (in particular in Articles 23 and 24), in the International Covenant on Economic, Social and Cultural Rights (in particular in Article 10) and in the statutes and relevant instruments of specialized agencies and international organizations concerned with the welfare of children,

Bearing in mind that, as indicated in the Declaration of the Rights of the Child, "the child, by reason of his physical and mental immaturity, needs special safeguards and care, including appropriate legal protection, before as well as after birth",

Recalling the provisions of the Declaration on Social and Legal Principles relating to the Protection and Welfare of Children, with Special Reference to Foster Placement and Adoption Nationally and Internationally; the United Nations Standard Minimum Rules for the Administration of Juvenile Justice (The Beijing Rules); and the Declaration on the Protection of Women and Children in Emergency and Armed Conflict,

Recognizing that, in all countries in the world, there are children living in exceptionally difficult conditions, and that such children need special consideration,

Taking due account of the importance of the traditions and cultural values of each people for the protection and harmonious development of the child,

Recognizing the importance of international co-operation for improving the living conditions of children in every country, in particular in the developing countries,

Have agreed as follows:

PART I

Article 1

For the purposes of the present Convention, a child means every human being below the age of eighteen years unless, under the law applicable to the child, majority is attained earlier.

Article 2

1. States Parties shall respect and ensure the rights set forth in the present Convention to each child within their jurisdiction without discrimination of any kind, irrespective of the child's or his or her parent's or legal guardian's race, colour, sex, language, religion, political or other opinion, national, ethnic or social origin, property, disability, birth or other status.

2. States Parties shall take all appropriate measures to ensure that the child is protected against all forms of discrimination or punishment on the basis of the status, activities, expressed opinions, or beliefs of the child's parents, legal guardians, or family members.

Article 3

1. In all actions concerning children, whether undertaken by public or private social welfare institutions, courts of law, administrative authorities or legislative bodies, the best interests of the child shall be a primary consideration.

2. States Parties undertake to ensure the child such protection and care as is necessary for his or her well-being, taking into account the rights and duties of his or her parents, legal guardians, or other individuals legally responsible for him or her, and, to this end, shall take all appropriate legislative and administrative measures.

3. States Parties shall ensure that the institutions, services and facilities responsible for the care or protection of children shall conform with the standards established by competent authorities, particularly in the areas of safety, health, in the number and suitability of their staff, as well as competent supervision.

Article 4

States Parties shall undertake all appropriate legislative, administrative, and other measures for the implementation of the rights recognized in the present Convention. With regard to economic, social and cultural rights, States Parties shall undertake such measures to the maximum extent of their available resources and, where needed, within the framework of international co-operation.

Article 5

States Parties shall respect the responsibilities, rights and duties of parents or, where applicable, the members of the extended family or community as provided for by local custom, legal guardians or other persons legally responsible for the child, to provide, in a manner consistent with the evolving capacities of the child, appropriate direction and guidance in the exercise by the child of the rights recognized in the present Convention.

Article 6

1. States Parties recognize that every child has the inherent right to life.

2. States Parties shall ensure to the maximum extent possible the survival and development of the child.

Article 7

1. The child shall be registered immediately after birth and shall have the right from birth to a name, the right to acquire a nationality and, as far as possible, the right to know and be cared for by his or her parents.

2. States Parties shall ensure the implementation of these rights in accordance with their national law and their obligations under the relevant international instruments in this field, in particular where the child would otherwise be stateless.

Article 8

1. States Parties undertake to respect the right of the child to preserve his or her identity, including nationality, name and family relations as recognized by law without unlawful interference.
2. Where a child is illegally deprived of some or all of the elements of his or her identity, States Parties shall provide appropriate assistance and protection, with a view to speedily re-establishing his or her identity.

Article 9

1. States Parties shall ensure that a child shall not be separated from his or her parents against their will, except when competent authorities subject to judicial review determine, in accordance with applicable law and procedures, that such separation is necessary for the best interests of the child. Such determination may be necessary in a particular case such as one involving abuse or neglect of the child by the parents, or one where the parents are living separately and a decision must be made as to the child's place of residence.
2. In any proceedings pursuant to paragraph 1 of the present Article, all interested parties shall be given an opportunity to participate in the proceedings and make their views known.
3. States Parties shall respect the right of the child who is separated from one or both parents to maintain personal relations and direct contact with both parents on a regular basis, except if it is contrary to the child's best interests.
4. Where such separation results from any action initiated by a State Party, such as the detention, imprisonment, exile, deportation or death (including death arising from any cause while the person is in the custody of the State) of one or both parents or of the child, that State Party shall, upon request, provide the parents, the child or, if appropriate, another member of the family with the essential information concerning the whereabouts of the absent member(s) of the family unless the provision of the information would be detrimental to the well-being of the child. States Parties shall further ensure that the submission of such a request shall of itself entail no adverse consequences for the person(s) concerned.

Article 10

1. In accordance with the obligation of States Parties under Article 9, paragraph 1, applications by a child or his or her parents to enter or leave a State Party for the purpose of family reunification shall be dealt with by States Parties in a positive, humane and expeditious manner. States Parties shall further ensure that the submission of such a request shall entail no adverse consequences for the applicants and for the members of their family.
2. A child whose parents reside in different States shall have the right to maintain on a regular basis, save in exceptional circumstances, personal relations and direct contact with both parents. Towards that end and in accordance with the obligation of States

Parties under Article 9, paragraph 2, States Parties shall respect the right of the child and his or her parents to leave any country, including their own, and to enter their own country. The right to leave any country shall be subject only to such restrictions as are prescribed by law and which are necessary to protect the national security, public order *(ordre public)*, public health or morals or the rights and freedoms of others and are consistent with the other rights recognized in the present Convention.

Article 11

1. States Parties shall take measures to combat the illicit transfer and non-return of children abroad.
2. To this end, States Parties shall promote the conclusion of bilateral or multilateral agreements or accession to existing agreements.

Article 12

1. States Parties shall assure to the child who is capable of forming his or her own views the right to express those views freely in all matters affecting the child, the views of the child being given due weight in accordance with the age and maturity of the child.
2. For this purpose, the child shall in particular be provided the opportunity to be heard in any judicial and administrative proceedings affecting the child, either directly, or through a representative or an appropriate body, in a manner consistent with the procedural rules of national law.

Article 13

1. The child shall have the right to freedom of expression; this right shall include freedom to seek, receive and impart information and ideas of all kinds, regardless of frontiers, either orally, in writing or in print, in the form of art, or through any other media of the child's choice.
2. The exercise of this right may be subject to certain restrictions, but these shall only be such as are provided by law and are necessary:
(a) for respect of the rights or reputations of others; or
(b) for the protection of national security or of public order *(ordre public)*, or of public health or morals.

Article 14

1. States Parties shall respect the right of the child to freedom of thought, conscience and religion.
2. States Parties shall respect the rights and duties of the parents and, when applicable, legal guardians, to provide direction to the child in the exercise of his or her right in a manner consistent with the evolving capacities of the child.
3. Freedom to manifest one's religion or beliefs may be subject only to such limitations as are prescribed bylaw and are necessary to

protect public safety, order, health or morals, or the fundamental rights and freedoms of others.

Article 15

1. States Parties recognize the rights of the child to freedom of association and to freedom of peaceful assembly.
2. No restrictions may be placed on the exercise of these rights other than those imposed in conformity with the law and which are necessary in a democratic society in the interests of national security or public safety, public order *(ordre public)*, the protection of public health or morals or the protection of the rights and freedoms of others.

Article 16

1. No child shall be subjected to arbitrary or unlawful interference with his or her privacy, family, home or correspondence, nor to unlawful attacks on his or her honour and reputation.
2. The child has the right to the protection of the law against such interference or attacks.

Article 17

States Parties recognize the important function performed by the mass media and shall ensure that the child has access to information and material from a diversity of national and international sources, especially those aimed at the promotion of his or her social, spiritual and moral well-being and physical and mental health. To this end, States Parties shall:

(a) encourage the mass media to disseminate information and material of social and cultural benefit to the child and in accordance with the spirit of Article 29;

(b) encourage international co-operation in the production, exchange and dissemination of such information and material from a diversity of cultural, national and international sources;

(c) encourage the production and dissemination of children's books;

(d) encourage the mass media to have particular regard to the linguistic needs of the child who belongs to a minority group or who is indigenous;

(e) encourage the development of appropriate guidelines for the protection of the child from information and material injurious to his or her well-being, bearing in mind the provisions of Articles 13 and 18.

Article 18

1. States Parties shall use their best efforts to ensure recognition of the principle that both parents have common responsibilities for the upbringing and development of the child. Parents or, as the case may be, legal guardians, have the primary responsibility for the

upbringing and development of the child. The best interests of the child will be their basic concern.

2. For the purpose of guaranteeing and promoting the rights set forth in the present Convention, States Parties shall render appropriate assistance to parents and legal guardians in the performance of their child-rearing responsibilities and shall ensure the development of institutions, facilities and services for the care of children.

3. States Parties shall take all appropriate measures to ensure that children of working parents have the right to benefit from child-care services and facilities for which they are eligible.

Article 19

1. States Parties shall take all appropriate legislative, administrative, social and educational measures to protect the child from all forms of physical or mental violence, injury or abuse, neglect or negligent treatment, maltreatment or exploitation, including sexual abuse, while in the care of parent(s), legal guardian(s) or any other person who has the care of the child.

2. Such protective measures should, as appropriate, include effective procedures for the establishment of social programmes to provide necessary support for the child and for those who have the care of the child, as well as for other forms of prevention and for identification, reporting, referral, investigation, treatment and follow-up of instances of child maltreatment described heretofore, and, as appropriate, for judicial involvement.

Article 20

1. A child temporarily or permanently deprived of his or her family environment, or in whose own best interests cannot be allowed to remain in that environment, shall be entitled to special protection and assistance provided by the State.

2. States Parties shall in accordance with their national laws ensure alternative care for such a child.

3. Such care could include, *inter alia,* foster placement, *kafalah* of Islamic law, adoption or if necessary placement in suitable institutions for the care of children. When considering solutions, due regard shall be paid to the desirability of continuity in a child's upbringing and to the child's ethnic, religious, cultural and linguistic background.

Article 21

States Parties that recognize and/or permit the system of adoption shall ensure that the best interests of the child shall be the paramount consideration and they shall:

(a) ensure that the adoption of a child is authorized only by competent authorities who determine, in accordance with applicable law and procedures and on the basis of all pertinent and reliable information, that the adoption is permissible in view of the child's status concerning parents, relatives and legal guardians and that, if required, the persons concerned have given their informed consent to the adoption on the basis of such counselling as may be necessary;

(b) recognize that inter-country adoption may be considered as an alternative means of child's care, if the child cannot be placed in a foster or an adoptive family or cannot in any suitable manner be cared for in the child's country of origin;

(c) ensure that the child concerned by inter-country adoption enjoys safeguards and standards equivalent to those existing in the case of national adoption;

(d) take all appropriate measures to ensure that, in inter-country adoption, the placement does not result in proper financial gain for those involved in it;

(e) promote, where appropriate, the objectives of the present Article by concluding bilateral or multilateral arrangements or agreements, and endeavour, within this framework, to ensure that the placement of the child in another country is carried out by competent authorities or organs.

Article 22

1. tates Parties shall take appropriate measures to ensure that a child who is seeking refugee status or who is considered a refugee in accordance with applicable international or domestic law and procedures shall, whether unaccompanied or accompanied by his or her parents or by any other person, receive appropriate protection and humanitarian assistance in the enjoyment of applicable rights set forth in the present Convention and in other international human rights or humanitarian instruments to which the said States are Parties.

2. For this purpose, States Parties shall provide, as they consider appropriate, co-operation in any efforts by the United Nations and other competent intergovernmental organizations or non-governmental organizations co-operating with the United Nations to protect and assist such a child and to trace the parents or other members of the family of any refugee child in order to obtain information necessary for reunification with his or her family. In cases where no parents or other members of the family can be found, the child shall be accorded the same protection as any other child permanently or temporarily deprived of his or her family environment for any reason, as set forth in the present Convention.

Article 23

1. States Parties recognize that a mentally or physically disabled child should enjoy a full and decent life, in conditions which ensure dignity, promote self-reliance and facilitate the child's active participation in the community.

2. States Parties recognize the right of the disabled child to special care and shall encourage and ensure the extension, subject to available resources, to the eligible child and those responsible for his or her care, of assistance for which application is made and

which is appropriate to the child's condition and to the circumstances of the parents or others caring for the child.

3. Recognizing the special needs of a disabled child, assistance extended in accordance with paragraph 2 of the present Article shall be provided free of charge, whenever possible, taking into account the financial resources of the parents or others caring for the child, and shall be designed to ensure that the disabled child has effective access to and receives education, training, health care services, rehabilitation services, preparation for employment and recreation opportunities in a manner conducive to the child's achieving the fullest possible social integration and individual development, including his or her cultural and spiritual development.

4. States Parties shall promote, in the spirit of international cooperation, the exchange of appropriate information in the field of preventive health care and of medical, psychological and functional treatment of disabled children, including dissemination of and access to information concerning methods of rehabilitation, education and vocational services, with the aim of enabling States Parties to improve their capabilities and skills and to widen their experience in these areas. In this regard, particular account shall be taken of the needs of developing countries.

Article 24

1. States Parties recognize the right of the child to the enjoyment of the highest attainable standard of health and to facilities for the treatment of illness and rehabilitation of health. States Parties shall strive to ensure that no child is deprived of his or her right of access to such health care services.

2. States Parties shall pursue full implementation of this right and, in particular, shall take appropriate measures:

(a)   to diminish infant and child mortality;

(b)   to ensure the provision of necessary medical assistance and health care to all children with emphasis on the development of primary health care;

(c)   to combat disease and malnutrition, including within the framework of primary health care, through, *inter alia,* the application of readily available technology and through the provision of adequate nutritious foods and clean drinking water, taking into consideration the dangers and risks of environmental pollution;

(d)   to ensure appropriate pre-natal and post-natal health care for mothers;

(e)   to ensure that all segments of society, in particular parents and children, are informed, have access to education and are supported in the use of basic knowledge of child health and nutrition, the advantages of breast-feeding, hygiene and environmental sanitation and the prevention of accidents;

(f)   to develop preventive health care, guidance for parents and family planning education and services.

3. States Parties shall take all effective and appropriate measures with a view to abolishing traditional practices prejudicial to the health of children.

4. States Parties undertake to promote and encourage international co-operation with a view to achieving progressively the full realization of the right recognized in the present Article. In this regard particular account shall be taken of the needs of developing countries.

Article 25

States Parties recognize the right of a child who has been placed by the competent authorities for the purposes of care, protection or treatment of his or her physical or mental health, to a periodic review of the treatment provided to the child and all other circumstances relevant to his or her placement.

Article 26

1. States Parties shall recognize for every child the right to benefit from social security, including social insurance and shall take the necessary measures to achieve the full realization of this right in accordance with their national law.

2. The benefits should, where appropriate, be granted, taking into account the resources and the circumstances of the child and persons having responsibility for the maintenance of the child, as well as any other consideration relevant to an application for benefits made by or on behalf of the child.

Article 27

1. States Parties recognize the right of every child to a standard of living adequate for the child's physical, mental, spiritual, moral and social development.

2. The parent(s) or others responsible for the child have the responsibility to secure, within their abilities and capacities, the conditions of living necessary for the child's development.

3. States Parties, in accordance with national conditions and within their means, shall take appropriate measures to assist parents and others responsible for the child to implement this right and shall in case of need provide material assistance and support programmes, particularly with regard to nutrition, clothing, and housing.

4. States Parties shall take all appropriate measures to secure the recovery of maintenance for the child from the parents or other persons having financial responsibility for the child, both within the State Party and from abroad. In particular, where the person having financial responsibility for the child lives in a State different from that of the child, States Parties shall promote the accession to international agreements or the conclusion of such agreements as well as the making of other appropriate arrangements.

Article 28

1. States Parties recognize the right of the child to education, and with a view to achieving this right progressively and on the basis of equal opportunity, they shall, in particular:

(a) make primary education compulsory and available free to all;
(b) encourage the development of different forms of secondary education, including general and vocational education, make them available and accessible to every child, and take appropriate measures such as the introduction of free education and offering financial assistance in case of need;
(c) make higher education accessible to all on the basis of capacity by every appropriate means;
(d) make educational and vocational information and guidance available and accessible to all children;
(e) take measures to encourage regular attendance at schools and the reduction of drop-out rates.

2. States Parties shall take all appropriate measures to ensure that school discipline is administered in a manner consistent with the child's human dignity and in conformity with the present Convention.

3. States Parties shall promote and encourage international cooperation in matters relating to education, in particular with a view to contributing to the elimination of ignorance and illiteracy throughout the world and facilitating access to scientific and technical knowledge and modern teaching methods. In this regard, particular account shall be taken of the needs of developing countries.

Article 29

1. States Parties agree that the education of the child shall be directed to:

(a) the development of the child's personality, talents and mental and physical abilities to their fullest potential;
(b) the development of respect for human rights and fundamental freedoms, and for the principles enshrined in the Charter of the United Nations;
(c) the development of respect for the child's parents, his or her own cultural identity, language and values, for the national values of the country in which the child is living, the country from which he or she may originate, and for civilizations different from his or her own;
(d) the preparation of the child for responsible life in a free society, in the spirit of understanding, peace, tolerance, equality of sexes, and friendship among all peoples, ethnic, national and religious groups and persons of indigenous origin;
(e) the development of respect for the natural environment.

2. No part of the present article or Article 28 shall be construed so as to interfere with the liberty of individuals and bodies to establish and direct educational institutions, subject always to the observance

of the principles set forth in paragraph 1 of the present Article and to the requirements that the education given in such institutions shall conform to such minimum standards as may be laid down by the State.

Article 30
In those States in which ethnic, religious or linguistic minorities or persons of indigenous origin exist, a child belonging to such a minority or who is indigenous shall not be denied the right, in community with other members of his or her group, to enjoy his or her own culture, to profess and practise his or her own religion, or to use his or her own language.

Article 31
1. States Parties recognize the right of the child to rest and leisure, to engage in play and recreational activities appropriate to the age of the child and to participate freely in cultural life and the arts.
2. States Parties shall respect and promote the right of the child to participate fully in cultural and artistic life and shall encourage the provision of appropriate and equal opportunities for cultural, artistic, recreational and leisure activity.

Article 32
1. States Parties recognize the right of the child to be protected from economic exploitation and from performing any work that is likely to be hazardous or to interfere with the child's education, or to be harmful to the child's health or physical, mental, spiritual, moral or social development.
2. States Parties shall take legislative, administrative, social and educational measures to ensure the implementation of the present Article. To this end, and having regard to the relevant provisions of other international instruments, States Parties shall in particular:
(a) provide for a minimum age or minimum ages for admission to employment;
(b) provide for appropriate regulation of the hours and conditions of employment,
(c) provide for appropriate penalties or other sanctions to ensure the effective enforcement of the present article.

Article 33
States Parties shall take all appropriate measures, including legislative, administrative, social and educational measures, to protect children from the illicit use of narcotic drugs and psychotropic substances as defined in the relevant international treaties, and to prevent the use of children in the illicit production and trafficking of such substances.

Article 34
States Parties undertake to protect the child from all forms of

sexual exploitation and sexual abuse. For these purposes, States Parties shall in particular take all appropriate national, bilateral and multilateral measures to prevent:

(a) the inducement or coercion of a child to engage in any unlawful sexual activity;

(b) the exploitative use of children in prostitution or other unlawful sexual practices;

(c) the exploitative use of children in pornographic performances and materials.

Article 35

States Parties shall take all appropriate national, bilateral and multilateral measures to prevent the abduction of, the sale of or traffic in children for any purpose or in any form.

Article 36

States Parties shall protect the child against all other forms of exploitation prejudicial to any aspects of the child's welfare.

Article 37

States Parties shall ensure that:

(a) no child shall be subjected to torture or other cruel, inhuman or degrading treatment or punishment. Neither capital punishment nor life imprisonment without possibility of release shall be imposed for offences committed by persons below eighteen years of age;

(b) no child shall be deprived of his or her liberty unlawfully or arbitrarily. The arrest, detention or imprisonment of a child shall be in conformity with the law and shall be used only as a measure of last resort and for the shortest appropriate period of time;

(c) every child deprived of liberty shall be treated with humanity and respect for the inherent dignity of the human person, and in a manner which takes into account the needs of persons of his or her age. In particular, every child deprived of liberty shall be separated from adults unless it is considered in the child's best interest not to do so and shall have the right to maintain contact with his or her family through correspondence and visits, save in exceptional circumstances;

(d) every child deprived of his or her liberty shall have the right to prompt access to legal and other appropriate assistance, as well as the right to challenge the legality of the deprivation of his or her liberty before a court or other competent, independent and impartial authority, and to a prompt decision on any such action.

Article 38

1. States Parties undertake to respect and to ensure respect for rules of international humanitarian law applicable to them in armed

conflicts which are relevant to the child.

2. States Parties shall take all feasible measures to ensure that persons who have not attained the age of fifteen years do not take a direct part in hostilities.

3. States Parties shall refrain from recruiting any person who has not attained the age of fifteen years into their armed forces. In recruiting among those persons who have attained the age of fifteen years but who have not attained the age of eighteen years, States Parties shall endeavour to give priority to those who are oldest.

4. In accordance with their obligations under international humanitarian law to protect the civilian population in armed conflicts, States Parties shall take all feasible measures to ensure protection and care of children who are affected by an armed conflict.

Article 39

States Parties shall take all appropriate measures to promote physical and psychological recovery and social reintegration of a child victim of: any form of neglect, exploitation, or abuse; torture or any other form of cruel, inhuman or degrading treatment or punishment, or armed conflicts. Such recovery and reintegration shall take place in an environment which fosters the health, self-respect and dignity of the child.

Article 40

1. States Parties recognize the right of every child alleged as, accused of, or recognized as having infringed the penal law to be treated in a manner consistent with the promotion of the child's sense of dignity and worth, which reinforces the child's respect for the human rights and fundamental freedoms of others and which takes into account the child's age and the desirability of promoting the child's reintegration and the child's assuming a constructive role in society.

2. To this end, and having regard to the relevant provisions of international instruments, States Parties shall, in particular, ensure that:

(a) no child shall be alleged as, be accused of, or recognized as having infringed the penal law by reason of acts or omissions that were not prohibited by national or international law at the time they were committed;

(b) every child alleged as or accused of having infringed the penal law has at least the following guarantees:

   (i) to be presumed innocent until proven guilty according to law;

   (ii) to be informed promptly and directly of the charges against him or her, and, if appropriate, through his or her parents or legal guardians, and to have legal or other appropriate assistance in the preparation and presentation of his or her defence;

   (iii) to have the matter determined without delay by a competent, independent and impartial authority or judicial body in a fair hearing according to law, in the presence of legal or other appropriate assistance and, unless it is considered not to be in the best interests of the child, in particular, taking into account his or her age or situation, his or her parents or legal guardians;

(iv) not to be compelled to give testimony or to confess guilt; to examine or have examined adverse witnesses and to obtain the participation and examination of witnesses on his or her behalf under conditions of equality;

(v) if considered to have infringed the penal law, to have this decision and any measures imposed in consequence thereof reviewed by a higher competent, independent and impartial authority or judicial body according to law;

(vi) to have the free assistance of an interpreter if the child cannot understand or speak the language used;

(vii) to have his or her privacy fully respected at all stages of the proceedings.

3. States Parties shall seek to promote the establishment of laws, procedures, authorities and institutions specifically applicable to children alleged as, accused of, or recognized as having infringed the penal law, and, in particular:

(a) the establishment of a minimum age below which children shall be presumed not to have the capacity to infringe the penal law;

(b) whenever appropriate and desirable, measures for dealing with such children without resorting to judicial proceedings, providing that human rights and legal safeguards are fully respected.

4. A variety of dispositions, such as care, guidance and supervision orders; counselling; probation; foster care; education and vocational training programmes and other alternatives to institutional care shall be available to ensure that children are dealt with in a manner appropriate to their well being and proportionate both to their circumstances and the offence.

Article 41

Nothing in the present Convention shall affect any provisions which are more conducive to the realization of the rights of the child and which may be contained in:

(a) the law of a State Party; or

(b) international law in force for that State.

PART II

Article 42

States Parties undertake to make the principles and provisions of the Convention widely known, by appropriate and active means, to adults and children alike.

Article 43

1. For the purpose of examining the progress made by States Parties in achieving the realization of the obligations undertaken in the present Convention, there shall be established a Committee on the Rights of the Child, which shall carry out the functions hereinafter provided.

2. The Committee shall consist of ten experts of high moral standing and recognized competence in the field covered by this Convention. The members of the Committee shall be elected by States Parties from among their nationals and shall serve in their personal capacity, consideration being given to equitable geographical distribution, as well as to the principal legal systems.

3. The members of the Committee shall be elected by secret ballot from a list of persons nominated by States Parties. Each State Party may nominate one person from among its own nationals.

4. The initial election to the Committee shall be held no later than six months after the date of the entry into force of the present Convention and thereafter every second year. At least four months before the date of each election, the Secretary General of the United Nations shall address a letter to States Parties inviting them to submit their nominations within two months. The Secretary-General shall subsequently prepare a list in alphabetical order of all persons thus nominated, indicating States Parties which have nominated them, and shall submit it to the States Parties to the present Convention.

5. The elections shall be held at meetings of States Parties convened by the Secretary-General at United Nations Headquarters. At those meetings, for which two thirds of States Parties shall constitute a quorum, the persons elected to the Committee shall be those who obtain the largest number of votes and an absolute majority of the votes of the representatives of States Parties present and voting.

6. The members of the Committee shall be elected for a term of four years. They shall be eligible for re-election if renominated. The term of five of the members elected at the first election shall expire at the end of two years; immediately after the first election, the names of these five members shall be chosen by lot by the Chairman of the meeting.

7. If a member of the Committee dies or resigns or declares that for any other cause he or she can no longer perform the duties of the Committee, the State Party which nominated the member shall appoint another expert from among its nationals to serve for the remainder of the term, subject to the approval of the Committee.

8. The Committee shall establish its own rules of procedure.

9. The Committee shall elect its officers for a period of two years.

10. The meetings of the Committee shall normally be held at United Nations Headquarters or at any other convenient place as determined by the Committee. The Committee shall normally meet annually. The duration of the meetings of the Committee shall be determined, and reviewed, if necessary, by a meeting of the States

Parties to the present Convention, subject to the approval of the General Assembly.

11. The Secretary-General of the United Nations shall provide the necessary staff and facilities for the effective performance of the functions of the Committee under the present Convention.

12. With the approval of the General Assembly, the members of the Committee established under the present Convention shall receive emoluments from United Nations resources on such terms and conditions as the Assembly may decide.

Article 44

1. States Parties undertake to submit to the Committee, through the Secretary-General of the United Nations, reports on the measures they have adopted which give effect to the rights recognized herein and on the progress made on the enjoyment of those rights:
   (a) within two years of the entry into force of the Convention for the State Party concerned;
   (b) thereafter every five years.

2. Reports made under the present Article shall indicate factors and difficulties, if any, affecting the degree of fulfilment of the obligations under the present Convention. Reports shall also contain sufficient information to provide the Committee with a comprehensive understanding of the implementation of the Convention in the country concerned.

3. A State Party which has submitted a comprehensive initial report to the Committee need not, in its subsequent reports submitted in accordance with paragraph 1(b) of the present Article, repeat basic information previously provided.

4. The Committee may request from States Parties further information relevant to the implementation of the Convention.

5. The Committee shall submit to the General Assembly, through the Economic and Social Council, every two years, reports on its activities.

6. States Parties shall make their reports widely available to the public in their own countries.

Article 45

In order to foster the effective implementation of the Convention and to encourage international co-operation in the field covered by the Convention:
   (a) the specialized agencies, the United Nations Children's Fund, and other United Nations organs shall be entitled to be represented at the consideration of the implementation of such provisions of the present Convention as fall within the scope of their mandate. The, Committee may invite the specialized agencies, the United Nations Children's Fund and other competent bodies as it may consider appropriate to provide expert advice on the implementation of the Convention in

areas falling within the scope of their respective mandates. The Committee may invite the specialized agencies, the United Nations Children's Fund, and other United Nations organs to submit reports on the implementation of the Convention in areas falling within the scope of their activities;

(b) the Committee shall transmit, as it may consider appropriate, to the specialized agencies, the United Nations Children's Fund and other competent bodies, any reports from States Parties that contain a request, or indicate a need, for technical advice or assistance, along with the Committee's observations and suggestions, if any, on these requests or indications;

(c) the Committee may recommend to the General Assembly to request the Secretary-General to undertake on its behalf studies on specific issues relating to the rights of the child;

(d) the Committee may make suggestions and general recommendations based on information received pursuant to Articles 44 and 45 of the present Convention. Such suggestions and general recommendations shall be transmitted to any State Party concerned and reported to the General Assembly, together with comments, if any, from States Parties.

PART III
Article 46
The present Convention shall be open for signature by all States.

Article 47
The present Convention is subject to ratification. Instruments of ratification shall be deposited with the Secretary-General of the United Nations.

Article 48
The present Convention shall remain open for accession by any State. The instruments of accession shall be deposited with the Secretary-General of the United Nations.

Article 49
1. The present Convention shall enter into force on the thirtieth day following the date of deposit with the Secretary-General of the United Nations of the twentieth instrument of ratification or accession.
2. For each State ratifying or acceding to the Convention after the deposit of the twentieth instrument of ratification or accession, the Convention shall enter into force on the thirtieth day after the deposit by such State of its instrument of ratification or accession.

Article 50
1. Any State Party may propose an amendment and file it with the Secretary-General of the United Nations. The Secretary-General

shall thereupon communicate the proposed amendment to States Parties, with a request that they indicate whether they favour a conference of States Parties for the purpose of considering and voting upon the proposals. In the event that, within four months from the date of such communication, at least one third of the States Parties favour such a conference, the Secretary-General shall convene the conference under the auspices of the United Nations. Any amendment adopted by a majority of States Parties present and voting at the conference shall be submitted to the General Assembly for approval.

2. An amendment adopted in accordance with paragraph 1 of the present Article shall enter into force when it has been approved by the General Assembly of the United Nations and accepted by a two-thirds majority of States Parties.

3. When an amendment enters into force, it shall be binding on those States Parties which have accepted it, other States Parties still being bound by the provisions of the present Convention and any earlier amendments which they have accepted.

Article 51

1. The Secretary-General of the United Nations shall receive and circulate to all States the text of reservations made by States at the time of ratification or accession.

2. A reservation incompatible with the object and purpose of the present Convention shall not be permitted.

3. Reservations may be withdrawn at any time by notification to that effect addressed to the Secretary General of the United Nations, who shall then inform all States. Such notification shall take effect on the date which it is received by the Secretary-General.

Article 52

A State Party may denounce the present Convention by written notification to the Secretary-General of the United Nations. Denunciation becomes effective one year after the date of receipt of the notification by the Secretary-General.

Article 53

The Secretary-General of the United Nations is designated as the depositary of the present Convention.

Article 54

The original of the present Convention, of which the Arabic, Chinese, English, French, Russian and Spanish texts are equally authentic, shall be deposited with the Secretary-General of the United Nations.

APPENDIX 3

RESERVATIONS AND DECLARATIONS OF THE UNITED KINGDOM TO THE UN CONVENTION ON THE RIGHTS OF THE CHILD

(As amended*)

Upon signature:

The United Kingdom reserves the right to formulate, upon ratifying the Convention, any reservations or interpretative declarations which it might consider necessary.

Upon ratification:

Declarations:

(a) The United Kingdom interprets the Convention as applicable only following a live birth.

(b) The United Kingdom interprets the references in the Convention to "parents" to mean only those persons who, as a matter of national law, are treated as parents. This includes cases where the law regards a child as having only one parent, for example where a child has been adopted by one person only and in certain cases where a child is conceived other than as a result of sexual intercourse by the woman who gives birth to it and she is treated as the only parent.

Reservations:

(c) The United Kingdom reserves the right to apply such legislation, in so far as it relates to the entry into, stay in and departure from the United Kingdom of those who do not have the right under the law of the United Kingdom to enter and remain in the United Kingdom, and to the acquisition and possession of citizenship, as it may deem necessary from time to time

...

(e) Where at any time there is a lack of suitable accommodation or adequate facilities for a particular individual in any institution in which young offenders are detained, or where the mixing of adults and children is deemed to be mutually beneficial, the United Kingdom reserves the right not to apply article 37 (c) in so far as those provisions require children who are detained to be accommodated separately from adults.

. . .

* On 18 April 1997, the Government of the United Kingdom of Great Britain and Northern Ireland informed the Secretary-General that it had decided to withdraw the following reservation made upon ratification:

(f) In Scotland there are tribunals (known as "children's hearings") which consider the welfare of the child and deal with the majority of offences which a child is alleged to have committed. In some cases, mainly of welfare nature, the child is temporarily deprived of its liberty for up to seven days prior to attending the hearing. The child and its family are, however, allowed access to a lawyer during this period. Although the decisions of the hearings are subject to appeal to the courts, legal representation is not permitted at the proceedings of the children's hearings themselves. Children's hearings have proved over the years to be a very effective way of dealing with the problems of children in a less formal, non-adversarial manner. Accordingly, the United Kingdom, in respect of article 37 (d), reserves its right to continue the present operation of children's hearings.

Further, on 3 August 1999, the Government of the United Kingdom of Great Britain and Northern Ireland informed the Secretary-General of the following:

[...] the following reservation entered upon ratification in respect of the United Kingdom of Great Britain and Northern Ireland is hereby withdrawn:

[(d)] Employment legislation in the United Kingdom does not treat persons under 18, but over the school-leaving age as children, but as "young people". Accordingly the United Kingdom reserves the right to continue to apply article 32 subject to such employment legislation.

The United Kingdom's reservations to article 32 in respect of its overseas territories, formerly referred to as "dependent territories", set out in the Declarations dated 7 September 1994, are unaffected.

INDEX